THE ARABS IN ISRAEL

The Institute gratefully acknowledges the comments and suggestions of the following who read the manuscript on behalf of the Research Committee: Dr Abner Cohen, Professor Elie Kedourie, Professor P. J. Vatikiotis.

THE ARABS IN ISRAEL

A POLITICAL STUDY

Jacob M. Landau

Issued under the auspices of the
Royal Institute of International Affairs
OXFORD UNIVERSITY PRESS
LONDON NEW YORK TORONTO

Oxford University Press, Ely House, London W.1
GLASGOW NEW YORK TORONTO MELBOURNE WELLINGTON
CAPE TOWN SALISBURY IBADAN NAIROBI DAR ES SALAAM LUSAKA ADDIS ABABA
BOMBAY CALCUTTA MADRAS KARACHI LAHORE DACCA
KUALA LUMPUR SINGAPORE HONG KONG TOKYO

First published 1969
Reprinted 1970

PRINTED IN GREAT BRITAIN

For

Zipora, Ronit, and Iddo

CONTENTS

ABBREVIATIONS ix

PREFACE xi

1 INTRODUCTION: SOME BASIC DATA 1
Historical Data, 1; Demographic and Ecologic Factors, 3; The Religious Communities, 7

2 ADAPTATION OR ALIENATION 19
Villagers and Townspeople, 19; The Bedouins and the Patterns of Change, 25; Problems in Adaptation, 28

3 CULTURAL CHANGE AND ITS REFLECTION IN POLITICS 39
Arab Education, 39; Arab Intellectuals and Israel, 43; The Arab Students, 49; The Crisis Reflected in the Press and Literature, 57

4 POLITICAL ORGANIZATIONS 69
New Political Trends, 69; Israeli Arabs and the Political Parties, 71; Communist Activity, 81; The *al-Arḍ* Group, 92

5 THE ARABS IN PARLIAMENTARY ELECTIONS 108
Elections to the First *Kneset*, 1949, 108; Elections to the Second *Kneset*, 1951, 112; Elections to the Third *Kneset*, 1955, 116; Elections to the Fourth *Kneset*, 1959, 122; Elections to the Fifth *Kneset*, 1961, 129; Elections to the Sixth *Kneset*, 1965, 135; Main characteristics, 149

6 THE ARABS IN LOCAL AND TRADE UNION ELECTIONS 156
The Arabs and Local Elections, 156; The Arabs in Trade Union Elections, 178

7 LEADERSHIP AND FOCI OF POLITICAL ACTIVITY 184
Arab Political Leadership in Israel, 184; National and Local Leadership, 185; The Arab Members of the *Kneset*, 190; Religious Leadership, 201; Foci of Political Activity, 205

8 CONCLUDING REMARKS 220

APPENDICES 221

A Rustum Bastūnī on Integrating the Arabs in Israel 221

B Manifesto of the Arab Students' Committee 225

C Tawfīq Ṭūbī on the Arabs in Israel 226

D *Al-Arḍ's* Memorandum on the Arabs in Israel 228

E Excerpts from the *Israeli Arab Awareness* 231

F Amnōn Līn on the Arabs and the Sixth *Kneset* Elections 237

G Some Resolutions of the Tenth Congress of the *Histadrūt* 249

H First Speech by an Arab Member of the *Kneset* 251

I *Al-Rābiṭa* asks the Arab Minority: 'Quo Vadis?' 253

J Editorial in *The Message of the Club* in Ṭīra 255

K The Questionnaire 257

L Interviewing the Arabs—Some Conclusions 261

GLOSSARY 278

SELECT BIBLIOGRAPHY 280

A Arabic 280

B Hebrew 281

C Other Languages 283

~~INDEX~~ ~~289~~

MAP 301

End of T. of C.

ABBREVIATIONS

CBS:	Central Bureau of Statistics
JP:	*Jerusalem Post* (Jerusalem, daily).
MḤ:	*Ha-Mizraḥ he-Ḥadash* (Jerusalem, quarterly).
MK:	Member of *Kneset.*
Moslems, Christians, & Druzes:	Israel, CBS, *Moslems, Christians and Druzes in Israel, data from stage 'a' and 'b' of Census,* 1964.
NO:	*New Outlook* (Tel-Aviv).
Stat. Ab.:	*Statistical Abstract of Israel.*
YA:	*Yĕdī'ōt aḥarōnōt* (Tel-Aviv daily).
YSY:	*Yarḥōn sṭatīsṭī lĕ-Yisra'el* (Israel statistical monthly).

End of Abbreviations

Page Roman 10 is blank

XI

PREFACE

ONE of the major problems in the political life of every polyethnic State is the relationship between majority and minority—a relationship which conditions nearly every aspect of society. This is particularly true of new States, where this relationship determines both the formal structures of the political system and the patterns of political behaviour.

Understanding this relationship requires thorough knowledge of the characteristics of both majority and minorities. While much has been written about the Jewish majority in the State of Israel, only little has been published on the Arab minority. Indeed, many articles dealing with the Arabs in Israel may be found in periodicals and in the daily press, but most of these are journalistic in nature, since they refer mainly to the temporary and transitory.

Books which discuss the Arabs in Israel are either general accounts by tourists,[1] or short informative publications by government agencies,[2] or political propaganda by various interested groups.[3] The social[4] and economic[5] aspects of the Arabs in Israel, with many of the statistical data and demographical implications involved, have been adequately dealt with by a number of scholars. In contrast, the special political problems of the Arabs in Israel have not yet been exposed to systematic research. This phenomenon is not surprising, due to two reasons: firstly, because many of the Arab politicians who lived in Palestine during the British Mandate did not remain here after the establishment of the State of Israel—on 14 May 1948—and many of the Arabs who did stay on revealed, in the first years of the State's existence, a considerable amount of indifference to political affairs. Secondly, when in recent years, a growing number of Israeli Arabs began to participate in politics increasingly, objective study of their political behaviour became comparatively difficult, because of the deep feelings involved in every discussion on this subject. It is

[1] Such as Walter Schwarz, *The Arabs in Israel* (1959). See bibliography below, p. 280 ff. for fuller details in this and other instances.

[2] e.g. Ministry for Foreign Affairs, *The Arabs in Israel* (1961) (an earlier edition was publ. in 1958).

[3] A recent example: Ṣabrī Jiryis, *ha-'Aravīm bĕ-Yisra'el* (1966).

[4] e.g. Henry Rosenfeld, *Hem hayū fallaḥīm* (1964); Abner Cohen, *Arab border-villages in Israel* (1965); and Emmanuel Marx, *Bedouin of the Negev* (1967).

[5] e.g. Y. Ben-Porat, *The Arab labor force in Israel* (1966). A work of smaller scope but in some respects more up to date is S. Zarhi & A. Achiezra, *The economic conditions of the Arab minority in Israel* (1966).

not surprising, that these feelings were related (at least in part) to considerable ignorance of the subject.

This study does not claim to give a complete answer to all the questions relating to the political behaviour of the Arabs in Israel, and *a fortiori* does not aim to present an overall picture of the various aspects of their life. In the present condition of research about this subject, this first contribution to so comprehensive a theme can but hope to describe and analyse several significant phenomena relating to the political behaviour of the Israeli Arabs, based on available materials, and then attempt to reach some intermediate conclusions. Moreover, the partisan approach prevailing in many of the publications touching on the Arabs in Israeli politics has put considerable obstacles in the way of objective research. Nevertheless, I have striven to keep a balanced approach, without any bias. One may be permitted to hope that better knowledge of the subject will contribute to a rapprochement between Jews and Arabs.

As to the period covered in this study, it was determined by the nature of the subject. As a starting point I chose 14 May 1948. It was then that the State of Israel was officially proclaimed and the Arabs became a minority group in the new State; furthermore, as will be shown, the Arabs in Palestine (that is, before 1948), have already been studied by various scholars. As to the *terminus ad quem*, the end of the year 1966 was originally decided upon, as the date when the military administration in all Arab areas was terminated. The 'six days' war' in June, 1967, changed the situation markedly, by bringing another million Arabs within the orbit of Israeli rule. When this happened, the manuscript of the present study was almost complete, and could not take into account changes which necessitate the preparation of another full-sized book. As to the Arab minority living in Israel prior to the 'six days' war', their loyalty to the State during this war remained unflinching, with very few exceptions.[6]

This book is based on an examination of considerable printed material in Arabic, Hebrew, and other languages—written by the Arabs in Israel, and about them. I refer to the literary output of the Israeli Arabs as well as to their articles in the daily press and periodicals; to the considerable newspaper material about them; to statistical data concerning their participation in parliamentary, local and trade-union elections, etc. The conclusions have been verified, as far as possible, by interviewing Arabs, in a manner and with results described in Appendix L. The Select Bibliography does not aim at

[6] Cf. Atallah Mansour, 'Fear of war and faith in peace', *NO* (Tel-Aviv), July–Aug. 1967, 26–29.

including everything relating to the subject, for an exhaustive list would have called for an additional volume. It includes only select books and articles in periodicals (not the daily press), which perhaps can help to broaden and complete the picture; references to more specific items may be found in many instances in the footnotes. Transliteration has followed approved forms, except in cases of generally known place names or of persons who have already used a form of their own in print.

I would not have been able to complete this book without the encouragement and assistance I was fortunate in obtaining. The Rockefeller Foundation and the Wenner-Gren Foundation for Anthropological Research, both in New York, have allocated generous grants for carrying out the research. The Faculty of Economics and Social Sciences, the Hebrew University, Jerusalem, and the Export Bank, Tel-Aviv, have added funds which have helped me in technical matters. Various colleagues at the Hebrew University have shared their knowledgeable experience with me. At different stages of this research, my assistants were—chronologically—Dr Subhi Abu Ghosh and Messrs Ori Stendel, Joseph Binya, and Sami Dibbini. It is not a coincidence that two of them are Jews and two Arabs. The Royal Institute of International Affairs has unstintingly given me the benefit of its experience: Mr Andrew Shonfield, Director of Studies, Miss Hermia Oliver, editor, and Miss Kay Jerrold, administrative assistant, all offered valuable advice. I thank all the above, although, of course, the responsibility for every opinion expressed as well as for every imperfection is mine alone.

March 1968 Signed J.M.L.

End of Preface

I

INTRODUCTION: SOME BASIC DATA

SOME basic data are needed for understanding the development of political consciousness and the main patterns of political behaviour of the Arabs in Israel. These may be divided into historical, demographic, and religious.

HISTORICAL DATA

The historical presentation is brief, since it is related only in part to the situation in the State of Israel. Besides, in 1947 (just when the British Mandate was approaching its end) two books appeared, summing-up the history of Palestinian Arabs during that period.[1] Later several other works were published,[2] dealing with a number of aspects concerning Palestinian Arabs. It might well be said that the most significant factor, which led to tragic complications, both in Israel and the Middle East, was the fact that two national movements arose simultaneously and progressed rapidly in the period between the two world wars, within the borders of one land. The World Zionist movement, encouraged by the Balfour Declaration (2 November 1917), made considerable efforts to encourage Jewish immigration and prepare political, economic, and later even military conditions, for establishing a Jewish State in Israel. The Arab national movement in Palestine, although less widespread in character and centred within an influential socio-economic group, had no less extremist demands. From the very start, the role of the British administration was very difficult, not to say well-nigh impossible: whenever it leaned towards either of the two national groups, it was accused by the other; if it tried to remain neutral, it was denounced by both. True, the British did not attempt to bring Jews and Arabs nearer to one another. However, their attitude was generally based on two factors: a well-conceived *Realpolitik*—following their own point of view—and the fact that Jewish efforts to reach political

[1] Y. Shimoni, *'Aravey Ereṣ-Yisra'el* (The Arabs of Palestine) (Tel-Aviv, 1947). Y. Waschitz, *Ha-'Aravīm bĕ-Ereṣ-Yisra'el* (The Arabs in Palestine) (Merhavya, 1947).

[2] Such as M. Asaf, *Hit'ōrĕrūt ha-'Aravīm bĕ-Ereṣ-Yisra'el w-brīḥatam* (Awakening of the Arabs of Palestine and their Flight) (Tel-Aviv, 1967); A. L. Tibawi, *Arab education in mandatory Palestine, a study of three decades of British administration* (London, 1956).

understanding with the local Arabs, in order to establish a bi-national State, did not gain much backing from either side.[3] The political cleavage between Jews and Arabs in Palestine was highlighted by the almost complete lack of social contact, since each of the two communities lived almost wholly by itself—even in mixed towns.

The Arab riots in Palestine in 1920 and 1929 were brief and local; but the 1936 riots broke out all over the country and continued intermittently for three years. Throughout these riots in the late 1930s the Palestinian Arabs received help from the Arabs in neighbouring countries. This help was parallel to the aid given the Jews in Palestine by their brethren abroad. Here was yet another indication that the conflict widened and deepened. At the end of the second world war, after a lull, the clashes were renewed, but with a difference: this time Jewish military organizations as well as Arab ones used terror and obstruction against the British authorities. The decision of the United Nations to end the British Mandate in Palestine (29 November 1947) started an armed conflict between Arabs and Jews in Palestine. Both sides tried to occupy strategic positions, to control the main roads and other means of communication, to annex land, to seize abandoned British camps, to import arms, and to train a regular army. The British evacuation (14 May 1948) and the proclamation and establishment of a Jewish State named Israel, on the same day, served as a signal for the regular armies of Egypt, Jordan, Syria, Lebanon, Iraq, Saudi Arabia, and Yemen, to go to war against Israel. The avowed aim of these armies was to crush Israel. They failed in this, but the Gaza Strip came under Egyptian control; and King 'Abd Allah of Jordan annexed a considerable part of the fertile land on the western bank of the Jordan river. In the rest of Palestine, the State of Israel continued to exist, with a Jewish majority and an Arab minority. The latter not only remembered vividly that it had been a majority in the recent past, but also felt keenly that in the confrontation with the Jews, it was facing a victor, more advanced in material civilization and speaking a different language. Side by side with the political confrontation, a desire for cultural imitation arose and was soon followed by the fear of losing Arab identity through assimilation.

One of the more arduous problems resulting from the Arab-Israeli War was that of the military administration imposed for

[3] Aharon Cohen, in his *Yisra'el vě-ha-'ōlam ha-'aravī* (Israel and the Arab World) (Merhavya, 1964), maintains that in addition to Jewish circles, there were also Arab circles in Palestine prepared to coexist. Actually, these were tiny Arab groups with no public support.

security reasons in Galilee, the Little Triangle (the region east of the coastal plain, north of Tel-Aviv, near the middle of the Israel–Jordan frontier), and the Negev; namely, in all the areas close to the borders, and inhabited mainly by Arabs. Legally, the military administration was based on the British emergency regulations of 1945–6. Although its authority and scope were restricted, it remained a subject of dispute not only among the Arab, but also among the Jewish, population, until it was abolished in 1966.[4] The main power vested in the military administration enabled the arrest or deportation of troublesome elements and the defining of closed areas, thus compelling their inhabitants to obtain travel-permits when wishing to enter or leave such areas. These restrictions applied to Jews as well as to Arabs, and, in fact, only a few Arabs and Jews were closely affected. And even they could apply to Israel's Supreme Court, sitting as a High Court of Justice, for redress. However, it was not only the practical side that annoyed the Arabs, but the principle as well.[5] From both these points of view the military administration served for years as a target for propaganda and argument, in Israel and abroad.[6]

DEMOGRAPHIC AND ECOLOGIC FACTORS

Upon the establishment of the State of Israel, there were nearly 1,300,000 Arabs and 650,000 Jews in the area defined as Palestine. Among these Arabs, some 700,000 lived in an area which actually became the State of Israel,[7] while others remained under Arab rule (about 100,000 in the Gaza Strip, and almost 500,000 in the territory annexed by Jordan). When the fighting ended, in the autumn of 1948, there remained some 156,000 Arabs within the borders of

[4] For details see, e.g., *Ma'arīv* (Tel-Aviv, daily), 18 Feb. 1966. A few remaining vestiges were abolished in 1967, cf. A Rubinstein, in *ha-Areṣ* (Tel-Aviv, daily), 16 Nov. 1967.

[5] Much has been written for and against the military administration. One of the best-balanced summaries of these views is by Y. Palmōn, in *ha-Areṣ*, 4 Feb. 1966. One may note that a novel in Hebrew on the military administration was published in 1967. It is by B. Giṭlīṣ, and its name is *ha-Mōshel ha-mĕkhō'ar* (The ugly Governor).

[6] Among the pamphlets written abroad, complaining of Israel's treatment of its Arab minority, one may note *The Arabs of Israel* (n.d., prob. 1955); J. A. Nasser, *The resentful Arab* (1964) (esp. ch. 8: 'The cruel oppression of the Arabs in Israel'); Sami Hadawi, *Israel and the Arab minority* (1959); Centro Arabo di Informazioni, Rome, *La minoranza araba nella Palestina occupata* (n.d.). Some books and pamphlets on the subject appeared in Arabic too, for which see the bibliography, p. 280 below. Of these, the Arab League's *al-Aqalliyya al-'arabiyya fī ẓalām Yisrā'īl* (1960) and Kanafānī's *Adab al-muqāwama fī Filasṭīn al-muḥtalla* (1966) deal solely with our subject, while others devote a chapter or more to the Arabs in Israel.

[7] Alex Weingrod, *Israel, group relations in a new society* (London, 1965), 15, based on Don Patinkin, *The Israel economy, the first decade* (Jerusalem, 1960).

Israel.[8] The others became refugees: nearly 200,000 in the Gaza Strip; others in the territory annexed by Jordan; and the rest in Lebanon.

Since the establishment of Israel[9] there have been far-reaching statistical and demographic changes among the Arabs in this country.

The most outstanding of those changes was the great increase in the Arab population in Israel, reaching 300,000 by the end of 1965.[10] This increase averages 4 per cent a year and is one of the highest in the world. Some reasons for this appear to be: (1) A high birth-rate (three times higher than that of the Jewish population in Israel). (2) A sharp decline in disease and mortality, as compared to the period of the British Mandate, as well as to some Arab States nowadays. This is a result of efficient health services, particularly in preventive medicine. (3) A reuniting of families, leading to the return of about 40,000 Arabs to Israel in the 1950s. (4) The meagre Arab emigration from Israel, if one does not consider the very small number of Christian families who left Israel[11] (as part of a general migration of Christians from the Middle East) and individual students who remained in the countries where they had studied.

As a consequence of this numerical growth, the Arab minority attained a ratio of about 12 per cent of the State's entire population in December 1966, despite the flow of Jewish immigration into Israel. During recent years there has been a steady increase, percentage-wise, of the Israeli Arabs, and this becomes gradually more evident, due to the decrease in Jewish immigration into Israel.[12] This is shown in the table on p. 5.

Not surprisingly, the growth of the Arab minority in Israel, both in absolute and relative numbers, strengthens its sense of oneness

[8] These details and many of the subsequent ones are based mainly on two official, nationwide censuses, both carried out methodically by Israel's CBS, the first in November 1948, and the second in May 1961. The data pertaining to non-Jews, which was obtained from the second census, may be found in *Moslems, Christians & Druzes*. After 1961 the CBS published estimates, which may be found in the annual *Stat. Ab.*

[9] See data and analysis in E. Ben 'Amram, in *MḤ*, 1965, 7–24.

[10] On 31 Dec. 1965 there were 300,227 non-Jews in Israel, cf. *Stat. Ab. 1965*, 41. These were all Arabs, with the exception of some 1,600 Circassians (of Slavic origin) and a few hundred Aḥmadīs (from Iran). The Circassians are Sunnite Muslims. About 7,000 of the Christians are not Arabs but Armenians, Copts, Christian priests and monks, etc.

[11] This happened mostly in times of unemployment such as mid-1966 (see *ha-Areṣ*, 10 Aug. 1966). The number of Arab emigrants from Israel for 1967 is estimated at about 1,500 (see R. Priester, ibid. 24 Mar. 1967, suppl.)

[12] This changing ratio alarmed some Jewish leaders in Israel. They feared the Jews would eventually become a minority in Israel. Perhaps the most outspoken was Sh. Peres, then political secretary of the RAFĪ party (ibid. 30 Apr. 1967).

and adds weight to its demands as a unit.[13] The character of these demands is also influenced by the relatively young age of its members. Because of its high birth-rate it is comprised of a relatively young

Year	*Percentage of Arabs in total Israeli population*
1957	10·8
1958	10·9
1959	11·0
1960	11·1
1961	11·3
1962	11·3
1963	11·3
1964	11·4
1965	11·3
1966	12·0

age-group; more than half the Arabs in Israel were born after the establishment of the State. They cannot remember the British Mandate; therefore much of their political behaviour is conditioned by the dynamics of life in Israel.

The Israeli Arabs' sense of oneness is further strengthened by the location of their residential areas and their concentration therein. It is true that the Arabs live in 104 towns and villages of their own, and in six mixed towns with a large Jewish majority[14] (Acre, Haifa,[15] Tel-Aviv—Jaffa,[16] Lydda,[17] Ramle, and Jerusalem). Yet almost 60 per cent of the Israeli Arabs live in Galilee, including the two all-Arab towns of Nazareth and Shafā 'Amr. More than 20 per cent of the Israeli Arabs centre in the Little Triangle. Two smaller centres, each with almost 7 per cent of the Arab population, may be found in the Haifa area and in the Negev (especially to the east of Be'er Sheba).

The Arab centres in Galilee, the Little Triangle, and the Negev present two significant common characteristics: all three centres are

[13] Extremist Arabs in Israel have told me on various occasions that they should aim at becoming a majority in the State, through natural increase. However, it is by no means certain that this view is generally accepted.

[14] See *ha-Areṣ*, 27 July 1966.

[15] Cf. ibid. 22 Oct. 1965 suppl. and 6 Jan. 1967 suppl.

[16] See Dan Margalīt's articles, ibid., 31 Mar. 1965, 27 May 1966, & 11 Nov. 1966.

[17] Details in *Davar* (Tel-Aviv, daily), 4 May 1965.

very near the land-borders of Israel with the Arab States (prior to the June 1967 war); they are Arab quasi-monolithic groupings with very few Jewish settlements in the area. In view of security risks and political dangers involved, the Israeli authorities maintained the military administration, though gradually reducing its impact and seemingly substituting a planned policy aimed at converting Galilee into a Jewish region. An example of this was adding a Jewish Nazareth near Arab Nazareth, and also founding a new town named Carmiel in the very heart of Upper Galilee, etc. Steps have also been taken to bring about a permanent settlement of the Bedouins. This has already succeeded in Galilee as well as in the Negev.

Another important factor is that the Arabs in Israel are divided into three main ecological groups—towndwellers, villagers, and Bedouins. In fact, almost three-quarters of the Israeli Arab population live in villages (while of the Jewish population, more than 87 per cent is urban). The economy of the Arab villages is chiefly based on agriculture, and aims at being self-sufficient. The mobility of the Arab villagers is relatively small, and very few of them change their residence after marrying and settling down; even those villagers who work in near-by towns, usually return home in the evening, or every weekend.

Of the two all-Arab towns, we may consider Nazareth, with nearly 28,000 inhabitants, as a town, whereas Shafā 'Amr, with a little over 8,000 inhabitants, still has the character of a large village. Nazareth is the centre of Arab economic and political life. Although part of the Israeli Arabs live in the six mixed towns, those six bear markedly the stamp of Jewish towns, because of the small number of Arabs living in each. A possible exception is Acre, where the Arabs form a quarter of the population in the town.

The Bedouins live in Galilee and in the Negev. There are twenty-five Bedouin tribes in Galilee, numbering approximately 10,000 persons altogether. These tribes, as already mentioned, are undergoing a rapid process of sedentarization and they are assisted by both State and local authorities, in planning their homes, dividing the new lands, and obtaining services and financial aid.[18] In the Negev alone, there are 18 or 19 Bedouin tribes (more precisely remnants of tribes), numbering about 20,000 persons. These differ from the Bedouins in Galilee, for they still follow their ancestors' way of life.[19] However, on account of the political boundaries between Israel and

[18] A. Dōlb, in *Ma'arīv*, 18 Dec. 1964 suppl., and Y. Arī'el, in *ha-Areṣ*, 25 Feb. 1966.

[19] Cf. *ha-Areṣ*, 5 Aug. 1966 suppl.; and Marx, *Bedouin of the Negev.*

its neighbours, they are unable to wander as before. The Israeli Government has shown that it is interested in stability. It has offered the Bedouins health services, education, facilities, aid in financing marriages,[20] and even compensation for damage by drought. It has also induced them to look for new sources of income (nearly a third of these Bedouins work in near-by Jewish settlements)[21] and encouraged them to approach a state of sedentarization, by stages. This process is slower in the Negev than in Galilee. Many Bedouins in the Negev still object to living in permanent settlements planned by the Israeli authorities[22] and are still accustomed to wandering. In years of severe drought, they move northwards into pasture lands which they lease, or simply occupy,[23] thus clashing with the farmers in that area.[24]

THE RELIGIOUS COMMUNITIES

The non-Jewish minorities in Israel are divided into several communities, each with a religion of its own. This religious division is an outcome of the schisms in early Christianity on the one hand, and of the Arab conquest on the other. This turned the area, to a great extent, into a Muslim region, with its own schisms. The fact that the Ottoman Government, and later the British Government, granted a measure of autonomy of several religious communities (particularly in enforcing laws in matters of personal status and administering religious institutions) has given permanence to the existence of these communities as social and political entities.

The Muslims in the State of Israel are divided into two main groups: (1) the Sunnites,[25] who follow orthodox Islam and form almost 70 per cent of all the minorities; (2) the Druzes, a sect which broke away from orthodox Islam about a thousand years ago. They form almost 10 per cent of all the minorities.

The Christians, who number about 20 per cent, make up the rest of the Arab population in Israel. They, also, are divided into several denominations. According to the 1961 census, the main groups are: (percentages in round figures):

[20] Sh. Giv'ōn, in *Ma'arīv*, 15 July 1966.

[21] Among their new professions—the first Bedouin medical student at the Hebrew University in Jerusalem (cf. 'Ū. Benzīman in *ha-Areṣ*', 7 Jan. 1966 suppl.).

[22] L. Lebhart, 'The fate of the Beduin', *Ner* (Jerusalem), Dec. 1954–Jan. 1955, 40–41; M. Arṣī'elī, in *ha-Areṣ*, 17 Jun. 1966.

[23] E. Yanōv, in *Ma'arīv*, 21 Dec. 1965.

[24] D. Mīrqīn, in *ha-Areṣ*, 24 Mar. 1966. On the Bedouin in Israel see also E. Marx's articles in *MḤ*, 1956, 89–98; 1957, 1–18.

[25] On whose characteristics see 'Abd al-Karīm Nāṭūr, in *Ner*, Feb.–Apr. 1958, 25–29.

Christians in Israel

	Per cent
Greek Catholics	42
Greek Orthodox	32
Latins	15
Maronites	6
Others (Protestants, Armenians, Copts,* &c.)	5

* On the Copts in Nazareth cf Ṭ. Karmel, in *Ma'arīv*, 17 Feb. 1965.

The religious structure of the Arab community shows two main characteristics:

1. The denominational division in both Christianity and Islam occurred over a long period of time. Although in time the importance ascribed to the causes for these splits has decreased, their consequences are still noticeable in the mosaic of the religious communities in the State of Israel.

2. During the Ottoman rule (a period of roughly four centuries, up to the first world war), an elaborate congregational organization developed, with specific autonomous patterns, expressed by the *millet* system. According to this system, the Ottoman Government granted several communities judicial autonomy in matters of personal status, *waqf*, and the autonomous administration of their religious institutions and courts. The system was based on the Muslim concept recognizing the special status of 'protected' communities and their right to live according to their beliefs. Thus a system of autonomous religious institutions arose and a tradition of community organization developed. This structure remained unchanged despite changes of government in Palestine. It was confirmed anew at the end of the British Mandate; then it became an integral part of Israel's institutional framework.

In the political arena, too, the community serves as a reservoir of power for its leaders. The community's sense of unity derives from its religious belief, while the *ḥamūla*, or larger family—based on patrilineal association—is kept together by kinship and several rights and obligations.[26] Nowadays religious belief alone does not suffice to establish and maintain political power; the support of a solid institutional framework is needed as well. An inner organization of the community is essential for maintaining its power, while the economic status serves as its foundation. However, judicial autonomy, probably

[26] Abner Cohen's book has described very adequately the social structure of the *ḥamūla* and the relations within it in contemporary Israel. I shall not repeat his conclusions, but concentrate on the political aspects involved.

less crucial, also serves to bolster the sense of obligation felt by the community's members towards it.

The amount of economic power and the dependence on the judicial system make up the differences between the various religious communities, in their relative impact on the political system. This can be seen, first and foremost, in the organization of the community as such.

The Muslims were organized in a community framework only during the British Mandate period. Before that Islam served as the State religion; therefore Muslims did not constitute a 'religious community', in the meaning of the term, as defined in art. 2 of the Inheritance Order, 1923, and art. 3 of the Palestine Order in Council, 1939.[27] The position changed during British rule in Palestine, when the Muslims were granted a special status with certain privileges. However, the fact remains that they acquired their organizational experience during that period only. Thus their organization differed from those of previously-established religious communities. The financial sources at the disposal of the Muslim community in Israel are comparatively meagre. That, together with the absence of established 'foreign relations', limits the community's influence as a united, closely-knit political factor.

The Druze community developed in its own way. The fact that it was not recognized as a religious community by either Ottoman or British rule led it to express loyalty to Israeli rule—the first to grant it community status.

Many Christian denominations, though not all, have a long history of organization in recognized religious communities—this being one of their more important sources of experience in political power.

One may classify the political structure of the various communities according to four criteria: economic status, judicial system, sociocultural institutions, and 'foreign relations'.

1. *The Muslims*

Islam is the religion of most of the Arabs in Israel. The population census in 1961 showed there were 170,830 Muslims, who made up 7·8 per cent of the entire State's population, and about 69·1 per cent of the non-Jewish population. In 1966 their number was estimated at more than 200,000. Compared with the period under British rule, their relative number in the Arab population has decreased.[28] In

[27] M. Zīlberg, *Ha-Ma'amad ha-īshī bĕ-Yisra'el* (Personal Status in Israel) (Jerusalem, 1961), 33.

[28] Shimoni (*'Aravey Ereṣ-Yisra'el*, 63), estimates that Muslims formed 90 per cent of the Arab population in Palestine in 1947.

more recent years the proportion of Muslims is slightly but constantly on the increase, mainly because of their higher birth-rate.

Since nearly all Muslims in Israel are Sunnites, the traces of the schisms in Islam are hardly found in Israel (with the exception of the Druze community). Nevertheless, the Muslim community is far from being a homogeneous unit, ecologically at least. The following types of settlement are shown by the population and housing census of 1961:

	Per cent
In rural settlements	67·3
In urban settlements	16·9
Bedouins, in various stages of nomadism	15·8

Source: Moslems, Christians & Druzes, p. 19.

Most of the Israeli Muslims, then, live in villages; a part of the urban Muslim population left Israel during the 1948 war. More than half the Muslims live in the northern region of Israel. All the Arabs in the Little Triangle and the Negev are Muslims—a fact which augments the homogeneity of this group. This homogeneity, together with the awareness of being the largest minority in Israel, and that beyond the borders of Israel there are many more millions of Muslim Arabs, give part of the Israeli Muslims a majority-feeling, even in Israel.

The Muslim community in Israel has considerable judicial autonomy.[29] Its courts have exclusive and extensive jurisdiction in matters of personal status. This authority was inherited from Ottoman rule, and confirmed in art. 52 of the Palestine Order in Council, 1922, and reconfirmed by the State of Israel. Significantly, the authority of the Sharī'a court judge, the *qāḍī*, is greater than that of Rabbinical or Christian courts, for the latter do not have exclusive powers in any matter other than personal status, while other cases are brought before them only in the case of both litigants agreeing, within a framework of parallel judicial authority. Nevertheless, the political role of the *qāḍīs* in Israel, even within their own circle, is not important. While their political influence is far from insignificant, there is little doubt that the *qāḍīs* or other Muslim holders of religious office in Israel do not constitute important components in the political leadership of their community. The judicial institutions of the Muslim community were affected by the 1948 war. During the fight-

[29] Cf. A Layish, 'Muslim religious jurisdiction in Israel', *Asian & African Studies* (Jerusalem, annual), i (1965), 49–79 and 'The Muslim waqf in Israel', ibid. ii (1966), 41–76.

ing many religious leaders, judges, lawyers of the Sharīʿa courts, and members of the Supreme Muslim Council left the country. Shaykh Ṭāhir al-Ṭabarī was the sole *qāḍī* who remained in Israel. Indeed, he had considerable influence on the Muslims in Israel because of his proficiency in legal matters and the high position he held. However, the fact is that no other Muslim religious leader who could equal al-Ṭabarī's standing remained in Israel. On the contrary, in a very few instances their good character was tainted, when they were involved in corruption, as in the case of Shaykh Ṭāhir Ḥāmid, the former *qāḍī* of Jaffa.

Ever since the State of Israel was founded, there have been constant efforts to buttress its institutional structure and crystallize the patterns of the services offered by the community. A *Qāḍīs*' Law was passed by the Israeli *Kneset* (Parliament), as part of the trend to regulate all the processes relating to the appointment of such judges in Israel. The law prescribes the text of the *qāḍī's* oath of allegiance to the State, and defines the conditions of his appointment, which terminate only upon his death, retirement, or change of employment. Four *qāḍīs* head the Sharīʿa courts in Nazareth, Acre, Jaffa, and Ṭaiyyba. In addition, there is a Court of Appeal. Procedure in all these courts was legalized in April, 1963.

Although in Israel there is no Muslim political leadership comparable to that of the Supreme Muslim Council, led by the ex-Mufti Ḥājj Amīn al-Ḥusaynī in the 1930s, it seems that the internal affairs of this community are still a factor to be reckoned with in political life. Even the Communist Party does not refrain from using the community's religious feelings to strengthen its own position; thus it has accused the Government of following a policy of harbouring a plot against the institutions of the Muslim community! Similarly, during the parliamentary and press debates about the bill regulating the Muslim *waqf*,[30] the Communist Party opposed the bill violently, stressing the importance that the *waqf* represented for the Muslim community.[31]

This interest in the Muslim community and its institutions on the part of outside political factors was stimulated by the special character of the Arab national movement in the Middle East. This was frequently inspired by Islam, and it even seems that there was an overlapping between Islam and the Arab national movement. No wonder, then, that in Israel Islam is a factor which crystallizes Arab national sentiment. The change in values challenges the foundations upon

[30] *Ha-Areṣ* & *Davar*, both of 28 July 1959.
[31] *Qōl ha-ʿam* (Communist daily), 17 May 1961.

which the Christian communities in Israel are built; this process does not have the same impact on the sense of identification of the Muslims. Sometimes the parallel between religion and Arabism, as it seems to exist in the consciousness of Muslim Arab youth in Israel, is evident. Hence one notices indications of a trend towards an Islamic revival, such as soliciting funds for building a mosque, or growing a beard in the style of the 'Muslim Brethren'.[32] Thus, the al-Salām Mosque in Nazareth was built by the inhabitants of the town's Eastern Quarter, who themselves covered all the expenses of this magnificent building.[33] Similarly, when Muslim Arab students in Israel are asked to state the components of the Arab national movement, they mention religion as the dominant factor; but they become confused when asked whether Christians are not Arabs.[34] It is interesting to note that many of these Muslims do not see any inconsistency between their strong religious sentiment and membership in a dynamic, secular State like Israel.

2. *The Druzes*

The Druzes form a separate religious entity in Israel and elsewhere—i.e. in Syria and Lebanon. Most Israeli Druzes[35] live in Western Galilee and on the slopes of the Carmel. In 1961, there were 24,282 Druzes in Israel, about 1 per cent of the entire population and 10 per cent of the minorities.[36] In 1966 they numbered about 30,000, that is approximately the same proportion. Most of them, some 91 per cent, are villagers, dependent on agriculture. However, in their case, too, an increasing number do not subsist on agriculture but rather on outside work in other, larger, settlements. This process seems to offer, in the case of the Druze community in Israel, two characteristics.

First, most Druze villages lie in distant places, not easily accessible. This peculiar trait is rooted in a background of long, cruel persecution, to which the Druzes were subjected by their Muslim neighbours. As a result of constant tension between Druzes and Muslims in the Ottoman period, the Druzes preferred to build their villages in the mountains, which they felt they could more easily defend. Tension was aggravated during the nineteenth century, and much of

[32] Cf. referendum among the younger Israeli Arabs, in *MḤ*, 1965, 86.

[33] *Ha-Areṣ*, 21 Dec. 1965.

[34] Cf. the above referendum in *MḤ*.

[35] On whom see the following articles in *NO*: June 1962, 30–35, 53; Feb. 1966, 36–39; Mar.–Apr. 1967, 40–44—all by Salman Falah, himself an Israeli Druze. A bulletin on Druze affairs, edited by Y. Yĕhōshū'a, is issued regularly by the Israeli Ministry of Religions (another is edited by him on Muslim affairs).

[36] *Moslems, Christians & Druzes*, table 7.

the ill-feeling between Druzes and Muslim Arabs in the area originated during that time. In the State of Israel, when the situation changed, the remoteness and relative inaccessibility of the Druze villages are the cause for a comparatively slow pace of development of these settlements and their limited ties with urban centres. Hence in several Druze villages a proportionately smaller number of inhabitants go to seek work outside.[37]

Second, the Druzes serve in the Israeli army and in the border-defence units. Indeed, they are the only minority in Israel (besides a small number of Circassians) to do so. The military enlistment detaches the young Druzes from their own society and enables them to form new contacts with a different way of life.

It has already been said that neither the Ottoman Government nor the British authorities in Palestine granted the Druzes the status of a recognized religious community. It followed that in all legal rulings they were subject to the decisions of Muslim jurisdiction. All the demands of the Druzes to the contrary were not considered. In contrast, the Druze community in the State of Israel was granted official, recognized religious status, equal to that of all other communities. Israel felt they deserved this status not only because they had constantly been persecuted by the Ottoman authorities and the neighbouring Arabs, but also as a tribute to the only minority that did not leave Israel in 1948, and even assisted the new State in its war against the Arab States, in that year. Again, in June 1967, they distinguished themselves in battle. Partly in consequence, it was decided at Government level, in December 1967, that in all administrative matters Druzes would address themselves through regular channels to the appropriate Government offices (while other minority groups would continue to deal with the minority departments of the same offices).[38] Thus, quasi-official approval was given to the claim made by Israeli Druzes that they did not consider themselves an integral part of the Arab minority in Israel.[39]

The official process of granting the Druzes recognized community status in Israel may be divided into three stages as follows: (1) In 1957 the Israeli Minister of Religions, acting on authority vested in him under 'The Religious Organizations Act, 1926', granted the Druzes separate status of an autonomous religious community. (2) In October 1961 the spiritual leadership of the Druze community was

[37] Such a village, for instance, is Yānūḥ (cf. M. Har'el, *Yānūḥ* (1959)).

[38] Details in *Ma'arīv*, 21 Dec. 1967.

[39] See *Bat-Qōl* (organ of the students in Bar-Ilan University, Ramat-Gan), 20 Feb. 1967.

organized as a Religious Council, and officially approved as such; the three-man council was presided over by Shaykh Amīn Ṭarīf, one of the Druze elders from the village of Jūlis in Western Galilee. (3) In December 1962 the *Kneset* passed a law approving the Druze courts; in 1964 the Druze Religious Council was appointed to serve as a Court of Appeal.[40] Since then, all members of this community apply to these courts in all matters pertaining to religious courts. Following a decision taken by the Druze Religious Council in 1961, the community's courts rule according to the code of personal status of the Druze community in Lebanon, adopted there in 1948. Since this code was adopted by the Druze community in Syria in 1953, it serves as the basis of litigation and legal decision in the three largest Druze communities—in Syria, Lebanon, and Israel.

In this manner, a new centre of power was formed within the Druze community in Israel. Its religious character in no way lessens its political significance. The establishment of the Druze Religious Council and the Druze religious courts was accompanied by violent conflicts, expressing strong competition among upper-class families jockeying for key positions in the new bodies. These conflicts show that the clash of interests within the Druze community is on two main levels: the local competition between the Galilee and the Carmel groups; and the family contest between the prominent families in both regions (particularly in the Carmel villages). The prominent families join one of the large *ḥamūlas*, for political reasons or for prestige, or sometimes due to past family history. This is very often the case in local affairs as well. The *ḥamūla* structure and its implications in Yirkā village are a case in point. There are thirteen Druze families in this village, but there has always been competition between the two large *ḥamūlas* of Mu'addī and Mullah. This modern version of the feud between Montagus and Capulets manifested itself by a marriage between the two rival families, by murder or imprisonment, and later unsuccessful attempts at appeasement. The other families take sides. This is fascinating for the student of local power politics to watch, but does not help in developing the village.[41]

Despite the dissension involved in the competition for key positions in the newly formed courts, it was precisely this creation of an autonomous judicial system that seems to have strengthened the age-long structure of the Druze community. Too little time has elapsed, however, so it is yet too early to gauge the full impact of the

[40] Layish, in *MḤ*, 1961, 258–62; Sa'īd al-Qāsim in *al-Yawm* (Jaffa, daily), 6 Nov. 1964.

[41] *Ha-Areṣ*, 31 Jan. 1965.

Druze religious courts on the community. In contrast to this factor, the dynamic development of Israel appears to shake the established framework, even in the most remote and isolated villages. Compared with the other minorities in Israel, fewer breadwinners leave their villages for outside work (estimates are around 45 per cent).[42] However, this is more than balanced by the influence of two years of army service. There, not only do the Druze youths come into close contact with an entirely different civilization, but their previous notions become irrelevant. Thus the rivalries between the *ḥamūlas* lose their significance. This sharp change of values undermines the loyalty of the Druze youth to the *ḥamūla* framework, and this affects the structure of the community as a whole.

Consequently, when the demobilized Druzes return to their villages, they co-operate in matters of general importance, such as local development and education, regardless of the conflicts between families.[43] Sometimes they form agricultural co-operatives, imitate Jews in methods of cultivation, and try to take over the local government in order to achieve their objects. They often fail owing to the efforts of the established leadership, which uses its influence—internal dissensions notwithstanding—to stand together and oppose the formation of new political organizations no longer based on kinship.[44] Thus in Yirkā, during the campaign for the election of a local council in 1959, young demobilized Druzes succeeded in presenting an independent list of candidates. However, the two large *ḥamūlas*, afraid of being defeated, agreed to boycott the elections. Later they refused to co-operate with the local council, they paid no taxes and sabotaged its activities—so that the newly elected local council could not operate. This was, admittedly, an extreme instance. In other cases, demobilized Druzes show a marked tendency not to return to their villages, looking for new places to settle in. So a small Druze group settled in Eilat, composed entirely of ex-soliders. In any case, in very recent years there has been a visible increase in the pace of development in the Druze villages: roads were built, linking remote mountainous places, water pipes were laid down, and telephone cables were connected.[45]

[42] Cf. *Ma'arīv*, 31 Jan. 1965.

[43] In 1966, during the economic recession, this organization assisted demobilized Druzes in finding jobs (see Z. Schiff, in *ha-Areṣ*, 13 Feb. 1967).

[44] *Ma'arīv*, 31 Jan. 1965. Cf. Sh. Shamīr in *MḤ*, 1961, 246–7.

[45] See *Ma'arīv*, 8 June 1966. This has not prevented radical demands on behalf of Druze youths; see series of articles on this subject, in *ha-Areṣ*, 11, 13, & 14 Nov. 1966. Cf. the reaction of a young Druze, Maḥmūd Yūsuf, in a letter to *ha-Areṣ*, 22 Nov. 1966.

3. *The Christian Communities*[46]

In 1961, 50,543 Christians of all denominations were counted, namely 20·5 per cent of the minorities in the State of Israel. In 1966 there were about 60,000. The larger communities have already been mentioned. The Greek Catholics form not only the largest community; they derive much of their power from their loyal ties with the Vatican, and were led until 1967 by a capable man of action, the Archbishop George al-Ḥakīm. In contrast, the Greek Orthodox community is headed by Greek priests, while most of the other members of this community are local Arabs, a factor which often causes friction all around. These two communities differ from each other, and from other Christian denominations. In particular, the differences are in connexion with the Papacy, ritual, and the language of prayer. However, differences have become more acute due to centuries-long rivalry, in the whole of the Middle East.

The members of the Christian communities prefer to live together in certain areas, as is the case in other minority groups in Israel. These Christian centres are in the north of the country. However, unlike the Muslims and Druzes, most Christians do not inhabit rural areas. In 1961 61·3 per cent of the Christians lived in urban centres, and more than half the remainder dwelt in large villages. Christians form about half the population in Arab Nazareth, 44 per cent of the inhabitants in Shafā 'Amr, and a majority of the Arabs in Haifa and Ramle (about 70 and 60 per cent respectively). Nazareth is the main Christian centre in Israel. Religious and educational institutions are located there, as well as churches, visited by thousands of pilgrims every year.

It may be that the marrying age of the Christians in Israel is higher than that of the Muslims and Druzes, due to the ecological division. The rate of child mortality is lower, too. Compared to the other minority groups, more Christians are educated and, proportionately, hold more jobs which require training. Their relations with the Arabs in the neighbouring countries are more direct: priests have often crossed the borders, and Christians were regularly permitted at Christmas and Easter to visit those holy places which until the June 1967 war were part of the Kingdom of Jordan. By way of contrast, the Muslims in Israel are not allowed by the Arab States to cross the

[46] Y. Zīper, in *MḤ*, 1951, 197–208. On the press of these communities, cf. Y. Ben-Ḥananya (pseudonym of Y. Yĕhōshū'a), ibid. 1959, 24–28. The Israeli Ministry of Religions issues a bulletin regularly, named *Christian News from Israel*, ed. by Chaim Wardi, which contains much useful information.

borders—not even in order to perform the pilgrimage to Mecca. All this goes to explain why the Israeli Christians are comparatively more interested in politics than the Muslims or Druzes, and also participate actively in political affairs. This is particularly true of the two large Christian communities, the Greek Catholics and the Greek Orthodox; it is less applicable to the Latins, Maronites,[47] and other small groups.

The authority of the Christian courts is more limited than that of the Sharī'a courts. Hence, dependence on them is more limited. But their power of jurisdiction is still considerable and their scope of activity quite important. They have sole jurisdiction in matters pertaining to marriage, divorce, alimony, and probate of wills. However, in other matters of personal status, the courts of the Christian communities have only parallel authority; the litigants must, therefore, agree to accept their jurisdiction. None the less, each recognized Christian community possesses considerable autonomy in organizing its own judicial system. This organization functions in co-ordination with the centres of the community outside Israel. These ties with the community abroad characterize the Christians in Israel, distinguishing them from Muslims and Druzes. This is connected with the visits of Israeli Christians to Jordan, and with growing Christian tourism into Israel. The Christian communities themselves are strengthened as a result of building inns and hostels for these pilgrims. Members of these communities guide the pilgrims on their visits to Israel, and they also take care of their sacred places. In this way, spiritual and economic interests combine to encourage the Christian communities to tour Israel. Thus complete uniformity of interests exists between them and the Israeli Government, in one important field at least.

Politically, the foreign relations of these Christian communities have more complicated consequences. These contacts with their churches abroad strengthen the position of the leaders of the Christian communities in Israel; they serve them as an important source of political power, both within their own community and in their relations with the Israeli Government. Sometimes these contacts are used as a means of attack on the Israeli Government, and, in consequence, this strengthens their own political or personal standing. For example, during the Pope's visit to Israel, this tendency was revealed through the presentation of a memorandum about the conditions of the Christians in Israel. Thus the contacts of the

[47] On whom see Sh. Rapapōrt, in *Ma'arīv*, 26 May 1966.

Christian communities with the Israeli authorities become interwoven with Israel's international relations.

The bonds of the Christian communities in Israel with their centres abroad have other implications, too, especially in the Arab States. The rigid subordination of many community leaders in Israel to their superiors in the Arab States has already created a strong feeling against this inflexibility, and a tendency among these leaders to free themselves from this framework and have direct contact with the Pope or Patriarch.

Another issue under the same heading was, until June 1967, the crossing of Christians into Jordan, usually during the Christmas holy days. Neither Israel nor Jordan approved all applications for crossing over, but this crossing enabled Christians to compare the extensive economic progress in Israel, from which they, too, benefited, with the situation in Jordan. Sometimes they themselves realized that in Israel a marked change had taken place in their own cultural values and their own way of thinking.

2

ADAPTATION OR ALIENATION

VILLAGERS AND TOWNSPEOPLE

BACK in 1950, an Israeli Arab described the attitude of his community towards the State of Israel as that of sons towards their step-mother.[1] This seems to hold good nowadays too. However, one should ascertain whether these sons have meanwhile learnt to live in peace with their step-mother, or whether they would rather she were dead.

The political behaviour of the Arabs in Israel is, to a great extent, a reflection of their general development in all fields. Its description is perforce an attempt at evaluating a still incomplete process; and because of the swiftness of change, it appears that the process of change itself is its most striking characteristic. Although not all the details in this process of change are evident, there is little doubt that Arab society in Israel is passing through a stage of modification in outlook and daily life. The traditional structure is gradually crumbling, although the pace of this process varies in every settlement, region, community, and social group.

The Arab village has changed in its exterior appearance and in its way of life.[2] Perhaps the most outstanding change is the transfer of the sources of livelihood from village to town. According to the 1961 census, 50·3 per cent of all non-Jews employed in profit-bearing work earned their livelihood outside their regular place of residence.[3] This applies particularly to the villagers. The constant outflow of Arab villagers, seeking work in near-by urban centres, closely affected the internal change in the means of production within their villages. This is a direct outcome of the decrease in landholdings and of the special features of the labour market in Israel.[4] Up to the economic recession of 1966, the demand for labour in Israel was so great that Arab villagers could obtain town jobs easily, and they became waiters, drivers, or unskilled workers in the building trade.

[1] Cited in *Ner*, 28 Apr. 1950, 7. On other 'rebellious thoughts' among the Arabs in Israel, cf. ibid. 27 Oct. 1950, 9–10.

[2] See B. Shidlovsky, in *MḤ*, 1965, 25–37. For an ably-written survey of Arab society in Israel, see S. N. Eisenstadt, *Israeli Society* (1967), 391–408.

[3] *YSY*, July 1963, 963 ff.

[4] Ben-Porat, *Arab labor force*

These Arabs would then forsake the agricultural occupation of their forefathers and move into an entirely different set of labour relations. However, in most cases this phenomenon of work outside their village was not accompanied by urbanization, for many of the villagers went home every evening, and others every weekend. In 1964 a referendum among 116 Arabs revealed that many of them returned home because they could not adapt themselves to the strange urban society.[5] Some of these Arabs were not content working in Jewish towns,[6] but they went on working there because of a high rate of pay compared with what they could earn in their own villages.[7] In the long run, this affected the Arab village in Israel, by drawing it closer to the town and weakening the structure of its established institutions. Their place was left empty, and it is difficult to fill this void.

The Arab-Israeli war of 1948 interrupted the continuity of the social, economic, and political development of the Arab population. This continuity was challenged by changing circumstances and new patterns, following the establishment of the State of Israel. Some of these changes were rooted in the period of British rule. In the Arab villages the local focal points of political power are still dependent on the rules established by custom—even if their authority has diminished. Indeed, most of the organized parties and political groups formed in the days of the British Mandate have disappeared. But various local notables have nevertheless retained some of their power. At least one political party, the communists, is a direct successor of the pre-1948 Communist Party. During the period of the British Mandate the distribution of Arab political forces conformed almost invariably to the social framework. Indeed, the Communist Party, which was the only exception to this, lacked real influence, and had to act through various front organizations; even so it had little success in the Arab villages and towns. Most of the power was centred in the hands of notable landowners, whose families held key positions and competed with one another. Rival camps were always made up of the same families in varying alignments. This traditional distribution of political forces was largely based on the socio-economic

[5] A. Ben-Tzur, in *ba-Sha'ar*, July 1964, 13–23.

[6] As expressed, for instance, in a short feature-film, produced in 1966 and called *I am Aḥmad*, which stirred up considerable public controversy. See estimate of H. Bōshes in *ha-Areṣ*, 17 Jan. 1967, and Y. Shavīṭ, in *YA*, 17 Feb. 1967.

[7] The same phenomenon continued, but with more modest proportions, after the beginning of the economic recession in 1966 (see Mīrqīn in *ha-Areṣ*, 20 Feb. 1966; Mansour, ibid. 26 July & 30 Oct. 1966, & 10 Mar. 1967; Y. Dar, in *Davar*, 24 Mar. 1967).

structure of the Arab population in Palestine and Israel. The village was the mainstay of economic power. In the past, it had little connexion with the town. The material culture of the village has slowly altered but its inhabitants continued to depend on the land and the landlords, who still owned large estates. In the days of British rule, though some lands were divided among the heirs of previous owners, the socio-economic polarization did not change basically. The division of lands hit the small owners hardest. Thus owning land continued to be the key to socio-economic power, and hence to political power. Indeed, the *ḥamūlas* competing for supremacy were actually part of the rural aristocracy.[8]

The competition between the *ḥamūlas* cut through the social and political structure of the Arab population. However, during the second half of the period of British rule, the impact of this competition weakened for two reasons: first, the growth of a middle class of landowners; and secondly, the growing prominence of the Arab towns, in which alternating forces began to rise. Even then, local village leadership continued to be connected with similar ruling circles in national Arab leadership. The elders of the *ḥamūlas* served as mediators who also represented the village *vis-à-vis* the Government. In fact, they were the self-appointed managers of the village, responsible for all its dealings with the outside world. This mediation was called *wāsṭa* in colloquial Arabic. The heads of the *ḥamūlas* were recognized by the Government and that further strengthened their position. The *mukhtār* of the village was the head of the strongest *ḥamūla*; sometimes there were two rival *mukhtārs*. In some Arab villages in Israel one can still find members of these major *ḥamūlas* in influential positions.

Even the Arab political parties, which developed since the 1930s, were groups of influential families, so that the *ḥamūla* structure still served as the basis for party organization. In fact, there were no deep ideological differences between the parties; if there were differences of opinion, they concerned tactics rather than principles. The same characteristics applied to political forces in the towns too. A certain neighbourhood generally included members of the same *ḥamūla*, religious community, or occupation. Each neighbourhood thus became a part of the political alignment. It was only during the last decade of the British Mandate in Palestine that new groups began to form: young intellectuals, workers, newly-established manufacturers, and others. The Arab townspeople showed a growing political

[8] Shimoni, *'Aravey Ereṣ-Yisra'el*, 168, Waschitz, *ha-'Aravīm bĕ-Ereṣ-Yisra'el*, 44–45.

awareness; the workers in the towns served as a special target for the eager onslaught of communist propaganda.

This cross-section of internal relations in the villages (and to a lesser extent in the towns) was maintained even after 1948. Despite the turn of events caused by the Arab-Israeli war, traditional rivalries are still influential in the competition between the *ḥamūlas*. However, despite the continuation of these factors locally, they have lost their impact in the struggle for power on a countrywide scale. Because of the absence of recognized national leadership within the Arab population in Israel, the ties which had connected various *ḥamūlas* throughout Palestine are now broken. Rivalry between *ḥamūlas* is still common, for instance in Yirkā,[9] Rāma, Kafr Kannā,[10] Beyt-Jān, Jatt,[11] and other Arab villages; but—it should be stressed again—only on a *local* scale. These *ḥamūlas* compete for power, and unite in order to block the rise of new elements when they endanger the traditional structure. True, a new scale of values operates in the Arab village in Israel, rejecting timeworn concepts; young intellectuals and workers holding jobs outside the village are among the advocates of change. Nevertheless, the transition is still in full swing, and age-hallowed tradition serves as a moderating force. This transition compels the traditional circles to adapt themselves to change. Results vary: in a number of cases there is a radical change in the balance of power between the *ḥamūlas*.[12] Hence the break-up of the traditional structure; the head of the *ḥamūla* loses much of his power and the elders of the main families take his place; minor *ḥamūlas* transfer their loyalty to a rival *ḥamūla*, which thus strengthens its position—but temporarily only, for it is threatened from within by the same process.

This process of change cannot be analysed in detail, for lack of space.[13] It suffices to say that it varies in every village, depending on a number of factors, the most important being the distance of the village from the nearest large town; its proximity to the border; the existence of Jewish settlements in its neighbourhood; its size; and its religious components. All these factors combine to make up the intellectual level of the villagers and their pursuit of outside work—the two main variables which actually determine the extent of *ḥamūla* power. Since the *ḥamūla* rule, though divided within itself,

[9] *Ha-Areṣ*, 27 Oct. 1965.

[10] Ibid., 20 Feb. 1966; *Ma'arīv*, 25 Feb. 1966.

[11] *Ha-Areṣ*, 3 Jun. 1966, suppl.

[12] See, about relevant events in Kafr Kannā and Ṭur'ān, *ha-Bōqer*, 21 Sept. 1959 and *ha-Areṣ*, 22 Apr. 1966.

[13] For additional details, cf. Abner Cohen, *Arab border-villages*.

is probably the single most important factor which shows up the development of the village,[14] it follows that trends of modernization may clash with the interests of the *ḥamūlas*. While the Israeli authorities do not take any concerted action to lessen the influence of the *ḥamūlas*, it is weakened anyway by the very existence of a modern, dynamic State. The direct influence of State institutions is expressed mainly in the following manner: (1) Establishing direct contact with individuals, not necessarily through the head of a *ḥamūla* or the chief of the religious community; thus the above *wāsṭa* loses much of its significance. (2) Raising the level of education, by founding boys' and girls' schools in every village, thus putting the 'compulsory, free education law' into effect. (3) Maintaining the rule of law against inherent practices, e.g. discouraging polygamy, divorce without a wife's consent, prohibiting blood-feuds[15] and violence, imposing taxation without any preferential treatment. (4) Developing the village, by introducing agricultural machinery, expert advice, improvement of road communications, or installing water and electricity; all these measures require the co-operation of the villagers and their influence is felt for a long time. (5) The formation of local councils through democratic elections—general, secret, direct, equal, and proportional.

Of the above-mentioned, the most important item is the introduction of democratic elections, and we shall deal with it at greater length later. In former times the head of a *ḥamūla* attained this position either by succession, or due to his wealth, or by successfully manipulating the support of the family chiefs.[16] The heads of the *ḥamūlas* decided who would be the *mukhtār* representing the village *vis-à-vis* the authorities; if they could not agree, the village had more than one *mukhtār*. Nowadays, direct and secret elections are held and all the villagers have equal rights of participation, including women; hence the candidates are now more dependent on their voters than they were previously. By the weakening of the position of the heads of *ḥamūlas*, as already described, elections enabled the expression of opposition to the established leadership. Their secrecy protected rebels who would not have dared to express opposition openly. The heads of the *ḥamūlas* are of course aware of this threat to their authority, and try to maintain their positions of power by putting pressure on the voters. They often succeed, despite opposition, in

[14] See A. Khalfōn, representative of the Israeli Ministry of the Interior in the northern district, in *ha-Areṣ*, 13 Aug. 1959.

[15] e.g. ibid. 8 Feb. 1966.

[16] Shimoni, *'Aravey Ereṣ-Yisra'el*, 173.

maintaining their power, but generally achieve more favourable results in local elections than in parliamentary elections.

In the Arab population, traditionalism is closely knit into the social structure, within two basic interconnected loyalty structures.[17] The *ḥamūla* is based on kinship, and the religious community rests on ties of faith. Often the two structures are identical, particularly in villages of mixed minorities, where the division between the *ḥamūlas* is according to faith.[18] However, in general, the religious community is much larger, and the *ḥamūlas* frequently compete with its framework. Despite changes, both the *ḥamūla* and the religious community have maintained much of their own character. It may be worth summing up this process of change in both.

The *ḥamūla* or the religious community is the basic unit in the traditional political alignment. As long as this alignment is tightly knit, all differences of opinion are kept within these units; they become apparent only when a new factor comes into being, as the result of family rivalry. The *ḥamūla* or religious community is founded on three main elements: (1) economic dependence upon the chiefs who own the land as well as the means of cultivation and marketing; (2) the *wāsṭa*, the means of negotiation between single individuals and all outside bodies; (3) the power of age-long habit, hallowed by continuity and upheld by local opinion. All three elements, which supplied the 'cement', were shaken by rapid development in the State of Israel. The villagers' work outside their village diminished their dependence on the *ḥamūla* chiefs; workers could themselves save the *mahr*,[19] or the price they had to pay the prospective bride's father. Close relations exist between the heads of *ḥamūlas* and religious communities on one side, and the government agencies and outside groups on the other. In addition to the former leaders, many other Arabs come into contact with government offices, the police, the *Histadrūt* (General Federation of Labour), etc. The hold of established institutions is still strong, mainly in the Muslim and Druze villages, but the younger people frequently meet in groups belonging to different *ḥamūlas* or communities—for sports, card games, watching TV,[20] and political activities.

It is not surprising that heads of the Muslim *ḥamūlas* and leaders of the Christian and Druze religious communities understand the value and importance of these new trends. As a result they have

[17] See Rosenfeld, *Hem hayū*, 77—on family ties and religion.

[18] Cf. Shamīr, in *MḤ*, 1961, 242.

[19] L. Ben Dor, 'Parliamentary report—Jews, Moslems and the law', *JP*, 24 June 1966. Cf. *ha-Areṣ*, 23 June 1966 and ha-Rĕ'ūvenī in *Ma'arīv*, 3 July 1966.

[20] See *MḤ*, 1965, esp. 92.

varied the sources of occupations they could offer—e.g. within the Greek Catholic community—and looked for ties with new socio-economic and political forces which have been penetrating the Arab countryside and towns in the State of Israel. New social and cultural structures were planned. At election time, for instance, even the old leadership adopted slogans not only of local but also of national import, viz., they attempted to awaken local loyalties and to create new ones, though with no ideological framework.[21]

THE BEDOUINS AND THE PATTERNS OF CHANGE[22]

In the northern part of the Negev there are many Bedouin tribes, made up of more than 20,000 people. A large part of the area they inhabit lies along the Israel–Jordan frontiers. Most of the Bedouin tent camps are pitched in the valleys between Be'er Sheba and 'Arad, since this is the main rainwater reservoir of the mountainous region which surrounds them.

The social structure of these Bedouin tribes is based more on age-long custom than that of the villagers and townspeople. This is precisely the reason why the process of change characterizing the whole Arab population in Israel is more pronounced in Bedouin society. The establishment of the State of Israel created new borders, thereby limiting the wide open spaces in which the Bedouins roamed; it also broke up their ties with other Bedouins across these borders. The tribes were thus split up; since some of the chieftains were living on the other side of the frontier, the social structure was also affected. Because of all this, the Bedouins take great interest in the fortunes of their brethren across the border; smuggling was carried on in these underpopulated areas with considerable profit. Nevertheless, since the year 1948, the Bedouins have undergone far-reaching changes. These were a direct result of their contact with the settled population in their dependence on outside work and in the development of public utilities in the Bedouin areas.

Palestinian Bedouins took on outside work as early as the first

[21] Patterns of change in the Arab village have been described and analysed in recent years, e.g. in a number of articles in *NO*: Feb. 1959, 37–42; Mar.–Apr. 1959, 14–23; Jan. 1961, 36–49; Mar.–Apr. 1962, 93–112; Jan. 1967, 5–9, 18; Oct. 1963, 23–31; Nov.–Dec. 1963, 65–73; Feb. 1964, 54–58; Sept. 1964, 10–25; Oct. 1964, 29–32, 50; Sept. 1966, 29–32; May 1967, 52–54.

[22] For the general patterns, see Marx's articles in *MḤ*, 1956 & 1957. Contrast, for another area in Israel, G. Golany, *Beduin settlements in the Alonim-Shfar'am hill region* [1967]. Cf. various articles in *NO*, esp. Sept. 1958, 17–24; Oct. 1958, 25–31; June 1960, 28–31; July–Aug. 1960, 37–40; Sept. 1960, 15–18; Sept. 1965, 24–28. J. Chelhod, 'L'organisation judiciaire chez les Bédouins du Négueb', *Anthropos*, lx (1965), 625–45.

world war years, when they were employed in constructing the railway to 'Awja al-Ḥafīr. Again, during the second world war the Bedouins found full employment in building army camps, constructing roads, and erecting military fortifications. Nowadays about one-third of the Bedouin breadwinners are salaried workers, working outside their camps. This ratio is smaller than in the Arab villages, but the resulting impact is more meaningful. Bedouin youths are gradually removed from the daily influence of the tribe. When they go home, they no longer wish to return to the same ways of life they were accustomed to. Their sense of value has changed; both the traditional law of the tribe, the *'urf*, and the tribe itself, seem strange to them. However, they still feel part of their tribe and have a sense of belonging to it, so they do not rebel against its authority. In the State of Israel, the process discussed above applies particularly to the Bedouin in the Negev. The development of this area has transformed Be'er Sheba into a fair-sized town; and the new towns of Dimona and 'Arad are growing rapidly. Industrial plants were constructed in this region, and many new roads built to shorten distances. Members of the Bedouin tribes found employment. In a number of cases, some Bedouins switched from stock-breeding to agriculture. The most significant fact is that they are no longer isolated and they are learning the ways of western civilization, and may even imitate them. The Israeli *Histadrūt* has organized special courses among them, training them to become skilled workers, such as drivers and craftsmen. Successive years of drought in the 1960s strengthened the tendency of the Negev Bedouins to seek more permanent employment.

The development of public services among the Negev Bedouins is no less significant. It forms new points of contact between the Bedouin and twentieth-century civilization. There is a central clinic for Bedouins in Be'er Sheba, as well as smaller clinics in their main encampments. The *Histadrūt* undertakes various activities there, such as a labour exchange, which protects the wages of the Bedouins and prevents possible delays in payment; offices for information and instruction; clubs and libraries. Professional courses, organized for Bedouin youths, assist them to get better conditions in the labour market. Most important is the progress of the educational system in the Negev. Under British rule there was one central school for the Bedouins in Be'er Sheba and only nine other schools elsewhere. Today each tribe has its own school, and many Bedouins study in schools in Be'er Sheba, Nazareth, and the Little Triangle. The first Bedouin medical student at the Hebrew University in Jerusalem is well on his way to becoming a doctor. True, the drop-out of Bedouin pupils is still considerable, but nevertheless the widening of education has already resulted in a conflict of values. Furthermore, most of the teachers in the Bedouin schools come from Galilee or the Little Triangle, thus serving as a link between the Negev Bedouins and the rest of the Arabs in Israel. It is quite likely that these teachers spread new ideas, not devoid of political content.

This closer contact with the outside world has brought about some remarkable changes in the Bedouins' way of life, accompanied by a rise in the standards of living and the consumption of commodities previously unknown. Nutrition, clothing, and household articles have changed. Cigarettes have taken the place of tobacco, the tasty *samne* comes in tins, men (and sometimes women, too) start wearing 'European' clothes; tin containers and plastic bowls are used instead of copperware and earthenware. Even more significant is the change in dwelling quarters. The costly encampment no longer suits present conditions. It is superfluous, since sedentarization is near and roaming is limited anyway. The general tendency is to change over to tin huts. Frequently permanent houses are built, in order to take possession of certain lands. As a result, nowadays a Bedouin encampment in the Negev is a mixture of tents, shacks, and tin huts, thus reflecting this transition stage in Bedouin life.

Politically, western civilization has penetrated into tribal life via the parties, trade unions, the press, and the courts—all of which challenge tribal authority. Internal relations in the tribe are changing; though the tribal shaykh still maintains his position of leadership, his authority is gradually diminished, as many matters cease to be under his control. An interesting case in point is the rivalry between Bedouin tribes, as expressed when facing new challenges, such as parliamentary elections. During the elections to the sixth *Kneset*, in November 1965, ballot polls were placed in several Bedouin tribes. The Huzayl tribe considered some of these socially inferior Bedouins. As a result, the elders of this tribe refused to vote, and only 40 per cent of the registered electors cast their vote (as compared to 80 per cent in the previous election).[23]

Indeed, the conflict between the old political structure and the new forces has much the same character as the clash between generations in Bedouin society. Many youths have acquired new accessories and commodities. They are strongly inclined to imitate western civilization. They wish to be economically independent, by terminating their financial subjection to their fathers or to the chieftain of the tribe. The problem of land should be mentioned here too.

[23] *Ha-Areṣ*, 29 Nov. 1965.

Owning land is a source of power for the elders, and helps them maintain their sway over the whole tribe. They claim vast areas in the Negev, where they once used to roam; but they know well that their legal position is frail, since there has never been a methodical land registration in the Negev.[24]

PROBLEMS IN ADAPTATION

The political alignments of the Arabs in Israel develop amidst various cross-currents. Inside and outside influences are at work on the Arab population. The complex reality in which the Arabs live in Israel highlights the contrasts and contradictions within their own community. These are expressed both in their reaction to social change and their political integration into the State of Israel.

Inevitably, an essential contradiction arises from the new political situation in the country after 1948. These make it difficult for the Arabs to accept reality; such acceptance, however, is necessary as a pre-condition to integration. Non-acceptance is expressed by refusing to consider themselves as a minority in the State of Israel; they prefer to identify themselves with the Arab majority in the Middle East and North Africa. The Israeli Arabs themselves are aware of this contradiction in their position. They often stress their difficulties of adaptation as a minority, while often passing over their identification with the Arab majority across the borders. An illustration may be found, for instance, in a symposium about the Arabs in Israel, held in Jerusalem at the end of November 1962.[25] One of the most interesting lectures was given by an educated Arab, Salīm Jubrān, on 'How does an Arab see himself in Israel?' In his introduction he stated: 'We, the Arabs in Israel, were a majority, while the Jews were a minority; it is not so simple to change from being a majority to a minority within a short time.' He then added: 'The problem of the Arab citizens in Israel is unique. I do not know of any other instance where a national minority exists in an environment surrounded by peoples of the same nation, without a state of peace between them.'[26] The speaker mentioned a focal point, but his general tone was moderate. His lecture stressed a desire for the integration of Arabs into the State of Israel, while expressing a strong hope for the solution of this contradiction he had pointed out. He put it in this way:

[24] On this problem, see Arṣī'elī, ibid. 17 June 1966.

[25] It was presided by the Israeli Minister of Police, the late B. Shīṭrīṭ, and attended by a number of journalists. The following is from the mimeographed stenographic report.

[26] The translation is given verbatim. The speaker's meaning is clear, even though his style is somewhat rhetorical.

'Everyone in the world must support the movement to liberate his own people; one should explain to the Arabs of Israel that loyalty to this State does not clash with the liberation movement of the Arab people.'[27]

The position of nationalist Arabs in Israel is diametrically opposed to this, since they reject any suggestion of adaptation. The most extremist even refuse to acknowledge the existence of the State of Israel, others disavow its post-1948 frontiers. An unusual illustration may be found in a geography booklet, written and published in 1957 by an Arab ex-teacher from Nazareth, in which he outlined Israel's borders as those defined by the UN 1947 partition plan only—as though the State of Israel did not exist at all. We shall have more to say, later, about the political activities of nationalist Arabs in Israel. Let us now attempt to show the main reasons for the alienation of many Arabs in Israel.

1. *Cultural Non-Identification*

One can understand the alienation of the Arabs in Israel better, if one remembers that many of them find it difficult to consider themselves part of the new State. They feel much more in common, as a nation having the same language and, mostly, the same religious beliefs and the feelings of a common history, with their brethren across the borders. This is the main cause of their identification with the Arab national movement and the reason for their failure to integrate—far more than the socio-educational and ecological disparateness from the Israeli Jews would have warranted. This national identification is particularly evident among the young Arab intellectuals in Israel. They are bolder in emphasizing this and in drawing the full conclusion. A Muslim Arab named al-Ṣa'īdī wrote a series of articles entitled 'The viewpoint of an Arab'. He expressed himself with complete frankness in this respect, declaring incisively: 'I am simply against the military service of Arabs in the Israel Defence Army. I am not willing to fight my brethren in other Arab countries, since I am an integral part of the Arab nation.'[28] Then he added: 'I am ready to fight for the State of Israel, if it is threatened by a foreign Power such as Russia, the USA, Great Britain, or France.' However, since he seemed aware of the fact that he would not be requested to serve in the Israel defence forces, he concluded: 'If I say that I

[27] Quoted from the unpublished minutes of the meeting, p. 4. Cf. Rustum Bastūnī in *MH̱*, 1965, esp. 1, 3; and 'Abd al-Muta'āl al-Ṣa'īdī in *Ḥerūt* (Tel-Aviv, daily), 13 Feb. 1964.

[28] The Arab original reads: '*juz' la yatajazza*'.'

agree to serve in that Army in order to show loyalty, it would mean I am a hypocrite—something I would never agree to be.'[29] And, indeed, Israel prevented the danger of schizophrenia by drafting the Druzes only, while excusing all members of other minorities from service.

2. *Consanguinity across the Borders*

Kinship between relatives in Israel and abroad also strengthens their desire to ignore the political borders. Many family meetings were arranged officially, and were then held near the Mandelbaum gate in Jerusalem.[30] It is easier for the Christians, because they have permission to celebrate Christmas in the Old City of Jerusalem. In a number of cases, blood-ties served as a basis for forming spy rings inside Israel. The intelligence services of the Arab States are well aware of the potency of kinship and use it for their purposes. The Israeli Arab faces a difficult dilemma, when confronted by a relative infiltrating from abroad and asking for refuge in his house; experience shows that he does not always lock him out.[31]

3. *Proximity to the Frontiers*

Many Arab villages and Bedouin camps are situated near Israel's land borders. Some are on the very border itself, a fact which for them wipes out its significance: in spite of the demarcation lines, it is quite easy to hold conversations across the border. Villages which were divided by the border still seem to form a natural unit—even though strict measures have been taken against fraternizers in recent years. In one case, until the year 1955, a common *mukhtār* ruled both sides of the village Barṭa'a in the Menashe mountains, as if it had remained one unit; the women of the village pumped water from the same well, and the men prayed together in the same mosque on Fridays. Finally, the *mukhtār* was arrested in Jordan and convicted of smuggling; villagers from both sides sent funds to Jordan to pay for his defence in court. Since then, the frontier seems to have deepened in meaning there.[32] However, all along the Little Triangle the frontier remained unreal. Thus people frequently crossed the border accidentally. For instance, in September 1961 two Jordanian Inspectors of Education arrived, by mistake, at the Arab village of

[29] In *Ḥerūt*, 13 Feb. 1964.

[30] For such meetings see e.g. 'O. Alyagōn's report in *Ma'arīv*, 17 June 1966.

[31] e.g. Murshid al-Khaṭīb, a spy from Lebanon (see below), obtained food and lodging from his cousin at Kafr Yāṣīf. At his trial, the prosecution proved that the spy had led a comfortable life in Israel (cf. *ha-Areṣ*, 8 Feb. 1966).

[32] Cf. ibid., 17 June 1955; *ha-Bōqer*, 21 June 1955.

Muqaybala in Israeli territory; they went to the school headmaster and wished to visit the classes. During the ensuing conversation it transpired that they were acting *ultra vires.*[33]

4. *The Impact of the Arab-Israeli War*

The 1948 war was a traumatic experience for those Arabs who experienced it. Some of the consequences are still felt. The war broke up families and ruined some of them. It appears that many Israeli Arabs are aware of their own leaders' responsibility for this war and the ensuing defeat, and often admit it. However, as they cannot demand reparations from these leaders, their resentment is sometimes expressed in their attitude towards the State of Israel. Another of the direct consequences of the war has been the land problem. A great number of Arabs lost part of their lands because of the war and the new situation. It is impossible to calculate precisely the influence of this factor, but there is little doubt that it is considerable, even though compensation has been paid for expropriated land, and the Arab population has benefited from the general economic progress in the State of Israel.

5. *The Influence of Mass Communication*

Radio and television serve as a powerful impetus to strengthen the Arabs' sense of identification arising from kinship, and—as a result—increase the alienation to the State of Israel. These media eliminate distances, bypass political borders, and establish tight contacts between the Arab citizens in Israel and the propaganda machine of the neighbouring States. Through these means of communication, every Arab home in Israel is directly aware of the prevailing political climate in the Arab State. These transmit special programmes aimed at forming a national Arab consciousness, alien or even hostile to the State of Israel. While the Israeli radio services fight back, the television of the Arab States has had a field-day, for Israel had no TV until 1968, except for an educational programme. This fact is particularly important, as compared with the constant increase of the TV networks outside Israel, considering that the broadcasts from Egypt, Syria, Lebanon, or Jordan are received quite clearly in Israel. The quality of reception varies, according to the location of the TV set, the power of the transmission, and the time of day.

The Egyptian TV is particularly strong. It reaches sets throughout the Middle East, transmitting continuously, from 4 p.m. to mid-

[33] *JP*, 17 Sept. 1964.

night (Israel time).[34] Many Arabs in Israel watch Egyptian TV, since its programmes are markedly better than those of other Arab countries. 'Abd al-Nāṣir is frequently seen on the screen; the very immediacy of seeing and hearing him gives added significance to his speeches. Syrian TV and radio follow an extremist tone both in their presentation (sarcasm, incitement) and choice of material (spy trials, etc.)—particularly in the programmes directed to Israel. In contrast, the tone of Lebanese TV is moderate, as it devotes most of its broadcasting to entertainment and advertising. The number of TV sets increases constantly among the Israeli Arabs, more rapidly, indeed, than among the Jewish population. Perhaps this, again, points at the tendency of Israeli Arabs to identify with the Arab national movement in the Middle East. TV is especially popular in times of tension, and influences the mood of the Arabs in Israel even more. Coffee-houses are quite crowded on such days. Some programmes are intentionally directed at the Arabs in Israel, urging them to support the Arab national movement. They sometimes contain definite instructions. For example, on the eve of the 1959 parliamentary elections, the Egyptian radio and TV stations called to the Arabs in Israel to abstain from the polls.[35] On that occasion, the heavy Arab participation in the voting served as proof that this call received little support. Nevertheless, there is little doubt that the radio and TV of the Arab States penetrate the home of the Israeli Arab and bolster up the feeling of alienation.

6. *Reaction to Attitudes of the Jewish Population*

The adaptation and alienation of the Arabs in Israel have been conditioned, in no small degree, by the attitudes of the Jews. The original official stand seems to have been that the problems of the Arab population in Israel were of a temporary nature, and that as soon as the Rhodes armistice agreements gave way to a formal peace settlement, the fate and place of the Arabs in Israel would be settled by mutual agreement. Hence the military administration and other measures were imposed provisionally. Peace remained remote; but official circles, faced with what they considered more pressing matters, became accustomed to regarding the affairs of the Arabs in Israel as temporary only. In consequence, they were in no hurry to

[34] The Arab TV stations use these hours more and more, as this is the most popular period for listening. Sometimes this turns into a 'TV war' (cf. *ha-Ares*, 16 Aug. 1965).

[35] See ibid. 12 July 1959. The same was repeated in the 1965 parliamentary elections.

put forward permanent solutions;[36] the postponement of decision-making gradually became the unavowed key-stone of policy.

However, unofficial Jewish attitudes have probably had a deeper impact on the Arabs in Israel. These attitudes have been coloured by the wide range of opinions prevalent in Israeli society and politics on most issues. In the early years of the State of Israel, some extremists held that the Arab minority had no right to live there and should be encouraged to leave, with due compensation.[37] Many others, with a more liberal approach, maintained that those Arabs who had remained in Israel were not responsible for the Arab-Israeli situation and ought to be treated on equal terms with their Jewish neighbours.[38] As the years have passed, the Jewish majority appears to have accepted the Arab minority as a part of the State's population, acquiescing in the possession by the Arabs of all political rights. The issue, as the Jewish majority in Israel came to see it, ceased to be the continued existence of the Arabs as a part of Israel's citizen body. This had become an agreed fact; but security-minded Jews were not sure whether they could fully trust the Arab minority. Nevertheless, among both official circles and Jewish public opinion, liberal attitudes triumphed. The termination of the military administration, in December 1966, was received with approval not only by Jews who had been demanding its abolition for years, but also by those who had been doubtful about the necessity for its continuation.

Social and economic current attitudes, however, were frequently more relevant. Even in mixed towns Jews and Arabs continued to live apart. A few met socially, but this was the exception rather than the rule. In general, social mixing and economic co-operation, on an individual level, were infrequent; and, in several such instances, Arabs were quick to take offence, even when the other side meant well. The barriers of language and custom were not easy to overcome. While it is difficult to generalize, in the absence of comprehensive research on this point, it is possible that the mutual separateness may have helped in preventing tensions and flare-ups. On the other hand, however unintentionally, it has tended to breed resentment among the Arab minority and contributed to its alienation.

All these factors combined—cultural and linguistic non-identification, consanguinity across the borders, proximity to the frontiers, the impact of the Arab-Israeli war, the influence of mass communication,

[36] A. Rubinstein, 'Aravey Yisra'el: gīsha mĕṣī'ūtīt', *Kalkala wĕ-ḥevra,* June 1966, 29–31.

[37] J. Kimchi, in *Davar,* 26 Nov. 1950; A. Sharōn, ibid. 25 June 1951.

[38] A. S. Stein, ibid. 13 July 1951.

and the attitude of a part of the Jewish population—do not encourage a sense of belonging to the State of Israel in its Arab citizens. Indeed, the alienation of a section of the Arab population is expressed quite strongly, by reacting in three different ways.

(*a*) *Flight*. A certain tendency to 'escape' into the neighbouring countries is found among Arab youth, particularly in times of personal tension or public excitement. Some youngsters cross the borders, hoping to find there a suitable political climate.[39] They take with them maps, photographs, and books, with the intention of assisting the intelligence agencies in their intended country of refuge. However, they are frequently induced or compelled by those same intelligence agencies to return to Israel clandestinely, in order to collect further information, so that they sometimes lose their lives while crossing the border in one or the other direction. Such a death immediately becomes the topic of conversation among the Arabs in Israel, so that the chain reaction continues.[40]

(*b*) *Assistance to spies*. There have been cases when Arab inhabitants helped foreign intelligence officers and spies who had crossed into Israel, to collect military and other information. Such a case was revealed at the trial of a Lebanese spy named Murshid al-Khaṭīb. During his visit to Israel, no less than thirteen people in the Arab village of Kafr Yāṣīf co-operated with him; they invited him to hide in their homes, provided him with food, and offered him means of communication.[41]

(*c*) *Chauvinist incitement*. Written material is often employed by alienated Arabs in Israel for extremist national expression. This will be dealt with in greater detail in the next chapter. Poems, articles, and manifestoes are often used for this purpose. In Acre, in the summer of 1964, manifestoes in Arabic were pasted on the walls, the chief slogans being: 'Palestine must be liberated, the Zionist conqueror should be driven out!' or 'Long live the Arab national liberation movement!' After the hanging of Eli Cohen in Damascus for spying for Israel, some Israeli Arabs distributed manifestoes against him in Arabic, saying 'Shame on Eli Cohen!' and 'All Jews ought to be hanged!'[42] In the village of Tarshīḥa swastikas appeared.[43] There is no doubt that only a few youths were responsible for such extremist

[39] For the psychological elements involved, see Ṣ. Elgat in *Ma'arīv*, 3 Dec. 1964; cf. ibid. 8 July 1966.

[40] For Arab youths killed near the Gaza Strip in 1961, see *Ma'arīv*, 9 Feb. 1962 and *YA*, 24 Nov. 1964.

[41] *Ma'arīv*, 8 Feb. 1966. Cf. the aid to spies in Naḥf village, *ha-Areṣ*, 17 May 1963.

[42] *Ma'arīv*, 21 June 1965. [43] Ibid. 5 Jan. 1966.

expressions, but it is symptomatic that the same phenomenon can be found in wider circles, with varying degrees of intensity. The communist paper *al-Ittiḥād*, an Arabic bi-weekly, publishes rousing poems regularly;[44] these are sometimes read aloud at weddings, funerals, and other gatherings. There are even several books, in poetry or prose, criticizing the very existence of the State of Israel.

It is wrong to assume, however, that the whole Arab population in Israel lends itself to such extremist views. Many Arabs regard the existence of Israel as a fact, and acknowledge the State's major share in the economic prosperity and development which they enjoy. So that, together with a marked sympathy for the Arab States across the borders, there exists a natural desire to integrate and profit from the material advantages offered by Israel. These mixed feelings are at the bottom of the basic contradiction between national aspirations and political reality. As no easy solution exists, the loyalties of the Israeli Arab remain divided, even if he takes sides. The *de facto* situation almost nullifies his freedom of decision and leaves him sitting on the fence. Furthermore, the uncompromising attitude of most Arab States increases the complexity of adaptation versus alienation among the Israeli Arabs. Most enlightening, in this respect, are the words of Rāshid Ḥusayn[45] one of the most notable men of letters among Arabs in Israel. He attended the meeting of non-aligned States in Belgrade in 1960, and after returning home, wrote:

> I went to Belgrade to cover the conference of non-aligned nations . . . Of course, I did not expect the Arab reporters to embrace me, but I was not prepared to read in their eyes, and certainly not to hear them express in words, the very same charges that are levelled against me in Israel. Only there, in Belgrade, did I fully realize the extent of the tragedy of the Israeli Arabs. I realized that we suffer from the consequences of the 1948 war no less—perhaps even more—than the refugees. In Belgrade I no longer knew who I was, a nationalist Arab loyal to his people, or a suspect Israeli citizen. The accepted concepts became confused in my mind. Only one notion remained starkly clear: that I was one of the 250,000 Arabs trusted by neither the Arab countries nor by the Israel Government.[46]

The same doubts very probably assail other Israeli Arabs, perhaps subconsciously. Despite the basic contradiction, resulting from circumstances, the integration of the Arab minority in the State of Israel has become more apparent. The willingness to adapt to new

[44] e.g. Maḥmūd Darwīsh's poem in *al-Ittiḥād*, 3 May 1963.

[45] On whom cf. E. Marmorstein, 'Rāshid Ḥusain: portrait of an angry young Arab', *Middle Eastern Studies* (London), Oct. 1964, 3–20. See also *Maʿarīv*, 28 Dec. 1965.

[46] See his 'I am an Israeli Arab', *NO*, Dec. 1961, 35.

realities has seemingly grown, even if the basic factors have not altered. Moderate political groups within the Israeli Arab population have been spreading their influence in their own community. Significantly, they seldom attempt to blunt the edge of the above basic factors; they stress them rather than otherwise, to serve their tactical purpose and improve their own position. From their point of view, their way appears easier, as they have succeeded in determining their stand, without openly compromising with the State authorities. However, even they are not of one view and differ as to practical solutions. Actually, because of their stand, a large number of Israeli Arabs turn away from them, preferring 'the middle of the road', despite its obvious contradictions. Hence, since 1948, the Israeli Arabs have been more and more integrated into the life of the State, though not in all fields and not at any set pace.

In recent years this process has gathered momentum and is particularly evident in the economic field.[47] Lately, even intellectual circles tend to find some ideological expression for what they consider the necessary co-operation between Arabs and Jews in Israel, though trying to tackle focal problems first. As a result, a few Arab notables met early in 1965 and published an interesting pamphlet,[48] aimed at finding a sort of 'formula for the existence of the Arabs in Israel', or—as one of the editors put it—a way to explain 'Arabic awareness in Israel' and a way to answer the question: 'Can an Arab be loyal to the State of Israel and be proud of his Arabism, both at the same time?' The affirmative answer to this is simple for them; they attempt to find the basis for it through historical review of the friendly relations between Arabs and Jews; they criticize the policy of 'divide and rule' fostered by the British authorities in Palestine; they blame the local Arab leaders for the 1948 war, for the riots, and for the mass flight of the Arab refugees. They boldly maintain that 'we shall sin if we ignore these facts. The young generation does not know these facts, for they were not born yet.' Then they add that the only way open to the Arabs in Israel is 'to support the Government and the State, which will make further progress and development possible, and to strive for even greater achievements for the sake of our sons'. Peace is emphasized as essential for continued development; a breach of the peace would endanger the Arab minority in Israel, first and foremost. Recognition of Israel's existence is the basis for peace: 'as for us, we believe in the historical right of the

[47] For the case of the Arabs in Haifa, *Davar*, 12 July 1961.

[48] *Al-Fikra al-'arabiyya al-isrā'īliyya* (1964). For excerpts, see App. E, pp. 231–6 below.

Jewish people to return to its State. We do not see any contradiction between this right and our loyalty to the Arab peoples.'

In March 1965, shortly after this pamphlet was published, the Arab mayor of Nazareth, Sayf al-Dīn Zu'bī, held a press conference, in which he expressed the same view, asserting that

> should war break out between the Arab States and Israel, we will be the first victims . . . fate has made us a minority in the State of Israel and, like every other minority throughout the world, we have no choice in the matter. Our obligations as citizens compel us to be faithful to the State in which, and under whose flag, we live.[49]

Sayf al-Dīn Zu'bī and the authors of the above pamphlet represent a considerable number of those Arabs in Israel who have become reconciled to new political realities. However, it appears that even they are torn between two points: the logic of accepting the new situation and benefiting from the economic development, educational progress, and high standard of living in Israel (as compared to that of its neighbours); and their sentiments, which would have them choose to live in less favourable conditions in a State with an Arab majority. Hence the relatively small number of Israeli Arabs who come into the open with such views and their hesitation to be completely reconciled to new realities and fully integrate into the State of Israel.[50] Their task is not facilitated by the opponents among the Arab population; nationalists who pounce on every instance of discrimination, real or imaginary,[51] and use it as a lever to brand the moderate Arabs as the 'tails of the Government' (Arabic: *adhnāb al-ḥukūma*). They criticize the moderates sharply, since the acceptance of the new political situation negates the very *raison d'être* of an Arab national movement within the State of Israel. There seems to be no easy way of bridging the gap between 'acceptance' and 'rejection', or—one might say—between adaptation and alienation. The fact remains that a great part, most probably the greater part, of the Arab population in Israel, is undecided, unwilling to take a definite stand for either side.

The continuous alienation of the Arabs in Israel has been a subject of concern to both Arabs and Jews. Private individuals have contributed towards mutual understanding, such as Mrs Nīna Dī-Nūr in Tel-Aviv, who opened her home to Arab workers in that urban area as well as to others who were willing to discuss problems of mutual

49 *Ma'arīv*, 25 Mar. 1965.

50 See about this hesitation, for instance, in *ha-Ṣōfeh* (Tel-Aviv, daily), 7 July 1961.

51 Cf. examples in *The Scribe, the Arab Review* (Cairo), Dec. 1963, 18–21.

interest.[52] In July 1966 a leading Hebrew daily, *Davar* (Matter), organ of the *Histadrūt*, arranged a symposium on 'attitudes to the Arab minority in Israel', which was held on its premises. Leading Jewish and Arab personalities aired their opinions frankly, and the proceedings were then published in *Davar*.[53] In September 1966, on the anniversary of the death of Martin Buber—the Jewish philosopher who had constantly advocated an Arab-Jewish rapprochement—a seminar was held in the *kibbūtz* Giv'at Ḥavīva. Jews and Arabs met in the peaceful surroundings of this collective settlement, with the intention of discussing ways and means for advancing peace between Israel and the Arab States. In fact, the debate turned into an inquiry about Jewish-Arab attitudes in Israel[54]—perhaps another sign of the urgency of the problem. In January 1967 the 'ideological circle' of MAPAI (Israel's largest political party) devoted special sessions to analyse the situation of the Arabs in Israel and the ways of helping them to integrate.[55] To these one may add many articles and readers' letters in both the Jewish and the Arab press,[56] lectures, public debates, etc. Not all of these referred to the alienation of the Israeli Arabs; the communist publications were apparently the most vociferous in this respect. Others, however, also expressed anxiety about the situation, proposing various ways for easing the tension between minority and majority in the State of Israel and for ensuring minimum loyalty among Israel's Arabs by their integration. One of the more meaningful results of this was the setting up of a public Arab Committee for Israel, presided over by the architect Rustum Bastūnī, numbering Arabs as well as Jews (mostly from Haifa), who—during 1966 and 1967—worked at recruiting public opinion to bring about a fuller understanding between Jews and Arabs in Israel. As a start, their main effort was to organize joint cultural events, which were fairly successful.[57]

[52] Details by Mansour in *ha-Areṣ*, 7 Apr. 1967, and Sh. Har-Gīl in *Ma'arīv*, 25 May 1967. The discussions at a large meeting of Arabs and Jews in Mrs Nīna Dī-Nūr's home, in Mar. 1964, have been mimeographed in a booklet, called *The first day*.

[53] 22 & 29 July 1966.

[54] Summary by Ḥ. Kna'an in *ha-Areṣ*, 12 Sept. 1966.

[55] Reported by M. Meysels in *Ma'arīv*, 10 Jan. 1967.

[56] Among the most noteworthy: Mansour, *ha-Areṣ*, 2 Apr. 1965; L. A., *Ma'arīv*, 17 Jan. 1966; Sh. Tōleydānō, ibid. 4 Mar. 1966; N. Lustig, *JP*, 6 May 1966; M. Dayyan, *ha-Areṣ*, 24 June 1966; Mansour, ibid. 8 July 1966; Palmōn, ibid. 14 Sept 1966.

[57] Mansour, ibid. 8 July 1966; Bastūnī, *ha-Yōm* (Tel-Aviv, daily), 19 Aug. 1966; A. Nesher, *ha-Areṣ*, 17 Mar. 1967.

End of Chap 2

3

CULTURAL CHANGE AND ITS REFLECTION IN POLITICS

ARAB EDUCATION

BOTH central and local authorities in the State of Israel have invested considerable effort in broadening and improving Arab education, with the intention of bringing it up to the standard of Jewish education. This has been a formidable task, in view of the slow advance in Arab schooling, especially in the villages, during the thirty years of British rule in Palestine. (The Jews had maintained a semi-independent network of schools, at their own cost, during that period.)

One of the first aims of the State was to include all Arab school-children, along with the Jews, in the Compulsory Education Law (one year of kindergarten, followed by eight years of primary school—all free of charge). Schools were built in practically every village, as well as in the main Bedouin encampments. Old teachers attended refresher courses and new ones were trained[1] in the Arab teachers' seminar, which was first located in Jaffa, then in Haifa. The Ministry of Education and Culture took real pains to improve the curriculum in both the primary and the high schools. This entailed the preparation of many new textbooks for various subjects at the various levels of learning.[2] Obviously this huge operation to extend and improve Arab education could not be completely successful in every detail. Critics of the Government—in both Arab and Jewish circles—have constantly pointed out every unsolved problem and every failure.[3] Some of this criticism was justified; nevertheless, it can be said that

[1] An interesting aspect is that, when we consider the division of the Arab population in Israel into religious communities, we find that there is a relatively large number of Christian teachers, while the pupils are mostly Muslim.

[2] Further details in Rasmī Bayādse's article in *al-Yawm*, 12 Sept. 1965. Cf. J. S. Bentwich, in his *Education in Israel* (1965), esp. 170–84; part of his chapter on Arab education appeared as 'Arab education in Israel', *NO*, July–Aug. 1963, 19–23. Earlier works on the subject: Y. L. Ben-Or, in *MḤ*, 1951, 1–8; id. & Sh. Salmon, in *Mĕgammōt* (Jerusalem), Jan. 1957, 90–97; Ben-Or, 'Some problems of Arab education', *NO*, Oct. 1957, 24–27; R. Hussein, 'The Arab school in Israel', ibid. Nov.–Dec. 1957, 44–48; M. Avidor, *Education in Israel* (1957), 100–6.

[3] This includes some works published outside Israel; cf. Mūsà Zayd al-Kīlānī, *Sanawāt al-ightiṣāb, Yisrāʾīl 1948–65* [1966?], esp. 114–15.

Arab education in Israel has been fairly successful, despite the numerous difficulties that beset it.

These difficulties were considerable,[4] and though typical of a developing country, were in this case the outcome of exceptional pressures. The 1950s were a period of Jewish mass immigration to Israel, when the new State had to face an overall shortage of teachers and schools. Nevertheless, the attention given to schooling of Arab children was equal to, if not greater than, that devoted to Jewish children. At the end of the year 1966, out of an Arab population numbering slightly over 300,000, about 70,000 were studying in primary schools and about 3,500 in governmental high schools.[5] Education experts were thus faced with a multitude of organizational and financial problems. They were fortunate in enlisting, in addition to the services of local Arabs, many Arabic-speaking Jewish teachers, new immigrants from Iraq. More difficult problems were involved in decisions of a pedagogical nature. Here questions of principle underlay educational methodology. Many parents, particularly in the Muslim village, opposed coeducation.[6] Older teachers could not be weaned from employing repetition as their staple method instead of adopting modern techniques of learning.

For example, it was ruled that Arabic would be the language of instruction in all Arab schools, the definition of such a school being one with a majority of Arab pupils. Hebrew would be taught from the fourth grade, and English from the sixth, as foreign languages only. Most of the teaching materials in the courses on literature and history would pertain to the Arab cultural heritage. Only very little information with Jewish content would be imparted. These decisions were based on a liberal point of view, which refused to compel Arab children to substitute Jewish civilization for their own rich and meaningful cultural heritage. The Israeli planners of this educational policy were under no illusions. They took into account the risk that the stress on the study of Arab civilization might encourage an Arab national awakening in Israel. This was particularly likely because in Arab schools male teachers outnumbered females by more than two to one.[7] (The opposite situation exists in Jewish schools.) It might be

[4] On some of these difficulties see Ben-Or, in *Middle Eastern Affairs* (New York), Aug.–Sept. 1950, 224–9; and S. D. Goitein, ibid. Oct. 1952, 272–5.

[5] The Bedouin children had their schools organized according to this centralized system, too (cf. on the ʿArab al-ʿArāmsha tribe, Arīʾel, ibid. 10 Feb. 1967).

[6] Quite a few Muslim parents still oppose this, esp. with regard to their daughters (cf. Elgat, in *Maʿarīv*, 31 Mar. 1967).

[7] In the year 1963–4 the ratio was 2·28:1—1,120 male teachers and 491 female (see *Stat. Ab., 1965*, 579, table T/8).

expected that some of these men would preach chauvinism to their pupils.

A similar problem arose in teaching the subject of civics. It was decided that in relation to the State of Israel and its institutions moral justification existed for teaching only facts. The assumption was that these could be taught in all frankness, while, in Arab schools, enforcing the study of values would be bound to breed hypocrisy on the part of both teachers and pupils.[8] Basically the same approach prevailed in the selection of materials for the Hebrew-language textbooks where, again, little—if any—of propaganda value was included. If anything, the textbooks emphasized the importance of co-operation.

A more practical experiment in co-operation between Arabs and Jews at school level was conducted just recently by the placing of pupils from both groups in the same high school. Earlier, indeed, some Arab school-children had happened to attend Jewish institutions, and it is difficult from these few cases to evaluate the impact of classroom co-operation on future identification with the State of Israel.[9] A more systematic experiment was recently initiated on the suggestion of Haifa's mayor, Abbā Ḥūshī, encouraged by the Ministry of Education. Classes for Arab pupils were created at a Haifa high school, parallel to the Jewish classes but conducting separate study programmes, as naturally the prior preparation of the pupils had been quite different (e.g. in their language of instruction). However, sports and social activities were often enjoyed in common. While it is too early to draw any conclusions from such experiments,[10] their contribution to integration might be viewed with qualified optimism.

More in evidence is the steep increase in the number of literate Arabs, particularly among the population who had gone to school in Israel[11] (though much less was done to encourage Arab adult education. Those in the age-group 19–29 usually know Hebrew, which they frequently need at work).[12] One should remember that this is also the group most prone to political agitation. It is natural that the Israeli

[8] In the first years of the State, raising the Israeli flag and singing the national anthem were not insisted upon. This did not prevent Arabs in Israel and abroad from complaining about it (see, e.g. the Arab League's *al-Aqalliyya al-ʻarabiyya fī ẓalām Yisrā'īl*, esp. 61–71).

[9] There is as yet no systematic study about this. For first impressions, see D. Harden, in *Ammōt* (Tel-Aviv, bi-monthly), Oct.–Nov. 1964, 29–41 (referring to the years 1963–4).

[10] Asaf considers it a failure (ibid. June–July 1965, 58–59).

[11] Data in *Moslems, Christians & Druzes*, ch. 6.

[12] Ibid. p. xliii.

Arabs, too, have perceived the direct relationship between the expansion of education and political alertness. On this, Yūsuf Khamīs, an Arab MK (member of the *Kneset*) on behalf of the MAPAM (socialist) party has commented:

> The wave of liberation and awakening which has swept the peoples of Asia and Africa and the Compulsory Education Law in Israel encouraged the members of the Arab minority in Israel to swim with the stream of progress in the modern age and to catch up with every development. Therefore, they flocked to educational institutions, to acquire knowledge.[13]

Ethnic minorities, particularly in States characterized by political alertness and the tension resulting therefrom, are sometimes apt to overemphasize the negative. Thus the introduction of modern textbooks may be less appreciated than the pleasant memory of the old, familiar ones.[14] Some people are not impressed by the quantitative advance and the development of new techniques, but rather by arguments against the Compulsory Education Law, especially when it compels girls to go to school (although of late one hears fewer complaints about co-education, even among Muslims). The rise in the standard of education and the emphasis on achievement do not compensate some young Arabs for the disappointment of failing in the matriculation examinations, where insistence on minimum achievements makes this crucially important. Without a certificate of matriculation, graduates of high schools are barred from higher studies as well as from jobs requiring it. In Israel this creates a problem which is more serious than would seem at first sight. In both absolute and relative figures, the number of those matriculating increases annually; however, many still fail. The latter tend, as a result, to live on the fringes of society; others adopt extreme political views, often anti-Israeli. The Ministry of Education is aware of the problem, but refuses to lower the requirements. It tries, rather, to improve further the quality of both teachers and textbooks and to encourage high-school students to engage in social activities, such as boy scouts. By inducing suitably-inclined graduates of the primary schools to continue in vocational or agricultural institutions, and thus improving selection at this level, it is hoped to raise the standard of Arab high-school pupils as well.

In recent years there has been a steady increase in the number of those Arabs employed in clerical work by the Government and other

[13] Official minutes of the *Kneset*, 6 Apr. 1959.

[14] See examples of such criticism in Schwarz, *Arabs in Israel*, 116 ff. Schwarz points out that similar objections are voiced regarding Jewish education, but that Israeli Arabs feel they are complaining about an *alien* Government (ibid. 117–18).

public bodies. A growing number works for enterprises financed by joint Jewish-Arab capital, such as the Israeli Arab Bank or the tinned citrus-fruit factory founded by Fāris Ḥamdān at the village of Bāqa al-Gharbiyya in the Little Triangle. Nevertheless many Arab graduates of high schools, teacher seminars, or universities remain unemployed if they do not wish to accept teaching positions, or are not offered what they consider suitable jobs. Their situation is further aggravated if they refuse low clerical work or manual labour (which they usually despise).[15] In other words, mass education at all levels in the State of Israel has raised a growing group of Arab high school or university graduates, dissatisfied[16] and ready to criticize the State and its Government, from nationalist or communist premises. Those who are unemployed, either by force of circumstances or personal choice, are even more inclined to extremism in their political attitudes.[17]

ARAB INTELLECTUALS AND ISRAEL

Any attempt to determine the main characteristics and political attitudes of the Arab intellectuals (*muthaqqafīn*) in the State of Israel is hindered by the fact that this group is undergoing a process of crystallization, and is meanwhile incessantly changing. An added difficulty lies in our need to consider these intellectuals together with their background. For example, the criteria required to determine the character of the intellectuals of a developing African State are different from those necessary for Great Britain or France.[18] Against the backdrop of Israeli Arab society—part of which still lacks formal education as the heritage of previous régimes, while another part is undergoing rapid transformation—some people will have to be labelled as intellectuals who would perhaps not be considered as such within another social frame of reference. In spite of these difficulties, it seems possible to indicate some rather interesting characteristics.

1. *The Young Age of the Intellectuals*

As mentioned, the majority of the Arab intellectuals, chiefly the Muslims, left Palestine during the Arab-Israel war of 1948. Indeed,

[15] Unemployment among Arab intellectuals is a severe problem. See on this subject Mansour, 'Arab intellectuals not integrated', *NO*, June 1964, 26–31. Mansour is a Christian Arab who tries to steer a middle course. He has also written a novel in Hebrew(!) about a love affair between an Arab and a Jewess, called, *Bĕ-ōr ḥadash* (In a new light) (Tel-Aviv, 1966).

[16] For some of their complaints about Arab education in Israel, cf. Y. Amīttay, in *ba-Sha'ar*, May 1960, 13–20.

[17] See E. Ben-Moshe, in *Ner*, Sept.–Nov. 1963, 26–31.

[18] For the difficulties in finding accepted definitions, cf. Charles Frankel, 'The scribblers and international affairs', *Foreign Affairs*, Oct. 1965, 1–14.

if we disregard a small number of Arab communists, mostly Christians, who remained behind (and whom we shall discuss later), we may say that almost the whole of the Arab intelligentsia in Israel is a 'local product', i.e. it was educated in the new State. This intelligentsia is young in age. Its members are in their late teens, twenties, and thirties, and few only are in their forties. These intellectuals are young not only in comparison with their Jewish counterparts in Israel, but also in comparison with those in various European countries. Their age structure is more similar to that of the intelligentsia in several Arab[19] and some new African States. This youthful character is reflected in the views and attitudes of the Arab intellectuals in Israel. The older generation remembers the situation during the British, or even Ottoman, rule; it may appreciate better, therefore, the improvement in education and general welfare in the State of Israel. The members of the younger generation, however, educated in Israel, most of whom have no clear memories from pre-1948 times, have other standards: they compare the situation of the Arab minority with that of the Jewish majority, and want complete equality, in practice as well as in theory. The authority of their parents, already in decline, binds them less, since they consider themselves better educated than their elders and more able to cope with new problems.

2. *The Small Number of the Intellectuals*

The precise number of Arab intellectuals in Israel cannot, of course, be calculated. However, if one includes those who completed their high school studies (counting in also those who sat for the matriculation examinations and failed), the Arab intelligentsia numbers several thousands. According to the calculation of A. Mansour,[20] an Arab journalist from Nazareth, almost 2,000 Arabs graduated from high school (passing all their examinations) in the years 1948–63. These figures point, then, to a numerically restricted intelligentsia, both absolutely and relatively. Their drive is perforce somewhat hampered. However, side by side with this large group, there is a larger public, which might be called a 'semi-intelligentsia'. These include the graduates of primary schools, drop-outs from high schools, and others. Intellectually aware of cultural and political life in Israel, they do not generally consider themselves as part of the Arab intelligentsia in Israel, nor do they co-operate with

[19] R. Makarius, *La jeunesse intellectuelle d'Égypte au lendemain de la deuxième guerre mondiale* (Paris, 1960).

[20] In *NO*, June 1964, 27. On Mansour himself, see above, n. 15.

it actively. Nevertheless, they are willing to listen to those who consider themselves intellectuals, or to read their works; in this lies their importance.

3. *The Components*

In contrast both to Jewish intellectuals in Israel and those in some of the neighbouring States, the Arab intelligentsia in Israel is influenced but little by religion.[21] Muslim sages and Christian priests are hardly noticeable within the group, which is mainly composed of teachers, journalists (some of whom work at the broadcasting station), and students. White-collar professions—lawyers, physicians, architects, etc.—are very sparingly represented. In general the group resembles an intellectual proletariat.[22] In a recent article on the Arab intelligentsia in Israel,[23] M. Asaf, a prolific Jewish journalist who has been writing on Arab affairs for many years, suggests broadening the application of the term. He defines Arab intellectuals in Israel as 'a group of citizens, who read books and newspapers; perceptive of current, public, and economic affairs; and demanding in economic, cultural, and political matters'. He would like to include within this framework university graduates, white-collar workers, MKs, mayors and members of municipal councils, teachers, officials, *qāḍīs*, and priests, as well as graduates of high schools including those who failed to pass matriculation.[24]

Even accepting Asaf's broader definition, it is still necessary to emphasize that teachers and students are the dominant elements among the Arab intellectuals. While the intellectuals in most ethnic minorities are politically alert, it is this particular composition that increases the articulateness of the Arab intelligentsia in Israel. A personal grievance, temporary or permanent unemployment, adds a special flavour of bitterness to the writings and conversation of some of these intellectuals. In 1963 A. Mansour intervewed 457 Arab high-school graduates, viz. a sample of almost a quarter of the total. In response to a question on current occupation he received the following replies:[25]

[21] However, religious dignitaries do voice their opinions in matters concerning the Arab minority in Israel, e.g. Shaykh Ṭāhir al-Ṭabarī, the *qāḍī* of Nazareth—acc. to *Ner*, Aug. 1953, 19–20.

[22] Cf. E. A. Simon, in *ba-Sha'ar*, May 1958, 34–35.

[23] In *Ammōt*, June–July 1965, 51–59.

[24] Ibid. 52.

[25] *NO*, June 1964, 28.

Continuing to study in Israel	57
at Universities abroad	55
Employed as teachers	142
as officials, clerks	76
as manual workers, etc.	29
Unemployed	89
No response	9
Total	457

The outstanding features of these figures are, firstly, the relatively large number of high-school graduates employed as manual workers (even higher by other estimates), and, secondly, the even larger number of jobless.

Mansour justly notes that the employment situation is better among university graduates. In spite of a marked inclination towards urban life, many of these intellectuals still consider themselves anchored in the Arab village, where their families continue to live. They are sentimentally attached to the village, and draw from it their financial resources—both for the completion of their studies and intellectual activities. Thus, characteristically, when young Druze intellectuals decided to organize, they chose a village, Kafr Yāṣīf, as their first meeting place.[26] The concentration of Muslim and Druze intelllectuals in rural areas may be explained by the fact that an overwhelming majority of both communities live in the village. This phenomenon is distinctive to Israel, contrasting with the position in Arab countries where practically all intellectual activity is centred in urban areas.

4. *The Intellectuals as Seen by the Public*

As far as may be ascertained, the influence of the Arab intelligentsia is growing in Nazareth as well as in some of the mixed towns. In the village, however, where most of the Arab population lives, its influence is mostly limited to its own circle.[27] By its very presence, it alters the intellectual level of the village; its overall impact affects the younger generation in particular. Intellectuals are often asked about the significance of events outside the village, but their opinion is very rarely solicited in decision-making in local affairs. The main reason for this situation would appear to be the prestige of the village elders, the long years they have maintained their positions, and the fact that

[26] *Ha-Areṣ*, 6 Nov. 1966.

[27] Some research has been carried on in this direction by Abner Cohen, *Arab border-villages*, and Sh. Shamīr, in *NO*, Mar.–Apr. 1962, 93–112.

many government offices and public bodies prefer to deal with them. Obviously, not all young Arab intellectuals accept this curtailment of their influence, which they consider is far from proportionate to their education. A characteristic reaction was expressed by a knowledgeable Druze, who said:

> We are intellectual and modern youths and will by no means agree to a situation where our elders, many of them illiterate, will dictate to us how to live and behave. . . . I am amazed at the fact that Government circles co-operate with these elders. The interest of the State of Israel is to encourage us, the young, as we constantly urge the community to integrate in the State and adapt to its life-rhythm, while the elders curb this process. . . .[28]

Nevertheless, in a number of cases the impact of the intellectuals who return to their villages is steadily (though slowly) increasing, even in local matters. This is due both to their wider social experience and even more probably—to their connexions with different influential bodies outside the village, such as some government offices, the *Histadrūt*, political parties, and others.

5. *The Intellectuals as Seen by Themselves*

Irrespective of their public appeal, the Arab intelligentsia in Israel is constantly preoccupied with itself and keenly conscious of its unique problems. The intellectuals are intensely aware that they are restricted in number and have only limited contact with the Arab public in Israel and less (if any) with the Jewish intelligentsia.[29] Although Arab intellectuals may be slow to admit it, they have themselves, in a great measure, to blame for their comparative isolation. In the villages, for instance, the local leaders are not the sole cause of their lack of influence. Arab intellectuals contribute but little to integration in the Arab village, whose backwardness they openly despise. On the contrary, they attempt, consciously or subconsciously, to detach themselves from the village—by their behaviour, speech, and mode of dress.

In consequence of their isolation, richer Arab intellectuals have tended to pursue their studies abroad, and some have remained there (as have certain Jewish students from Israel, but for other reasons). A number of those who could not afford travel tried to settle in the towns of Israel. Those who have succeeded in this seldom return to visit their villages. However, many have not been

[28] Reported in *Ner*, May–June 1962, 32. Stronger words were used by Muhammad Watad, 'The war of generations in the Arab village', *NO*, Oct. 1964, 29–32, 50.

[29] As acknowledged by K. Qāsim in *Ner*, Feb. 1953, 14–15.

able to adapt, socially and politically, to life in the mixed towns, so that they feel utterly rootless and displaced—a factor adding to their uncertainty. They are unsure whether they are Israeli Arabs or Arabs in Israel. Even the main spokesmen of this Arab intelligentsia cannot agree on the major questions confronting it. This confusion may be illustrated from the results of a limited referendum amongst them, conducted in 1962;[30] the impression received is that their only common ground is a feeling of *malaise*, resulting in a sense of crisis.

6. *The Crisis of the Arab Intellectuals*

A number of factors, therefore, contribute to the current crisis of the Arab intelligentsia in Israel, which is also connected with somewhat similar phenomena among other Arab intellectuals in the Middle East. There appear to be two main explanations for this crisis in the Arab countries. On the one hand, the alienation of these Arab intellectuals from a major share of their traditional heritage uncompensated by adequate satisfaction from foreign sources of inspiration results in a prevailing atmospherc of psychological rootlessness. On the other hand, the participation of many of them in the political, economic, and technocratic life of the Arab States, but frequently as yesmen of the prevailing régimes, implies subservience limiting their original creativity.

In Israel, the origins of the crisis among the Arab intellectuals are similar, but not identical. As already noted, many intellectuals in the Arab States seek inspiration from foreign civilizations (France, the Soviet Union, and others). The Arab minority in Israel also looks for inspiration across the borders, but its sources are rooted in its own culture. In the Israeli case the tension derives from the fact that the intellectual expression of the Arabs often comes into direct conflict with the national culture of the Jewish majority.[31] However, the Arab intellectuals in Israel are under no compulsion to become yesmen. Rather, this is a matter of free choice, to be resolved by a profound individual decision. Those Arabs who determine to compromise with the realities of life in Israel differ from those in the neighbouring States in that, although possibly advancing in the material sense, they still do not attain key positions in the political or economic system; on the contrary, they are apt to be accused by other Arab intellectuals of selling the interests of Arab nationalism for the fleshpots of personal profit. Whether an Arab intellectual integrates in Israel out of personal conviction or out of material

[30] 'Arab intellectuals on Israel', *NO*, Nov.–Dec. 1962, 55–64.

[31] On these difficulties of integration cf. ibid. June 1964, 26–31.

interest, he is going to be blamed by his fellow intellectuals for selling out. Hence, the crisis of the Arab intelligentsia in Israel is more severe and complicated. A pessimistic feeling of displacement appears to be the main common denominator among its spokesmen—just as in the Arab States, only more so. The feeling of displacement very probably springs from the break with the past, on the one hand, and the failure to come to terms with the present, on the other. As a result, Arab intellectuals in Israel are intensely politically minded, smarting under the injustice (real or imaginary) of the present[32] and passionately eager for a different future.

THE ARAB STUDENTS[33]

If the Arab minority as such is largely ethnocentric, this is particularly noticeable among the Arab students in institutions of higher learning. This is an easily excitable and very articulate group, even more so than other Arab intellectuals in Israel.[34] The number of Arab students increases every year, as does that of university graduates, although it is more difficult to trace the activities of the latter, who disperse after graduation.

At the Hebrew University of Jerusalem there were about 160 Arab students in 1964–5, 200 in 1965–6, and more than 250 in 1966–7 (including over a dozen women students).[35] At Tel-Aviv University there were 16 Arab students in 1966–7, at Bar-Ilan University 10 in the same year, and a few more at the Polytechnic Institute in Haifa. One of the main aims in establishing a City College in Haifa (for the time, affiliated to the Hebrew University of Jerusalem) was to enable Arab high school graduates from Western Galilee and the Haifa area to attend this College. Their number reached close on 150 in 1966–7. About half of the Arab students attending the Hebrew University during 1966–7 studied in the Faculties of Humanities and Social

[32] Details in Palmōn, *ha-Areṣ*, 14 Jan. 1966.

[33] This concerns Arab students in Israel. No reliable data are available concerning the hundreds of Arab students from Israel studying in Western Europe or the USA, some with the assistance of missionary groups, others with grants from the Israeli Government and various international organizations. See also B. Abū Manna, in *Ner*, Apr. 1955, 9, and his 'Spotlight on Arab students', *NO*, Mar. 1965, 45–48 (where he signs Abu-Muna).

[34] This is one of the interesting conclusions reached by Mr Y. Peres and Miss S. Levi, two sociologists who interviewed Arab students about their confrontation with Jews. They reported their findings in *Yĕhūdīm vĕ-'Aravīm—īsh bĕ-'eyney re'ehū* (Jews and Arabs—each in the eyes of the other) (Jerusalem, 1967, mimeo.).

[35] *News from the Hebrew University in Jerusalem*, 31 Oct. 1966, p. 4. Compared with the Jewish student-population, their number is small, but the ratio of Arab students is growing faster than the Jewish rate.

Sciences,[36] while a considerable number of the others studied Law.

Many Arab students at Israeli universities already have a taste for politics from the village—open as it is to outside propaganda—and the high school. Now their active interest in politics is due both to their young age and to the company of students which encourages discussion and self-expression. Moreover, many of these students have repeatedly asserted that they considered themselves as the intellectual vanguard of the Arab population in Israel. Although several of these students are financially supported by their families, many worked to pay their own way, before or during their university years; thus they seem to have acquired a stronger sense of independence and self-reliance.

Needy Arab students engage in part-time work during their studies, as do Jewish students.[37] Sometimes they find it more difficult to get certain jobs because they have not yet mastered Hebrew well enough. This, however, worries the Arab students less than their future. Most feel that after graduation they will be unable to re-adapt to village life with its narrow scope, the more so since they know that the positions they think they deserve are held by the dominant circle of their elders and are thus unattainable. Not surprisingly, they prefer to settle in the towns and work at their newly-acquired profession. Between the years 1948–66 all the Arab engineers, architects, lawyers, physicians, and agronomists,[38] as well as practically all the teachers, were easily absorbed in the Israeli labour market. However, conditions seem to be changing for the worse, in so far as opportunities for some Arab university graduates are concerned. A certain saturation (of teachers, lawyers) combined with the economic recession (affecting construction engineers and architects) is threatening their future. Some forms of employment are not yet open to them at all, such as in the Ministries of Defence and Foreign Affairs, while some other Government agencies, also, prefer to hire Jews for sensitive jobs. As yet, no one has checked statistics on a countrywide basis to discover whether Arabs are discriminated against in employment in comparison with Jews, who also have their problems in finding suitable jobs. However, the feeling that discrimination exists persists amongst Arab students and conditions their political attitudes and

[36] Ibid.

[37] Waleed Awwad Khoury [sic], 'The two main problems of Arab students', *JP*, 10 Apr. 1966. Abū Manna, one of these Arab students, calculated that approximately 15 per cent of the Arab students paid their own tuition fees (cf. *Ner*, Apr. 1955, 9).

[38] Incomplete data in *News from the Hebrew University in Jerusalem*, 26 June 1966, 4; cf. *Ma'arīv*, 20 Feb. 1967.

activities. Only rarely does their political activity reach such proportions as the extreme action of Badrān Jamīl Mish'al, who failed in his law examinations and decided to flee from Israel to Jordan; he jumped from a train and died from his injuries in December 1965.[39] This was a symptom of despair. Most other Arab students prefer to express themselves in organized, intense political activity. They react to anything that they consider relates to the Arab population in Israel, and particularly to the policy of the Government towards them, including political, judicial, economic and educational matters. Their most vocal demands may be summarized as follows:

(*a*) *The Military administration*

The Arab students were especially articulate in their demand for the abolition of the military administration, which they attacked relentlessly. When it was officially abolished, in December 1966, they felt free to devote their energy to other political matters.

(*b*) *Discrimination*

Apart from the feelings of some Arab students concerning preferential employment for Jews, they are very alert to any indication of discrimination in the field of civil rights, and immediately step up their campaign for complete equality, in theory and practice.

(*c*) *Freedom of expression*

Some students claim that Arab intellectuals in Israel are afraid of writing and speaking as they would like, as they may be blacklisted and suffer in their economic advancement in the future. Actually, the Arabic press and literature in Israel is replete with nationalist propaganda, part of which is so extremist that it openly incites against the State, its authorities and representative institutions. It appears that blacklisting has no basis in fact, except for the reasonable assumption that the State authorities would prefer to employ in public office an Arab (or a Jew, for that matter) who is reliable from their point of view.

(*d*) *The development of the Arab village*

Arab students are ready to admit that the general situation of the Arab village in Israel is noticeably better than that of its counterpart in the Arab States. Characteristically, they nevertheless demand full equalization of the Arab village to the Jewish one, in all material and cultural aspects.

[39] Mansour, in *ha-Areṣ*, 17 Dec. 1965; Y. ha-'Elyōn, in *Ma'arīv*, 17 Dec. 1965.

(*e*) *Expropriation of land*

British and Israeli laws enable the authorities to expropriate land for the sake of cultivation, development, and construction as well as for security considerations. The same laws stipulate the payment of adequate compensation. It is evident that even generous compensation cannot always erase a feeling by the dispossessed landowner of having been wronged. Arab students, practically all villagers themselves, feel this keenly. As they do not agree with security measures anyway, they maintain that land expropriation is not only a personal injustice but part of a plan to dispossess the Arabs in Israel.

(*f*) *Arab education*

Arab students in Israel cannot but admit that the level of education throughout the country has risen considerably since the establishment of the State. None the less, they contend that Arab education is not what it should be; again, one hears the same claim as that regarding the Arab village: Arab education in Israel ought to be absolutely equal to the Jewish.[40] This argument of the Arab students seems particularly poignant, since they feel themselves less prepared for higher studies than their co-students, graduates of Jewish high schools. Low marks sometimes cause bitter feelings of frustration.

(*g*) *Superior attitude of some Jews*

Even though few Arab students themselves have experienced an attitude of superiority by the Jewish population, such cases have probably occurred, perhaps due to the Jewish 'sense of majority' in Israel and the tense relationship with the Arab States, which may have caused some Jews in a few instances to identify Israeli Arabs with the Arabs in the neighbouring countries. By extension, Arab students have concluded that such an attitude is widespread and have tended to label it as contempt towards them.

(*h*) *Interest in foreign affairs*

Middle Eastern affairs loom large on the horizon of the Arab students in Israel. Many favour all-Arab unity, which is also bound to strengthen their own position. Hence they feel sympathy with 'Abd al-Nāṣir and are ready to defend him and his actions. However, most students hasten to add they are for peace and do not wish the State of Israel to be destroyed by an armed clash; they are aware

[40] This lends added interest to a letter to the editor of *Ma'arīv*, 22 May 1967, written by eight Arab students; they speak in favour of coeducation and think it should be compulsory.

that the Arab minority in Israel would suffer in a prolonged, bitter war between Israel and its neighbours. The sincerity of these oft-repeated views is difficult to evaluate, since much depends on the estimate these students have formed of the ratio of power between Israel and the Arab States.

(*i*) *The problem of loyalties*

In the present circumstances, the Arab student—as part of the Arab intelligentsia in Israel—has to make an inner decision as to his choice of loyalty. Is he to identify with the State of Israel, or with Arab nationalism, openly hostile to this State? While the whole question may remain academic as long as peace, even a tense peace, reigns, it becomes more immediate whenever war in the Middle East is imminent.[41] The Israeli Government is well aware of the complexity of this problem and refrains from demanding any formal identification with the State of Israel from the Arab students; with the exception of the Druzes, they are exempt from military service. There is therefore no compulsion upon them to renounce any nationalist sentiments they may possess. The inner conflict of these students is also known within the Arab States, whose reaction is the opposite to that of the Israeli authorities. Radio and television propaganda from the Arab States is aimed at the students, calling on them to prove their Arabism by taking up an anti-Israeli stance. These continuous, often violently-worded, appeals have succeeded in creating a nationalist atmosphere in the 'Arab street'. The younger generation, susceptible to this type of propaganda,[42] cannot but be influenced; hence the identification of a section of the Arab students with the Arab national movement outside Israel.

It may be deduced that many of the attitudes of the Arab students are determined emotionally, quite irrationally. Practically all of them try to behave as perfectly loyal citizens of Israel. However, their feelings of injustice and discrimination (real or exaggerated), together with deep sympathy with the Arab national movement, condition their atitudes as well as their oral and written expression. Furthermore, in the large town which is preponderantly Jewish, their sensitiveness becomes acute.[43] They are lonely in their new surroundings, and the use of Hebrew (a foreign language for them all) at the universtity and outside is for most an added strain.

[41] This problem bothered some people in Israel during the six-days' war in June 1967.

[42] Cf. Watad, 'Arab youth in Israel—today and tomorrow', *NO*, June 1964, esp. 23 ff.

[43] Details in G. Weigert, *ha-Areṣ*, 21 Dec. 1965.

These points briefly summarize the main problems and opinions of the Arab students in Israel, as gleaned from their writings and conversations with them. However, since many of them refuse to be interviewed, and it is possible that the replies of others are not always reliable, it is doubtful whether these views are truly representative. A brief discussion of the character, activities, and attitudes of the Arab Students' Committee may better reflect the political opinions of the majority of these students. While this committee represents the Arab students at the Hebrew University only, these form the very large majority of Arabs registered at institutions of higher learning in Israel. This committee, moreover, appears to be the only elected body in any of these institutions. In discussions with Arab students at the Hebrew University, one gains a definite impression that most of the Arab students there support the committee and even identify with it. Until the beginning of the academic year 1966–7, when a special assistant to the Dean of students at the Hebrew University was appointed to assist the Arab students, this committee was practically the sole source of advice or assistance for the Arab student.[44]

The first Arab Students' Committee was founded in 1958–9 by some Arab students, mainly studying law at the Hebrew University. Its avowed purpose was to assist and advise Arab students. The fact that this self-constituted body included a few extremist nationalists is reflected both in the written constitution of the committee and its activities. To a large extent, this character persisted in later years, when it was elected regularly by all the Arab students at the Hebrew University who cared to cast their vote. Most Arab students regard the committee as their sole representative, even though it is not officially recognized by either the authorities of the Hebrew University or the Students' Federation.

The Arab Students' Committee consists of seven members, the most important of whom are the chairman and the secretary. During 1965–6 the secretary was Muḥammad Maṣārwe, a remarkably dynamic young man, who proved how active a role the secretary could play. His successor was Khalīl Ṭu'ma, a student of law, who was detained later (in January 1968) and charged with harbouring in his home a leader of *al-Fatḥ* terrorist organization,[45] for which he was sentenced (March 1968) to nine months in jail. The committee is elected annually by all Arab students at the Hebrew University. Its

[44] As in the case of finding housing accommodation, cf. *Pī ha-Atōn* (students' journal), 11 Nov. 1964, 1.

[45] Details in *Ma'arīv*, 14 Jan. 1968.

meetings are open and held once a month. It is financed by donations from the Arab students; 'donations', not 'dues', since it may not impose dues, not being legally registered.

The founding members of the Arab Students' Committee intended it to retain its initial purpose and direction, and therefore defined its aims so that they could not be altered. The aims, particularly interesting for this reason, may be found in the third chapter of the constitution, the first article of which reads: 'The committee, which represents Arab students at the Hebrew University, will do its share in all forms of the struggle of the Arab nation in this land; for that, common fate and the single aim of all the sons of this nation will urge it on.' The wording here and in the rest of the constitution refrains from mentioning the State of Israel. Instead, as above, the Arabic term *bilād*, 'country' or 'land', is used—no doubt intentionally. The term 'the Arab nation' is employed very much as it is customarily used in the broadcasts and press of the Arab States. Other aims also, such as broadening the scope of Arab education or welfare to the Arab students, are formulated in a forceful, almost aggressive style.

The extension of the aims of the Arab Students' Committee beyond the social and cultural, to the political, may be seen from its activities. Actually, all its fields of activity are closely interrelated. A perusal of the minutes of the committee for the years 1964 and 1965 (later ones are not yet available) shows alertness to every public matter in Israel which has a bearing on the Arab minority. These are some of the major topics the committee debated: guest-lectures by its members in Arab high schools; protests against the military administration; expropriation of land; treatment of convicts; activities of the police; dismissal of Arab teachers; foundation of new Arab sports clubs; an appeal to ban the public showings of the film *Exodus* (which, the committee claimed, distorted the image of Palestine Arabs); the establishment of a countrywide organization of Arab graduates from institutions of higher learning; and instituting in Jerusalem a discussion group for Arab-Jewish understanding. The committee has indicated its intention to carry on international activity too. Thus it sent one letter to the UN Secretary-General about racial incidents in South Africa, and another on what it termed the denial of the rights of the Arabs in Israel. It also presented a note to the French Ambassador in Tel-Aviv protesting against the French nuclear tests. In 1965 the committee initiated a demonstration of Arab students before the British Embassy in Tel-Aviv to protest against the Government of Ian Smith in Rhodesia.[46]

[46] Mansour, in *ha-Areṣ*, 16 Jan. 1966.

When J.-P. Sartre visited Israel early in 1967, Khalīl Ṭu'ma met him and conveyed to him the political views of the Arab students.

The close correspondence of social, cultural, and political aims is also evident in the committee's day-to-day activity. It has financially assisted Arab students (accommodation and jobs); kept in touch with Arab and Jewish MK's in matters regarding the Arab minority; collected funds among the Arab population; sent Arab students to lecture in the Arab villages; and organized literary meetings. It has given careful consideration to every decision and, once carried, has tried hard to implement it. Some Arab students have tended to blame the committee for meddling in international affairs, while approving of its assistance to the local Arabs. The committee's demonstrations against the war in Vietnam, for instance, were not merely an imitation of a number of student bodies abroad. They were rather evidence of a certain amount of communist influence on the students. (Repeated abortive attempts have been made by communist students to take over the committee.)

The fact that the Arab Students' Committee is not an association in the legal sense of the term widens its room for manoeuvre. Indeed, the committee has felt free, at various times, to approach a number of political groups, in an attempt to gain their support. In this, as indeed in practically all its other activities, their political approach seems dominant. Thus literary meetings turn into nationalist incitement; the supply of jobs or accommodation becomes a subject with a political undertone. It is accordingly not surprising that in the tension felt by Arab students, lonely and uncomfortable in a new, urban environment, political activity tends to become extremist. Their political propaganda is sometimes so violent that Dr J. J. Cohen, director of the Jerusalem Beyt-Hillel students' club, had to warn them that they might not use the club for incitement against the State of Israel.[47] It is, of course, difficult to say how many Arab students are extremist or moderate. Obviously, extremist activity is more easily noticeable. An outstanding example is the passionate propaganda of Arab students *vis-à-vis* African students at the Hebrew University (which greatly annoys both the university and the Government, who between them pay the fees for tuition and for the maintenance of many of these African guests).

Extremism appears to be reflected also in the composition of the Arab Students' Committee for 1965–6. A new committee was elected

[47] This is particularly significant, since Dr Cohen has gone out of his way to assist the Arab students socially.

in February 1966. Students identify two of its members as 'extremist' and the others as 'moderate'. The new chairman, 'Azīz Shihāda, described his own attitude as constructive and said he wanted to co-operate with the university authorities and the Government. However, the first manifesto drafted by the committee on 26 February 1966, referring to the clashes between *ḥamūlas* in Kafr Kannā, was strongly worded and attacked the conduct of the Israeli police. Nevertheless, it seems that the new committee has been more moderate than its predecessor and does not surrender easily to the pressure of the extremist members, perhaps because of the tactical ability of Shihāda.

One of the main achievements of the committee has been to obtain the support and identification with it of most Arab students, and even of a section of the Arab population in Israel. Although a number of Israeli Arabs regard the committee and the extremism of its activities with a certain reserve, many others have assisted it with contributions (in 1965 £I3,000 were donated); responded to its appeal to demonstrate against the military administration; and asked for its intervention in personal matters bearing on public affairs, such as the expropriation of land.[48]

THE CRISIS REFLECTED IN THE PRESS AND LITERATURE

The literature of the Arabs in Israel is intended primarily for the local Arab population. Some of it is known beyond the borders. For instance, a selection by a Lebanese journalist, Ghassān Kanafānī, was published in Beirut in 1966 under the title *Adab al-muqāwama fī Filasṭīn al-muḥtalla* (The literature of resistance in occupied Palestine).[49] However, this is incidental only; one may repeat, this literature is chiefly produced for the local Arabs. Arabic-reading Israeli Jews only needed literature in this language (and indeed even contributed to its advance) during the early 1950s. In this period a large number of Jewish immigrants from Egypt, Iraq, and other Arabic-speaking countries came to settle in Israel. Since then, however, most of these have become accustomed to reading and writing Hebrew. There is certainly a market for Arabic literature in Israel, which may be estimated from the growing readership figures as well as from the profits involved: publishers not only sell various writings of Israeli Arabs, but reissue many works of Arab poets and writers outside Israel. Since 1948 the broadening of the scope of education

[48] See also App. B, p. 225 below.

[49] Cf. detailed review in *al-Ḥawādith* (Beirut, weekly), 29 July 1966, 24–25, and in *Ma'arīv*, 11 Nov. 1966, 19.

and the rise in standards have produced a relatively large group of potential readers of Arabic, whom we have labelled 'intelligentsia' and 'semi-intelligentsia'. Arabic is the only language most of them can read fluently and enjoyably.

An outstanding feature of Arab literature in Israel is that it has in no way been influenced by modern Hebrew writing. This does not necessarily indicate a lack of interest in what goes on in the near-by Jewish community. It is rather that spiritually and culturally, Israeli Arabs are much closer to Arab literature outside Israel than to Hebrew writing, which remains strange and foreign to them.[50] In the early years of the new State, most of the Arab literature was non-political. In so far as an attitude towards the Jews was expressed, it was in a vein of friendship and with a declared wish for mutual good-will and close co-operation; this was addressed to Arabs and Jews alike. More recently, especially in the 1960s, Arab literature in Israel is increasingly concerned (avowedly or indirectly) with the confrontation between Jews and Arabs, Zionism and Arab nationalism.

The Israeli authorities, acting on the assumption that the extremist tenor of Arab literature in Israel results from ignorance of the Jewish community, have repeatedly encouraged intellectuals to hold Jewish-Arab meetings and get acquainted.[51] The *Histadrūt* also, has acted in this direction, and under its sponsorship a number of conferences were arranged. It has also financially supported the publication of two volumes of modern Arabic and Hebrew prose and poetry, in both the original and a page-by-page translation.[52] The introduction to Volume I is a sort of 'credo', explaining the need for confrontation through mutual acquaintance and tolerance:

> The very publication of this anthology, incorporating the work of twenty Arab and Jewish writers, is simple and clear proof that there exists a possibility, and particularly that there is a sincere wish—at least among a certain circle of intellectuals from both peoples, including writers, poets and artists—to meet and converse, listen and understand, hear and be heard, learn and teach.[53]

However, despite this promising conception, both volumes, although very instructive in content, contain no controversial material. Hence their importance appears to lie more in paving the road towards a frank dialogue than in providing a full-sized confrontation.

[50] 'Abd al-'Azīz Zu'bī, in *ba-Sha'ar*, Feb. 1958, 17–19.

[51] *Government Yearbook*, *5725* (*1964/5*), 110.

[52] *Mifgash, qōveṣ sifrūtī 'ivrī 'aravī* (Hebrew & Arabic), i: May 1964; ii: Feb. 1966. A third vol. was scheduled for 1968.

[53] Ibid. i, preface.

The dominance of the political tone—one might say the politicization—of the writings of the Arabs in Israel may be explained by certain common characteristics of this literature, the principal of which may be listed as:

1. The young age of the writers, reflecting the youthfulness of the intelligentsia in Israel and the absence from the literary scene of pre-1948 authors, who live abroad, or have since died. Hence, Arab literature in Israel cannot be considered a continuation of Palestinian literary activity.

2. A marked degree of provincialism[54] differing from pre-1948 days. Then Jaffa, Jerusalem, and Nablus served as the main cultural centres of Arabic culture in British-ruled Palestine, secondary centres also existing in other towns. Nazareth was at the time, as it is today, rather provincial; this helps to explain why Arab authors living in Nazareth and smaller places are mainly preoccupied by local matters.

3. The traumatic experience of the 1948 war and the Arab defeat has undoubtedly overshadowed the literary work of the Arabs in Israel, and the effects of this trauma are still felt. Possibly, Arab defeats in 1956 and 1967 have added to the intensity of these feelings.

In consequence, a strong nationalistic, even chauvinistic, current runs through the poetry composed by the Israeli Arabs. Its moving spirit is alienation from Israel and its Government; its main aim—inflaming the passions of the reader; its *Leitmotiv*—the return of the refugees and re-establishment of Palestine (at the expense of Israel).[55] The prose is more moderate in tone, but this varies from one author to another.

The press, perhaps more than any other means of communication, reflects the politicization of Arab writing. The newspapers appearing in Israel in Arabic deserve more than a passing mention, as they voice more clearly the day-to-day opinions of journalists and their readers. In addition, the Arab minority in Israel uses the press as the main vehicle for its literary writing, despite the comparatively low circulation of Arabic newspapers. This low circulation may be attributed to the lack of fluent reading ability on the part of the older generation, while the younger frequently reads Hebrew newspapers. However, circulation does not necessarily reflect the size of readership: in several villages a newspaper is still passed from hand to hand (for example, in the coffee-house) or is read aloud and interpreted—

[54] Cf. M. Barqa'ī, in *Davar*, 10 June 1966, suppl.

[55] See Emīl Tōmā, in the Arabic monthly *al-Jadīd*, Jan. 1965, and comments of Asaf, in *Davar*, 26 Mar. 1965.

so that it actually reaches a wider audience. It is interesting to note that, while most of the newspaper readers are Muslims, most journalists and editors are either Jews (chiefly in organs that defend Government policy) or Christians (mainly in those which attack it). Another characteristic is that all newspapers and periodicals, when they are not governmental publications, are directly attached either to political parties or to religious communities, in most cases Christians.[56] These bodies frequently subsidize publication.

The principal Arabic newspapers and journals in Israel are:

1. *Al-Yawm* (The Day). This is the only daily in Arabic. Since 1948 it has been financially supported by the *Histadrūt*. This newspaper appears to have four aims: (*a*) Supplying current information to the reader of Arabic, mainly about events or developments in Israel and abroad, with an accent on Arab news. (*b*) Providing a forum for Arab writers and poets in Israel. (*c*) Emphasizing the positive achievement in the Arab policies of the Israel Government and its various departments. (*d*) Blunting the edge of the opposition press as well as of the broadcasts from the Arab States. The circulation of the newspaper is (1966) about 4,000 daily copies, with the Friday weekend-edition reaching some 5,000 copies.[57] This is considerable, but its impact appears limited. Many Arabs in Israel consider it the mouthpiece of the Government (and of the MAPAI ruling party). In consequence, they doubt its sincerity and suspect its attitude; they often point to the fact that most of its editors[58] and reporters are Jews.[59] *Al-Yawm*, indeed, has Arab correspondents throughout Israel, but these serve mostly to select information and send it on, rather than as journalists with any influence on editorial policy. Hence few consider *al-Yawm* as representative of Arab trends in Israel.

2. *Al-Mirṣād* (The Observation Post) is the Arabic weekly of the MAPAM party, appearing twice a week before general elections. It has appeared since 1951, closely following the party line. This weekly reflects the dilemma of MAPAM in its attitude to Jews and Arabs in Israel. The party has continuously advocated a policy of befriending the Israeli Arabs and granting them full social equality as well as economic incentives. It has therefore taken issue with MAPAI Arab policy though it has joined most coalition Govern-

[56] As already noted by Weigert, in the monthly *Mōlad*, Nov. 1959, 577–9.

[57] Mansour in *ha-Areṣ*, 4 Mar. 1966. Cf. *Davar*, 10 June 1966, suppl.

[58] Including the editor in chief. During 1959–66 this was Nissim Rejwan, an intellectual Jew from Iraq.

[59] See accusations, in this respect, in *al-Ittiḥād*, 18 May 1965.

ments headed by MAPAI since the establishment of Israel, including the coalition established early in 1966. As a result, MAPAM has generally had to go along with MAPAI in its policy guidelines, including those applying to the Arabs in Israel. MAPAM and its Arabic weekly *al-Mirṣād* have attempted to solve this dilemma by consistently advocating the abolition of the military administration and by continuous assistance to the local affairs of the Arabs in Israel. *Al-Mirṣād* has employed a large number of Arab editors and journalists, at policy-making as well as at lower levels, and has opened its pages to Arab writers, generally of leftist inclinations conforming to MAPAM ideologies.[60]

3. *Al-Ittiḥād* (Unity). This communist organ originated under British rule as early as 1944. It has appeared in its present form since 1954. It is a bi-weekly, efforts to change it into a daily having failed. Following the break-up of the Communist Party in the summer of 1965 (to be described in the next chapter), *al-Ittiḥād* remained the organ of RAQAḤ, i.e. of that communist group, most of whose leaders and members are Arabs. At the same time MAQĪ, the communist group with a Jewish majority, published a fortnightly in Arabic, named *Ṣawt al-sha'b* (The Voice of the people).

Al-Ittiḥād is more like an Arab newspaper than the others. This is noticeable in its editorial board, staff, and contributors, in its polished style, and in its socio-economic and political orientation. Although it sometimes accepts for publication literary work of non-communist Arabs, *al-Ittiḥād* is completely geared to the party propaganda. Incitement is its regular tactics, and the use of nationalist slogans the means of achieving it (resulting, however, in its periodic closure). It continues publication in the shadow of significant ideological and political conflicts: between East and West (naturally, it is anti-Western), the Soviet Union and China (it is pro-Soviet), Jews and Arabs in Israel (it supports the Arabs all the way), Israel and the Arab States, and the latter among themselves (it favours the so-called progressive Arab States). This bi-weekly has consistently opposed the Israeli Government and most of its policies. In particular, it has deplored the Government's non-identification with the Soviets and has blamed on it what it regards as the discrimination against the Arab minority in Israel. *Al-Ittiḥād* is ably edited: the use of different colours, the headings and wording all help to achieve the emphasis which the party wants to convey. Its circulation, estimated at between 3,000–6,000 is evidence of its growing popularity.

[60] See also Marmorstein, in *Middle Eastern Studies*, Oct. 1964, 3–20.

4. *Periodicals in Arabic.* Quite a large number of these appear in Israel,[61] and most have a political or semi-political character. They all have literary pretensions, which in some cases are justified.

The periodicals of the Christian communities are somewhat high-brow. Foremost among them is the monthly *al-Rābiṭa* (The Bond), which first appeared in January 1944, and later renewed its publication in Israel, since May 1952. This is the organ of the Greek Catholics, though it deals but little with community affairs. It is more concerned with general politics in the area, chiefly with those of the Arab minority in Israel. This monthly gains importance from being the mouthpiece of Archbishop George al-Ḥakīm, who was not only the spiritual leader of the Greek Catholic community in Israel until 1967, but also a leading personality within his own right.[62] At times, *al-Rābiṭa* has assumed nationalist slogans and an extremist tone which have enabled it to attract those Arab nationalists in Israel unwilling to write for the communist periodicals. For a time this increased its popularity among Israeli Arabs. However, as it was not easy to compete with the communists, and as al-Ḥakīm has drawn nearer to Government circles since the late 1950s, its tone has mellowed considerably in recent years.

The main rival of *al-Rābiṭa* is an Anglican missionary monthly, *al-Rā'id* (The Pioneer), which began publication as early as 1926. It was called *al-Akhbār al-Kanā'isiyya* (Church News) until 1957, when it changed its name. This monthly, also, lays emphasis on those political aspects which appeal to its Arab readers in Israel. As a result, it succeeds in attracting different contributors, some of whom are Muslims.

Of the secular magazines in Arabic, the only one which is wholly independent of the influence of political parties is the weekly *al-Muṣawwar* (The Illustrated), appearing in Jaffa since 1955. Its name was originally *al-'Ālam al-muṣawwar* (The Illustrated World). Although its virulence varies, it is not infrequently a titillating combination of photographs bordering on eroticism, if not pornography, and extremist political articles indiscriminately besmirching the Israeli Government. The tone of *al-Muṣawwar* reached its peak,

[61] Further details in two articles in Hebrew and Arabic by S. Moreh in *MḤ*, 1958, 26–39; and 1964, 296–309. Cf. as well his recent article 'Arabic literature in Israel', *Middle Eastern Studies*, Apr. 1967, 283–94.

[62] Archbishop George al-Ḥakīm has shown himself as a leader of Israeli Arabs in general, not only of his flock. See Sh. Rapapōrt in *Ma'arīv*, 21 Nov. 1967. Archbishop al-Ḥakīm was chosen as the Greek Catholic Patriarch on 22 Nov. 1967, thus becoming the spiritual mentor of all Greek Catholics in the Middle East, including those in Israel.

apparently, in the years 1960–2; since then it has been somewhat less aggressive.

Many periodicals affiliated to certain political parties are ephemeral. Some of them appear for a short time only, during the campaign preceding parliamentary elections, and compete for the Arab vote. Others are less temporary and mainly of a literary character: examples are the now defunct monthlies *al-Fajr* (The Dawn), published for a few years, by MAPAM, since 1958, and *al-Hadaf* (The Target), issued by the *Histadrūt* and probably sponsored by MAPAI, during 1960–2.

The communist journals in Arabic seem more durable. From the literary and linguistic point of view they are frequently on a higher level too. The monthly *al-Jadīd* (The New) started in October 1951, at first as a supplement to the bi-weekly *al-Ittiḥād*. This magazine publishes translations of communist works into Arabic, as well as reprints of articles and stories from the leftist press in the Arab countries, and original works by Israeli Arab communists or sympathizers. Otherwise, the orientation of *al-Jadīd* follows closely that of *al-Ittiḥād*. It constantly attacks the Israeli authorities, which it accuses of pro-western and imperialist tendencies, on one hand, and a policy of internal discrimination, on the other. *Al-Jadīd*, however, publishes different material from *al-Ittiḥād* and includes no news items.[63] Another communist monthly in Arabic, *al-Ghad* (Tomorrow) presents Marxist literary material, intended for youth. In addition, *al-Ghad* prints materials dealing with youth activities throughout the world, especially in the Eastern block. *Al-Darb* (The Path) is another communist Arabic periodical, a quarterly which deals with Leninist-Marxist theory.

Before the parliamentary elections of November 1965, the *ha-'Ōlam ha-zeh* Movement made preparations for the publication of an Arabic weekly, which has appeared regularly since February 1966. Its name is *Hādhā'l-'ālam*, an exact translation of the Hebrew weekly's title, *ha-'Ōlam ha-zeh* (both mean 'This World'). Moreover, the Arabic magazine is, in great part, a translation from the Hebrew, adapted to the taste and views of its Arab readers. The Arabic weekly's first editor was Samīḥ al-Qāsim, a Druze in his thirties, a teacher and a poet sympathetic to Arab nationalism. After his dismissal, a younger ex-teacher, no less extremist, 'Uthmān Baransī, was appointed editor. Not surprisingly, *Hādhā'l-'ālam* violently attacks the Government of Israel and most of its Ministries and

[63] For a selection of some articles in *al-Jadīd*, cf. the bibliography, pp. 280–1 below.

departments, attempting in this manner to increase the number of its sympathizers among the Arab population.[64]

To sum up, Arabic newspapers, magazines, and periodicals in Israel serve mainly as a vehicle for discussion or as a mirror reflecting accomplishments within the State of Israel or by its authorities. Whether informative or literary, they may be divided into two categories: (1) those intended to defend the policy of the Israeli authorities in general and towards the Arabs in particular. In these an apologetic tone is frequently discernible. (2) Those intended to criticize the official policy. Among the latter, the organs of MAPAM, often mild in their criticism, may be distinguished from the communists, characterized by sharp attacks. While this is not always the case (for instance, at election time, MAPAM newspapers become extremist, too), a perusal of the Arabic press in Israel verifies this differentiation in general. Another characteristic applies to the tone of these publications. The communist press in Arabic is apt, as a general rule, to label Israeli official policy as Machiavellian and tuned to imperialist western interests;[65] MAPAM is more selective in its criticism. While MAPAM's *al-Mirṣād* has consistently attacked the military administration and demanded full equality for the Arabs in Israel, it has its own approach to the sovereignty of the State and its future—which it does not hesitate to put forward. Thus, while *al-Ittiḥād* has continuously advocated the indiscriminate return of all Arab refugees who so desire, *al-Mirṣād* maintains that the State has the right to select the refugees who are to return.

From the above, one can see that the extreme politicization of Jewish public life in Israel—in the economic, social, and religious areas, not less than in the political—easily finds its counterpart among the Arab population in the same State. It is no mere chance that so few Arabic journals are published by the religious communities, while practically all are linked to political parties or organizations. Moreover, politicization is even more far-reaching among the Israeli Arabs than among the Jews in at least one respect. The literature of the Arabs in Israel is subordinate to politics, in both its choice of subjects and their presentation.

There is a definite connexion between the manifest political trends

[64] Mansour in *ha-Areṣ*, 23 Mar. 1966. Acc. to *Ma'arīv*, 22 Sept. 1966, both these editors had quarrelled with Ūrī Avnerī, leader of their movement and editor of the Hebrew weekly *ha-'Ōlam ha-zeh*, and they were dismissed.

[65] In order to revile the Israeli Government, *al-Ittiḥād*, oddly enough, attempts to boast of championing the *religious* interests of the Arab population in Israel; cf. *al-Ittiḥād*, 5 & 22 Nov. 1963; 3 Jan. 1964; 19 Jan., 2 Mar., 11 May, & 4 June. 1965.

in Arab literature in Israel and the way in which the Arabic publishing houses were established. As no Arabic publishing enterprises were carried over from the period of British rule in Palestine into the Israeli period, it was felt necessary to fill the vacuum with a supply of reading material in Arabic. This had to be printed in Israel, as no import-export trade has existed between Israel and the Arab States since 1948. Therefore, several publishing houses were established, mainly since 1954, appended to the Christian communities, the *Histadrūt* (MAPAI-inspired), and a number of political parties—in particular MAPAM and the communists.

Several of these publishing houses are also connected with the party newspapers. They have, in the last few years, reissued the best in both classical and modern Arabic literature, previously printed in the Arab States. They have also published various works by local Arab writers and poets, where the connexion between the publishing house and the political party has been crucial. The parties have initiated certain works and financed many more. This has increased politicization in a literature addressed to an Arab public, previously quite politically conscious under British rule and which has become more committed in Israel in response to the deep involvement in politics by the Jewish public.

Obviously, not all Arabic literature in Israel is political in nature. One may find fine lyrical poems. Stories and poems deal with non-political subjects such as change in society and tradition, the status of woman,[66] the problems of workers and farmers, and general human topics. However, even these are often connected, explicitly or implicitly, with present-day politics. More so, the response to current political events is seldom incidental: many Arab literary works reveal a direct, personal involvement in politics. In fact, every major event regarding the Arabs in Israel, the Middle East, or the world (apparently, in this order of importance) receives some reaction from Israeli Arabs, chiefly in their poetry. This has been the case particularly since the Sinai campaign of 1956. Matters have reached a point where one of the outstanding Arab poets in Israel, has commented on this as follows: 'I do not deny that poets have to write political poetry, but there is no need for everything they write to be politics. Most of our poets in Israel today are just expecting some tragedy or political event, so that they can compose a poem about it.'[67]

[66] A subject treated with great sensitivity by the Israeli Arab poet Jamāl Qa'wār in his collection of stories *Salmà*.

[67] Rāshid Ḥusayn, in an article in Arabic, publ. in *al-Rā'id*, i/4–5 (1957).

No less than poetry, the short story and the novel written by Arabs in Israel are to a great extent politically oriented. For example, one may mention the narrative stories of Tawfīq Mu'ammar, a lawyer who has woven into his literary works deep hatred for the State of Israel. This approach colours much of the literature with exaggerated emotionalism, little restrained by an objective evaluation of the present.[68] Since a central subject is the Arab-Jewish confrontation in Israel, perhaps one cannot expect otherwise. Rarely does one find an attempt at a neutral standpoint, which divides responsibility for this tragic confrontation, such as that of Najwa Qa'wār Faraḥ, wife of the editor of *al-Rā'id*, who wrote:

> You, and others like you, may ask yourselves, when you grow up, who is responsible for the tragedy of the refugees; and you will be told: the English, or the Arab leaders, or the Jewish leaders; and no doubt they are all responsible. But I shall teach you something more: fundamentally, the human heart is responsible, for it is the root of good and evil. . . .[69]

In general, when the Arabs in Israel refer to politics in their writings, they take a stand. Only rarely do they write in support of the Israeli Government and the considerable material advantages it has introduced into everyday life. These benefits are, indeed, appreciated by those Arab writers who have identified their future with the State of Israel; or by those submitting their literary work to competitions organized by bodies with a Jewish majority, such as the *Histadrūt*. Otherwise, much of the Arab literary production in Israel is characterized by dislike of the State and incitement against it—of the type collected in the previously mentioned anthology, *Adab al-muqāwama fī Filasṭīn al-muḥtalla*.

Many of the Arab poets and writers in Israel consider themselves as fighters on behalf of their brethren. The Arab defeat in 1948 and its consequences constitute typical themes for them. Those who are close to the communists constantly redefine the régime in Israel as a dictatorship supported by British and American imperialism. Even writers who do not repeat this tendentious definition are prone to emphasize the negative in Israel. Exaggerated stress is laid on such subjects as the military administration, the need for transit permits, unemployment and other economic problems, and judicial discrimination. The writer Faraj Nūr Salmān presents the Jew as a stranger, fanatically hating all Arabs; the next step is to upbraid

[68] See, in addition to the articles of Moreh (n. 61), an article by A. Yinon, *MḤ*, 1965, 57–84.

[69] Quoted by Yinon, ibid. English summary, xiii.

openly all Arabs guilty of collaboration with such Jews. Hence the very fact that the *mukhtār* of an Arab village co-operates with the Israeli authorities leaves him open to be accused, *post factum*, of abandoning the Arab cause disgracefully, even treasonably. The logic underlying this approach is that only two types of values exist, the good and the evil. In this context, Arab literature in Israel returns again and again to the theme of the Arab refugees. The spirit is usually that of nostalgia to the lost generation, to which bitterness at the lack of any solution is frequently added. In the literary exposition of this theme, all nuances may be found, from the moderate to the violent. Thematically, there is usually a sentimental description of the longing for the divided family, the lost house and land. The Arab is generally presented as the acme of perfection, as a good, altruistic neighbour of the Jews (e.g. in one of Tawfīq Mu'ammar's stories), or as a hero, ever ready to fight an injustice brought about by the authorities (e.g. in the work of Samīḥ al-Qāsim, already mentioned as editor of *Hādhā'l-'ālam*). The reader is left with the impression that a community consisting of such characters will never yield until it succeeds in freeing itself from the 'Israeli yoke'.

This approach, although common and typical, is by no means the only one. There are many nuances in dealing with the subject. However, except for a few cases, most Arab writers in Israel present the confrontation between Jew and Arab in what amounts to a strong spirit of alienation towards the new State and its Jewish majority; as the second side of the same coin, these same writers identify themselves fully with the special problems of the Arab minority as well as with national sentiment across the borders. It is symptomatic of this that even an author and journalist such as A. Mansour, the Christian Arab correspondent of the *ha-Areṣ* Hebrew daily in Nazareth, cannot free himself from a feeling of alienation. He was the first Israeli Arab to write a Hebrew novel. It is named, characteristically, *Bĕ-ōr ḥadash* (In a new light). Although the plot revolves round a love affair in a *kibbūtz* between an Arab and a Jewish girl, namely a bridge between the two peoples in Israel—the whole book is nothing but a continuous cry of despairing alienation, as felt by the Israeli Arabs versus the new reality.

Alienation finds place, even more, in the literature produced in Arabic. Suspicion or hatred is frequently an ingredient. An extreme example is a collection of stories by Tawfīq Mu'ammar. Named *Bithūn* (Never Mind!), this volume is written in literary Arabic mixed with the vernacular, which adds to an appeal, mainly achieved through its contents and approach. Mu'ammar sees the Israeli

Government through dark spectacles. According to these stories, the Israeli rulers govern thanks to British-American support and are cunningly ruthless regarding their Arab citizens: they persecute them, in order that the Arab States will retaliate by oppressing the Jews living there, resulting in their emigration to increase Israel's human potential! Everything done by the Government of Israel for its Arab population—paving roads, supplying water and electricity, granting social welfare, old-age pensions and sickness insurance, broadening education, and encouraging the economy—is comparable to the delicacies given the condemned in their last meal. If the condemned remain alive, taxation will impoverish and compel them to emigrate. Injustice is rampant in employment opportunities and in the freedom of political association (but not in the judicial system, fair even by Mu'ammar's standards). Mu'ammar adds a lawyer's reasoning to his selective approach; he is particularly effective in his satire, which is inspired by popular Arab humour.

This attitude presupposes malice aforethought for every governmental decision and action in Israel. Other Arab writers, less pessimistically alienated, seem less bitter. Thus Yaḥyà Fāhūm does not hesitate to protest against what he considers as the heavy taxation on the farmers. However, he considers this a necessary evil, due to disappear when matters improve in the course of time. Other Arab writers, like Maḥmūd 'Abd al-Qādir Kanā'ne and others who have accepted the new conditions in Israel, estimate the situation in Israel in a more hopeful spirit and sometimes go so far as to praise it. The adaptation of these Arab writers to Israel is often based on a better acquaintance with their Jewish neighbours and a sincere willingness to co-operate with them. Their works show that not all Jews in Israel are arrogant and Arab-haters, as some of the more extremist Arab writers in Israel would have their readers believe.

End of Chap 3

4

POLITICAL ORGANIZATIONS

NEW POLITICAL TRENDS

DURING the days of British rule in Palestine, the local Arabs were already divided among themselves, politically, according to their institutionalized social structures. The development of the towns and the rise of a budding proletariat assisted in the formation of new political forces: the small Communist Party was the most vocal, but others, also, were beginning to crystallize. The decline in the power of the *ḥamūlas* has already been described.[1] In the vacuum left by the weakening of the age-long structures, new political groups were trying to assert themselves, eagerly competing with the elders of the *ḥamūlas*, the leaders of the villagers, and the chiefs of the religious communities. This process, begun in Palestine, developed rapidly in Israel.

The factors which have assisted in this process have already been analysed for their socio-economic significance, but it is worthwhile to recapitulate briefly and reconsider them in their *political* context:

1. The constant expansion of the group of salaried workers has endangered their economic ties with the village and their dependence on it; this group, in turn, is frequently subject to the impact of western civilization in the town. The growth in the number of these workers has paved the way for the rise of new political organizations which base themselves on individual recruitment, while striving to break up previously existing structures. Among these workers, *dispersed* as they are, one may notice various political influences at work, quite different from those emanating from the *ḥamūla* or the religious community. The communists were among the first to benefit from this situation.

2. Arab workers, having jobs in near-by towns, bring some of the influence of urban civilization back into their villages. Thus the impact of new political ideas and trends is broadened. The almost total absence of urbanization and the regular return of the workers to their villages bring them, sooner or later, in conflict with the established local leaders. This conflict may reach its peak in a contest for local power and political leadership.

[1] See above, ch. 2.

3. A new class of young intellectuals has arisen as a direct result of the wider scope of education and the rise in its level. These have a completely different *Weltanschauung* from their elders. Systematic education had endowed them with new ways of thinking, tools of analysis, a sense of relationship to western values and an even keener one to the Arab national movement. They are desirous of developing their newly-acquired skills and using them for personal advancement. This class serves, no less than salaried workers, as a natural recruiting area for political organizations, which may even find among these Arab intellectuals suitable candidates for future leadership.

4. The penetration of the Israeli way of life, based on an egalitarian philosophy and expressed in democratic institutions, has made an impact on the Arab population. The leadership in the Arab villages has had to adapt. It has not always been able to keep pace with swift modernization, however, and has sometimes clashed with the new concepts (such as that of general elections) and their protagonists. This has opened the way for new political forces—more flexible and speedily adaptable to the new set of values in Israel. These forces have rapidly learnt to make use of the new processes for attaining power.

5. The same causes which strengthen the Arab nationalist consciousness among Israeli Arabs serve to undermine their attachment to the older structures of loyalty towards the *ḥamūla*, the tribe, or the religious community.

6. The sharp rise in the standards of living has resulted in more leisure time. This, in turn, has increased the use of modern media of communication, in particular the radio and television. Thus contact with current opinion beyond the borders has been maintained, and in many cases even intensified. This contact has not improved the image of the traditional structures, tending to make them appear too narrow and antiquated.

We have already stressed that this is a period of transition. Hence the expression and activities of the new political forces among Israeli Arabs are often ambiguous or even confused. A case in point is the split vote in Arab villages, in parliamentary and local elections (to be discussed later). Arab communists and nationalists, in a number of villages, who voted for the communist slate in parliamentary elections, voted the same day for the *ḥamūla* elders or other local personalities in local elections.[2] This occurred in the 1965 elections in several villages of the Little Triangle, with a consistency that elimi-

[2] Cf. Abner Cohen, *Arab border-villages*, 9.

nates the possibility of a coincidence.[3] The split vote suggests that loyalty to the *ḥamūla* is still strong, even among the young; and that this loyalty was translated into support at the polling booths, whenever the *ḥamūla* succeeded in standing together and overcoming less inclusive forms of loyalty. These phenomena, however, are only indications of the period of change: the structure and strength of the *ḥamūla* have not yet been destroyed, but they are declining. During the period of the British Mandate, the political attitudes of the Palestinian Arabs were determined by the *ḥamūlas*—in both local and national affairs. Thus during the countrywide conflict between the Ḥusaynīs and the Nashāshībīs, divided loyalties were unknown. At that time, the *ḥamūla* was a tightly knit, all-comprehensive organism. The individual was literally absorbed into it; the range of his decisions was very limited, and his independent opinion was hardly ever expressed in local and Arab national politics. All this is changing in Israel.

ISRAELI ARABS AND THE POLITICAL PARTIES

Except for a few instances (to be mentioned later in this chapter), the active participation of Arabs in Israeli political parties has been and remains still quite modest. One of the publications of the League of Arab States has attempted to explain the phenomenon in somewhat superficial terms: The Arabs in Israel are prevented from forming their own political parties.[4] In fact, numerous reasons exist why so few Israeli Arabs join political parties, the main ones being the following:

1. Basically, the ideologies of most political parties in Israel hardly encourage the local Arabs to join them wholeheartedly and integrate within them. With the exception of the communists, all Jewish parties were originally Zionist groupings in pre-State days. Zionist ideology is still axiomatic to all political parties in the State of Israel, even if the emphasis varies; it still dominates the activities of Jewish parties outside the new State. Not surprisingly, even those Israeli Arabs who wanted to adapt to the new situation could hardly hope to integrate easily into all-Jewish, openly-Zionist political parties.[5]

[3] See *Ma'arīv*, 11 Feb. 1965.

[4] Hadawi, *Israel and the Arab minority*, 36. Cf. for an opposite view, I. Koplewitz, in *ha-Dōr* (Tel-Aviv, daily), 14 Sept. 1949.

[5] For Jewish political parties in Israel, their ideology and activities, see M. Seliger, 'Ideologie und Politik in Israel', *Geshichte in Wissenschaft und Unterricht, Zeitschrift des Verbandes der Geschichtslehrer Deutschlands* (Stuttgart), Sept. 1967, 513–41. E. E. Gutmann, 'Some observations on politics and parties in Israel', *India Quarterly* (New Delhi), Jan.–Mar. 1961, 3–29. A. Arian, Voting and ideology in Israel', *Midwest Journal of Political Science*, Aug. 1966, 265–87.

2. The political parties themselves, with the exception of the communists and MAPAM, have not encouraged Arabs to seek membership. They are, in their orientation and composition, characteristically Jewish, and seem content to continue in this way. Their only concession has been to organize lists of Arab candidates allied with them as a vote-catching tactic prior to elections.

3. The Israeli Arabs themselves have apparently been in no hurry to enter politics, in general, and most have refrained from joining any of the existing parties. Factors (1) and (2) may have played a part in their calculations. Moreover, the very large majority of the Arab population, namely most of the villagers, had had no real share in politics during British rule in Palestine. During that period, the main political activities were a few party workers belonging to the more important families. Following the 1947–8 struggle, even the few who had been involved in politics had become discredited as a consequence of their failure. Others blamed the partisan approach of the Palestinian Arabs for the lack of unity to which many of them attributed the Arab defeat.[6] Others again were still suffering from the effects of shock, after the reversal of fortune in 1948 and their change of status from an Arab majority to a minority in a Jewish State. In these new conditions, the Arab masses lacked the guidance of their political leaders, most of whom had left the country either before the Arab-Israeli war of 1948, or during it. For these reasons, many preferred to sit and wait. Only a few sought—and obtained—membership in MAPAM or the Communist Party. Some others preferred to approach political parties who had ruled the Government-coalition for some time, such as MAPAI. They did not join these as full members (and the parties did not invite Arab membership), but collaborated with them and probably reaped material advantages as a result.

4. In consequence, some Israeli Arabs have tried to establish purely Arab parties. These attempts date from recent years, with the gradual disappearance of the effects of the shock brought about by defeat. They may also be seen as the result of perception and adoption by the Arabs in Israel of some of the methods by which a democratic régime permits—or even encourages—free expression and association. Early experiments with founding independent Arab parties proved to be total failures. The first attempt shortly after the establishment of the new State was by a rich Arab in Jaffa, named Abū Laban. His efforts were unsuccessful, probably because he lived far away from the main Arab centres in Israel. Another attempt to

[6] Asaf, in *MH*, 1949, esp. p. 5; Waschitz, ibid. 1950, 259.

establish a People's Party by a Christian Arab called Dā'ūd Khūrī, also failed. The party's main *raison d'être* was to fight against the laws governing absentee property; the chiefs of the party which was envisaged wanted to repossess the immovable property abandoned by their relatives who had left the State.[7] A third attempt to found an Arab political party was made by Niqūlā Ṣābā, a Christian Arab from Nazareth, who tried to establish a Democratic Party in 1951–2. He was apparently backed by the General Zionists, one of the Jewish political parties. Ṣābā's group was centred in Haifa, where they could act freely, away from the area controlled by the military administration. Few Arabs showed interest in the Democratic Party, and it soon dispersed.

A more serious effort was made by the lawyer Nimr al-Hawārī. This dynamic personality had already been politically active during the period of British rule in Palestine. Following the Arab-Israel war in 1948, he was the representative of the Arab refugees in the Israeli-Arab armistice negotiations on the island of Rhodes. In 1951 he was allowed to return to Israel. The Israeli authorities apparently hoped that he might found and lead an Arab political party, moderate in character. Hawārī tried, with Archbishop George al-Ḥakīm and others, to establish a slate of candidates for the 1951 *Kneset* elections. Following the failure of this plan, Hawārī revealed extremist tendencies;[8] he headed a small but articulate group of Arab nationalists, prominent among whose members were the Druze 'Abd Allāh Khayr and the Christian Arab lawyer Eliyās N. Kūsā. The latter is quite well known for his able, sometimes fervent, defence of Arabs in the law courts and for his numerous letters to the press, in which he advocates full equality for the Arab minority in Israel. In his articles, Kūsā has enunciated his views clearly and boldly: the State of Israel has to prove, by its actions, its intentions regarding the Arab minority; it has to change its policy in this respect, that is, to allow Arabs to move freely everywhere and to reunite families by letting Arabs return;[9] even if the general situation of the Arabs in Israel is good, all social discrimination against them should cease.[10] When the Hawārī–Khayr–Kūsā group proved unable to attract sufficient Arab backing,

[7] *Ha-Areṣ*, 19 Mar. 1965.

[8] R. Moṣeyrī, ibid. 24 July 1951, for the list of candidates. For Hawārī's accusations, see e.g. *Ner*, 20 Apr. 1951.

[9] e.g. his articles *Ner*, 6 Jan. 1951, 20–21; 20 Apr. 1951, 19–20; Sept. 1951, 19–21; June 1952, 22–23. Cf. his open letters, ibid. Feb.–Mar. 1952 *passim*; July 1952, 20–22; Nov. 1952, 21–23.

[10] See his article in the New York *al-Bayān*, summarized in *al-Mirṣād*, 25 Sept. 1964.

Kūsā established his own Israeli Arab Bloc which he then tried to expand into an Israeli Arab Party. Founded in 1955, the main activity of this party consisted in calling upon the Arabs in Israel to boycott the parliamentary elections, held the same year. Its efforts were unsuccessful, although it distributed handbills among the local Arabs, and sent letters of protest to the Israeli and foreign press. Perhaps because of the intransigent attitude of Kūsā,[11] the so-called party remained a tiny group, which soon disappeared from the political scene.

In the period immediately preceding the elections to the fourth *Kneset*, in 1959, two MKs previously allied to MAPAI, who had been dropped from the new pro-MAPAI slate of Arab candidates, attempted to run on their own; they failed to collect enough support. In the late 1950s and early 1960s, the same fate befell two political groups (which will be analysed at greater length further on), the Popular Arab Front and *al-Arḍ*. Each tried to establish an independent Arab party and later a slate of candidates for the *Kneset*. They, too, failed.

In practically all these attempts the newly-founded Arab political groups were oppositionist to the Government. This fact alone did not, apparently, endear them sufficiently to the Arab population in Israel. Obviously also the older political parties saw no reason to encourage rivals, which might conceivably rob them of a share of 'their' votes in future elections; so these parties did everything within their power to discourage the formation of new political groups. The same attitude seems to have been held by the Government, though of course it could not openly discourage the establishment of an Arab party. The first intimation of such a policy dates only from the beginning of the year 1967. Even then it was not expressed in a public statement by any official spokesman of the Government. Instead, the policy was announced by Amnōn Līn, chief of the Department for Arab Affairs in the Alignment (i.e. the combined MAPAI and *Aḥdūt ha-'avōda* (Unity of Labour) parties). In the course of a press conference in Haifa, Līn explained the position and activity of the alignment in the municipal elections held in Nazareth at the end of 1966. What he said on that occasion is so instructive, that the relevant phrases merit full translation into English:[12]

[11] For an illustration, cf. his call to the Minister of Defence in 1955, challenging him to let all the Arabs emigrate from Israel, and take their money with them (*Ner*, Feb.–Mar. 1955, 34–36).

[12] Acc. to *ha-Areṣ*, 5 Jan. 1967. Meanwhile Līn has become a member of the *Kneset*. See also Mansour, ibid. 17 Feb. 1967.

There is great danger in the very existence of an Arab party, not allied with any Jewish party. Experience in the Middle East shows that extremist elements always get the upper hand within a nationalist party; then they remove the moderates by labelling them 'traitors' . . . A nationalist party which does not identify with the State is liable to bring disaster upon the Arab population in Israel.

Continuing, Līn declared that no one required the Arabs in Israel to become Zionists; however, it was desirable to persuade them to identify with the State and to resist chauvinistic propaganda, that is to prevent them from banding together in a party with subversive aims. From Līn's words, it may be deduced that—in so far as he represents the views of the MAPAI party—the Government of Israel has tended to suspect that an independent Arab party might well turn to anti-State activities. We shall later discuss the measures taken against the attempt of the *al-Arḍ* group to organize itself as a political party.

Though few Arabs in Israel have joined political parties, they nevertheless appear well aware of their tenor and activities as well as of their bid for electoral support. Understandably, many Arabs have maintained some contact with one or other of the parties, without formally joining them. A characteristic example is the usual formation of lists of Arab candidates, allied with MAPAI, before parliamentary elections. The generally high-sounding titles of these lists have only partially revealed their nature; examples include the Democratic List of the Arabs of Israel, Agriculture and Development, Co-operation and Brotherhood, Progress and Development, etc. In general, MAPAI has supported two or three such allied lists of candidates for each electoral campaign. The first few names in every list—that is, those standing a chance of being elected to the *Kneset*—were those of Muslim, Christian, and Druze personalities, divided by the same ratio as their approximate numerical share in the minority population.[13] The lists have also taken into account the competing interests of the main *ḥamūlas*, as well as representation of

[13] This was the original intention; but it did not always turn out that way. For example, after the *Kneset* elections in 1955 a noisy quarrel broke out between the main candidates in a MAPAI-sponsored list, called the Democratic List of the Arabs in Israel. The first candidate was Sayf al-Dīn Zu'bī, a Muslim; the second Mas'ad Qasīs, a Greek Catholic; the third Jabr Mu'addī, a Druze. The group obtained only two seats in the *Kneset*. The Druzes claimed that their group had secured numerous Druze votes, and demanded that Qasīs stand down. This was bitterly opposed by the Greek Catholics, who argued that in this case they would be left without any representative in the *Kneset*, while the Druzes already had a 'safe' MK on another list, allied with MAPAI. Finally, Qasīs and Mu'addī agreed to divide the four years of *Kneset* office between them, equally.

various regions: frequently, one list would be headed by candidates from Nazareth and Eastern Galilee, another from the Druze villages and the Little Triangle. The number of lists reflects, in addition, the unwillingness of the main candidates to compromise on a characteristically personal matter, i.e. the chance to be elected to the *Kneset*.[14]

The prominent candidates in these lists were usually rich notables, connected with MAPAI by similar interests. They had an almost identical approach to politics, with slight variations. The nature of these variations depended on the nature and tenor of their requests to MAPAI (the majority party in the Government) concerning betterment of the condition of the Arab minority in Israel. The common denominator of all these personalities was that they considered themselves the only ones able to improve the situation of the Arabs in Israel, the only means being full co-operation with MAPAI and the State authorities. In plain words this meant that, thanks to their connexions, they would be in a position to recommend certain measures desired by their fellow villagers or the members of their religious community. Some of these Arab notables proved to be opportunists, mainly concerned with prestige or personal advancement; others supported MAPAI and the Israeli Government out of conviction. The latter would repeatedly explain to any would-be listener that only the continuation of MAPAI preponderance in the Government guaranteed stability; and that only this kind of stability protected the Arab community from undesirable agitation. Such a presentation of the problem reveals the undoubted vested interest of these Arab notables in the political *status quo*.[15]

It may be claimed that these Arab 'lists' allied with MAPAI resemble personal groups rather than political parties. Their main role consists of gaining electoral Arab support for MAPAI, on the one hand, and supporting it in crucial parliamentary votes, on the other. And indeed, the Arab MKs allied to Jewish MAPAI have cautiously refrained, in general, from discussing the military administration or Israel's relations with the Arab States. Rather, they have preferred to dwell on the local and communal problems of the Arabs in Israel. Occasionally, MAPAI has experimented with organizing an Arab party, allied to it, but had to give up the idea because of the bitter rivalry among those slated to head it. MAPAI has indeed had

[14] B. Akzin, 'The role of parties in Israeli democracy', *J. of Politics*, xvii (1955), esp. 538 ff.

[15] Cf. the frank views of Fāris Ḥamdān, Arab MK (allied to MAPAI) in the 2nd and 3rd *Knesets*, in an interview with Schiff, publ. in *ha-Areṣ*, 15 July 1955.

to be satisfied with a substitute: the lists of candidates for election. Since these lists are totally inactive between electoral campaigns, they may well be considered as *ad hoc* groups rather than political parties, even in a loose sense of the term. However, their very existence hinders the establishment of rival independent lists of Arab candidates. Obviously, the peculiar character of the lists allied with MAPAI is well known both to their supporters and opponents among the Arabs. One of the latter, a young, self-confessed nationalist, describes these Arab candidates for the *Kneset* as follows:

> These are not our representatives. They ignore the interests of the Arab population. Together with the local Arab politicians, they are more dangerous to the State than to the Arab population itself, because the Arab problem cannot be solved through a separate struggle, or a separate Jewish struggle, but only through a common struggle. They are opportunists, and hence negative characters.[16]

MAPAI has set up special committees to decide on the party's relationship with the Arab minority in Israel. Their role includes dealing with the Arab lists of election candidates, allied with MAPAI, as well as with those who were elected as MKs. Responsibility is shared by three committees:

1. A committee for minority affairs, which is in direct contact with the central committee of MAPAI (in recent years, its chairman has been Abbā Ḥūshī, the mayor of Haifa). This committee meets on an *ad hoc* basis and determines the party's general policy towards the Arabs in Israel. It keeps in touch with the MAPAI co-ordinating committee for minorities in the *Kneset*; and passes on directives to the party's Arab department.

2. A co-ordinating committee for minorities in the *Kneset*, which is composed of five Jewish MAPAI MKs, whose task is to meet when needed and maintain contacts with the Arab MKs allied with MAPAI, listen to their claims, and to co-ordinate their speeches and votes with those of the other MAPAI MK's.

3. The Arab Department of MAPAI is the body which carries out all the current activity of MAPAI regarding the Arab minority in Israel. The function of the department is to keep itself aware of the changing moods in the Arab street and to retain permanent representatives in the major Arab villages. These representatives are expected to maintain uninterrupted contact with the Arabs, which is achieved through MAPAI members and sympathizers, Jews and Arabs alike. In recent years, in addition to fostering relations with *ḥamūla*

[16] Reported in *YA*, 17 Feb. 1967.

leaders and other notables—very useful in vote-getting—MAPAI's Arab Department has increasingly employed younger Arabs. This approach appears to indicate a growing consciousness among MAPAI decision-makers of the imminent need for younger reserves from the Arab population. Among the relatively new Arab faces that have become prominent in MAPAI activities during the 1960s may be mentioned George Sa'd, who headed the Alignment's list of candidates for the trade union elections in Nazareth (a part of the national elections of the *Histadrūt*; 'Ārif Rushdī from Haifa, who manages the employment bureau in Umm al-Faḥm; Salīm Jubrān, secretary of MAPAI's Arab Department; Kamāl Manṣūr, a Druze from the village of 'Isfiyya, near Haifa, director of the Government's information services in the Haifa area; and others. All these are comparatively young men, aged 35–40.[17]

Other political parties besides MAPAI have also tried either to found parties or to organize lists of candidates at election time—usually the latter. Thus early in 1949 MAPAM assisted an allied slate of Arab candidates to run for the first *Kneset*; but this Arab Popular Bloc, as it was called, failed to win even one parliamentary seat. In response, MAPAM soon set up a new section within the party, to draw Arabs closer to MAPAM,[18] with full membership in view. Before the 1951 elections to the second *Kneset*, the General Zionist Party appealed to Arab landowners, whose interests might have been hurt by the government monopoly on the marketing of farm produce; their vote was solicited in an attempt to force economic liberalization. In view of their lack of success in gaining the Arab vote, the General Zionists attempted before the 1955 elections to the third *Kneset* to establish an allied Arab party. This was, in practice, a list of candidates for the *Kneset* consisting of Arab notables (which incidentally failed to obtain a single parliamentary seat). Before the 1959 elections to the fourth *Kneset*, the *Aḥdūt ha-'avōda* party tried to found an allied political group, called the Israeli Arab Labour Party (in Arabic: *al-'Amal*); it also published an Arabic periodical bearing the same name. This, like previous efforts, failed to collect enough Arab votes. The conclusions drawn by the various political parties from the successive failures of the Arab lists (those allied with MAPAI excepted) have been somewhat different. The Communist Party was alone in accepting from its inception Jews and Arabs alike into its ranks.[19] MAPAM opened its membership to Arabs in 1954. Other

[17] For additional details see Mansour, in *ha-Areṣ*, 11 Feb. 1966.
[18] *'Al ha-Mishmar*, 29 Nov. 1949.
[19] We shall discuss the Communist Party and the Arabs in Israel later.

parties were content with restricting most of their political acitivity among the Arabs in Israel to electioneering. They even placed Arab personalities on their own lists of candidates, but always placed them sufficiently low to stand no real chance of being elected. (In Israel, the candidates become MKs in the order in which they appear on the slate.)

MAPAM is still attempting to resolve an inner ideological conflict concerning its attitude to the Arab minority in Israel, as well as to discover the most effective way of presenting the party's image[20] to Arab voters. MAPAM's desire to persuade the Israeli Arabs that it is their true friend and protector conflicts with the fact that it is a Zionist party, some of whose slogans differ considerably from those of the Arab national movement. This remains so, in Arab eyes, despite the *Leitmotiv* argument in MAPAM's dialectics that the misunderstanding between Zionism and Arab nationalism is temporary only and that it can be solved by co-operation between the socialist progressive forces in both camps; their joint action will aim at achieving peace in the Middle East, by neutralizing the whole area politically and banning the use of atomic weapons in it. Nevertheless MAPAM has failed to convince most of the Arabs in Israel that it opposes the Arab policy of the Government, as it has repeatedly participated in the Government coalition.

In its propaganda among the Arabs, MAPAM is in continuous competition with two other parties: on the one hand with MAPAI which has larger means and, as permanent majority party in the Government coalition, can grant material benefits more easily; and on the other with the communists, whose appeal to the Arabs is in the image of a non-Zionist (often anti-Zionist) party, consistently opposing Government policy towards the Arab minority in Israel.[21] Between MAPAI and the communists, MAPAM is in danger of falling between two stools in order to compete. MAPAM is forced to keep up constant activity among the Arabs in Israel. Responsibility for this work is divided between the party's central organs and its Arab Department. MAPAM's Arab Department was headed for some years by Simḥa Flapan, and more recently by Ya'aqōv Eytan—both Jews, assisted by Arabs. The *kibbūtzīm* of MAPAM, also, are extremely active in maintaining a close relationship with neighbouring Arab villages and aiding them with expert advice. MAPAM's Arab activities extend regularly into four regions: Eastern Galilee, Western Galilee, the Little Triangle, and the Negev (where its centre is

[20] See also, on MAPAM's Arabic newspaper, *al-Mirṣād*, above, pp. 60–61.

[21] Cf. Waschitz, in *ba-Sha'ar*, Apr. 1960, 18–22.

Be'er Sheba). Apparently, the party's activity is more intense in Galilee than in the Little Triangle. MAPAM's local branches consist of small units, organized according to occupation. Since 1954, when the party opened its ranks to Arab members, they have shared formally in much of the party's work. Their number, however, is unknown to outsiders (all Israeli political parties are very chary about releasing membership figures).

Since the second *Kneset*, elected in 1951, the MAPAM parliamentary group has always included an Arab MK. In the second *Kneset* he was Rustum Bastūnī, a young Christian architect (who later left MAPAM). From the third *Kneset* to the fifth, that is, during the years 1955–65, MAPAM's Arab MK was Yūsuf Khamīs, also a Christian Arab. In the sixth *Kneset*, i.e. since 1965, it was 'Abd al-'Azīz Zu'bī, a Muslim from Nazareth, belonging to the large and influential Zu'bī *ḥamūla* in that town.[22] These MKs have assisted, to a great extent, MAPAM's propaganda among the Arab population in Israel.

MAPAM also undertakes activities which are not formally political and whose scope includes Arabs who are not party members. It sponsors various educational activities, between evening classes, courses of instruction (including special ones for women—such as handicrafts), builds clubs, organizes visits, and so forth. One of its most imaginative projects concerned the establishment of a semi-informal organization called the Arab Pioneer Youth.[23] This movement was founded during 1954 and seems to have been disbanded ten years later. Modelled in great measure on the Jewish youth movements, the Arab one was intended to become a pioneer group, meant to oppose the traditional structure in the Arab settlements. Most of the activities of this movement were aimed at the villages, a few at the towns. The age of the youths was between 15 and 20. When the movement was established, it contained about 300 youths, in 1958 some 800, and in 1959 it reached a peak of approximately 1,500 (according to MAPAM's data). This movement has a close relationship with MAPAM's all-Jewish *ha-Shōmer ha-ṣa'īr* (the Young Watchman) organization—as expressed in joint outings, visits, sports activities, etc. Another connexion was forged between Arab pioneer youths and various *kibbūtzīm*, with the aim of giving those young Arabs vocational or agricultural training as well as some insight into life in a collective settlement. This arrangement solved

[22] In every single case, MAPAM's central committee decided who would represent the Arabs in a safe place on their list of candidates for the *Kneset*.

[23] Further information by Ben-Tzur in *ba-Sha'ar*, Dec. 1959, 7–10.

many of their employment problems for these youths, too. Later on, the Arab Pioneer Youths were encouraged to establish small co-operatives, of 6–10 members, in various Arab villages: in Kafr Yāṣīf a farmers' co-operation; in Ma'īlyā pig breeding; in 'Ar'ara construction blocks; in Ṭaiyyba transportation; and in Ṭīra an agricultural and a transportation co-operative.

MAPAM's emphasis on educational activities among the Arabs is evident in its efforts to gain support among the Arab intelligentsia. Obviously its Arab organ, *al-Mirṣād*, plays a central role in this. In addition, MAPAM's publishing house issues reprints of Arabic literature (by a photographic process) as well as offering an opportunity of publication to Arab writers in Israel. MAPAM arranges meetings and discussions among teachers, young intellectuals, and others—Jews and Arabs. It has established an Institute for Arab and Afro-Asian Studies in Giv'at Ḥavīva, where Arab and Jewish intellectuals study together. The central figure in this institute is an enthusiastic MAPAM member, much concerned with the Arabs, Yosef Waschitz. All this activity contributes to the image MAPAM would like to foster among the Arabs in Israel. Perhaps the concept was best expressed by the MAPAM MK, 'Abd al-'Azīz Zu'bī, while he was still living in Nazareth and was a prominent member in municipal affairs there: 'Thus a true front of workers and intellectuals was established against the reactionary front supported by the representatives of the Government in Israel.'[24] Even if this characterization is not entirely accurate in all its details, it exemplifies the intention of MAPAM to appear among the Israeli Arabs as the ally of the workers and intellectuals. In this area MAPAM has been forced into direct competition with the communists.

COMMUNIST ACTIVITY

Alongside MAPAI and MAPAM (or, rather, in opposition to them) the communists are intensively active among the Arabs in Israel. This activity displays a number of characteristics:[25]

1. The communists began political activities among the Arabs earlier than any other party. During the period of British rule[26] communist nuclei operated among the Palestinian Arabs, both

[24] Zu'bī, in an article for *Sefer ha-shana shel ha-'ittōna'īm* (Journalists' yearbook), *1963*, 159–61.

[25] For further details, cf. M. M. Czudnowski & J. M. Landau, *The Israeli Communist party and the elections to the fifth Knesset, 1961* (1965), and works cited in the footnotes.

[26] See Y. Pōrat's article in *MḤ*, 1964, 354–66. Cf. W. Z. Laqueur, *Communism and nationalism in the Middle East* (London, 1956), *passim.*

openly and clandestinely. At the time they faced considerable difficulties, mainly because of the opposition of both the rich landowners and the nationalists. Although the communists failed to recruit meaningful cadres from among the Palestinian Arabs at that time, the experience they gained was invaluable later, in the State of Israel. Under it their political activities became legal and unhindered, just as those of the other parties. Thus as soon as the State of Israel was established, the Communist Party prepared to fill the political vacuum, created by the hasty departure of the previously prominent leaders and the break-up of former parties.

2. In their propaganda, the communists were the sole party which could point out that their ideology was not Zionist. Therefore, it claimed, the communists alone had the real interests of the Israeli Arabs at heart, and could be trusted to guard these interests against the nefarious intentions of the Government.[27] (Their opponents wryly pointed out that the communists could promise anything; there was little chance of their achieving a position where they would have to fulfil their promises.) This, then, was the essence of the image the communists tried to build up, generally avoiding too detailed a discussion of Marxist theories, which were rather complicated for part of their audience and obnoxious to the remainder, pro-nationalist as it was. To enhance its appeal the Communist Party praised the volte-face of the Soviet Union, after its original support at the United Nations for the establishment of Israel, and stressed its unflagging support for the Arab States in more recent years. Communist propaganda put to good use many international events, both important and trivial. Frequently this propaganda used different arguments when addressing Arabs and Jews respectively.[28]

3. The party's composition reflects its political approach. It is the sole party in Israel during the whole period of Israel's existence that has included both Jewish and Arab members. MAPAM, as already stated, accepted Arab members only after 1954, and the number of Arabs in this party is still comparatively small. Other Israeli parties do not encourage Arabs to join (some may let in a minute number). The situation is different in the Israel Communist Party, or MAQĪ as it was called before the 1965 rift. If one is to believe the party's report at its 14th national congress in 1961,[29] there existed then a ratio of 25·7 per cent Arab members to 74·3 per cent Jews. Although

[27] Cf. D. Peretz, 'The Arab minority of Israel', *Middle East Journal* (Washington, D.C.), spring 1954, 149–50.

[28] Examples in *'Al ha-Mishmar*, 30 Aug. 1959.

[29] MAQĪ's *ha-Vĕ'ida ha-arbā' 'esreh* (The 14th congress), 112.

the absolute numbers were not impressive—as the party seemingly had at the time a membership of about 3,000 only[30]—the proportion of Arabs is certainly significant. Even numerically this is important, as these are very probably young, devoted members.[31]

It should also be remembered that among the minorities in Israel the Communist Party has obtained most of its support from the Christians. Only in the 1960s has it made headway among Muslims and Druzes. Since the establishment of the State the party's outstanding leaders have been Christians: Tawfīq Ṭūbī, Emīl Ḥabībī (both MKs) and Emīl Tōmā (the party's theoretician). Christian support is even more marked in the two wholly-Arab towns of Nazareth, where the communists have strong support among the Greek Orthodox, and Shafā 'Amr, where they receive considerable electoral support thanks to the vote of Christians from various communities. This is understandable, in view of the relative social advance of the Christians in Israel (less committed to established structures); their better education (through their congregational schools); and their political alertness. Realizing this, the communists have tried, in recent years, not only to keep up their propaganda among the Christians but also to concentrate on penetrating the Druze and Muslim villages. They are particularly interested in the younger generation. This trend has been intensified since 1961, when MAQĪ adopted some of the nationalist slogans to which Muslims were sympathetic; it even tried to organize a General Muslim Congress in Acre (June 1961), to oppose the *Qāḍīs* Law. MAQĪ's argument was that the law appointed a committee to nominate *qāḍīs*, consisting of Muslims and Jews—and that this would give 'atheists' power to decide in matters of Islam. Not surprisingly, the board elected at this congress to defend Islam consisted of 23 members, 20 of whom were MAQĪ men. The party shrewdly exploited this for propaganda purposes among Muslims in Israel.

Similarly, the sympathy of Israeli communists for the nationalist movements in the Arab States coincides with the party's desire to bolster up its image among Israeli Arabs in general, and Muslims in particular. The admiration of many of these for the charismatic leadership of 'Abd al-Nāṣir was properly exploited in party propaganda; praise, however was duly rendered also to 'Abd al-Nāṣir's attempts to solve Egypt's economic problems, which the party warmly appreciated.

In accordance with these tendencies, the Communist Party has

[30] *Ann. suppl. to the Bolshaya Sovetskaya Entsiklopediya, 1962*, 252.

[31] Data about age in Czudnowski & Landau, *The Israeli communist party*, 18–19.

continually shown its empathy for the Arabic minority in Israel, and has consistently striven to penetrate it. The year 1948 witnessed the reunion of the party's two branches, ending a five-year-old conflict over Arab-Jewish rivalries within the party. Old opponents co-operated in MAQĪ, the guiding principle of all being concern for the Israeli Arabs. In the 11th national congress of the party (October 1949), the first to be held after the establishment of Israel, Me'īr Wīlner declared in his speech:[32] 'Upon this country becoming binational . . . we have changed our programme according to the new circumstances, and we come forth with the slogan of independence for both peoples in this land!' Suitably enough, the congress then adopted a resolution which 'recognized the justified hopes of the Arab nation in Palestine for independent political life, as well as *its natural and legitimate right for self-determination. We fight* [the resolution added] *for the establishment of an Arab State, independent and democratic, in the other part of Palestine.*'[33] This standpoint of the party has changed but little since, even if emphasis has been laid, in varying degrees, on other matters. Thus at MAQĪ's 12th national congress a resolution stated that the final goal of the Arabs in Israel was the achievement of their independence, in order to put into practice 'the right of nations to self-determination, up to the point of seceding and founding an independent State'.

Over the years, with Israel a *fait accompli*, and part of the Western Bank of the Jordan river annexed to the Kingdom of Jordan, MAQĪ has spoken less about an independent Arab State in Palestine.[34] Instead, it has stressed the need to allow the Arabs in Israel autonomous management of their national, political, and economic affairs, while closing the ranks of Jewish and Arab workers, in Israel and abroad. MAQĪ rarely appeals to the Governments of the Arab States, usually addressing itself to the Israeli Government. On these occasions, it criticizes the latter for (what MAQĪ terms) its rigidity in preventing agreements with the Arab States because of the support it receives from the imperialist States. Hence the Communist Party has striven to protect what it considers the oppressed Arab minority in Israel. It has ceaselessly proclaimed the equal rights of the Arabs, mainly regarding the military administration, land expropriation, demands for education, employment, and various improvements in their standard of living.

[32] Reported also in *Qōl ha-'am*, 21 Oct. 1949.

[33] Italics in original.

[34] The party opposed this idea even after the 1967 six-days' war (cf. *al-Ittiḥād*, 12 & 15 Sept. 1967).

The full identification of MAQĪ's Jewish members with the Arab minority in Israel and even with the Arab national movement outside served to cement the party for a few years. However, the sharp conflict between Arabs and Jews within the party during the 1940s was still smouldering. Leading Arab members, as well as rank and file, could not help being excited by the swelling waves of Arab nationalism abroad; possibly some of them may have smarted under the preponderantly Jewish leadership of MAQĪ. After 1958, apparently, the conflict became more acute: in July of that year a MAQĪ-supported public meeting in Acre elected a wholly-Arab public committee to protect the rights of the Arabs in Israel.[35] Ferment continued in MAQĪ circles,[36] the main bone of contention being the party's opinion on Israel's stand in its confrontation with the Arab national movement.[37]

This conflict became public knowledge in consequence of the 1965 rift in the party which broke up largely on Jewish-Arab lines. In the first week of August 1965 two national party congresses were held, each upbraiding the other.[38] The rift in the party was preceded by an internal quarrel which had been growing more bitter month by month. Differences of opinion had previously existed on certain points and had brought about the secession of small groups, for example after the 20th congress of the Communist Party of the Soviet Union in 1956. The 1965 rift was, however, the first serious one in Israel and resembled, in many respects, the rift in the communist camp in Palestine in 1943. As then, the party split chiefly along Jewish-Arab lines, bitterly divided as to the attitude towards Zionism and the Arab national movement. For some years the leading Arab members of MAQĪ, especially Tawfīq Ṭūbī and Emīl Ḥabībī, had worked towards identifying MAQĪ with the Arab national movement—while some leading Jewish party members had been hesitant.[39]

After MAQĪ split, its leadership remained Jewish, the key figures being the former MAQĪ secretary, Shmū'el Mīqūnīs, and the journalist-orator Moshe Sneh. A few Arabs were willing to continue in MAQĪ, such as Muḥammad al-Khaṭīb and Muḥammad Ḥasan

[35] *Ma'arīv*, 27 Aug. 1958.

[36] Cf. Kna'an in *ha-Areṣ*, 7 July 1959.

[37] A summary of the major arguments may be read in articles by Kna'an, ibid. 24 May 1965, and Meysels, in *Ma'arīv*, 2 Aug. 1965.

[38] 'Opportunism' was one of the derisive words used (cf. Ṭūbī and Ḥabībī in *al-Ittiḥād*, 10 Aug. 1965; see ibid. 13 Aug. 1965).

[39] The course of events has been described in detail by Meysels, in *Ma'arīv*, 23 June 1966.

Jabbārīn; but most of these later retired from active membership.[40] MAQĪ kept the Hebrew daily *Qōl ha-'am* (Voice of the People) and its organs in some other languages, for example in Polish. The secessionists at first called themselves The Jewish-Arab List, then changed into The New Communist List (or RAQAḤ).[41] It was led by Arabs and a few Jews (notably Wīlner); but its members and supporters were almost entirely Arabs. RAQAḤ took over the communist bi-weekly *al-Ittiḥād*, later adding a Hebrew periodical.

It is important to understand the differences of opinion in MAQĪ on the eve of the rift, since they reveal a picture of the previously undisclosed seething quarrels[42] and were responsible for the serious result of splitting the party. According to the 'theses'[43] for the 15th national congress in 1965, the Arab-led faction attacks the Israeli Government, which—so it claims—carries on imperialist activities against the movement of liberation of the Arab peoples; while Israel prepares for aggression against the Arab States, the latter draw increasingly closer to the socialist camp, thus moving away from a tendency to war; any improvement in the situation of the area is dependent on a turn-about in Israeli policy.[44] In opposition, the Jewish-led faction maintains that even if Israel breaks its ties with imperialism, this will not by itself guarantee the success of the struggle for peace; this struggle should be the starting-point which ought to aid in breaking the hold of imperialism; not all Arab States are against imperialism—as the examples of Jordan, Lebanon, Lybia, and Morocco prove, and 'Abd al-Nāṣir himself has imprisoned communists in Egypt.

An ingredient in this debate might have been personal rivalries between the party chiefs and their competition for present and future leadership. These, however, only highlighted the ideological rift and the differences in tactics.[45] The Jewish-led faction recognizes the rights of the Arabs in Israel and is in sympathy with the struggle of some Arab States towards socialism; it considers the change of

[40] *Al-Ittiḥād*, 10 Sept. 1965.

[41] The term 'list' was chosen since the new party's most pressing job was to stand for the coming *Kneset* elections of Nov. 1965. The name stuck, although RAQAḤ maintains *it* is the Communist Party in Israel.

[42] Although the conflict found its way into the press (cf. Mīqūnīs in *Qōl ha-'am*, 12 Feb. 1965, and E. Wīlensqa in *Zō ha-derekh*, June 1965).

[43] First, both factions agreed on joint 'theses', fully printed in *Zō ha-derekh*, Mar. 1965. Then they disagreed again and printed their separate theses in *Qōl ha-'am*, 19 May 1965.

[44] These views have been summed up by Tōmā, in *Qōl ha-'am*, 8 June 1965, and 'Alī 'Āshūr, in *al-Ittiḥād*, 17 Aug. 1965.

[45] Cf. Tōmā in RAQAḤ's report of its 15th national congress, 1965, 16.

leadership in Israel—Ben-Gurion's retirement from the Government—as a proper time for the communists to recognize Israel's rights to existence[46] and thus gain popularity in Jewish circles. In contrast, the Arab-led faction attacks Israel's Arab policy without reservation; it attaches greater significance to the struggle of the Arab peoples towards socialism and to their movement of liberation, and prefers to seek popularity in Arab circles.

The break-up of the Communist Party became definite after the two separate congresses in August 1965, with each part declaring itself to be the sole true Israeli communist congress.[47] In consequence, the new RAQAḤ party became the only one in Israel with a majority of Arab members, estimated at at least 70 per cent in 1965–6,[48] as compared with practically none in MAQĪ. We shall give further details of its activities when considering its share in recent parliamentary and municipal elections. For the moment, let us briefly consider RAQAḤ's organization. Most of the party's possessions remained in the hands of MAQĪ, except for the bi-weekly *al-Ittiḥād*. However, the party branches were generally not divided between MAQĪ and RAQAḤ; the secretary of each branch decided its future allegiance. Thus all Arab branches and a few Jewish ones (e.g. that of Petah-Tiqva) passed over to RAQAḤ. This was organized very much on the same pattern as MAQĪ. At the top is the party's central committee, consisting (in 1966) of ten Jews and nine Arabs. Various other committees co-operate with this body, such as the political bureau, the committee for communist youth, and others. RAQAḤ's central committee controls the regional committees, which in turn are in charge of the local branches. The main regional committees are, in practice, those in Galilee (Nazareth) and the Little Triangle (Umm al-Faḥm), with the latter responsible for the local branches in Umm al-Faḥm, Ṭaiyyba, Ṭīra, Kafr Qāsim, and other villages. Branches are subdivided into cells, the number of which is related to the size of membership. In the village Barṭa'a, for example, RAQAḤ's local branch had only one cell, since the number of members was not more than ten (1966). In Kafr Yāṣīf, however, there are more RAQAḤ members, so that they are divided into an ideological, a woman's, a youth cell, etc. The regional com-

[46] Thus they claim that Syria's 'Warming-up' the borders is no less detrimental to peace than Israel's doing so; their opponents, however, put the blame on Israel alone.

[47] See editorial in *Qōl ha-'am*, 4 Aug. 1965.

[48] This is an approximation. Estimates of Jewish membership in RAQAḤ vary between 15 and 40 per cent of the total. Either way, RAQAḤ is not an all-Arab party, like *al-Arḍ* group (to be considered later).

mittee supervises all activity in its area—such as co-ordination of common matters, joint meetings of members from various villages, and the like. The branch committees deal with current local activity and average one session a week, in which decisions are taken on internal and external affairs. The former are concerned with matters of organization, sale of newspapers, information and propaganda, collecting dues and donations. The latter refer to the recruitment of new members and the introduction of such services as electricity, running water, sewerage, and roads. The branch committees are fairly independent in dealing with most purely local matters, but need the approval of RAQAḤ's central committee and the regional committee for political decisions such as putting up candidates for local elections.

While Wīlner, a Jew, still has an important share in RAQAḤ's decision-making, most key-figures are Arabs, all of them dedicated communists. The names of Tawfīq Ṭūbī and Emīl Ḥabībī have already been mentioned. Both are trusted party-members from pre-Israel days. Together with Wīlner, they represent RAQAḤ in the sixth *Kneset*, elected in November 1965. Other prominent members are Ḥannā Naqqāra, a Haifa lawyer; 'Uthmān Abū Ra's, RAQAḤ's secretary in the Little Triangle; Ṣalībā Khamīs, nicknamed 'the red boss of Nazareth'; Salīm al-Qāsim, a veteran workers' agitator, and Mun'im Jarjūra, scion of a large, rich family in Nazareth.

Both MAQĪ and RAQAḤ[49] claim to represent the true interests of Jews and Arabs alike. Nevertheless, there exists a basic difference between the parties in their approach to the question of the Arab minority in Israel, running parallel to their respective views (already noted) concerning Israel and the Arab States. MAQĪ maintains its original opinion, viz. that the Arabs in Israel form a national minority within the State, entitled to equal rights in all spheres. RAQAḤ, however, considers the Israeli Arabs an integral part of a larger entity, the Palestinian Arab nation, and hence a component in an even more comprehensive entity—the entire Arab nation. Or, in the words of *al-Ittiḥād* (17 Aug. 1965). 'The Arabs in Israel regard themselves as an integral part of the Palestinian Arab people, which has national rights in Palestine, equal to the national rights of the Jewish people.'[50] It should be stressed that the differences between RAQAḤ and MAQĪ are not merely in phrasing and definition, but in their fundamental attitudes (RAQAḤ appears to have reservations even about Israel's right to exist) as well as in their tactical moves

[49] See *al-Ittiḥād*, 10 & 13 Aug., 10 & 17 Sept. 1965.

[50] The use of 'Palestine' instead of 'Israel' is intentional.

(obviously, RAQAḤ's arguments are tailored to attract the support of many Israeli Arabs). Thus RAQAḤ may be seen as a direct continuation of that group within the earlier ranks of MAQĪ, which sought to identify completely with the Arab minority in Israel and appear as its champion. This has been forcefully propounded by Tawfīq Ṭūbī, who said: 'The Arab communists are proud to stand in the vanguard of the just struggle of the Arab people in Israel against oppression, land robbery, and military administration; they teach the Arab masses and the youth to maintain their rights and struggle for them.'[51]

This image was cultivated by MAQĪ, and since the year 1965 by RAQAḤ, among the Arab population, both locally and on a country-wide scale. The communists have made strenuous efforts to spread themselves widely—which, related to the tiny size of their party, seem more impressive than those of MAPAI and MAPAM. They have systematically attempted to open a local branch, or at least a small cell of active members, in every Arab village, or group of contiguous villages. One of their first steps is always to establish a 'cultural home', to serve as a base for the party's activity in the area. The party's central institutions as well as its branches organize communist propaganda, whether written or oral—by means of meetings,[52] literary gatherings, and street demonstrations,[53] as well as other forms of appeal to the Israeli Arabs to fight for their rights (under the guidance of the Communist Party). The parliamentary activity of MAQĪ, and later of RAQAḤ, has been no less intensive. The party's MKs, both Arabs and Jews, exploit every opportunity to raise demands for Arab rights. The fact that the party's frequent motions and interpellations are regularly rejected makes no real difference to its admirers, who appreciate its tenacity and articulateness in its self-imposed crusade for the defence of the Arabs in Israel. Single-mindedness on this point is the more remarkable, seeing that in many other respects, the party has repeatedly changed its mind. The often lone stand of the communist MKs in voting on such matters as the Sinai war in 1956[54] or the six-days' war in 1967 provides even greater cause for admiration by the party's members and supporters.

Inevitably, many of the claims and demands made by the communists in the *Kneset* are mirrored in the party's press. *Al-Ittiḥād* has been especially aggressive in this respect, to a point where it

[51] Ibid. 10 Aug. 1965. For a fuller exposé of Ṭūbī's views, see App. C, below, pp. 226–7.

[52] Examples in *al-Ittiḥād*, 31 Aug., 8 Oct., & 1 Nov. 1965.

[53] Examples ibid., 14 Sept. & 12 Oct. 1965.

[54] See *Qōl ha-'am*, 30 Oct. 1956.

seems that its violent style is chosen with intent to appeal to a growing circle of Arab readers. This newspaper has consistently blamed the military administration for most evils—preferential treatment, refusal of travel permits,[55] interference in education,[56] land expropriation,[57] and provocations of all kinds.[58] Much of the information is selective; thus *al-Ittiḥād* omits to mention that Jewish lands, also, have been expropriated for security considerations, and that fair compensation was offered to both Arabs and Jews. Sometimes, facts are exaggerated,[59] as when complaining about the unemployed Arabs. Any economic argument, true or false, serves for nationalist propaganda.

Indeed, in recent years one may notice an escalation in the nationalist, even chauvinistic attitude first of MAQĪ, and then of RAQAḤ. This is increasingly evident in communist appeals to the Arabs in Israel. Any sign of injustice and discrimination, significant or insignificant, real or imaginary, is immediately pounced upon by communist propaganda and exaggerated by all its mouthpieces. In spite of varying emphasis at different times, this line of propaganda praises highly both 'Abd al-Nāṣir and his development plans—often in contrast to what the communists term the 'imperialist bourgeois' policies of the Israeli Government. This is a clear indication of the intention of the Israeli communists to gain the sympathy (and, at election time, the votes) of those local Arabs who identify themselves emotionally with 'Abd al-Nāṣir's brand of nationalism and his claims to all-Arab leadership. The difference in emphasis is due to the variations in 'Abd al-Nāṣir's relations with the Soviet Union (generally described as amicable) and the United States (usually explained as tactical moves), all the while completely ignoring the persecution of communists in Egypt and their imprisonment for long periods. This approach is consistent. In order better to exploit the nationalist sentiments of some Israeli Arabs and gain their support, the information and interpretation supplied first by MAQĪ, then by RAQAḤ, were regularly presented as a *schwartz-weiss Politik*: all the activities of the Israeli authorities were violently

[55] e.g. *al-Ittiḥād*, 16 Feb., 22 Apr., & 16 July 1965. The newspaper refused to acknowledge the significance of easing travel restrictions, cf. ibid. 21 & 28 Jan., 11 Feb. & 25 Mar. 1966.

[56] e.g. ibid. 13 Apr., 4 June, 3 Sept. 1965.

[57] Ibid., 8, 15, 19, & 22 Jan., 2, 12, 16, & 23 Feb., 5 & 23 Mar., 6 & 9 Apr., 14 & 25 May, & 26 Oct. 1965.

[58] e.g. ibid. 5 & 15 Jan. 1965, 1 & 25 Feb. & 16 Aug. 1966.

[59] Examples ibid. 8, 15, 19, & 22 Jan., 12, 16, 23, & 26 Feb., 5 & 23 Mar., 6 & 9 Apr., 25 May, & 26 Oct. 1965; 28 Jan., 15 Feb., 1 Apr., 3 & 20 May 1966.

criticized, with no mitigating circumstances; all those of 'Abd al-Nāṣir were extolled, without reservation.

In summing up communist activity in Israel, it should be stressed that their propaganda appeals continuously to all sections of the population, both Jewish and Arab, and employs all available media of communication. The smallest cells are exhorted to sell or distribute free of charge the party publications; to organize meetings and lectures; and to work hard in electioneering, as the occasion offers. An example of the intensification of communist activity may be seen in the case of the Druze community in Israel. The sympathy for communism among certain Christian circles has already been mentioned. MAQĪ, then RAQAḤ, has frequently attempted to attract Muslims by deferring to their pro-Arab national feelings. The Druze community, however, has generally been considered loyal to the State of Israel and thus apparently immune to communist propaganda. Undaunted RAQAḤ started—at its formation in August, 1965—to increase its activity in many Druze villages, addressing itself to youth in particular. Some immediate results were evident. Thus the RAQAḤ branch in the Druze village Mughār was so successful that in the November 1965 *Kneset* elections, 221 people voted for RAQAḤ! In the 1966 local elections, in the same village, the head of the RAQAḤ list succeeded in being elected to the local council—an unprecedented achievement in Mughār.[60]

Previously it was stated that MAQĪ, then RAQAḤ, directed their propaganda at the whole Arab population in Israel. This statement requires qualification in that this propaganda actually varied in intensity. Naturally, communist propaganda could not hope to gain identical support among all strata of the population, certainly not among those with conflicting economic interests. Therefore the communists in Israel directed their propaganda principally at Arab workers, giving particular attention to villagers who were employed in towns and felt lonely and forlorn there. Their situation made them suitable targets for communist propaganda. Circumstances seemed to play directly into RAQAḤ's hands: with the start of an economic recession in Israel in 1966, many builders had to lay off their workers and numerous Arab villagers had been employed in this trade. The Israeli Minister of Labour, Yig'al Allōn, insisted on the inclusion of many Arab villages in specially initiated development projects, whose budget provided jobs. There remained, nevertheless, unemployed or semi-employed Arabs, whose bitterness RAQAḤ ably exploited.

[60] See Dar, in *Davar*, 15 July 1966.

In addition to directing propaganda at the workers, MAQĪ, and more recently RAQAḤ, has been concerned with Arab intellectuals, in particular teachers and students. Arab teachers are regarded by the communists as open to persuasion because they are better educated, and worth while influencing, since they are directly responsible for moulding the views of schoolchildren. In this context, communist propaganda generally attempts to exploit the conflict of values and the perplexity of many Arab educators in Israel: on the one hand, they are employees of the Israeli Ministry of Education and Culture, and therefore expected to be loyal to the State; on the other, they are confronted by the call of Arab nationalism. MAQĪ tried and succeeded in establishing a Democratic Teachers' Association, which was a typical front organization. It is not surprising that the communists obtained more than 2 per cent of the vote of Arab teachers in the elections to the countrywide teachers' federation (1961–2). This is particularly noteworthy in view of the fact that the Israeli Ministry of Education and Culture does not in practice encourage the employment of communist teachers.

Out of similar considerations, MAQĪ and RAQAḤ attempted to win support among Arab youth.[61] They invested considerable effort in Arab students, fully conscious that they were probably gambling on the future leadership of the Arabs in Israel. It is practically impossible to obtain accurate data about the measure of their success, but something may be gathered about the general tenor of communist propaganda among the Arab students. Since the national sentiments of these students appeared to be the one common factor, unifying them over and above differences in origin, class, community, and interests—communist propaganda employed a definitely chauvinistic tone. While RAQAḤ has failed to take over the Arab Students' Committee, its relentless propaganda seems to have won over a number of students. Its organs have supported and encouraged every sign of dissatisfaction among the Arab students and consistently presented the party as the natural ally of the young intelligentsia against the village heads and the *ḥamūla* leaders.

THE AL-ARD GROUP

To anyone interest in politics, the crystallization and fortunes of *al-Arḍ* is one of the most fascinating chapters in the development of the Arab minority in Israel. The foundation of this small all-Arab political group was the culmination of efforts to establish a non-communist political organization which would represent extreme

[61] Mansour, in *ha-Areṣ*, 1 Dec. 1965; cf. ibid. 22 July 1966, suppl.

nationalist trends among the Arabs in Israel. A few such attempts proved abortive in the early years of the State (and have been described at the beginning of this chapter). The first such effort of real significance was the Popular Front. The founders of this front learnt their lesson from the fate of previous experiments, which failed because of lack of popular support. In order to remedy this situation, a meeting was held by a number of MAQĪ leaders and other Arab personalities. Among the latter were the laywer E. N. Kūsā;[62] the chairman of the Kafr Yāṣīf local council, Yānī Yānī; the mayor of Shafā 'Amr, Jabbūr Jabbūr, and others. They all agreed there was a need to establish some sort of comprehensive organization, in which different opinions prevalent among Israeli Arabs could coexist. The opportunity arose in 1958, when an Arab First of May demonstration clashed with police forces in Nazareth. With the participation of Kūsā, Yānī, and Jabbūr an Arab Public Committee for Protection of the Imprisoned and Exiled (namely those jailed during the demonstration) was formed. On 6 July 1958 this committee initiated the establishment of the Arab Front, later called the Popular Front.[63] It was founded in MAQĪ's club in Nazareth,[64] and indeed the communists soon became the guiding spirit of the front. Even the declared aims of the front were identical with the nationalist theses of MAQĪ, though omitting the socio-economic demands of the communists. The *modus operandi* of the front, also, resembled MAQĪ's: festive gatherings to celebrate international events, memorial meetings, distribution of manifestoes, publication of pamphlets (with such themes as 'the front's road', 'the front's unity' or 'the front's banner').

The Popular Front, incidentally, proved one of MAQĪ's rare successes in attempting to identify with the Arabs in Israel. Between July 1958 and February 1959 branches of the front were established in various towns and villages, chronologically as follows: Kafr Yāṣīf, Ṭaiyyba, Wādī Nisnās, Ramle, Lydda, Bi'na, and others. Dedicated efforts were made to lend the front a character of mass support. Thus large quantities of manifestoes were distributed, huge advertisements appeared, mass rallies were convened, and many Arab personalities were appealed to and invited to join. This activity was clearly aimed at making the Popular Front (as MAQĪ's organ put it) 'the basis for uniting the ranks of the Arab people in Israel'.[65] Actually, success

[62] See above, pp. 73–74.

[63] *Qōl ha-'am*, 7 July 1958. Cf. Schiff in *ha-Areṣ*, 19 Sept. 1958.

[64] The Nazareth branch of *al-Arḍ* was officially inaugurated on 3 Aug. 1958 (see *Qōl ha-'am*, 3 Aug. 1958).

[65] Editorial in *al-Ittiḥād*, 6 Mar. 1959.

was rather limited in this direction, as soon became apparent, both because of competition with other parties and groups and because many suspected that the Popular Front was a front organization for MAQĪ. Indeed, the honeymoon between the communist and nationalist components of the Popular Front continued for not more than a year. Even this was achieved solely through a tacit agreement to avoid decisions concerning attitudes to foreign policy; and, on the contrary, to stress those internal problems on which agreement existed. Working together proved relatively easy, during this brief period, due also to the apparent identity of interests between 'Abd al-Nāṣir and the Soviet Union. However, when 'Abd al-Nāṣir attacked Syrian communists 'for endangering Arab unity' in a speech at Port Said at the end of 1958 and another early in 1959, the repercussions could be felt in the Popular Front as well. Furthermore, the 1959 conflict between 'Abd al-Nāṣir (the nationalist tendency) and Iraq's 'Abd al-Karīm Qāsim (whom Moscow tended to support in this conflict) left the Popular Front badly shaken.

It appears that nationalist Arabs in the Popular Front, admirers of 'Abd al-Nāṣir, refused to follow MAQĪ's line, particularly as communism did not necessarily appeal to them, anyway. It is also possible that they were not over anxious to co-operate with MAQĪ's leadership, which was after all Jewish-Arab. These differences of opinion could not be left unresolved, if the front were to run with a mutually accepted platform in the parliamentary elections scheduled for the end of 1959.[66] The Israeli authorities, for their part, took steps to discourage the political activity of the front, which they regarded as potentially subversive. The military administration refused to grant some front activists travel permits, which resulted in their being unable to attend meetings or lectures far from their regular residence; a few were even detained for investigation. When the Popular Front requested legal registration as an Ottoman association, the Haifa district commissioner refused, replying that Ottoman law prohibited the establishment of associations which aim at influencing the political activity of the various communities.[67]

These restrictions imposed by the Israeli authorities appear to have been a less decisive factor in the disintegration of the Popular Front than the rift between the two components. The front broke up into its nationalist and communist elements. The former seceded, forming an independent political group, to become the nucleus of *al-Arḍ*. The rift was first revealed by Emīl Ḥabībī, a MAQĪ leader, in his column in *al-Ittiḥād* (10 July 1959), when he wrote, 'A small

[66] *Ha-Areṣ*, 7 Jan. & 11 Oct. 1959.

[67] Schwarz, *Arabs in Israel*, 58.

number of friends, co-operating with us in the Popular Front, secretly attack us; such a situation cannot continue.' Several days later the division within the front was public knowledge and became final when the seceding group officially asked the Israeli authorities for a permit to publish a journal of its own. The leaders of the new group were intellectuals; some of them had literary interests; others had studied law. Outstanding was Manṣūr Qardōsh, a Greek Orthodox who had been an active member of the front and now openly declared that the rift in it was a direct result of the political conflict between 'Abd al-Nāṣir and Qāsim.[68]

While some of the early history of this group—which was soon known as *al-Arḍ*—is still obscure, much is known thanks to the Israeli press and to a book in Arabic written by one of its young but prominent members, Ṣabrī Jiryis.[69] From the very beginning the new group had to contend with three opponents, each stronger than itself.

1. The Israeli Government and its various departments. The new group was founded on the premise of non-recognition of the authority of the State of Israel, at least not within its 1948 frontiers. It openly clamoured for changes in the political map of the Middle East.

2. The traditional structure of the Arab population, from which a number of the group's founders originated. These thought (and rightly so) that the traditional structure was supporting the régime politically; they therefore set about purposefully to widen the rifts in this structure, in order to speed up its breakdown.

3. MAQĪ, within whose sponsored Popular Front the group originated. Compared with *al-Arḍ*, MAQĪ was older and larger, more experienced, and better known. However, both organizations appealed for the backing of the same elements within the Arab population in Israel. This soon set MAQĪ up in arms against *al-Arḍ*. In order to reveal its true nature, *al-Arḍ* stressed its all-Arab character, thus possibly implying a slur on MAQĪ, whose membership had a Jewish majority. Again, when the new group called for the boycott of the parliamentary elections of 1959, this was justly interpreted as calling on the Arabs not to vote for MAQĪ either.

For its extremist propaganda, *al-Arḍ* needed a newspaper or periodical, in which to compete with other political views. Its first overt political act was therefore to ask for a permit to publish a journal.[70] When this was delayed, the group started publication

[68] *Ha-Areṣ*, 8 July 1959.

[69] *Ha-'Aravīm bĕ-Yisra'el* (1966), esp. 117 ff. On the author cf. his interview with Mansour, *ha-Areṣ*, 12 Dec. 1965.

[70] *Ha-Areṣ*, 14 July 1959. However, it seems that this group only applied for a permit officially in Aug. 1959.

without a permit, as from October 1959. Its weekly thus appeared for thirteen weeks. Unconfirmed reports estimated circulation at about 2,000 copies.[71] The magazine tried to create for the group an image of the sole and real defender of the Arab minority in Israel and its interests; to praise pan-Arabism and its main exponent 'Abd al-Nāṣir, while defaming his opponents, including Israeli leaders. The weekly attacked the State of Israel and even covertly threatened its Jewish inhabitants, writing, for instance, 'Live and let your fellow-men live, so that you may live with them!' It appeared each time under a different name, but its last name was *al-Arḍ* (the Earth); hence the group's appellation,[72] which caught popular fancy. Every issue, besides having a different title, also had a different responsible editor.[73] The group thus tried to circumvent the law, which imposes the requirement of a permit to publish more than one issue of the same newspaper or periodical. When the editors became careless and repeated themselves, they were hauled into court and fined (March 1960).[74] The weekly ceased publication. One member of *al-Arḍ* commented on this, in a conversation which was printed later, saying: 'Are the Jews interested in learning the real views of the Arabs about their life in this country, or do they want the Arabs to play the game of life in Paradise?'[75] Here was a clear exposition of the image the group had of its own role: the members regard themselves as representatives of the Arabs in Israel and express their views. This approach was consistently followed by the contributors to and editors of the group's weekly in 1959–60. Among the latter, the moving spirit was Ḥabīb Qahwajī, previously a member of the Popular Front's executive committee.

The name of *al-Arḍ* stuck to the group, which adopted it willingly, wishing to demonstrate their close connexion with the earth of Israel and their wish to protect it from expropriation by the Government.

In June 1960 seven active members of *al-Arḍ* established a company under the name of *al-Arḍ* Ltd, which they tried to have legally registered. The registrar of companies refused to do this, 'due to considerations of security and the public good'.[76] Manṣūr Qardōsh then appealed against this decision to the High Court of Justice in

[71] Ed. Eytan, in *YA*, 31 July 1966.

[72] Acc. to Mansour, in *ha-Areṣ*, 9 Sept. 1964. In a conversation, Mansour told me that he had been mixed up in the publication of this weekly, but soon left the group when he became aware of its extremist nature.

[73] *Ha-Areṣ*, 2 Nov. 1960.

[74] Ibid. 31 Jan. 1960. Acc. to ibid. 14 Jan. 1963, Ṣāliḥ Barānsī was sentenced to a short term in jail.

[75] *Ner*, Feb.–Apr. 1960, 16–17.

[76] *Davar*, 15 Jan. 1961.

Jerusalem, asking for an order *nisi* against the registrar of companies. The Supreme Court, sitting as High Court of Justice, considered the attitude and reasoning of the registrar of companies. He claimed that according to art. 14 of the Companies' Law, the Minister of Justice had absolute discretion to grant permits to companies; and that he had transferred part of his authority to the registrar of companies. This argument notwithstanding, the High Court decided that the appeal of *al-Arḍ* was a case justifying its intervention as it doubted good faith in this use of the discretionary authority. After due consideration, the court upheld the request of *al-Arḍ*, made the order *nisi* absolute, and ordered the registrar of companies to accede to *al-Arḍ*'s request.[77] The registrar of companies, through the Government's Attorney-General, asked for a second hearing. This was granted, early in 1962, before a panel of five (instead of three) Supreme Court justices, who however concurred in the previous decision and again made the *nisi* order absolute.[78] Thus *al-Arḍ* Company Ltd. was registered as a company, the avowed aims of which were: 'to concern itself with all types of printing, publication, translation, press, import of books and all kinds of printed matter'. In this manner *al-Arḍ* developed from a mere group of people with political initiative into a political body, officially registered as a limited company; this transformation had been achieved by cleverly exploiting the due process of law in the State of Israel. Undoubtedly the Supreme Court decision encouraged *al-Arḍ* to continue its political activity.

The predominance of the political element was evident throughout its activities. It also determined its tactics. All the activities of *al-Arḍ* may be understood in the light of its aim to become a fully-fledged political party. After registration it first increased its capital from £I500 to £I20,000, by offering shares for sale among the Arab population in Israel.[79] Secondly, it asked for a permit to publish a newspaper of its own; when this was refused by the district commissioner in Haifa, it again appealed to the High Court of Justice. However, this time it failed, as the court ruled that the matter was beyond its jurisdiction; it considered the decision to be well within the authority granted to the district commissioner by the British emergency regulations.[80] The frustration of its attempts to spread its message within Israel did not prevent *al-Arḍ* from carrying on international activity. In September 1961 it cabled the Secretary-

[77] High Court of Justice, 241/60, *Qardōsh* v. *the Registrar of Companies.*

[78] Ibid. 16/61, the *Registar of Companies* v. *Qardōsh.*

[79] *Ha-Areṣ*, 21 Mar. 1963.

[80] High Court of Justice, 39/64, *al-Arḍ Co. Ltd.* v. *the Haifa District Commissioner.*

General of the United Nations regarding some Arab youngsters who had tried to cross from Israel into the Gaza Strip. Later, in July 1964, it sent a memorandum, written in English, to U Thant, the foreign embassies in Israel, and the editors of several important newspapers abroad. The memorandum enumerated in detail all *al-Arḍ*'s claims, with emphasis on the military administration, expropriation of land, and the condition of Arab culture in Israel.[81]

Two weeks later *al-Arḍ* wrote to the district commissioner in Haifa and informed him of the establishment of an *al-Arḍ* Movement, as an Ottoman association, according to a law dating from the year 1909; they also appended the articles of association. The district commissioner replied that he could not officially confirm their association, which was illegal because of its intention to harm the State of Israel. The leaders of *al-Arḍ* then appealed yet again to the High Court of Justice for an opinion on the legality of the existence of the movement. Their main argument was that the district commissioner had no competence whatsoever to determine whether an association was legal or not; and that, in any case, there was nothing in the aims of *al-Arḍ* which could be construed as an intention to harm the State of Israel.[82]

However, it is clear that *al-Arḍ*, apart from its legal struggle (to which we shall return), considered its activity among Israeli Arabs as the main task. True, members of *al-Arḍ* worked for their cause among the Jewish population, too—but mainly as individuals, not as a group: they participated in debates, gave interviews to Jewish newspapers, or wrote letters to editors. Among the Arabs *al-Arḍ* acted as a group, though not continuously, none the less systematically and energetically. It tried to enlist the support of Arab students; and was not unwilling to co-operate with MAQĪ, at the beginning of 1961, against what it considered as the Government's intention to expropriate Arab land. However, *al-Arḍ*'s main efforts were devoted to disseminating propaganda among the Arabs in Israel and collecting funds from them. For instance, in August 1964 it organized a meeting in Jaffa, attended by about a hundred persons, which sent a cable to Archbishop Makarios, President of Cyprus, expressing support for him in his struggle against the Turks. In October of the same year it distributed locally the Arabic translation of the memorandum it had sent to the UN and others in July. *Al-Arḍ* paid special attention to

[81] See App. D, pp. 228–30 below. The memo. aroused interest in the Arab press outside Israel, e.g. in Jordan: *al-Jihād*, 16 July 1964; *al-Manār*, 17 July 1964; *al-Difā'*, 19 July 1964. Acc. to the Jordanian daily *Filasṭīn*, 31 Dec. 1964, the Palestine Liberation Organization distributed copies of this memo.

[82] *Davar*, 3 Aug. 1964.

enlisting the support of Arab youth, trying to infiltrate into the cultural and sports clubs of the Arab population.

Some of these activities were cited in the case before the Supreme Court sitting as High Court of Justice, in November 1964, to consider the request of *al-Arḍ* to be registered as an association according to the Ottoman law. After profound consideration, the court rejected the request.[83] The main points of its reasoning were: in spite of the obvious desirability of granting a permit to every association—including those which intend to change the *status quo*—a permit should not be granted to an association that does not recognize the State within which it operates, and which opposes the free régime in it. In this connexion the court remarked that the term 'Israel' was not even mentioned in the articles of association of *al-Arḍ*. It also referred to art. 3, where *al-Arḍ* stated that it desired to solve the Palestinian problem by considering the country as an indivisible unit, according to the wishes of the Arab people—which the court understood to mean as totally disregarding the wishes of the Jewish people. Thus in refusing to grant *al-Arḍ*'s request, the court also held that its very establishment was inappropriate within Israeli democracy. These conclusions of the Supreme Court are especially significant in view of its strictness in upholding the freedom of association in Israel. Its reasoning and decision obviously indicated its opinion that *al-Arḍ* endangered Israel democracy.[84]

Three days after the ruling, three of *al-Arḍ*'s leading members were arrested: Manṣūr Qardōsh and Ḥabīb Qahwajī, as well as Ṣabrī Jiryis, a graduate of the Faculty of Law at the Hebrew University in Jerusalem. According to the press, they were arrested as a result of the capture of infiltrators from across the border, with orders to contact the leaders of *al-Arḍ*, who had been seized in Israel. At the end of November 1964 an order signed by the Israeli Minister of Defence was published in *Rĕshūmōt* (official gazette of the Government); in it, according to the authority granted to him by the emergency regulations of 1945, he banned *al-Arḍ* stating: 'The group of people known as *al-Arḍ* group, or *al-Arḍ* movement, its name whatever is from time to time, as well as the group of people organized in *al-Arḍ* Company . . . are an illegal association.'[85] With the publication of this order, the legal existence of *al-Arḍ*, as well as its activity as a group, came to an end. Its last stand together was before the

[83] High Court of Justice, 253/64, *Jiryis* v. *the Haifa District Commissioner.*

[84] Detailed report also in *ha-Areṣ*, 12 Nov. 1964.

[85] *Yalqūṭ ha-pirsūmīm* (Israel's official record of orders, etc.), no. 1134, 23 Nov. 1964, 638. Cf. *Ma'arīv*, 24 Nov. 1964 & *Davar*, 27 Nov. 1964.

District Court in Haifa, where Ṣabrī Jiryis and the lawyers of the other members unsuccessfully opposed the Attorney-General's application to wind up the assets of *al-Arḍ* Company. The district court concurred that it was an illegal association and ordered that it be wound up.

The escalation of *al-Arḍ*'s political activity between January 1962 and November 1964 carried extremism to a point at which, according to official circles, some contact was established with Israel's enemies across the borders; this led directly to the banning of the group's activity and the winding up of its assets. Special interest attaches to the fact that MAQĪ was the sole organized political body to criticize the ban on *al-Arḍ*. This party declared that, although it did not subscribe to *al-Arḍ*'s views, it regarded with anxiety the ban on political activities of any group. Both *al-Ittiḥād* and *al-Jadīd* vigorously demanded the cancellation of the order banning *al-Arḍ* and the release of those group leaders who had been held for questioning.[86]

The last act in the political activity of *al-Arḍ* was unfolded before the 1965 parliamentary elections, when some leading members presented a slate of candidates for the *Kneset*. This was a retreat from the group's earlier attitude, according to which any kind of participation in elections was tantamount to granting recognition to the State of Israel. Now the candidates wanted to be elected to the *Kneset* and thus obtain parliamentary immunity for their political activity, in addition to the prestige attached to the status of an MK. However, the Central Elections Commission refused to register their slate, called the Arab Socialist List (September 1965), arguing that this was an illegal association, denying the very existence of the State of Israel.[87] The representatives of the Arab Socialist List appealed to the Supreme Court, which upheld the decision of the Central Elections Commission. A majority of the justices agreed with the reasoning offered by the Attorney-General that *al-Arḍ*, which had initiated the presentation of the Arab Socialist List for parliamentary elections, was a group liable to sabotage the State by attempting to exploit any loophole in the law for the realization of its political aims.[88] The justices agreed with the findings of the chairman of the Central Elections Commission that the list denied the existence of the State and wanted to cause its destruction. Mr Agranat, President of the Court, added that he did not deny the right of any of the candi-

[86] *Al-Jadīd*, Nov. 1964; *al-Ittiḥād*, 27 Nov. & 1 Dec. 1964, and cf. ibid. 4 June 1965.

[87] *Ha-Areṣ*, 30 Sept. 1965.

[88] *Davar*, 10 Oct. 1965; *ha-Areṣ*, 13 Oct. 1965.

dates on the list to be elected individually, or as candidates on other slates. However, he pointed out, the present system of election was by slates, that is by groups each having a common political objective; hence a list defined by the chairman of the Central Elections Commission as subversive *a priori* loses its right to share in the process of crystallizing the wishes of the people and therefore cannot participate in the elections. The President of the Court also added that he was aware of democratic principles and the accepted processes for a change of régime, but he quoted in this context a ruling by Mr Justice Wītqōn,[89] that no free régime would grant assistance and recognition to a movement undermining its own existence.[90]

As already stated, the activity of *al-Arḍ* as an entity actually ended with the order of the Minister of Defence outlawing it and the district court winding up its assets. Any attempt of the group to act as a body would undoubtedly have incurred legal proceedings. As a result, only part of the group's leaders entered their names as candidates on the Arab Socialist List for the sixth *Kneset* in 1965. Since their slate was not approved, the former *al-Arḍ* members continued their political activity as individuals. For instance, Ṣabrī Jiryis participated in debates and made speeches; he also published a book on *The Arabs in Israel* (1966), the first of its kind in Hebrew written by an Israeli Arab. The book was translated into Arabic by the Jordanian bureau of the League of Arab States and issued in a mimeographed form. Other members of the group tried to exploit for political purposes the Arab sports clubs in the Little Triangle and other institutions which had occasionally served previously for Arab nationalist propaganda.[91] Thus Ṣāliḥ Barānsī, from Ṭaiyyba, attempted to establish a sports and cultural club there and to register it as an association, according to Ottoman law. Although Barānsī prudently refrained from including his name among those sponsoring the registration of the Ṭaiyyba sports club as an association, the Israeli authorities maintained that he was behind the move; and also that all the seven members proposed for the management of the projected association were known as supporters of *al-Arḍ* (they had all signed their names as supporting the Arab Socialist List of candidates for the *Kneset* in 1965). None the less, in the request for registration of the club as an association its aims were described as cultural and educational (15 May 1966). Since the district com-

[89] Given regarding *al-Arḍ's* application for registration as an association.

[90] Elections appeal 1/65, *Y. Yardō̱r* v. *the chairman of the Central Elections Commission.*

[91] *Al-Ittiḥād*, 29 Sept. 1964.

missioner delayed his reply, the lawyer who had submitted the club's request advised opening the club *de facto*. The military administration reacted with characteristic vigour. The club managers, together with Ṣāliḥ Barānsī, were confined to their homes, and the activities of the club practically ceased—presumably acting on the assumption that the club could be used as a centre for incitement.[92] In this manner, the Israeli authorities continue to control any sign of renewed political association inspired by *al-Arḍ* members or supporters. Several of these Arabs were detained for a few days when war broke out in the Middle East, in June 1967. Later, in December 1967, three were charged with organizing a terrorist cell connected with *al-Fatḥ*; at the end of January 1968 a court found them guilty and imposed stiff prison sentences on them.

It is not difficult to define and analyse the aims of *al-Arḍ*. Its name indicates its preoccupation, and in an interview with the Tel-Aviv weekly *Etgar*,[93] Manṣūr Qardōsh maintained that the group's main struggle was against the expropriation of Arab land. However, even Qardōsh could not mention more than one instance in which the group had worked in this direction. In fact, it would be more correct to describe the group's aims as extremely nationalistic ones. They are revealed in its early publications, its articles of association, memoranda, and the speeches of its leaders at various political gatherings. The third article of its articles of association is particularly revealing and important for appraisal of its aims. This is the very article criticized by the Supreme Court, and on account of which it rejected the group's application to register as an association in accordance with Ottoman law. Because of its relevance, it merits translation in full:

Art. 3. The Association will act to achieve the following aims or a part thereof:

1. Raising the educational, scientific, health, economic, and political level of its members.

2. Bringing complete equality and social justice among all strata of the people in Israel.

3. Finding a just solution for the Palestinian problem, through its consideration as an indivisible unit—in accordance with the wish of the Pales-

---

[92] Ibid. 23 Sept. 1966; Y. Avī'am in *Ma'arīv*, 25 Sept. 1966; M. Stein, in a letter to the editor, ibid. 18 Oct. 1966; Mīrqīn, in *ha-Areṣ*, 30 Oct. 1966; *ha-'Ōlam ha-zeh*, 22 Mar. 1967.

[93] 7 Mar. 1963. This is the organ of a small group, mostly Jews, named 'the Semitic action'; it advocates the complete integration of Jews and Arabs in the Middle East.

tinian Arab people; a solution which meets its interests and desires, restores to it its political existence, ensures its full legal rights, and regards it as the first possessor of the right to decide its own fate by itself, within the framework of the supreme wishes of the Arab nation.

4. Supporting the movement of liberation, unity, and socialism in the Arab world, in all lawful ways, while considering this movement as the deciding power in the Arab world—a factor which should make Israel regard it in a positive manner.

5. Acting to make peace prevail in the world in general, and in the Middle East in particular.

6. Supporting all movements of progress everywhere in the world, opposing imperialism, and assisting all peoples desirous of freeing themselves from it.

Briefly, the essential aim of *al-Arḍ* is to struggle for Palestinian Arab nationalism, ignoring the will of the Jewish majority in Israel as well as the State's authorities. This echo of 'Abd al-Nāṣir's formulation of Arab nationalism[94] is re-formulated with admirable frankness in various of its publications. In the group's first issue of its weekly, for instance, *al-Arḍ* calls for the recognition of the Arab national movement as the decisive force in the Middle East. Perhaps this voices only a sense of national pride, serving as a psychological outlet for frustrated Arab youths, who have failed on the material plane. However, its effect is to identify *al-Arḍ* fully with the Arab national movement outside Israel, on one hand; and, on the other, uncompromisingly to object to all the policies of the Israeli Government, and in particular to those concerning the Arab minority. *Al-Arḍ*'s criticism of the Israeli Government is characterized by one-sidedness (stressing the negative side and completely ignoring all Government assistance to the Arab minority), aggressiveness (often emotionally loaded), and sincerity (frank expression of admiration for 'Abd al-Nāṣir and incitement of the Israeli Arabs). Such an attitude may be considered as extreme, for in considering the solution of the area's problems it wholly ignores the interests of the Jewish majority in the State of Israel and sees Palestine solely as a part of the united Arab nation.

Its uncompromising stand in all political matters was a potentially significant source of power for *al-Arḍ*; it ultimately induced the authorities to ban it and restrict the political activities of its erstwhile leaders. In order to appreciate more clearly the attitudes of this group, it is worth perusing excerpts from a characteristic talk by one of its noteworthy spokesmen, the ex-teacher Ṣāliḥ Baransī. He repre-

[94] Even verbatim, in some instances.

sented *al-Arḍ* in a symposium organized by the Tel-Aviv English monthly *New Outlook*, early in 1963. The subject under discussion was 'New paths to peace between Israel and the Arabs'. After attacking the Israeli Government and what he considered as its identification with Western imperialism, Ṣāliḥ Barānsī scathingly described his conception of official Israeli policy towards the Arab population in Israel, saying:

> . . . Last but not least, there is the policy of the Israeli Government towards the Arabs in Israel. The humiliating military rule, sowing corruption and dissension between the Arabs, favouring the most reactionary elements, spying on everybody, maintaining economic and political pressure on those whose behaviour the military Governor does not like . . . [95] and, in short, administering, although unofficially, all Arab affairs: economic, political, labour, etc., in a military fashion.
>
> The confiscation of land. . . . About 65 per cent[96] of the land of the Arabs in Israel has been confiscated in the name of the law. A new kind of refugee has thus been created . . . inside Israel.
>
> The miserable level attained by education as a result of bad administration, the interference of security agents, military personnel and party members . . . who are really the real administrators from behind the scenes; the vague curriculum, the prohibition of Arab youth to organize itself, to publish a newspaper of its own; shutting the doors of governmental and public offices in the faces of the Arab intellectuals . . . all these came from the same source.
>
> The Arabs began to see in them a sign proving the impossibility of two nations living in peace here. They were also taken to mean, or to show, the intention of the Israeli Government to get rid of the Arab community here and so to add a new large number of homeless distressed Arabs.[97]

It is difficult to ascertain the exact numerical sphere of influence of *al-Arḍ*. When they left the Arab Popular Front, they were convinced of the difficulty of recruiting mass support in the way the Popular Front had tried and briefly succeeded in doing. They preferred to establish a small, but efficient, organization, to prepare the ground by written and oral propaganda. The founders distributed among themselves the twenty founders' shares of *al-Arḍ* Company Ltd, which together commanded 76 per cent of the votes; while they distributed in other quarters 400 ordinary shares, which together commanded 24 per cent of the votes only. The owners of the founders' shares actually became the group's secretaries of the nuclei in various regions. The list of the owners of the regular shares—roughly equivalent to the group's members and supporters—was

[95] This, and subsequent . . .—in the original.

[96] A typical gross exaggeration.

[97] *NO*, Mar.–Apr. 1963, 66–67.

kept by these secretaries and its secrecy jealously guarded (to prevent its falling into the hands of the Israeli police or security service).

As far as is ascertainable, *al-Arḍ* was a small élitist group, particularly concerned with recruiting Arab intellectuals. During most of its existence, the number of its members does not appear to have been much more than a score.[98] Even among these, there were few remarkable personalities. In spite of incomplete information, it is possible to describe briefly the main participants; the data refer to the time when the group broke up, in 1964.

1. Manṣūr Qardōsh, 43 years old, a Greek Orthodox who owns a coffee-house in Nazareth.[99] He does not speak Hebrew. He is the oldest member of the group and was apparently considered by most of the members as its leader and as the planner of the group's lines of action.[1]

2. Ḥabīb Nawfal Qahwajī, 33 years old, a Maronite, born in the village Fassūṭa in Galilee. He was a teacher at the Greek Orthodox school in Haifa, then taught in an elementary school, from which he was dismissed. He has some literary talent and often wrote poetry.

3. Maḥmūd Surūjī, 30 years old, a wholesale shopkeeper from Acre.

4. Sulaymān ʻAwda, a Nazareth merchant.

5. Ṣāliḥ Baransī, 36 years old, is the son of a farmer. He is a Muslim and was born in Ṭaiyyba. Baransī was a teacher, but was dismissed at the end of 1961 and has apparently been unemployed for a number of years. He was considered as an orator and the main spokesman of the group (see *New Outlook* symposium above).[2]

6. Ṣabrī Jiryis, 25 years old, a Greek Catholic from Fassūṭa, who graduated from an Israeli high school, and later from the Hebrew University's Faculty of Law, becoming a lawyer himself. He was active in representing the group, chiefly in its lengthy litigation.[3]

7. Eliyās Muʻammar, 32 years old, from Nazareth, a graduate of the Hebrew University's Faculty of Medicine.

8. Muḥammad ʻAbd al-Raḥmān ʻĪsà, a Muslim from the village of al-Makr, in Western Galilee, also a university graduate.[4]

Most of the group's members were young, in their 30s with

[98] See *ha-Areṣ*, 20 Aug. 1964. According to *Qōl ha-ʻam*, 28 July 1964, *al-Arḍ* numbered some tens of members only.

[99] About him and his family, see Alyagōn in *Maʻarīv*, 17 June 1966.

[1] Cf. his article 'For a Palestinian Arab state', *NO*, May 1966, 43–44.

[2] See about him G. Sharōnī, in *Maʻarīv*, 11 Nov. 1966.

[3] In addition to his book, *Ha-ʻAravīm bĕ-Yisraʼel*, see his interview with Mansour in *ha-Areṣ*, 12 Dec. 1965.

[4] About others, see ibid. 22 July 1966, suppl., esp. p. 6.

Manṣūr Qardōsh the eldest and Ṣabrī Jiryis the youngest. They carried on their meetings and activities in the main centres of Arab population in Israel: the Little Triangle, Upper Galilee, and the Acre–Haifa area. They were all middle-class intellectuals, and the majority were teachers or members of other liberal professions.

The number of overt supporters reached more than a few hundreds, to judge from the participation in the various public meetings organized by *al-Arḍ*. However, this figure may not be taken as the full extent of its support among the Arabs in Israel. It is necessary to take into account the increase of *al-Arḍ* Company's capital, first, from £I500 to £I20,000 and, later (March 1963), to £I100,000. This expansion, due to the shares sale which financed the activity of *al-Arḍ*, is proof that the group enlisted considerable sympathy and support among the Arabs in Israel. One gathers that the population, especially the young people, were impressed. *Al-Arḍ* offered no crystallized political ideology, except for a few ideas inspired by 'Abd al-Nāṣir's version of nationalism and socialism combined. This represented the minimum programme upon which the leaders of *al-Arḍ* could unanimously agree. However, the simplicity of the group's ideology, its familiarity (due to Cairo's previous broadcasts), and its sentimentalism appealed to a section of the Arabs in Israel. This standing was a significant achievement, in view of the group's size and political inexperience; true enough, the opponents of *al-Arḍ* unwittingly aided its renown.[5]

There were periods of co-operation between *al-Arḍ* and MAQĪ, even after their separation and the breaking up of the Popular Front by *al-Arḍ*. The relationship between the two political groups tended to be one of love-hate, deriving, at least in part, from identity of aims regarding defence of the Arab minority in Israel. MAQĪ and *al-Arḍ* co-operated several times, for example in the protest meetings during 1961 against what they considered as the discrimination against Israeli Arabs. Mutual recriminations finally put an end to the quasi-harmonious relationship. The rifts became deeper, due to ideological differences: *al-Arḍ* as a nationalist movement could not but oppose the universal principles of communism. However, of even more significance was the rivalry between the two for the support of the Arabs. The implications of the competition between *al-Arḍ* and MAQĪ were more far-reaching than those of its conflicts with other groups or parties. As may be recalled, in the very first

[5] Starting with the statement by the Prime Minister's adviser for Arab affairs, Dīvōn, at a news conference, saying that he saw serious danger in this group's activities (early 1960) (cf. *Davar*, 1 Feb. 1960).

issue of its weekly, *al-Arḍ* called on the Israeli Arabs to boycott the 1959 parliamentary elections. Had this call been successful, MAQĪ would have lost considerable electoral support. MAQĪ seemed to have feared the increase of *al-Arḍ*'s influence on the Arabs; it therefore, called on it, repeatedly to reunite with MAQĪ. Upon the failure of these appeals MAQĪ turned to attacking *al-Arḍ*, and the latter responded in kind. Nevertheless, MAQĪ resisted any governmental attempt to suppress *al-Arḍ*.[6] Its lone protest in this matter was perhaps prompted not only by principle but by possible apprehension of a similar fate some day.

[6] e.g., *Qōl ha-ʻam*, 28 July 1964.

End of Chap 4

5

THE ARABS IN PARLIAMENTARY ELECTIONS

PERHAPS the best way to evaluate Arab voting behaviour is to examine Arab attitudes to and participation in each of the six Israeli parliamentary elections, chronologically, that is: 1949, 1951, 1955, 1959, 1961, and 1965; then to compare these and the results achieved by the various parties competing for the votes of the Arabs in Israel.

The struggle for Arab support is in many respects similar to that for Jewish votes: competition between a relatively large number of lists; the efforts of candidates to have their name put in a safe place on the lists; and rebelliousness within those parties which had dropped candidates or down-graded them to unsafe places on the lists. Nevertheless, these characteristics differ from one *Kneset* election to the other.

ELECTONS TO THE FIRST *KNESET*, 1949

1. *The Arabs before the Elections*

The 1949 parliamentary elections were held under the impact of the Arab-Israel war. This was no less the case for the Israeli Arabs than for the Jews. The defeat of the Arab armies, Israel's victories in the battlefield, large-scale Jewish immigration, the imposition of military administration in some of the Arab-inhabited areas left many Israeli Arabs numb with shock.[1] Moreover, they had been left leaderless, culturally and politically. Therefore they raised no particular demands which could weigh significantly in the electoral campaign. A few isolated voices requested economic improvements, chiefly regarding production and marketing; others asked for unrestricted travel throughout the State.[2]

2. *The Political Parties and the Arabs, 1949*

The Arab minority showed considerable suspicion of the Jewish parties in this election. This was not only a consequence of the

[1] Acc. to Waschitz, 'Arabs in Israeli politics', *NO*, Apr. 1962, 33 ff.

[2] See also Jon Kimchi, in *ha-Areṣ*, 2 Aug. 1948; and A. Gelblum, ibid. 10 Dec. 1948.

1948 war and Arab resentment towards the leaders and parties, who had failed them, but also of a more basic phenomenon. They simply had had no previous experience of parliamentary elections. Many of them were wary of political organization, and afraid to initiate activity of their own.[3]

The Israeli political parties, though mainly concerned with the vote-getting among the larger, politically-alert Jewish public, invested efforts in varying degrees to obtain electoral support among the Arabs too. Most of the parties were ill prepared for systematic electioneering among them. Because no oral propaganda was permitted in the border areas, written propaganda was widely used; since many Arabs were illiterate, however, much of the printed material they received was meaningless to them.

(*a*) *MAPAI and the allied Arab lists*. MAPAI, the largest Jewish party in pre-State days (very moderately left of centre), was hardly equipped for electioneering among the Israeli Arabs. At the time, most of its energies were devoted to the electoral campaign among the Jews, as well as to conducting many of the affairs of State. Moreover, MAPAI's widely-proclaimed accusation that the Arab States started the 1948 war[4] hardly endeared the party to those local Arabs who sympathized with their brethren across the recently established frontiers. Hence MAPAI preferred to campaign among the Arabs through an Arab-Jewish Alliance of Palestinian Workers (established as early as 1929) and through newly formed groups, or 'lists of candidates', made up of notables. These were put together by MAPAI according to criteria of local influence, *ḥamūla* leadership, and religious affiliation.

(*b*) *MAQĪ*, or the Israel Communist Party. In November 1948, two months before the elections to the *Kneset*, the Jewish and Arab communists, previously two warring factions, united in MAQĪ. The main reason for the merger—among others—was the Soviet Union's support for the establishment of the State of Israel. MAQĪ's platform for the 1949 parliamentary elections called for the foundation of an independent, democratic Arab State in the other part of Palestine; full equal rights for the Israeli Arabs; the return of the Arab refugees; and the abolition of the military administration and all travel restrictions.[5]

(*c*) *Other parties*. These started their electoral propaganda among the Israeli Arabs only shortly before election time. MAPAM (left of

[3] Cf. Asaf, in *MḤ*, 1949, 2–7.
[4] M. Argōv, in *Gesher* (Tel-Aviv, quarterly), Dec. 1959, 24 ff.
[5] *Qōl ha-'am*, 10 & 13 Dec. 1948.

centre) tried to group candidates for an allied list. The religious parties (which desired to safeguard the orthodox way of life of Israel) apparently promised material benefits, as did the General Zionists, a Jewish party of bourgeois economic interests; while parties composed of Oriental Jews (that is, immigrants from Afro-Asian countries) put to good use their knowledge of Arabic. The *Ḥerūt* (Freedom) party (right-wing, extreme nationalist) made only half-hearted attempts to influence the Arab vote, for obvious reasons.

3. *The Results*[6]

Parliamentary elections in Israel are general, direct, secret, and proportional, with the vote cast for one of the lists of candidates. The whole country is considered as one constituency. Election day was 25 January 1949. The number of those eligible to vote was 505,567, among them about 33,000 Arabs. The following are general data about the distribution of the vote of the Arab minority on election day.[7]

The Arab Vote, 1949 (in percentages)

Participation out of those eligible to vote	*MAPAI*	*Religious parties*	*Ḥerūt*	*MAPAM*	*Party of Oriental Jews*	*General Zionists*	*Arab lists**	*MAQI*	*Others*
79·3	9·6	0·6	0·4	0·2	11·4	3·6	51·7	22·2	0·3

* It is a fair assumption that all votes for the various Arab lists were given by Arabs.

The Vote for the Arab Lists, 1949

Name of list	*Affiliation*	*No. of votes*	*Percentage of total vote*	*Kneset seats*
Workers' bloc	with MAPAI	3,214	0·7	—
Democratic List of Nazareth	,, ,,	7,387	1·7	2
Popular Arab bloc	,, MAPAM	2,812	0·6	—

[6] These and the following results are based on the official data published by the CBS.

[7] It is difficult to separate Arab from Jewish votes in mixed towns. Hence, unless otherwise stated, all the data here and further on refer to electoral results in the all-Arab localities, which contain the greatest part of the Arab population in Israel (about nine-tenths).

In general, the 1949 elections reveal a considerable lack of interest on the part of the Arab voters. This is primarily revealed in their low participation, 79·3 per cent out of the number of those having the right, as compared with a countrywide ratio of 86·9 per cent. None the less, several indications were present of an initial awareness by the Arab electorate of its role in parliamentary elections. In 1949 it encountered, for the first time, the democratic process of elections and the impact of media of mass communication on the electorate. The Arab minority was no doubt impressed by its very participation in the elections and by the entry of Arabs into the *Kneset*. A number of patterns emerged, to evolve in future elections: Arab political groups were formed, which identified their political future with that of certain Jewish parties, thereby hoping to improve their own position. The 1949 elections and the campaign which preceded them gave an impetus to Arab demands for complete equality.[8] Several other characteristics were already evident, particularly the spate of election-eve promises by all political parties and the formation of Arab lists of candidates, allied with Jewish parties, usually with MAPAI.

The distribution of the Arab vote is shown in the above tables, which reveal MAPAI and its allied lists, as well as MAQĪ, as the main gainers.

(*a*) MAPAI and its two allied Arab lists, the Workers' Bloc and the Democratic List of Nazareth, obtained together 61·3 per cent of the Arab vote, i.e. an absolute majority. This result was largely due to maximum exploitation of the influence of tradition, kinship, *ḥamūla* authority, and obedience to the traditional leaders in voting; MAPAI successfully contacted those who could, and did, influence the Arab electors. Similarly, its alliance of Palestinian workers put to good use previous connexions, chiefly in the Haifa area.[9]

(*b*) MAQĪ emerged from the 1949 *Kneset* elections second only to MAPAI among the Arab minority, obtaining 22·2 per cent of its votes. This result was even more remarkable in comparison with its countrywide vote, which was only 3·5 per cent. The main reason lay in the character of MAQĪ as a Jewish-Arab party (indeed, Tawfīq Ṭūbī then became one of its MKs). Its platform supported all the demands of the Arab minority, including even that for a separate State in Palestine. Last but not least, its experienced cadres from pre-State days were better known among the Arabs than the repre-

[8] Acc. to Asaf, in *MḤ*, Oct. 1949.

[9] *Qōl ha-'am*, 17 Jan. 1949. The accusations of Jiryis (*Ha-'Aravīm bĕ-Yisra'el*) have never been substantiated.

sentatives of most other political parties, who became prominent only shortly before the elections.[10]

(*c*) Other political parties benefited from earlier personal contacts (MAPAM) or the creation of new ones (Oriental Jews). Not a few ballots bore the imprint of a lunatic-fringe vote—probably indicating the total lack of previous electoral experience.

Another interesting feature was the publication of a great many newspapers and journals in Arabic. These were initiated and financed by the political parties directly interested in the results of the Arab vote, mainly MAPAI, MAQĪ, and MAPAM. The Arab religious communities published their own periodicals. The fact that most of these periodicals, appearing just prior to the elections, continued publication afterwards may be an indication that political consciousness was reawakening, and possibly intensifying, among the Arabs in Israel.

ELECTIONS TO THE SECOND *KNESET*, 1951

1. *Background to the 1951 Elections*

Each *Kneset* is elected for four years, but the first *Kneset* sat in session hardly more than half that time before new elections were held. It had to contend with two serious parliamentary crises, in the one case due to economic difficulties and in the other to religious differences of opinion. The crises highlighted the dependence of the coalition Government on the vote of small parliamentary groups—a lesson which was not lost on the Arab MKs.

In June 1949, as a result of the Israel-Arab armistice agreements of Rhodes, a number of minor territorial changes increased the Arab population of Israel: in the Jerusalem area, about 2,000 Arabs were included, while the addition of the 'Little Triangle' to Israel brought about 30,000 more.[11] These, together with Arab refugees who had infiltrated back and been allowed to stay, increased both the Arab population and its feeling of importance. In November 1950 the Arabs in the mixed towns had participated in municipal elections;[12] in the villages material development and improvements in education were beginning to be felt. All these factors contributed to a growing interest in politics among Israeli Arabs.

Various observers in 1951 noted that a feeling of perplexity pervaded the recently-enlarged number of Arab voters. Before election time many were in doubt about the basic differences of approach

[10] See also Waschitz, in *NO*, Mar.–Apr. 1962.

[11] H. Z. Hirschberg, in *Qamah* (annual), *1949–50*, 213–22.

[12] *Al-Yawm*, 22 Sept. 1950. Cf. Moşeyrī in *ha-Areṣ*, 24 July 1951.

between the various political parties. Others said 'We do not know whether we really are full citizens in this State and whom should we vote for?'[13] Two main trends of opinion seemed to prevail, according to the way in which the question was answered. A tiny minority of Arabs tended to ignore the elections, so as not to be considered 'traitors to the Arab cause' by their brethren across the borders. Most, however, were resigned to the existence of the State of Israel, and considered how to employ their vote for bettering the general status of the Arab minority or improving their own, personal situation.[14]

2. *The Political Parties and the Arabs, 1951*

In view of the considerable increase in the number of potential Arab voters, to about 70,000, there was a systematic rush by practically all Israeli parties to win Arab support. As the system of parliamentary elections in Israel is proportional, with the whole country considered one electoral district, the Arab votes could evidently be a significant source of strength. Further, since 1949 most parties had had time to prepare for an onslaught on the Arab electorate. Most of the larger political parties arranged mass meetings and festive dinners and organized trips for potential Arab voters.

(*a*) *MAPAI and the allied Arab lists*. Before the 1951 parliamentary elections MAPAI increased and diversified its activities among the Israeli Arabs, without, however, allotting their problems any special space in its own platform. Apparently, MAPAI's pragmatic assumption was that deeds spoke better than ideologies. Hence, in addition to festive meetings, new roads were paved in Arab settlements, running water was installed, and so forth. Three Arab lists of candidates, allied with MAPAI, worked for it among the Arabs; they were named Agriculture and Development, the Democratic List of the Arabs of Israel, and Progress and Work. The first addressed itself to voters in the Little Triangle; the second to Nazareth and Galilee; the third to Western Galilee and the Druzes. This notwithstanding, each of these lists presented itself to the Arab electorate as a national countrywide slate. But, since local loyalties were very strong, MAPAI hoped thus to gain votes for these Arab lists which otherwise would have gone to the national lists of rival political parties. Socially, most candidates on these lists (and all those in safe places) were from the upper stratum of the local notables and close collaborators with the Israeli Government and MAPAI. Out of the 23 candidates, 17 were villagers; the other 6 were drawn from the liberal professions.[15] The

[13] Cf. *ha-Areṣ*, 22 July 1951. [14] Acc. to Moṣeyrī, in *ha-Areṣ*, 24 July 1951.
[15] Waschitz, ibid. 26 June 1951.

election platforms of these lists were almost identical, except for varying emphasis on matters of local development; they all demanded and, by implication, promised, material improvements, the reuniting of Arab families, progress in education, and a more extensive use of Arabic as an official language.

(*b*) MAQĪ. The essence of this party's platform was expressed by its secretary-general, Mīqūnīs, when he opened the party's electoral campaign. In a speech in Nazareth he said: 'The defence of the Arab minority by the communists is the defence of democracy'.[16] Additional points,[17] in the party's propaganda during this campaign, were the abolition of the military administration, State credits for agriculture, and complete equality of rights and obligations—including that of compulsory military service. This was the only political party with a number of Arab candidates in safe places (Ṭūbī was a candidate in the second place, Ḥabībī in the fourth). Combined with its vocal propaganda against the Government's Arab policies, the effect was to improve considerably MAQĪ's image among the minorities in Israel.

(*c*) *MAPAM*. A few months before the 1951 elections, MAPAM had decided in principle to accept Arab members, but the decision remained unimplemented because of the strong opposition of a minority group. However an Arab, Rustum Bastūnī, was placed tenth on its slate of candidates to the *Kneset*.[18] Shortly before the elections, MAPAM was apparently the first party to introduce limited canvassing from house to house among the Arabs.

(*d*) *Other parties*. Of the other political parties, the General Zionists were the only ones who attempted, with some drive, to campaign among the Arabs. Some of their leaders visited Druze villages and influential farmers in the Little Triangle, stressing socio-economic interests, such as a promise of help in the marketing of their produce.[19] The religious parties attempted to obtain the support of Archbishop George al-Ḥakīm, the Greek Catholic leader, but the latter refused to side with them. Attempts to organize an independent, all-Arab slate of candidates failed.[20]

3. *The Results*

The elections to the second *Kneset* were held on 30 July 1951; 924,885 people were eligible to vote, among them approximately 80,000 Arabs. The Arab vote was distributed as follows:

[16] *Qōl ha-'am*, 2 July 1951.
[17] Acc. to *ha-Areṣ*, 22 July 1951.
[18] Ḥīram, ibid. 18 June 1951.
[19] Ibid. 1 June 1951.
[20] Ibid. 21 June 1951.

The Arab Vote, 1951 (in percentages)

Participation out of those eligible to vote	*MAPAI*	*Religious parties*	*Ḥerūt*	*MAPAM*	*Party of Oriental Jews*	*General Zionists*	*Progressive party**	*Arab Lists*	*MAQĪ*	*Others*
85·5	11·7	0·7	0·4	5·6	0·3	9·8	0·2	54·8	16·3	0·2

* This was a small Jewish party with a liberal ideology.

The Vote for the Arab Lists, 1951

Name of list	*Affiliation*	*No. of votes*	*Percentage of total vote*	*Kneset seats*
Democratic List of the Arabs of Israel	MAPAI	16,370	2·4	3
Agriculture and Development	,,	7,851	1·1	1
Progress and Work	,,	8,067	1·2	1

One of the new phenomena, perhaps the most noteworthy, is the sharp increase in the voting participation of the Arabs in Israel, from 79·3 per cent in 1949 to 85·5 per cent in 1951. Several causes were responsible:[21] the rise in political activity and propaganda among Israeli Arabs, the cumulative effect of the 1949 parliamentary elections and the 1950 municipal elections, and the heavier voting of women (much of it influenced, even guided, by their husbands). Another significant feature is the increased employment, by practically all political parties, of young Arabs—for propaganda canvassing, etc.; this proved, in due course, to be another blow to the authority of the *ḥamūla* elders.

(*a*) MAPAI. In terms of relative success of the political parties in vote-getting,[22] a salient feature is the rise in the over-all vote for MAPAI and its allied Arab lists: 66·5 per cent, as compared to 61·3 per cent in 1949. This rise may be attributed, at least partly, to the increase in the number of Arab voters. The population of the Little Triangle, recently added to Israel, had not been exposed to the propaganda of MAQĪ, MAPAI's chief rival; many Bedouins in the Negev, who voted for the first time in 1951, apparently tended to favour the ruling party.

[21] Cf. Y. Avī'elī, in *ha-Areṣ*, 6 Aug. 1951.
[22] See Waschitz, in *NO*, Mar.–Apr. 1962.

(*b*) MAQĪ lost ground in 1951 and obtained only 16·3 per cent of the Arab vote, as against 22·2 per cent in 1949. However, a closer analysis reveals that its main failure to obtain votes occurred in those villages or Bedouin camps which voted for the first time. Among those Arabs who had participated in the 1949 election, the vote for MAQĪ actually rose, in some places quite impressively: in Ṭaiyyba, for instance, from 0 to 752 votes (or about 35 per cent of the total vote). This support was gained by the fostering of an image of an Arab-Jewish party with the interests of the Arab minority at heart and no scruples about anti-Government declarations, strikes, and the like. MAQĪ's incessant activity among the Arabs, in which it was frequently represented by dynamic young workers or intellectuals, also assisted the party's increase in popularity.

(*c*) MAPAM was not as yet an important factor among Israeli Arabs, but it had already made some remarkable headway and raised its support from 0·2 to 5·6 per cent. MAPAM had steadily maintained its activity among the Arabs, since 1949. The *kibbūtzīm* of MAPAM had assisted neighbouring villages, and its representatives canvassed Arabs at home before the 1951 elections. The fact that MAPAM included an Arab among the candidates for safe places in the *Kneset* doubtless improved its image.

(*d*) Other political parties reaped the fruit of their characteristic neglect to foster ties with the Arabs in Israel until the eve of the election. The only exception proved to be the General Zionist Party which succeeded in obtaining 9·8 per cent of the Arab vote—as compared to 3·6 per cent in 1949, chiefly thanks to their promises to encourage private initiative as well as an economy with no controls, and to fight against government monopolies. Landowners and rich farmers who were impressed apparently voted for it, along with their families and retainers. In contrast, other parties obtained very few votes. The failure of the Party of Oriental Jews is instructive, for it failed similarly among the Jewish electorate and then disappeared.

ELECTIONS TO THE THIRD *KNESET*, 1955

1. *Background to the Elections*

During the four years of the second *Kneset* a series of crises characterized the various coalition Governments. These crises, although less significant, seen from the perspective of later years, engendered much ill feeling. Mutual charges were often bandied about, and some were eagerly believed among the Government's critics, Jews and Arabs alike. The latter were particularly dissatisfied with two laws, passed by the second *Kneset*. The Citizenship Law required all non-Jews to prove that they (or their parents) had been residents in Palestine; some Arabs did not possess the necessary documents. Worse still, the Land Appropriation Law of 1952 was interpreted by the opposition as intended to expropriate Arab abandoned property as well as additional land.[23] A group of university Professors—including Ernst A. Simon and the late Martin Buber—were of this opinion and agitated against the law, starting publication of a journal, *Ner*, largely for this purpose.[24] All this found ready listeners among the Arab minority in Israel, some of whom petitioned the *Kneset*,[25] while others organized demonstrations.

There were other reasons for excitement among the Arabs in Israel. Increased infiltration from across the borders and sabotage in Israel caused some Arabs to wonder whether Israel was not on the brink of destruction (and some of them published handbills to this effect). The highest Muslim dignitary, Shaykh Ṭāhir al-Ṭabarī, *qāḍī* of Nazareth and Galilee, published in 1952 an appeal for an exchange of population between Israel and the Arab States. The result was to heighten general tension.[26] Neither the rise in material conditions, education, health and welfare services, nor the decision of all trade unions in Israel to accept Arab members eased the popular excitement among the Arabs.

To some extent, the attitudes within the Arab minority, on the eve of the 1955 parliamentary elections, reflected differences among the Jewish political parties. Although most of their own problems were of a different nature, many Arabs were drawn into these inter-party conflicts. Pressures within their own factions were partly responsible: Thus the three MKs of the MAPAI-allied Arab Democratic List of the Arabs Israel made a show of moving away from MAPAI, because of the latter's alleged neglect of the interests of the Arab minority in Israel. Along these lines, many Israeli Arabs began to consider the party issue in Israel as support for or rejection of MAPAI. The propaganda of many Jewish political parties, throughout Israel, strengthened this view. The fact that most of these parties became interested in the Arabs and their problems only on the eve of the election was now confirmed for the third time. It is hardly surprising that this attitude bred cynicism—and in several instances a desire for personal or family profit: employment, travel permits, etc. The vicious circle (in this case perhaps very vicious) was com-

[23] *Ha-Areṣ*, 10 Mar. 1953.
[24] Ibid. & 7 Jan. 1955. *Ner* still appears, though infrequently.
[25] Details in *ha-Areṣ*, 29 July 1953.
[26] K. Qāsim, ibid. 22 Jan. 1953.

pleted, when some of the parties noticed this growing trend among the Arabs in Israel, and acted accordingly to increase their chances of gaining votes. Repetition was to make this practice a fine art and permanent feature.

2. *The political parties and the Arabs, 1955*

During the 1955 electoral campaign most parties intensified their propaganda among the Arabs: they organized costly receptions and festive meetings; promised private benefits as well as public support for Arab demands (e.g. to abolish the military administration, to rescind the land appropriation law, and similar promises which they stood little, if any, chance, of accomplishing); threatened those assisting rival parties with loss of employment, deprivation of permits, etc.; and exaggerated minute local matters into significant questions of principle. Although these practices were by no means continuous and universal, knowledge of them was widespread and resulted in confusion among Arabs, who could not understand the radically different and mutually-exclusive attitudes of so many parties. In consequence, an atmosphere of apathy prevailed among a section of the Arab electorate, and one of cynical doubt about all promises another section. What alternative reaction was possible to coalition parties, which promised the earth, and to opposition parties, which swore to lift completely all restrictions on the Arab minority right away?[27]

(*a*) *MAPAI and the allied Arab lists.* More than in previous electoral campaigns, MAPAI brought many of its leaders into action among the Arabs. They all pointed to the party's achievements in all fields, and to the material advance of the Arabs in Israel. Prime Minister Moshe Sharet called on them to vote for the allied Democratic List of the Arabs in Israel. No less eagerly, the Arab MKs and candidates in the allied Arab lists canvassed the Arab minority. There were, again, three lists bearing the same names as in the previous elections and directed at the same voters. However, in 1951 the Democratic List of the Arabs in Israel had obtained three MKs (as compared with one each for Agriculture and Development and Progress and Work). Hence, it was considered by MAPAI, in 1955, as a sort of central Arab list, designed to attract undecided voters. Accordingly, the first three candidates in the Democratic List of the Arabs of Israel were Sayf al-Dīn Zu'bī, a Muslim; Mas'ad Qasīs, a Greek Catholic; and Jabr Mu'addī, a Druze.[28]

[27] Schiff, ibid. 6 June 1955; cf. ibid. 20 June 1955.
[28] Further details in *Davar*, 10 June 1955.

(*b*) *MAQĪ* had recourse to strong nationalist propaganda, trying to create an image of a party sympathetic towards the extremist demands of the dissatisfied Arabs in Israel. It made frequent promises to act as their spokesman, expressing readiness to send future memoranda on their behalf to the United Nations. Its cadres, small but dedicated, had continued to work among the Arabs between elections and were fairly well known.

(*c*) *MAPAM*. Between the elections to the second and third *Knesets*, MAPAM had split: a less radical group, *Aḥdūt ha-ʻavōda*, left MAPAM. Although the acceptance of Arab members had not been a significant issue, one result of the split was the removal of opposition to this course[29] and in 1954 MAPAM threw open its doors. An Arab section was inaugurated, with twenty branches containing a few hundred Arab members. In the mixed towns Arabs could join the party on equal terms with Jews. An Arab Pioneer Youth was organized.[30] These moves were intended to create an image of MAPAM as the friend of the Arabs in Israel. MAPAM had apparently abandoned its previous hopes for a bi-national State (because of the small size of Israel) and indeed proclaimed the full equality of Israel's Arabs, together with reduction of the military administration to the minimum possible. As proof of its goodwill, MAPAM again included an Arab candidate in its slate for *Kneset*, in a fairly safe place, replacing Rustum Bastūnī by Yūsuf Khamīs.

(*d*) *The General Zionists* were somewhat more active among the Arabs than previously; this was particularly noticeable after 1953, when they joined the Government coalition.[31] They founded small party branches in Nazareth, Acre, and Abū Ghōsh (near Jerusalem), their main theme being the identity of interests between Arab and Jewish landowners and farmers. Towards the elections for the third *Kneset*, they established an allied Arab list, headed by a rich landowner in the village of Ṭīra (in the Little Triangle).

(*e*) *Other parties. Aḥdūt ha-ʻavōda*, after it broke away from MAPAM, decided to include an Arab in its slate of candidates (1955), but no suitable person was found.[32] The Progressive Party attempted to form an allied Arab list of candidates, led by one of the Zuʻbīs but later gave up the idea.[33]

[29] Knaʻan in *ha-Areṣ*, 8 Feb. & 8 Apr. 1955.
[30] On which see above, p. 80.
[31] Further details in *ha-Areṣ*, 22 Jan. 1953.
[32] Ibid. 13 June 1955.
[33] Ibid. 10 June 1955.

3. *The Results*

The elections to the third *Kneset* were held on 26 July 1955. 1,057,795 people were eligible to vote, including 86,723 Arabs. Of the latter, about 77,750 voted and their votes were distributed as shown on p. 121.

Again, Arab participation in *Kneset* elections rose visibly in 1955, reaching 91 per cent as compared with 85·5 per cent in 1951, and to a national 82·8 per cent in 1955. This was thanks not only to the cumulative effect of voting experience but to the growing political awareness of the Arabs in Israel in those years (general tensions, the Land Appropriation Law), combined with the bitter electoral campaign of most political parties in 1955.

(*a*) MAPAI and the allied Arab lists maintained their proportional strength with approximately the same results. This can be explained by the propensity of many Arab voters to support a major party, with a decisive say in most matters concerning them. The pro-MAPAI stand of Archbishop al-Ḥakīm, before the elections to the third *Kneset*, very probably influenced the heavy support given to MAPAI in Nazareth.[34] Charges of pressure, made by MAPAI's opponents, were never substantiated.

(*b*) MAQĪ's support dropped slightly, percentage-wise, among the Arabs. The reason may have been the over-exaggeration of its political attitude, which may have frightened away some of the floating votes.[35] MAQĪ's failure to maintain its position among the Arabs in 1955 is the more noteworthy in view of its increase in Jewish support which enabled it to gain six *Kneset* seats, as compared with five in 1951.

(*c*) MAPAM profited from MAQĪ's failure to gain Arab votes, and slightly increased its Arab electoral support in 1955, apparently as a direct result of initial improvement in image among the Arabs. As already noted, MAPAM accepted Arab members, placed Khamīs in a safe place on its list, and—in general—showed interest in the Arabs, including the establishment of employment opportunities and the aid given by MAPAM's *kibbūtzīm* to neighbouring Arab villages.[36]

(*d*) The General Zionists lost considerable ground among the Arabs. Their allied Arab list, named the Arab List—the Centre, did not succeed in electing any of its candidates. Apparently, few were impressed by their election-eve promises. In fact, the General

[34] Ibid. 28 July 1955. [35] Ibid. 10 Aug. 1955.
[36] *'Al ha-Mishmar*, 6 Aug. 1955.

The Arab Vote, 1955 (in percentages)

Type of settlement	*Participation out of those eligible to vote*	*MAPAI*	*Religious parties*	*Ḥerūt*	*MAPAM*	*Aḥdūt ha-'avōda*	*General Zionists*	*Progressive Party*	*Arab lists*	*MAQI*	*Others*
Arab towns	89·9	20·3	0·9	0	3·6	1·1	0·5	0·6	37·2	34·9	0·9
Arab villages & Bedouin tribes	92·1	11·7	2·3	0·5	7·3	1·7	0·8	0·8	57·9	15·6	1·4

The Vote for the Arab Lists, 1955

Name of list	*Affiliation*	*No. of voters*	*Percentage of total*	*Kneset seats*
Democratic List of the Arabs of Israel	MAPAI	15,475	1·8	2
Agriculture and Development	,,	9,791	1·1	1
Progress and Work	,,	12,511	1·5	2
Arab List—the Centre	General Zionists	4,484	0·5	—

Zionists had materially assisted some Arabs during their participation in the Government coalition. But, it was seemingly reasoned, if one decides to vote for Government, why then not support the *strongest* party, MAPAI?[37]

(*e*) Other parties obtained a few votes, perhaps because of their promises of material advantages, or just lunatic-fringe support.[38]

ELECTIONS TO THE FOURTH *KNESET*, 1959[39]

1. *Background to the Elections*

The turbulent events of 1955–9 had substantial implications for the Arabs in Israel. Perhaps the central event, from their point of view, was the Sinai campaign (October 1956), at the beginning of which occurred the Kafr Qāsim shooting. An Israeli army unit, ordered to enforce the curfew during the campaign, interpreted these orders in its own way and shot at residents of Kafr Qāsim (an Arab village in the Little Triangle), returning home from work. A few were killed, others wounded. Despite the immediate public outcry of indignation, from all sides (Jews as well as Arabs), and the subsequent trial and punishment of the guilty officers, the event long continued to mar Arab-Jewish relations in Israel and to serve as ammunition for the opponents to the Government, time and again in following years—with almost traumatic intensity.

A rising number of Arab youngsters attempted to 'escape' from Israel by fleeing across the borders (though they could have achieved their aim equally well by requesting passports, easily accessible to anyone). About a hundred cases were registered in the years 1957–8 alone. The fact that in many instances their parents had aided and abetted them added significance to the trend. Some of these youths fled because of family problems, but others had been influenced by rising nationalist sentiment and the incitement of the Egyptian broadcasting stations.[40]

Some of these factors were taken into account when, in August 1959, the Government decided to ease the restrictions imposed by the military administration. Liberalization included reduction of the

[37] Avī'eli, in *ha-Areṣ*, 10 Aug. 1955.

[38] Avī'eli, ibid. 28 July 1955.

[39] A more detailed analysis in Abner Cohen, *Arab border-villages*, esp. ch. 7; Don Peretz, 'Reflections on Israel's parliamentary elections', *Middle East J.*, xiv/1 (1960), 15–27; C. Solente, 'Attitudes israëliennes à l'égard du problème de la minorité arabe', *L'Afrique et l'Asie* (Paris), 52 (1960), esp. 42–43; and my 'Les arabes israéliens et les élections à la quatrième Knesset', *Internat. R. of Soc. Hist.* (Amsterdam), vii/1 (1962), 1–32.

[40] *Ha-Areṣ*, 26 Aug. 1956.

areas subject to military administration. Travel was eased—for instance, Arabs in the Little Triangle were allowed to move freely to the Jewish towns in the neighbourhood, and the Negev Bedouins could travel twice a week to Be'er Sheba. Assistance was provided for the sedentarization of the Bedouins. Payment of compensation for expropriated land was expedited.

Momentous events abroad were to exercise an influence on Israeli Arabs and, later, on their vote in the 1959 elections. The establishment of the union between Egypt and Syria, within the framework of the United Arab Republic, may have influenced the formation of the so-called Popular Front, discussed in the previous chapter. At that time, MAQĪ's popularity had reached its peak. The splintering of the extremist *al-Arḍ* group from the Popular Front was another indication of rising nationalist feeling among a section of Arab youth in Israel. The 1959 conflict between 'Abd al-Nāṣir and Iraq's Qāsim, as well as Moscow's support of the latter, injured the image of MAQĪ, the nationalists siding with 'Abd al-Nāṣir, and the communists with Qāsim. Also, some of the Christian admirers of MAQĪ may have been shocked by the pro-Muslim intrigues, sponsored by the UAR in Lebanon's communal strife during 1958–9. The major Israeli political parties were not slow to grasp the situation, and determined to take advantage of it to dislodge MAQĪ from its position among the Arab minority.[41]

2. *The Political Parties and the Arabs, 1959*

Electioneering among the Arabs during 1959 again demonstrated that few, if any, of the political issues among the Jewish public were meaningful for the Arabs, deeply engrossed by their own problems. This situation was exploited by the old parties as well as by new political groupings.

(*a*) *MAPAI and the allied Arab lists.* In its 1959 election manifesto, MAPAI presented Arab voters with a detailed programme for their complete integration in the State.[42] It intended to achieve this by increasing welfare services, developing the Arab village, and broadening the scope of education and employment openings for Arab youth. MAPAI pointed to its record of bringing progress to Arab villages: new roads, electricity, running water, and a general rise in standards of living. It emphasized that it was the party with sufficient power to

[41] Cf. ibid. 2 & 23 May & 3 Oct. 1958; 7 July 1959.

[42] For its platform and others in the elections to the 4th *Kneset*, 1959, see 'Party programs on the Middle East and foreign policy, on the Arab minority in Israel', *NO*, Nov.–Dec. 1959, 59–63.

implement its electoral promises, or in its own words, 'We promise and carry out what we promise; the others only promise, but we are able to fulfil!'[43]

As in previous election years, MAPAI made fresh efforts to establish allied Arab lists. At first it attempted to form a single all-Arab slate of candidates, but failed because of personal rivalries between the top candidates. Therefore, once again, it had recourse to three slates, adapted to local interests. At this point a new factor entered into the picture: MAPAI felt that it was time to replace the leaders of the allied lists with new faces, able to attract a larger share of popular support.[44] Some of the 'purged' MKs did not take this lying down. They put pressure on MAPAI to reinstate them, or else—they threatened—they would run for the *Kneset* at the head of independent Arab slates of candidates. As MAPAI did not retract, two of the ex-MKs, Ṣāliḥ Khneyfeṣ, a Druze from Shafā 'Amr, and Mas'ad Qasīs acted upon their threat. Despite MAPAI opposition, they ran for the *Kneset* at the head of separate Arab lists of candidates, enlisting all possible support from their *ḥamūlas* and neighbours.[45]

(*b*) *MAQĪ*. The situation in 1959 was not too favourable for MAQĪ's electoral prospects among the Israeli Arabs. A decline in popularity had followed its adoption of a pro-Qāsim line in the 'Abd al-Nāṣir–Qāsim rift. Aware of this, MAQĪ leaders decided, during 1959, to avoid the issue. Instead, their propaganda concentrated on an attempt to unite behind them all Arabs who opposed the Israeli Government and its policies. For their purpose, as an Arab commentator phrased it later, 'the communists' anti-Zionism gave them a monopoly over opposition votes among the Arabs'.[46] As in pre-State times, anti-Zionism was again emphasized by the party. Accordingly, they demanded, on one hand, the immediate and total abolition of the military administration; and, on the other, permission to all the Arab refugees to return. MAQĪ's propaganda pivoted upon the tragic events in Kafr Qāsim, during October 1956, and exaggerated their import. It bitterly denounced the Israeli share in the Sinai campaign, extolling Egypt (evidently hoping to gloss over its attitude in the 'Abd al-Nāṣir–Qāsim rift). As usual, MAQĪ also charged the Israeli authorities with economic discrimination against the Arabs.

(*c*) *MAPAM*. As already noted, MAPAM had worked hard, during the years 1955–9, to change its image among the Arabs in Israel—

[43] Mansour, 'Israel's Arabs go to the polls', ibid. Jan. 1960, 23.
[44] Schiff, 'Israel's fourth elections', ibid. Jan. 1960, 15–23.
[45] Mansour, in *ha-Areṣ*, 19 Aug. 1959.
[46] Mansour, in *NO*, Jan. 1960, 24.

by accepting them as party members, organizing Arab youth, and assisting their farmers. Over this period, MAPAM had also put forward a number of proposals favouring the Israeli Arabs, which it now repeated in its election propaganda, for example abolition of the military administration and employment for Arab intellectuals. It re-emphasized its peace plans, according to which Israel was ready to negotiate a peace with the Arabs directly; the assumption being the neutralization of the Middle East through its demilitarization. Despite these and other demands, not many in the Arab street were ready to support MAPAM, mainly because of its Zionist character. Those who did not accept MAPAM considered its supporters as 'Arabs of MAPAM'.

(*d*) *Aḥdūt ha-'avōda*. After spliting from MAPAM, *Aḥdūt ha-'avōda* had few chances of obtaining electoral support among the Arabs in Israel. The party, even while still a faction within MAPAM, had been known for its partiality to a tough foreign policy and its insistence on the priority of security considerations. Such policies were far from popular in the Arab street. Therefore, the party established an allied Arab list, the Israeli Arab Labour Party, with a weekly of its own, *al-'Amal* (Work or Labour).[47]

(*e*) *The General Zionists and Progressive Parties*. The former had learnt the lesson of their failure in the parliamentary election of 1955. Then they had established, on MAPAI lines, an allied Arab list of candidates which had not succeeded in obtaining even one seat. Now, four years later, they reverted to personal appeals; but their whole activity among the Arabs was more limited; they seem to have had no regular branches in any Arab town or village. The Progressive Party was a little more active among the Arabs, perhaps in an attempt to gain the previous positions of its rivals, the General Zionists. Its leaders established contact with some Arab notables in the Little Triangle, but apparently there was no follow-up. A few Arabs were included in this party's slate of candidates, but not in safe places.[48]

(*f*) *al-Arḍ*. The electoral campaign to the fourth *Kneset* gave this group an occasion for its first country-wide performance. They advocated boycott of the elections, for the alleged reason that the Zionist parties did not recognize the national existence of the Arabs; of course, the fact that the group was not competing may also have had some bearing on the boycott. The group's weekly actually published orders to abstain from voting. Some of these orders were

[47] Mansour, in *ha-Areṣ*, 2 Sept. & 3 Oct. 1959.
[48] See also ibid. 17 Aug. 1959.

modelled on similar ones broadcast by the radio stations of Egypt at the time (e.g. on 10 July 1959).

(*g*) *Other parties.* The religious parties started their activity among the Arabs a short while before the elections. Their representatives contacted various religious personalities, chiefly in Nazareth, Acre, Dāliyat al-Karmil, and Tarshīḥa—where they seem to have established (at least temporarily) branch offices. Most of their contacts, it seems, were with the Greek Orthodox community in Israel, who desired to obtain representation in the *Kneset* (which they apparently, could not achieve by alliance with MAPAI). *Ḥerūt* invested some efforts, also towards the eve of the election, in attracting part of the Arab vote: it obtained the co-operation of the *mukhtār* of Abū Ghōsh village and of some Druze families, mainly in Jūlis and Yirkā.[49]

3. *The Results*

On 3 November 1959, the elections to the fourth *Kneset* took place; 1,218,483 people were registered as being eligible to vote, among them 94,193 Arabs. While overall participation was 81·6 per cent, among the Arabs it reached 88·9 per cent. This was a reduction of more than 3 per cent compared with 1955, a decline that might have been caused, in part, by *al-Arḍ*'s propaganda. The distribution of Arab votes among the political parties is shown in the tables on pp. 127–8.

(*a*) MAPAI and its three allied lists together obtained about 52 per cent of the Arab vote in 1959; this was still a majority, but more than 10 per cent less than the 62·4 per cent of 1955.[50] The votes lost were apparently transferred to MAPAM and the two independent Arab lists, led by the ex-MKs Khneyfeṣ and Qasīs, who had been dropped by MAPAI and consequently stood against it. Both ex-MKs appealed to the same circles, often to the same people, who had previously voted MAPAI. In absolute numbers, MAPAI and its Arab allies lost about 3,500 Arab votes, a loss made more serious by the growth in the number of voters since 1955.

(*b*) MAQĪ. The decline in MAQĪ's strength among Arab voters may very probably prove the most significant result of the 1959 elections. While in 1955 the decline of its Arab support was proportionately small, in 1959 it fell from 15·6 to 10 per cent. Even more significantly, MAQĪ was placed third (after MAPAI and its allies, and MAPAM), whereas formerly it had always been placed second. Most of its votes probably went to MAPAM. The failure of MAQĪ

[49] Ibid. 28 Aug. 1959.

[50] *Davar*, 9 Nov. 1959, A Kapelyuk, in *'Al ha-Mishmar*, 13 Nov. 1959.

The Arab Vote, 1959 (in percentages)

Type of settlement	*Participation out of those eligible to vote*	*MAPAI*	*Religious parties*	*Ḥerūt*	*MAPAM*	*Aḥdūt ha-'avōda*	*General Zionists*	*Progressive Party*	*Arab lists*	*MAQI*	*Others*
Arab towns	88·9	4·3	2·0	1·0	11·3	0·7	0·3	1·0	51·6	26·5	1·4
Large Arab villages*	88·9	1·5	4·8	2·3	10·7	1·1	—	—	62·4	12·5	1·1
Small Arab villages	91·9	7·4	4·2	2·8	16·3	0·5	—	—	60·7	5·1	0·9
Bedouin tribes	80·6	10·0	1·5	1·5	30·5	1·2	—	—	46·0	0·9	5·1

* i.e. over 2,000 inhabitants; small villages: 2,000 or under.

The Vote for the Arab Lists, 1959

Name of list	*Affiliation*	*No. of voters*	*Percentage of total*	*Kneset seats*
Agriculture and Development	MAPAI	10,902	1·1	1
Progress and Development	"	12,347	1·3	2
Co-operation and Brotherhood	"	11,104	1·1	2
Independent List of the Arabs in Israel	Independent	3,818	0·4	—
Progress and Work	"	4,651	0·5	—
Israeli Arab Labour Party	*Aḥdūt ha-'avōda*	3,369	0·3	—

among the Arabs in Israel was a particularly hard blow to the communist leadership since their party had achieved a certain popularity in 1958, and lost some of it because of the rift between 'Abd al-Nāṣir and Qāsim.[51]

(*c*) MAPAM. The progress of MAPAM to second place among the Arab voters is another important feature in these election results. For the party, this was not only gratifying, but important, for it helped to compensate losses among the Jewish voters. The success may be partly attributed to MAQĪ's decline, but was partly, also, a result of continuous work among and for the Arab minority. In addition to the characteristics of previous campaigns, MAPAM initiated, between 1955 and 1959, the publication of books and periodicals in Arabic and the fostering of relations with Arab intellectuals in Israel.[52]

(*d*) *Aḥdūt ha-'avōda* failed to raise a substantial vote among the Arabs, and the Israeli Arab Labour Party, allied with it, did not succeed in gaining even one *Kneset* seat. Its failure was probably the result of a variety of causes. *Aḥdūt ha-'avōda* was not popular among the Arabs, and it had nothing to offer that MAPAI and MAPAM lacked. A serious blow to the group's hopes was the return to MAPAI of Maḥmūd Nāshif, who was supposed to lead the Israeli Arab Labour Party, but changed his mind and carried many of his friends with him.

(*e*) The two independent Arab lists. The very fact of their establishment and electoral campaign indicated that Arab independent

[51] Ya'arī, in *Davar*, 7 Dec. 1959; *Qōl ha-'am*, 13 Dec. 1959.

[52] As n. 51.

groups stood some chance of election. That this chance was rather slim was proved by their failure, probably due mainly to the lack of MAPAI's support in the competition with the larger, more experienced political parties.

(*f*) Other parties. Other Jewish political parties obtained only a small number of Arab votes: in the purely Arab localities, the National Religious Party received 2,700, *Ḥerūt* 1,500, the General Zionists 1,000 and the Progressive Party 800 (in rounded figures). Even these modest achievements seem to be in consequence of material expectations by the Arabs. For example, the relatively impressive vote for the National Religious Party in Bāqa al-Gharbiyya (15 per cent of all the vote in that village, as compared to only 2·1 per cent in 1955) was apparently a mark of gratitude for a commercial deal with orthodox Jews fulfilling the rules of the sabbatical year in agriculture (*shĕmiṭṭa*).[53]

ELECTIONS TO THE FIFTH *KNESET*, 1961

1. *Background to the Elections*

Twenty-one months only passed between the elections to the fourth and the fifth *Knesets*. Most of the problems preoccupying the Arab minority in Israel during this period were internal affairs; their common denominator was the increase in nationalist sentiment. There were several major outward signs. First, a rise occurred in the number of those young Arabs who 'escaped' to the Gaza strip, for reasons already discussed; those imprisoned or wounded and killed by border guards became near-martyrs and encouraged others to follow.[54] Secondly, a new Law for the Concentration of Land[55] was interpreted as directed against the Arabs in Israel, and was received among them with sharply articulate opposition, which had definite chauvinistic undertones.[56] Thirdly, overall economic progress in Israel made for dissatisfaction among the Arabs. Many Arab youths used the need for workers in the Jewish towns and the easing of the military administration to seek employment in building, gardening, and restaurant work; they were well paid, but as they found little in common with the Jewish urban environment, their alienation—and even hostility—was strengthened.[57]

[53] Ya'arī, in *Davar*, 5 Dec. 1959.
[54] Schiff, in *ha-Areṣ*, 8 Nov. 1960 and 9 Nov. 1961.
[55] See editorial in *Davar*, 27 Feb. 1961.
[56] Interview with Lubrānī (adviser to the Prime Minister on Arab affairs), in *ha-Areṣ*, 1 Sept. 1960.
[57] Y. Gilbō'a, ibid. 10 Oct. 1961. On young Arab villagers working in mixed towns and their problems, see also Mansour, ibid. 7 Apr. 1967.

The need for new parliamentary elections, before even half of the four-year term of the *Kneset* had lapsed, arose out of a conflict among the Jewish public. Its major theme was the 'Lavōn affair', a political and personal clash between MAPAI's leaders on the background of a military-security mishap. In this election year, the Arab minority, little interested in the Lavōn affair, was mainly concerned with its own matters. Its political alertness was now manifest in many of its attitudes. This was particularly evident in the politicization of the younger generation, educated in Israel, and now of voting age. Some of these youths actively campaigned on behalf of political parties, supplanting to some degree the role of their elders; others showed their independent political attitude at the polls. Many fully used their opportunity to discuss freely all political issues and to vote according to their convictions.[58] In the pre-election propaganda, the two basic attitudes of the Israeli Arabs reappear: adaptation to the new situation in the State, leading to support of the parties in the Government coalition, on the one hand; and, on the other, alienation leading to chauvinism and even non-acceptance of the State's authority. Within this context, the main demands made by the Arabs—with varying degrees of intensity—were: first, the abolition of the military administration; secondly, the suitable employment of young intellectuals; and, thirdly, the settlement of all land claims—both those of the Bedouins (who could not prove ownership) and of the farmers (who refused to accept compensation for expropriated land).[59]

2. *The Political Parties and the Arabs, 1961*

Written propaganda was employed more than in previous electoral campaigns. The circulation of the party press rose, special pages were added to existing newspapers, and new ones were founded. Many newspapers were distributed free of charge, or at very low cost. The number of handbills rose, too. This increase in the use of the written word indicates the awareness of all political parties of the rise in the scope and level of education among the Arabs in Israel. The terms in which much of the written propaganda was couched showed respect for the Arab intellectuals and Arab youth in general. The desire to win their support is further understandable in view of the entry of many of these young Arabs into political activity.

(*a*) *MAPAI and the allied Arab lists.* As in previous campaigns,

[58] Y. Qanṭōr in *Davar*, 29 June 1961.

[59] Q. Menaḥem (pseud. of Menaḥem Kapelyuk), in *Davar*, 8 Dec. 1961.

MAPAI enlisted the participation of many local leaders in meetings with Arab personalities and in speeches before large gatherings. These emphasized the party's achievements and promised additional progress. For example, Haifa's mayor, Abbā Ḥūshī, opening MAPAI's electoral campaign in Nazareth, promised foreign investment to improve the residential situation in the town. He also asserted that MAPAI planned to accept all Arabs as full party members, if the proportional-representation system of parliamentary election was altered to a plurality system. This combination of promises on the local and the national scale was characteristic also of the party's daily, *al-Yawm*, and of a new, *ad hoc* bi-weekly called *bi-Ṣarāḥa* (Frankly), distributed free of charge.[60]

There were only two Arab lists allied with MAPAI in 1961 (instead of three as formerly) and a few personal changes in their leadership. Otherwise they were composed on the same principles as previously. An attempt by some Druze notables to force MAPAI's hand, by presenting a slate of candidates as a *fait accompli*, failed completely.[61] Jabbūr Jabbūr, mayor of Shafā 'Amr, attempted to convene a 'congress of non-aligned mayors and chairmen of local councils', presumably in order to campaign as an independent Arab list, but this failed to materialize because of MAPAI's pressure on its adherents in the Arab local councils. However, MAPAI was not able to prevent another independent Arab list from running for the *Kneset*; nor could it hinder Khneyfeṣ, an erstwhile MK allied with MAPAI (who had run independently in 1959 and failed) from allying himself in 1961 with the National Religious Party.

(*b*) *MAQĪ*. The activity of MAQĪ during the electoral campaign of 1961[62] profited from the fact that the party's 14th national congress had been held just before the campaign started. The party initiated a series of organizational moves, intended to enlarge its membership, increase circulation of its newspapers, and collect funds.[63] Various front organizations were established, small in scope, but with such resounding and appealing names as the Movement of Intellectuals for the Defence of Democracy, the Movement of Workers and Farmers against Rising Prices and for a Rise in Salaries, the Movement of Arab Farmers against the Robbery of Lands, etc. The party's cadres attempted to foster frequent strikes and to take over those which others had initiated. This was accompanied by a noisy press cam-

[60] Election propaganda in *ha-Areṣ*, 3 July 1961, and Mansour, ibid. 25 July 1961.
[61] See Y. Darwīsh in *Davar*, 6 June 1961.
[62] Details in Czudnowski & Landau, *The Israeli communist party*.
[63] *Qōl ha-'am*, 3 Apr. & 31 May 1961; and *al-Ittiḥād*, *passim*.

paign, in which MAQĪ claimed credit for every move in favour of the Arab minority, while continuously attacking the rival parties. In its platform for the 1961 elections, oft repeated and elaborated by its spokesmen, MAQĪ demanded full equality for the Arab minority, no discrimination in employment, abolition of the military administration, agricultural and industrial development, and the encouragement of cultural activity.[64]

(*c*) *MAPAM.* As in previous electoral campaigns, MAPAM directed most of its activity, among the Arabs, against MAPAI and MAQĪ. It tried further to build up its image as their truest friend and best protector, pointing to its record of opposition to the military administration and to the assistance offered by its *kibbūtzīm*. It presented itself as the only peace party and accused others of war-mongering. Its Arabic newspaper *al-Mirṣād* increased in circulation. MAPAM enlisted, for its oral propaganda, the support of all its Arab adherents, together with a few nationalists, such as Nimr al-Hawārī—probably a move to counteract MAQĪ's offensive.[65]

(*d*) *Aḥdūt ha-'avōda.* This political party learnt the lesson from the failure of its allied Arab list in the 1959 parliamentary elections: in 1961 it decided to appeal directly to the Arab vote. For this purpose, it included an Arab candidate, a bank official from the village Ṭaiyyba, in the tenth place on its slate—a possible, but not certain, safe place. In this manner, *Aḥdūt ha-'avōda* was the third Israeli political party (after MAQĪ and MAPAM) to include Arab candidates in relatively safe places for *Kneset* elections. In addition, the party stepped up its propaganda among the Arabs, representing itself as an alternative party to MAPAI in the formation of future Government coalitions.[66]

(*e*) *The Liberal Party.* This was the name of the new union of the General Zionists with the Progressive Party. The Liberals issued a magazine, to introduce themselves to the Arabs. In it, as well as in personal contacts, the party stressed its liberal viewpoint in politics and private initiative in economics.[67]

(*f*) *The religious parties.* These, well aware of their relative failure in 1959, decided to change tactics. The largest, the National Religious Party, aided the formation of an allied Arab list, headed by Ṣāliḥ Khneyfeṣ, the same Druze chieftain who had failed to enter the *Kneset* independently in the 1959 elections.[68]

[64] *Qōl ha-'am*, 2 June 1961; cf. ibid. 7 Aug. 1961.
[65] *'Al ha-Mishmar*, 16 & 27 July 1961.
[66] Mansour, in *ha-Areṣ*, 27 July 1961.
[67] Cf. ibid. 19 July 1961. [68] Ibid. 27 July 1961.

(*g*) *Other parties*. These, such as *Ḥerūt*, made various, somewhat half-hearted attempts to obtain electoral support.

3. *The Results*

Election day for the fifth *Kneset* was 15 August 1961. The total number of those eligible to vote amounted to 1,271,285, out of whom 105,154 were Arabs; 81·6 per cent of the electorate participated. Among the Arabs participation reached 85·6 per cent, a slight decline (compared to 1959, not easily explainable). The distribution of the Arab vote was as follows:

The Arab Vote in 1961 (in percentages)

Type of settlement	*Participation out of those eligible to vote*	*MAPAI*	*Religious parties*	*Ḥerūt*	*MAPAM*	*Aḥdūt ha-'avōda*	*Liberal Party*	*Arab lists*	*MAQĪ*	*Others*
Arab towns	85·8	4·6	1·6	0·5	8·5	2·3	0·5	36·9	45·0	0·1
Large Arab villages	88·9	7·3	4·5	1·7	7·9	5·6	1·0	46·4	25·5	0·1
Small Arab villages	91·9	7·5	6·1	2·0	19·2	4·8	1·5	45·7	13·0	0·1
Bedouin tribes	80·6	18·4	1·9	0·9	14·4	5·1	1·8	54·2	2·7	0·7

The Vote for the Arab Lists, 1961

Name of the list	*Affiliation*	*No. of voters*	*Percentage of total*	*Kneset seats*
Co-operation and Brotherhood	MAPAI	19,342	1·9	2
Progress and Development	,,	16,034	1·6	2
Progress and Work	National Religious Party	3,561	0·4	—
Defenders of Democracy	Independent	335	0·0	—

(*a*) MAPAI and its allied Arab lists obtained together only 50·8 per cent of the Arab vote, their lowest proportional figure until then. A number of reasons was responsible, e.g. the brief period between elections, which did not allow the whole party machine to work smoothly in full action, for instance among the young Arabs who voted for the first time; personnel changes in the Arab department of MAPAI; changes in the candidates at the head of the Arab lists; and the unpopularity of the law for the concentration of land.[69]

(*b*) *MAQĪ*. The most impressive result in these elections, among Israeli Arabs, was the increase of MAQĪ's support by 122 per cent, as compared with the exceptional 1959 vote, although its success did not differ radically from that in parliamentary elections previous to 1959. In 1961 MAQĪ regained its strength and even advanced. It obtained 19,802 votes in the purely Arab settlements as compared to 8,813 in 1959.[70] These results are not necessarily connected with any sudden ideological change of attitude towards communism among Israeli Arabs. Rather they may be attributed to the following factors: in addition to all previously-mentioned lines of propaganda, in 1961 MAQĪ emphasized its nationalist image, attempting to represent itself as a sort of ally to and supporter of 'Abd al-Nāṣir; the party benefited from the close ties of 'Abd al-Nāṣir with Moscow at the time. Propaganda for the return of the Arab refugees was an invaluable vote-getter, as was MAQĪ's determined, articulate opposition to the law for the concentration of land. These arguments were put forward by dedicated young cadres, directed by the decisions of the party's national congress, held barely a few weeks before election day.

(*c*) MAPAM lost ground, declining from its peak of 12·5 per cent of the Arab vote in 1959 to 11 per cent, that is approximately to its usual relative strength among the Arab minority. It returned to third place after MAQĪ, which apparently gained from MAPAM's reversal. The fact that the party had shared in the Government coalition damaged its popularity in certain circles. Its former argument for the admission of Arabs as full members in the trade union organization had been rendered obsolete by their entry in 1959. The use of nationalist Arabs, such as al-Hawārī, for its election campaign, was less successful than expected: those Arabs liable to be attracted by leftist and nationalist propaganda were more apt to be responsive to MAQĪ propaganda, untinged with MAPAM's Zionist background.

(*d*) Other parties made little impression on the Arab voter. The Arab Independent list and the list allied with the National Religious Party obtained very modest support and did not manage to gain even one *Kneset* seat. The Jewish political parties somewhat improved their overall position by an increase in Arab voting strength, but their

[69] Cf. Asaf, *Davar*, 25 Aug. 1961.

[70] All in all, MAQĪ received about 21,000 Arab votes in the 1961 *Kneset* elections, in other words, half its total electoral support (cf. Czudnowski & Landau, *The Israeli communist party*).

achievements were none the less unimpressive. The National Religious Party was the only one to register a slight proportional gain: 3·7 per cent, compared with 3·1 per cent of the Arab vote in 1959. In varying degrees *Aḥdūt ha-'avōda*, the Liberal Party, and *Ḥerūt* suffered losses relative to 1959. Doubtlessly, the main reason, in all cases, was the neglect of the Arab voter between electoral campaigns.

ELECTIONS TO THE SIXTH *KNESET*, 1965

1. Background to the Elections

During the four years between the elections to the fifth and sixth *Knesets*, the Israeli party system changed substantially. MAPAI split, due to inner conflicts in its leadership. The breakaway faction, headed by D. Ben-Gurion, was named List of the Workers of Israel (or RAFĪ, according to its Hebrew initials). MAPAI came closer to *Aḥdūt ha-'avōda*, and they appeared as a joint group for the 1965 parliamentary elections, called the Alignment for the Unity of the Workers of Israel (briefly, the Alignment). In January 1968, over two years after the elections to the sixth *Kneset*, the Alignment and RAFĪ were to reunite, in an Israeli Labour Party; but for the moment they campaigned against each other. The Liberal Party, it will be remembered, was a union of the General Zionists and the Progressive Party, achieved before the 1961 elections. Before the 1965 elections they split again. The General Zionists, retaining the name of Liberals, joined *Ḥerūt* in a slate of candidates named the *Ḥerūt*-Liberals Bloc (known, by its Hebrew initials, as GAḤAL); while the erstwhile Progressive Party now called itself the Independent Liberal Party. As already noted, the Communist Party, or MAQĪ, had also been split, in the summer of 1965, into MAQĪ and RAQAḤ, largely on Jewish-Arab lines. Finally, a new slate of candidates was running, under the name of This World[71]—a New Force; it directed its electoral appeal to both Jews and Arabs.

The Arab minority seemed, in general, little concerned about inter-party conflict, except in so far as it was directly implicated. In fact, Israeli political conflicts were tangential to their problems which remained basically the same, but with different emphasis. With varying degrees of articulateness, the same old grievances were brought up again during 1961–5: Arab lands, village development, return of refugees, and the military administration. However, all these grievances seemed to have decreased in significance: land expropriation had practically ceased; substantial investments had

[71] Given the name of its Hebrew weekly, which was the rallying point of this new political group.

developed most villages; the problem of the Arab refugees, although still unsolved, had no new elements to offer; and the military administration's authority had been much reduced, and would clearly be abolished entirely after the 1965 elections.

Among more pressing grievances, and perhaps those most often voiced at the time, were, firstly, those of the Arab university graduates who could not always find employment in their field of specialization;[72] and, secondly, those of the Arab workers living in the mixed towns away from their villages in Galilee or in the Little Triangle. Their number was estimated during 1965 at approximately 33,000. Their problem, unlike the intellectuals, was not gaining employment, but a social one: they had difficulty in finding accommodation, particularly since they wanted to save most of their earnings, so they lived in squalor;[73] Jewish girls frequently refused to go out with them;[74] their employers were sometimes rude to them. (They were rude to their Jewish workers, too, but the Arabs, understandably, were more sensitive.) Few took real interest in them,[75] so that their circles naturally became centres for political debate and a focus of emotional nationalism.[76]

Arab intellectuals, workers, and others were mainly concerned with only a single aspect of the Israeli political situation—the rift in MAQĪ. As the Arabic *al-Ittiḥād*, now organ of RAQAḤ, pointed out several times, at last there existed a party which cared for Arab interests. The implication was clear: RAQAḤ was the *sole* Arab party. Perhaps it was this monopoly claim on the part of RAQAḤ that determined members of *al-Arḍ* group to attempt to run in a list of their own. As already described,[77] the Arab Socialist List was not approved by the Central Elections Commission (and its appeal to the Supreme Court failed). These steps did not increase the feelings of sympathy for the State authorities among the Israeli Arabs, and RAQAḤ was quick to seize advantage of these trends in vote-catching slogans. RAQAḤ's nationalist line outweighed its socio-economic demands (particularly as the economic situation in Israel was good).

[72] The problems of the Arab intelligentsia have already been discussed. See also Asaf, in *Ammōt*, June–July 1965, esp. 52–53.

[73] Cf. a description by Mīrqīn in *ha-Areṣ*, 18 & 20 Feb. 1966.

[74] Qāsim Zayd, in *'Al ha-Mishmar*, 16 Mar. 1965.

[75] One who did was Mrs N. Dī-Nūr (cf. Mansour in *ha-Areṣ*, 7 Apr. 1967).

[76] During 1966 a short Israeli documentary film was made. Its name was *Anī Aḥmad* (I am Aḥmad) and it purported to portray the problems facing an Arab villager working in Tel-Aviv. The film is biased, shows the negative side of the problems only, and exaggerates Aḥmad's alienation. However, its very filming is symptomatic. See also above, p. 20 n. 6.

[77] See above, pp. 100–1.

Characteristically, quite a number of the other parties attempted to emulate RAQAḤ's Arab nationalist line, explicitly or guardedly pandering to Arab sentiment.

2. *The Political Parties and the Arabs, 1965*

There were no significant changes in the 1965 electoral campaign beyond the new disposition of the political parties, already noted. House meetings, successfully employed for propaganda purposes among the Jewish public in 1961, were now increasingly employed among the Arab public, too: sympathizers of a political party would invite friends to their home in order to listen to a party representative and discuss the situation with him. Mass rallies, personal canvassing, and written propaganda supplemented these meetings.

(*a*) *The Alignment and the allied Arab lists.* The Alignment (of MAPAI—without RAFĪ—and *Aḥdūt ha-'avōda*) debated two alternative strategies for the 1965 electoral campaign. One view was that allied Arab lists should, as in the past, assist MAPAI. The other—supported by Ṭōleydānō, the Prime Minister's adviser for Arab affairs, and some trade union representatives[78]—maintained that allied lists should be dropped and, instead, that the Arabs ought to be encouraged to vote directly for the Alignment. Partisans of the second view held that the allied lists had spent much effort in attacking one another; and that the prestige of many MAPAI-sponsored Arab notables was at a low ebb. Eventually the first view prevailed: it was decided once more to form allied Arab lists, lest disgruntled notables change their allegiance to other parties, such as RAFĪ. In addition, the Alignment itself campaigned for the direct vote of the Arabs, no less than in previous electoral campaigns. Its main argument was the need for the continuation of stable government, possible only when led by the Alignment. An able move was obtaining the support of Archbishop al-Ḥakīm, which had marked influence over the vote of the Greek Catholic community.

Following the rift in MAPAI (and the establishment of RAFĪ) and the overall attack of the other political parties on the Alignment, the latter struck back in force. Government Ministers, MKs, and party representatives campaigned tirelessly, among Jews and Arabs alike. For instance, one Arab mass rally, early in October 1965, was attended by the Prime Minister, Levī Eshkōl, Ministers Yig'al Allōn and Bĕkhōr Shīṭrīṭ, the MAPAI secretary-general, R. Barqat, and the mayor of Nazareth, Sayf al-Dīn Zu'bī, all of whom spoke. Zu'bī,

[78] Cf. *Jewish Observer and Middle East R.* (London), 13 Aug. 1965. A fuller account in App. F, pp. 237 ff. below.

speaking as an Arab to his fellow Arabs, maintained that the constructive activity of the Alignment for the Arab village was more important than a hundred speeches. This assertion reveals the main line of the Alignment's propaganda in 1965. It was equally evident, for example, in a speech by Abbā Even, then deputy Prime Minister, before a rally of Arabs in the Little Triangle in mid-October 1965.[79] The main points in his speech were: (1) our main aim is to prevent war; (2) the present Government, led by Eshkōl, has achieved more than any of its predecessors in integrating the Arab minority; (3) emphasis in development has been given to the Arab village, by paving new roads, installing water and electricity, improving health services, broadening the school network, building new homes with public funds, encouraging agriculture, handicrafts and local industry; (4) full employment exists, and in the future it will embrace all Arab intellectuals, too; (5) suitable compensation will be offered for expropriated land; (6) full assistance will continue to be given to the Bedouins, to achieve their sedentarization, with all the services they may then need; (7) education, already improved, will advance further; (8) a further easing up in the restrictions imposed by the military administration is to be expected, reducing them to the bare minimum required for security purposes.

As in 1961, two allied Arab lists were sponsored by the Alignment. The first campaigned in Nazareth and Eastern Galilee, the second in the Little Triangle and Western Galilee. Progress and Development was led by Sayf al-Dīn Zu'bī, the 53-year-old mayor of Nazareth (who had already been a member of the first, second, and third *Knesets*); the next candidate was Eliyās Nakhla, a Greek-Catholic from the village of Rāma, also 53 years old (who had been a member of the fourth and fifth *Knesets*). Co-operation and Brotherhood was headed by Jabr Mu'addī, a 49-year-old Druze from Yirkā (a member of the second, third, and fifth *Knesets*), followed by Diyāb 'Ubayd, a 55-year old Muslim from the village Ṭaiyyba (a member of the fifth *Kneset*). These four, those with a real chance of being elected, were all respected notables, trusted allies of MAPAI in previous parliamentary elections. Their community affiliation (two Muslims, a Greek Catholic, a Druze), their residence (Galilee and the Little Triangle), as well as their family connexions ensured support for the Alignment among the Arabs (although some Druze notables requested the replacement of Mu'addī, who had voted in the fifth *Kneset* for the continuation of the disliked military administration).[80]

[79] Later published in Arabic, by the Alignment.
[80] Details in *Ma'arīv*, 10 Sept. 1965.

As formerly, the fact that the Alignment had formed slates of Arab candidates and was sponsoring their electioneering, both administratively and financially, conditioned the character of their propaganda. The candidates decided on a small number of local matters; otherwise the platform of both allied lists extolled the achievements of the Alignment and the advantages in supporting it and its Arab lists, as stablizing factors. Such delicate subjects as the military administration and the Arab refugees were avoided. Other parties (chiefly RAQAḤ, MAPAM, and RAFĪ) were attacked. However, these platforms were already well known, and greater importance attached to canvassing, personal visits, house meetings, and the like.

(*b*) *RAFĪ and its allied Arab list.* Since RAFĪ broke away from MAPAI only shortly before the 1965 *Kneset* elections, it had very little time to organize for electioneering, either among Jews or among Arabs. Nevertheless, RAFĪ tried hard to benefit from previous personal connexions with the Israeli Arabs. It sponsored an allied Arab list, called the List of Peace, led by Ṣuwayliḥ ʿAbd al-Hādī Manṣūr, a 45-year-old Muslim from Ṭīra, and an ex-chairman of the local council in that village. Chief of the largest of Ṭīra's fifteen *ḥamūlas*, with about 700 people, Ṣuwayliḥ ʿAbd al-Hādī Manṣūr emphasized the fact that he was the only one of Ṭīra's residents who was standing for election. Second on the list was ʿAwda Abū Muʿammar, chieftain of the ʿAzāzma Bedouin tribe in the Negev, the only Bedouin decorated for valour by Israel after the 1948 war.[81] Third was Ṣāliḥ Khneyfeṣ from Shafā ʿAmr, the same Druze notable who had broken his affiliation with MAPAI and unsuccessfully competed for a *Kneset* seat in 1959 (independently) and in 1961 (allied with the National Religious Party).

The main electioneering problem of RAFĪ and its allied List of Peace was that of its image among the Arabs in Israel. These identified RAFĪ's leaders—chiefly D. Ben-Gurion, Moshe Dayyan, and Shimʿōn Peres—as the main architects of the Israeli army. Many considered them responsible for thwarting Arab hopes. The spokesmen of RAFĪ and the List of Peace therefore skirted these issues, and based their speeches on more attractive themes: the need for changes in the election system (to give the Arabs larger representation), free high-school education, and a speedier modernization of the Arab village.[82] This propaganda was actually not very different

[81] See about him in *ha-Derekh la-tĕmūra* (RAFĪ's organ), 12 Sept. 1965. Cf. Arṣī'elī in *ha-Areṣ*, 17 Sept. & 1 Nov. 1965.

[82] Examples in *ha-Areṣ*, 12 Sept. & 14 Oct. 1965; *Maʿarīv*, 10 Oct. & 1 Nov. 1965.

from that of the Alignment; but its presentation was more superficial, due to lack of preparation and to financial limitation. Thus only three mass rallies (all with Moshe Dayyan's participation) were organized: in Ṭīra (Little Triangle), the Druze village Jūlis (Galilee), and in the Bedouin encampment of Shaykh 'Awda Abū Mu'ammar (Negev). Apart from these, the representatives of RAFĪ and the List of Peace visited many Arab localities in an attempt to attract support. Usually they chose those villages where *ḥamūla* influence was still strong, avoiding larger towns such as Nazareth, where their chances seemed minimal in any case. Thousands of handbills were distributed, and four issues of a newly founded Arab magazine, named *al-Salām* (Peace), appeared.

(*c*) *MAQĪ*. The party split, in the summer of 1965, occurred only a few months before the elections to the sixth *Kneset*. One of MAQĪ's premises, which had contributed to the rift, was that (contrary to RAQAḤ's view) the Arab minority in Israel was tending towards integration. As in former electoral campaigns, MAQĪ stressed its interest in the Arab minority and its struggle for its rights, particularly those of the workers.[83] However, in addition, MAQĪ made an effort to convince the Arabs in Israel that it was the only party actively interested in peace in the Middle East. The major difficulty facing MAQĪ was to persuade Arab voters to support it at the expense of RAQAḤ, which was meanwhile accusing MAQĪ of 'Jewish deviationism'. The main line of the MAQĪ speakers and of its new Arabic magazine *Ṣawt al-sha'b*[84] was to remind Israeli Arabs of MAQĪ's long-drawn-out struggle on their behalf, the implication being that only a strong MAQĪ could continue to work in their favour. RAQAḤ (so MAQĪ claimed) was so far removed from the Jewish public that it could not hope to assume any influential position,[85] or, in MAQĪ's own words, 'without the support of Jewish democratic forces, the Arab masses will be unable to effect the necessary change'.[86] MAQĪ's secretary-general, Shmū'el Mīqūnīs, charged RAQAḤ with postponing peace and thus harming one and all.[87]

In addition to the party's magazine *Ṣawt al-sha'b*, MAQĪ's representatives distributed handbills and organized house meetings and a few rallies. In general, MAQĪ met with varying degrees of indifference

[83] Broadcast by MAQĪ's representative, Fu'ād Ḥaqqāq, in Arabic, repr. in *Qōl ha-'am*, 16 Sept. 1965.

[84] Since *al-Ittiḥād* had been taken over by RAQAḤ, following the 1965 rift in the communist camp.

[85] *Qōl ha-'am*, 19 Sept. 1965. [86] Ibid. 29 Oct. 1965.

[87] *Ṣawt al-sha'b*, 13 Oct. 1965.

in 1965, as it had retained no Arab branches after the rift with RAQAḤ. Nazareth, formerly one of its strongholds, now seemed almost unmoved by its propaganda. For example, meetings in coffee-houses, in Nazareth, Qalansawa, Umm al-Faḥm, Ramle, and Abū Ghōsh were poorly attended. It appears that RAQAḤ persuaded many Arabs to boycott those MAQĪ functions, and then provokingly heckled speakers.[88] Not surprisingly, most of MAQĪ's propaganda was directed against RAQAḤ, while its struggle with MAPAM and the Alignment took second place.[89] In practice, MAQĪ's task was not facilitated by its inclusion of Arabs in unsafe places[90] on its list of candidates for the *Kneset*; even some of these were induced by RAQAḤ to retract publicly.

(*d*) *RAQAḤ*. This newly-formed party addressed the Israeli Arabs from a position of strength, not only in relation to MAQĪ but to all other political parties as well. It was the only party—and the first in all Israel's electoral campaigns—which could present itself in the image of an *Arab party*. The first ten candidates included five Arabs and five Jews; but in the first three positions were two Arabs (in the second and third places), Tawfīq Ṭūbī and Emīl Ḥabībī. The fact that the first candidate was a Jew, Wīlner, and that a few Jews were in key positions, was explained away as the party's 'internationalist approach' and did not prevent RAQAḤ from identifying itself with Arab interests and attitudes. The party's argument was that the Jews in RAQAḤ were well known for their support of the Arab cause. RAQAḤ's take-over of communist branches in the Arab towns and villages assisted it both administratively and in its claim that it was the true Israeli communist party—with all the credit that accrued from this claim. In Nazareth and Western Galilee, RAQAḤ claimed to have twenty-seven local branches. These and others were called upon for a swift financial drive.[91] Early in September, two full months before election-day, RAQAḤ started its electoral campaign entirely (so the party's spokesman claimed) on a voluntary basis. Mass rallies were held in Arab towns (chiefly in Nazareth)[92] and villages; house meetings were organized; its various publications were mailed to inaccessible places. These publications included the bi-weekly *al-Ittiḥād*,[93] to which an Arabic supplement was added,

[88] Cf. *Qōl ha-'am*, 16 & 19 Sept. 1965.
[89] *Ma'arīv*, 25 Oct. 1965.
[90] *Qōl ha-'am*, 9, 12, & 19 Sept. 1965.
[91] *Zō ha-Derekh*, 6 Jan. 1966.
[92] Cf. *al-Ittiḥād*, 8, 12, 15, & 19 Oct. 1965. See also *ha-Areṣ*, 13 Sept. & 1 Nov. 1965.
[93] *Al-Ittiḥād* led a very vigorous propaganda campaign to make the names of RAQAḤ's candidates known, see e.g. *al-Ittiḥād*, 1 & 29 Oct. 1965.

named *al-Ittiḥād for the Voter*; the party's *al-Jadīd* and *al-Ghad*; as well as a number of handbills.[94]

In its aggressive electioneering, RAQAḤ presented itself to the Arab voter as the only non-Zionist and Arab political party, the successor to MAQĪ in the struggle for Arab rights. The party's campaign was three-pronged: against MAQĪ, which it smeared as a Jewish deviationist group; against the Alignment, which it depicted as the ally of the *ḥamūla* elders and the enemy of the workers; and against MAPAM, which it accused of Zionism and hypocrisy in its alleged two-faced propaganda among Arabs and Jews. This propaganda successively exploited every single case of discrimination against Arabs (real or imaginary) for the sake of political capital and as an indictment of either the State authorities[95] or RAQAḤ's rival parties.[96]

(*e*) *MAPAM*. As in former electoral contests, MAPAM was again faced with the same dilemma: that it appeared among the Jewish public as a Zionist socialist party, an unsuitable image to present to the Arab minority. In 1965 its main rivals were the Alignment, which stood a better chance of fulfilling its electoral promises, and RAQAḤ, invested with a non-Zionist, Arab image. Hence MAPAM stressed its interest in the problems of the Arabs in Israel and promised to intensify it. In its platform[97] and in the speeches of its representatives, MAPAM emphasized its desire for an Arab-Israeli peace and the return of some of the Arab refugees consequent upon such a peace. The party drew attention to its efforts on behalf of the Arab intelligentsia in Israel, and in the provision of employment and assistance to development in the Arab villages. It claimed credit for opening up the trade union organization to Arab membership. It proudly pointed to its record—topped only by the Communist Party—in regularly placing an Arab candidate in a safe place on its slate for the *Kneset*. This time, their choice was 'Abd al-'Azīz Zu'bī, a 40-year-old MAPAM worker. Following graduation from the Arab college in Jerusalem, he had become secretary of the Government Workers' Union in Nazareth and, later, deputy mayor of this town and an active promoter of Arab culture in Israel.

Naturally enough, most of MAPAM's propaganda during the 1965 electoral campaign was directed against the Alignment and RAQAḤ.

[94] On these aspects of RAQAḤ's campaign, see Kna'an in *ha-Areṣ*, 17 Jan. 1966; cf. *Ma'arīv*, 20 Oct. 1965.

[95] Examples in *al-Ittiḥād*, 31 Aug. & 1 Nov. 1965.

[96] Cf. ibid. Oct. 1965.

[97] *'Al ha-Mishmar*, 15 Oct. 1965.

In writing and by word of mouth, MAPAM spokesmen accused the Alignment of discriminating against Arabs.[98] The Arab MKs allied with the Alignment were charged with passively ignoring Arab interests and neglecting to initiate legislation benefiting their brethren.[99] As to RAQAḤ, the representatives of MAPAM portrayed it as a small party, totally unable to fulfil its promises.[1] In contrast, MAPAM was described as the golden mean between the Alignment and RAQAḤ. This policy was outlined in a number of rallies in Arab settlements, including Bedouin camps in the Negev and Galilee. On such occasions, and on others, the party's magazine, *al-Mirṣād*, as well as other propaganda material, was distributed. However, MAPAM placed its main hopes on the effect of its continuous work among the Israeli Arabs, in which it resembled only the Alignment and the communist parties.

(*f*) *The religious parties.*[2] The only religious party active among the Arabs in Israel was the National Religious Party. It is possible that its increased activity was partly due to the moral it drew from the steady, though slow, rise of its electoral support among the Arabs. In 1965 the propaganda of this party increased among the Arabs. Its main arguments were the need for strengthening the faith and the identity of interest among followers of all religions—with suitable quotations from the Bible and the Qur'ān; the activity shown by the party in passing a law against raising pigs; the common interest in the continuation of religious marriages as the only recognized ones (i.e. against civil marriages). The party also reminded the Arabs of the special efforts on their behalf by the Ministers of the Interior, Social Services, and Religions (who represented the party in the coalition Government): enlargement of local government, assistance for the needy, erection of mosques,[3] encouragement towards community organization among the Druzes, improvement of relations with the Christians (the Pope's visit). Since the National Religious Party had no permanent branches in Arab towns and villages, it worked through representatives in various places, who were in direct communication with the party's central institutions in Tel-Aviv. These maintained contacts with the local Arabs, arranging meetings with the participation of religious dignitaries and other notables.

[98] *Al-Mirṣād*, 10 Sept. 1965.

[99] Ibid. 24 Aug. 1965; *ha-Areṣ*, 28 Oct. 1965.

[1] *Al-Mirṣād*, 15 Oct. 1965. Other parties were attacked too, e.g. RAFI (cf. *'Al ha-Mishmar*, 24 Oct. 1965).

[2] For their limited activity see *Ma'arīv*, 13 Oct. 1965.

[3] According to unconfirmed reports, the National Religious Party donated about £I1,000 for the repair of a mosque (see *al-Ittiḥād*, 7 May 1965).

Sometimes the party's leaders and MKs came too.[4] In Nazareth a few Greek Catholics, of the Mazzāwī and al-Ḥā'ik families, worked in the party's campaign.[5]

(*g*) *GAḤAL*. This political group, made up of *Ḥerūt* and the Liberals, was handicapped among the Arabs by the image of *Ḥerūt* as a chauvinistic, presumably anti-Arab, political party. GAḤAL's rivals spread the rumour that the new group wished to enlarge the State's frontiers (which had some basis in the introduction to GAḤAL's election platform) and to drive all Arabs out of Israel (which had no basis whatsoever). Since GAḤAL found it difficult to combat these rumours, it preferred to campaign not on ideological grounds, but on personal ones. Hence GAḤAL's representatives favoured personal canvassing with the Arabs, hoping to influence their vote. The topics in these discussions were thus more personal than political. Political matters, however, were touched upon in GAḤAL's new Arabic periodical, *al-Ḥurriyya* (Freedom), which claimed a circulation of 3,000, and in a number of speeches. GAḤAL courageously reiterated its opposition to the return of the Arab refugees, but claimed that it had been won over to abolition of the military administration.[6] A number of improvements were promised, should GAḤAL form the next Government. In this manner, GAḤAL attempted, in the Arab *milieu* as well as in the Jewish, to create an image of itself as the only alternative to the Alignment for governing the State. Representatives of GAḤAL explained this position in many Arab villages. However, since both *Ḥerūt* and the Liberals maintained their own Arab departments, despite the union, a certain duplication of effort and waste of energy were evident. Interestingly, much of *Ḥerūt*'s propaganda was directed at the Druzes, among whose villages the party had founded a number of clinics.[7]

(*h*) *The Independent Liberals*. As a small political party, the Independent Liberals' channels for propaganda among the Arabs were restricted. The party's main line of approach was that it could not hope for the votes of the extremists, but that the moderates might be made to understand that it was desirable to distinguish between the relations of Israel with the Arab States, and between those of Jews

[4] *Ha-Ṣōfeh*, 31 Aug. 1965.

[5] Acc. to Mansour, in *ha-Areṣ*, 24 Oct. 1965, this was an instance of horse-trading: the National Religious Party undertook to support the electoral campaign of these two families for the municipal council in Nazareth, on condition that they support the party in the *Kneset* elections.

[6] Y. Tamīr's speech in Kafr Qāsim, reported in *ha-Bōqer*, 19 Oct. 1965. The line was: abolish the military administration and enforce security by more suitable means.

[7] See also *ha-Areṣ*, 17 Nov. 1964.

and Arabs in Israel. The main principles of the party were expressed in an Arabic manifesto it distributed among the Arabs before election day. It called for a written constitution, full equality for all, energetic steps for integrating the Arabs in all walks of economic life, more housing for Arab workers, improvements in education, etc. Some original suggestions were for the appointment of an 'ombudsman' as well as the establishment of a special governmental Ministry for Peace. In addition to this manifesto, other written material was distributed, personal contacts were established, and house meetings arranged—chiefly in Nazareth, Acre, Haifa, and some villages. The leading spirit was Nissīm Elī'ad, a Jewish lawyer who was to become the party's secretary-general.

(*i*) *This World—New Force*. The party bearing this unlikely name (after its weekly) was a new one, but its magazine had been widely circulated among Hebrew-reading Arabs for some time. As a dedicated opponent of practically all Government policies, this Hebrew weekly had embraced the cause of the Arab minority, which it was to emphasize even more in an Arabic weekly it soon issued. The party leaders stressed the need for joint political action by Jews and Arabs. They claimed that since the rift in MAQĪ, their party was the only Jewish-Arab political organization. The party demanded the abolition of all laws discriminating against the Arab minority. Furthermore, it called for an overall imaginative effort for reattainment of a stable peace in the whole Middle East. The party was represented as the only group capable of bringing about a meaningful dialogue between the Jewish and Arab national movements.[8] The written propaganda was complemented by a mass rally in Nazareth, addressed by the party's leader (and weekly's editor), Ūrī Avnerī, and two 'peace caravans' into Arab villages. This notwithstanding, the party included only one Arab candidate, Aḥmad Maṣārwe, on its slate for the *Kneset*, and even he was in the last (and twentieth) place.

3. *The Results*

The elections to the sixth *Kneset* were held on 2 November 1965. The total number of those eligible to vote was 1,499,709, including 129,902 Arabs; 83·0 per cent of the electorate participated, among them 87·8 per cent of the Arabs or 110,978. In other words, among both Jews and Arabs proportional participation rose, with the latter maintaining their relatively heavier vote. In most Arab settlements, in Galilee and the Little Triangle, large queues formed, with the parties bringing prospective voters in specially-hired cars. In the Little

[8] *Ha-'Ōlam ha-zeh*, 20 Oct. 1965, 15. See also *ha-Areṣ*, 24 Oct. 1965.

Triangle, wholly Muslim, women helped their men to remind their friends to vote. Only the Bedouins experienced a lower level of participation, because of personal rivalries and conflicts of prestige between the tribes. The distribution of the Arab vote was as follows.[9]

(*a*) *The Alignment and its allied Arab lists.* The Alignment received 13,353 votes, making with its allied lists a total of 53,247 or about 50·1 per cent of all the Arab valid votes. If we consider the loss of RAFĪ and the addition of *Aḥdūt ha-ʻavōda* as approximately cancelling one another out, the Alignment and its Arab allies lost very little Arab support, compared with 1961 (when they obtained 50·8 per cent of the Arab vote). This can be construed as a notable success, considering the rift in MAPAI and the attack of all parties on the Alignment. It very possibly was a reflection of the economic prosperity in Israel and the Alignment's vigorous electioneering. Apparently, it was those interested in the continuation of the Alignment's government, for personal or other reasons, who voted for it. Conversely, the relatively low support for the Alignment in Nazareth pinpoints the force of nationalist sentiment there and envy of the rapid development in near-by Jewish Nazareth. Another salient feature is the relatively low vote for the two Arab lists allied to the Alignment in the towns—not only in Arab Nazareth but also in the mixed towns, where presumably the *ḥamūlas* have little influence.

(*b*) MAQĪ failed disastrously among the Arabs as compared with former parliamentary elections. Only 549 Arabs voted for it, or just about 0·5 per cent of all Arab valid votes. The reason for this is obvious. It lies in the break-up of the communist camp in Israel, and the success of RAQAḤ in convincing the Arab voters that MAQĪ was a Jewish, 'pro-Zionist' party. Those who voted for MAQĪ regardless were probably communists convinced of its stand.

(*c*) RAQAḤ, in contrast, received 24,069 Arab votes, or about 22·6 per cent of all valid Arab votes (and 3,344 Jewish votes only).[10] These figures refer solely to purely Arab settlements, but various signs indicate strong Arab support for RAQAḤ in mixed towns as well. RAQAḤ's success was particularly marked, if compared with the support for MAQĪ in 1961, in the larger Arab localities. This may be considered as a noteworthy achievement by RAQAḤ, considering that it had been established barely three months before the election to the sixth *Kneset* took place. The very fact that the rift occurred

[9] In addition to the official statistics, see also *al-Yawm*, 5 Nov. 1965; Dar, in *Davar*, 15 Nov. 1965; Schiff, in *ha-Areṣ*, 21 Nov. 1965; and Mansour, ibid. 1 Dec. 1965.

[10] RAQAḤ was active among Jews too; see examples in *Zō ha-Derekh*, 26 Aug. & 23 Sept. 1965.

The Arab Vote in 1965 (in percentages)

Type of settlement	*Participation out of those eligible to vote*	*Alignment*	*Religious parties*	*GAḤAL*	*MAPAM*	*Independent Liberals*	*RAFĪ*	*Arab lists*	*MAQĪ*	*RAQAḤ*	*This World*	*Others*
Arab towns	87·1	3·4	3·9	0·5	6·8	1·8	3·2	34·9	0·6	42·0	2·6	0·3
Large Arab villages	87·9	8·3	6·6	3·0	8·8	1·1	2·4	44·2	0·4	23·1	2·0	0·2
Small Arab villages	88·7	13·6	6·7	2·4	14·4	0·9	4·1	43·1	0·3	13·1	1·2	0·2
Bedouin tribes	66·0	12·0	1·9	2·0	18·3	2·8	2·8	49·9	1·6	4·5	2·2	2·0

The Vote for the Arab Lists, 1965

Name of list	*Affiliation*	*No. of voters*	*Percentage of total*	*Knesset seats*
Co-operation and Brotherhood	MAPAI	16,464	1·4	2
Progress and Development	,,	23,430	1·9	2
List of Peace	RAFĪ	5,536	0·5	—

among mutual recriminations of chauvinism had apparently increased electoral support for RAQAḤ among those Arabs who declined to vote for Jewish parties or for Arab lists allied with them. Hence the heavy Arab vote for RAQAḤ by non-party members may be considered as a protest vote against the State of Israel and its Government. It should also be remembered that Cairo radio called on all Israeli Arabs, shortly before election day, to vote for RAQAḤ, and *al-Ittiḥād* printed this call on its front page.

It is also possible that the easing of restrictions by the military administration encouraged some Arabs to vote according to their inclinations, without fear of possible reprisals, real or imaginary. The economic prosperity in Israel, which encouraged some grateful Jews and Arabs to vote for the Alignment in 1965, had a reverse aspect: because of this prosperity and the need for workers everywhere, some Arab voters may have felt less dependent for their livelihood on their family elders or on the local representatives of the State authorities. Hence the way was clear for an opposition vote. In so far as can be ascertained, a sizeable number of the under-30 Arabs, and particularly of those youths voting for the first time, voted RAQAḤ.[11] This applies not only to Christians (mainly Greek Orthodox) whose communist vote has already been noted, but to the Druzes, too, whose proportional vote for the communists rose.[12] It is not easy to explain this relatively new phenomenon in a community whose members are considered as enthusiastically loyal to the Establishment. Probably the RAQAḤ vote was by a number of youths who had quarrelled with the community elders and wanted to express their protest; or possibly by demobilized Druze youths who were experiencing difficulties in finding suitable jobs.

(*d*) MAPAM received 444 more votes in 1965 than in 1961, but owing to the increase in the number of voters, it lost proportionately 1·5 per cent over the country, receiving only 9·2 per cent of the vote in purely Arab localities. This decline was probably the result of several factors: MAPAM's work among the Arabs had been somewhat more restricted—e.g. it had disbanded the Arab Pioneer Youth;[13] RAQAḤ's success was at MAPAM's expense; overriding these, MAPAM's frequent declaration that it had definitely made up its mind to form a Government coalition with the Alignment probably lost the party some support among those Arabs who were anti-

[11] Cf. Amnōn Līn, quoted by Dar, in *Davar*, 15 Nov. 1965; cf. Schiff, in *ha-Areṣ*, 21 Nov. 1965.

[12] See *Davar*, 15 July 1966.

[13] The party machine probably failed in this instance (cf. *'Al ha-Mishmar*, 11 & 17 Nov. 1965).

Alignment.[14] (As for the supporters of the Alignment, they voted directly for it or for its allied Arab parties—anyway not for MAPAM.) Generally speaking, MAPAM's support decreased in the Little Triangle, concomitant with the rise of nationalism there. It declined more noticeably in smaller localities than in medium or large ones, most likely because it had failed to invest enough effort in them.

(*e*) Other parties obtained only modest electoral support among the Arabs in Israel, an outcome very similar to the results of former parliamentary elections. GAḤAL received some support among the Druzes, a major reason being that Quftān al-Ḥalabī, possibly annoyed at his clansman not being appointed a *qāḍī*, gave his vote, along with his *ḥamūla*, to GAḤAL. The National Religious Party received many scattered votes, most of them in Western Galilee, and improved upon its 1961 vote. Other parties—chiefly RAFĪ and its allied List of Peace (the latter got no *Kneset* seat), the Independent Liberals, and This World—obtained their few Arab votes in a small number of localities, probably those whose residents were candidates, or whose chiefs had been contacted by one party or another. Remarkably, This World received 1,926 Arab votes, which though amounting to only 1·8 per cent of the valid Arab votes, was proportionally a higher vote for this party than among the Jewish voters, a ratio emulated only by RAQAḤ—that is, by no other Jewish political party!

MAIN CHARACTERISTICS

1. *Trends in the Electoral Behaviour of the Arabs*

(*a*) *Significance of the Arab vote.* Without exception, all Governments in Israel have consisted of a coalition of parties. In certain political configurations, it could—and did—occur that small parliamentary groups held a considerably wider power than their size warranted. Natually, the larger such groups were, the greater their capability for manoeuvre. This is an added reason for the electoral struggle put up by all Israeli parties, each trying to get an additional *Kneset* seat. It was very worth-while to invest vote-catching efforts among the Arabs, as in most parliamentary elections they numbered almost a tenth of those eligible to vote. The Arab minority in Israel was not ignorant of these facts: Hence the sporadic efforts to establish an all-Arab party (which failed, however, to materialize); hence also their very heavy voting participation.

(*b*) *Heavy participation.* With the exception of the first *Kneset* elections, in 1949, when the Arabs were still overwhelmed by the

[14] Mansour, in *ha-Areṣ*, 1 Dec. 1965.

shock of defeat, their voting participation was consistently higher than that of the Jews, reaching a peak of 92·1 per cent in 1955. Several reasons seem to account for this. (1) A growing appreciation of the democratic process and a desire to benefit by participating in political elections. (2) The wish to react to legislation directly affecting them, such as to certain land laws. (3) The intensive activity of practically all political parties among the Arabs, openly intended for vote-catching. (4) The pressure and inducements of village *mukhtārs* and tribal shaykhs, on both men and women. (5) The very inclusion of Arabs on various slates of candidates, and the fact that some of these actually became MKs.

(*c*) *Constant addition of young voters.* While among the Jewish voters in Israel, the numerical increase from one *Kneset* election to the other includes new voters of all ages, due to immigration, this is not the case at all among the Arabs. These, indeed, rise in number from one parliamentary election to the next, but the addition is almost wholly composed of new age-groups, upon reaching the required voting specifications. Competition for the vote of these youngsters, voting for the first time, is one of the main tasks of those political parties which are regularly active among the Arabs. The parties strive to attract many of them, even as permanent party workers on the party's payroll.

(*d*) *The struggle between the old and the new.* The greater part of the Arabs in Israel reside in Galilee, the Little Triangle, and the Negev. In their quasi-monolithic settlements, they are under conflicting pressures. While the hold of custom-hallowed leadership is gradually losing ground, it is still strong and seeks allies among the Israeli authorities. Hence the competition in parliamentary elections between Arab slates composed of local notables and Arab candidates appearing on the slates of national Jewish parties.

(*e*) *Absence of a religious basis in electoral competition.* The political loyalties of the Arab minority in Israel are little connected with those of their faith or religious community. This differs from the practice of several other religious minorities in the Middle East, such as the Maronites in Lebanon. There is, probably, a double reason for this phenomenon in Israel: first the Arabs, irrespective of religion, have already linked their political activities and voting in parliamentary elections to the Jewish parties; secondly, the rising sentiment of nationalism among the Arab minority, particularly in view of the State's geographical situation, overshadows religious loyalties to a considerable extent.

(*f*) *Rising nationalism.* A part of the Arab minority in Israel could not but be attracted by the tide of Arab nationalism in the Middle East. This sentimental tie, only natural after all, was fostered by direct physical contact (infiltration into Israel) and even more by the tenacious radio and TV propaganda of the neighbouring States. As Israel is territorially contiguous to Arab countries, feelings of Arab irredentism, though not widespread, have been frequently expressed by the more extreme. Such alienation from the State of Israel was bound to influence voting behaviour in political elections; often, the refusal to integrate in Israel was expressed in a protest-vote for MAQĪ (in 1965 for RAQAḤ).

2. *Political Parties and Arab Electoral Support*

All Israeli political parties were active in the Arab minority, as demonstrated by their share of the Arab vote. However, a closer examination of the distribution of Arab votes immediately shows one characteristic feature: some parties always obtain a substantial part of the Arab vote, while others, just as regularly, get a very small share. This is not only a constant feature in all six parliamentary elections, but is valid also for most Arab residential areas, considered singly. Since all the Israeli political parties (with the possible exception of RAQAḤ in 1965) are either Jewish, or consist of Arab lists of candidates allied with them, the above characteristics appear odd at first glance.

In an article by Y. Waschitz,[15] an attempt has been made to distinguish in Israel between ideological and non-ideological parties, and to explain in this manner the discrepancy in the Arab vote. His classification is somewhat artificial, in so far as the Israeli system of political parties is concerned; and it seems rather unconvincing, if ideological considerations are taken as the main basis for Arab electoral support. Perhaps it would be more realistic to differentiate between the permanently-present and the election-eve parties, and to attempt to relate the Arab vote to these two categories.

The permanent parties are active among the Arabs in Israel all the year round between elections. They take an interest in the Arabs' problems and assist them culturally (with publications), agriculturally (expert advice) and with services. They have special party machinery to co-ordinate all these activities, and this is partly staffed by Arabs employed with full or at least part-time pay. Each of these parties has a well-defined, overall policy for the Arab minority. Arabs are included in their slates of parliamentary candidates in safe places or in allied lists with a real chance of election to the *Kneset*. They have

[15] *NO*, Mar.–Apr. 1962, 40–42.

accepted Arab members into the parties, or at least considered the issue and postponed the decision for the time being.

The election-eve parties see the Israeli Arabs as an object of their political activity, without expecting them to participate in any activity within the framework of these parties, with one exception—voting on election day. These parties are at best sporadically active among the Arabs; they show interest only for a brief while (a few months, at most) before political elections. Hence they have no regular party machinery and Arabic publications—these appear, *ad hoc*, before the elections. The election-eve parties have no consistent policy regarding the Arab minority, except perhaps dedicated vote-getting intended to increase the party's vote which is almost wholly based, anyway, on the Jewish public. If these parties include Arabs on their slates of candidates, it is only as a vote-catching device, with no intention of allowing them safe places. Sometimes, they attempt to organize allied Arab lists, but fail to gain the minimum number of votes ensuring even one *Kneset* seat.

The permanent parties are MAPAI (in 1965: the Alignment), MAPAM and MAQĪ (in 1965: RAQAḤ). All others are characteristic election-eve parties, which grant benefits in varying degrees, as a last-minute attempt to buy votes. The Arabs in Israel are, naturally, aware of this trend and try to use the situation to their advantage. As one of them recently put it, 'Would that every year were an election year!'[16] Interestingly, this affects but little their vote (which, of course, is secret). While a few votes may be swayed in this manner, the election-eve parties have continuously failed to rally significant electoral support among the Arabs. This feature is reflected in the following table.

The Arab Vote for the Permanent and the Election-Eve Parties (percentages)

	1st Kneset, 1949	*2nd Kneset, 1951*	*3rd Kneset, 1955*	*4th Kneset, 1959*	*5th Kneset, 1961*	*6th Kneset, 1965*
MAPAI and allied Arab lists	61·3	66·5	62·4	52·0	50·8	50·1*
MAQĪ	22·2	16·3	15·6	10·0	22·7	22·6†
MAPAM	0·2	5·6	7·3	12·5	11·0	9·2
Total, permanent parties	83·7	88·4	85·3	74·5	84·5	81·9
Total, election-eve parties	16·3	11·6	14·7	25·5	15·5	18·1
Grand total of Arab vote	100·0	100·0	100·0	100·0	100·0	100·0

* In 1965 the Alignment, i.e. plus *Aḥdūt ha-'avōda*, but without RAFĪ.
† The 1965 figures refer to RAQAḤ alone.

Source: Compiled on the basis of official data published by the CBS.

[16] Quoted in *la-Merḥav*, 29 Oct. 1965.

The table on p. 64 demonstrates that in all Israeli parliamentary elections, from 74·5–88·4 per cent of the Arab vote went to the permanent parties, while the election-eve parties, combined, never received more than 25·5 per cent of the Arab vote (in 1959), and usually considerably less. While there is always a certain floating vote from the permanent to the election-eve parties and vice-versa, as well as from one party to another, it seems relatively small. Sometimes the elders of a *ḥamūla* will move to support another party, and carry their followers along with them. Disgruntled voters may change their vote from one party to a rival one, as may a few who expect material rewards. However in many Arab villages and Bedouin camps, such changes are relatively infrequent and lead one to assume that the Arab vote is generally quite stable (as is a very sizeable part of the Jewish vote in *Kneset* elections).

The table on the Arab vote for the permanent and election-eve parties also shows a consistent ratio of support among the permanent parties. With the exception of the election results for the fourth *Kneset*, the permanent parties, between them, gained 81·9–88·4 per cent of the Arab vote. MAPAI,[17] combined with its allied Arab lists, demonstrates a clear, though moderate downward trend, since the elections to the third *Kneset* in 1955. MAPAM shows an upward trend until 1959, then a decline. MAQĪ[18] shows a clear downward trend until 1959, then picks up considerably. While the exact direction of the Arab floating vote cannot be ascertained, it is more than probable that MAPAM and MAQĪ were rivals: one's gain was the other's loss; MAPAI contributed to both by its decline, but only to a slight degree. The political correlations between the electoral achievements of the permanent parties among the Arabs in Israel may be expressed by the following model.

Correlation between Electoral Achievements among the Arabs by Permanent Parties

A MAPAI and allied Arab lists ↔ MAPAM + MAQĪ (RAQAḤ)

B MAPAM ↔ MAQĪ (RAQAḤ)

C Arab lists allied with MAPAI ↔ Other Arab lists

↙ ↓

D Permanent parties ↔ Election-eve parties

[17] In 1965—the Alignment. [18] In 1965—RAQAḤ alone.

Pair A of the diagram expresses the situation in which MAPAI and its allied Arab lists continuously obtain a majority of the total Arab vote in Israel. The main rivals are MAPAM and MAQĪ (in 1965: RAQAḤ). After 1951, their combined vote is steadily on the rise, fed (partly at least) by MAPAI's moderate decline. This correlation reaches its peak in the 1961 and 1965 elections, when MAPAI (or the Alignment) and its allied Arab lists barely receive slightly more than half of the total Arab vote, while MAPAM and MAQĪ (or RAQAḤ) receive between them about a third of the total vote. This seems significant, because it also demonstrates the relation between continuity and change, the former represented by MAPAI (or the Alignment) and its Arab allies among rural local leaders, the latter by MAPAM and MAQĪ (RAQAḤ) which seek younger and more politically-conscious allies among the Arabs. It is reasonable to assume, then, that the correlation in the electoral results is yet another facet of the weakening of long-established structures among the Israeli Arabs and the slow but steady advance of a newer approach to participation in politics. Relevantly, electoral support for MAPAI and its allied Arab lists is heaviest in the smaller villages; the larger the locality, the stronger, proportionally, is the support for MAPAI's main rival, MAQĪ (RAQAḤ), the best example being that of communist strength in Nazareth.[19]

Pair B reflects the constant relation between the strength of MAPAM and MAQĪ (RAQAḤ) among the Arabs, as shown by electoral results. Indeed, the interplay between them, although varying in scope, is steady: the rise of one is the decline of the other. This is probably the function of both being not only permanently present, but also ideological parties. They appeal to more or less the same elements in the Arab electorate with quite similar arguments and attempt to create among them practically the same image. Communist success in the last two parliamentary elections, those of 1961 and 1965, seems to indicate that lately MAQĪ, or RAQAḤ, has had better success in identifying itself with the Arab minority.

Pair C expresses the reciprocal relations of the Arab lists allied to MAPAI and those allied to other Jewish parties. Except for the direct Arab vote for the Jewish parties (including RAQAḤ in 1965), the Arab allies of MAPAI stand a good chance of monopolizing all the rest. In this, their main rivals are other Arab lists, either independent (i.e. led by ex-MAPAI MKs) or sponsored by Jewish parties other than MAPAI. In every single case, the rivals have failed dismally, not obtaining even one *Kneset* seat. However, their efforts

[19] Examples in Czudnowski & Landau, *The Israeli communist party.*

doubtless succeeded in attracting away votes from the Arab lists allied to MAPAI. Thus in the 1951 *Kneset* elections 4·7 per cent of all votes in Israel were given to the Arab lists allied to MAPAI (again, it is natural to assume that all are Arab votes). In 1955, an Arab list sponsored by the General Zionists obtained 0·5 per cent of the total vote in Israel, and the vote for the Arab lists allied to MAPAI declined to 4·4 per cent. In 1959 there were three other Arab lists competing with MAPAI's three Arab lists. The former obtained together 1·2 per cent of the total vote in Israel; the latter obtained altogether 3·5 per cent, which combined make up exactly the same 4·7 per cent of the total vote in Israel which the Arab lists allied to MAPAI received between them in 1951! In later *Kneset* elections, this correlation still holds true, but the Arab lists allied to MAPAI have lost votes, in addition to the other permanently present parties besides MAPAI, and (to a lesser extent) to the election-eve parties.

Pair D sums up the constant relation between the permanently present and the election-eve parties. The permanently present parties receive most of the Arab vote in *Kneset* elections. Again, reciprocity rules the ratio of votes obtained by each of these two groups in all six parliamentary elections.

End of Chap 5

p 156

Chap 6

THE ARABS IN LOCAL AND TRADE UNION ELECTIONS

THE ARABS AND LOCAL ELECTIONS

1. *Local Government and the Arabs*

Local government developed, over hundreds of years, in the West against a background of an increasing awareness of public life and relatively tolerant rule. Its purpose was to establish a formal framework for local autonomy and to enable the inhabitants to manage their own affairs. It is thus concerned with the general development of the area and the provision of indispensable services. The underlying principles of local government have been to increase the well-being of the inhabitants and to enable them to express their desire for public activity. With these aims in mind, the colonial States introduced local government into the Middle East during the late nineteenth and early twentieth centuries. Imported from the different socio-cultural background of Western Europe and superimposed on local rule initiated in the late Ottoman empire, the transplantation has not worked out too well.

During the period of British rule in Palestine, the Jewish population (a large part of which initially came from Europe) adapted more easily and rapidly than the Arab population to the new concepts of local government. The State of Israel has attempted to remedy this discrepancy. In a constantly growing number of Arab localities the Israeli authorities have gradually been introducing local councils, secretly elected by general suffrage. Both municipal councils and the smaller local councils have had increased connexions with Government offices and various public organizations such as the trade unions or the political parties. In this way, Arab localities in Israel were swiftly swept into the whirlpool of Israeli politics, without having had sufficient opportunity to adapt to the new situation.

The continual struggle for power in the Arab towns and villages becomes increasingly manifest on the approach of elections. People compete within the framework of the *ḥamūla*, and *ḥamūlas* compete with their rivals. Groups manoeuvre in order to gain more power, seeking influential allies outside their locality. Some Israeli experts, such as Y. Palmōn (who was the first adviser to the Prime Minister on Arab affairs), warned that the introduction of local government would foster strife in Arab villages.[1] Nevertheless, no one in Israel seriously envisaged the possibility of preventing the Arabs from electing their own local councils and sharing in the country-wide system of local government. On the contrary, this institution has sometimes channelled local jealousies and intrigues into the healthier climate of orderly debate within a democratically elected body.

Local elections shed light on the political behaviour of the Arabs in Israel. As elsewhere, local politics are connected with national politics but are quite revealing in their own right. In Israel, the relations between local and parliamentary elections are particularly close, as they have often taken place on the same day (in recent years this arrangement has been sanctioned by law). In practical terms, there is an essential difference between Jewish and Arab local elections. In the former, the national political parties are active on the local level, too, with a few additional groups in the larger cities (representing mainly local interests). In the latter, in contrast, local groups have a decisive share in local elections (even though many may be supported by national parties). The over-all impression is that many Arabs attempt to adapt to a new situation, while struggling to preserve most of their acquired power in local politics.

Therefore, particular attention is devoted to politics in local elections, but our discussion is relatively brief—for in Israel activity in local government is not considered as a step towards a political career on the national level, as in the United States of America, for instance. In this lies the reason for the reluctance shown by political personalities of stature when called upon to devote themselves to the management of local affairs. Exceptions are made only in the case of important municipalities, such as Jerusalem, Tel-Aviv, Haifa, or Nazareth. Even men such as Sayf al-Dīn Zu'bī (the Alignment) or 'Abd al-'Azīz Zu'bī (MAPAM) were not elected to the *Kneset* because of their role in the municipality of Nazareth, but rather as a result of their family standing and their political activities on behalf of their respective political parties.

2. *Arab Municipal and Local Councils*

(*a*) *Introducing local government*. In Israel, the development of local government proceeded more rapidly than in most other Middle Eastern countries.[2] When the State of Israel was established, there

[1] Cf. Palmōn, in *Ner*, Feb. 1953, 3–5.

[2] For which see W. H. Wickwar, 'Pattern and problems of local administration in the Middle East', *Middle East J.*, Summer 1958, 249–60.

were in its area two Arab municipalities (Nazareth and Shafā 'Amr) and one local council (Kafr Yāṣīf)[3]—for an Arab population numbering more than 150,000. Even these three were in a sorry state, because of budgetary difficulties and the lack of efficient, trained manpower. In accordance with his statutory powers, the Minister of the Interior started an energetic policy encouraging local government in the Arab villages. This policy appears to have had three main targets: (1) to form local councils which would, in the course of time, bring the level of Arab local government to the level of the Jewish, and thus serve as a suitable link between the villagers and the central State authorities; (2) to create tools to assist economic development, by giving the villagers a representation capable of acting in their best economic interests, negotiating loans, etc.; (3) to serve as a sort of safety-valve for long-standing envy and strife as well as for the feelings of frustration caused by sudden transformation into a minority. Therefore in the early 1950s fourteen additional local councils were established. This trend was continued, with varying pace. The larger villages, close to Jewish centres, were granted local government first. Among these may be found the most developed local councils in Abū Ghōsh (near Jerusalem), Ṭīra, and Ṭaiyyba (both in the Little Triangle). At the end of 1966 there were 2 municipalities, 38 villages with local councils, and another 17 within larger regional councils. By then, about 200,000 Arabs, or two-thirds of Israel's Arab minority, had been granted local government.[4]

(*b*) *In favour of local councils*. Quite frequently, the villagers themselves showed interest in a local council. Even older people were dazzled by the speedy municipal development of Tel-Aviv when they visited it. Their sons, chiefly the educated and the workers in the mixed towns, soon realized the archaic administrative structure of their villages, and hankered for a change. Arabs who noted that in the town the local authorities cared for education, health, water supply, garbage cleaning, and road-paving, soon demanded the same from their own *mukhtār*.[5] When he refused, being unable or unwilling to provide these services, the innovators would demand a local council instead of the *mukhtār*, pointing out near-by Jewish or Arab settlements as models of progress. They would then be supported by all those who wanted to settle accounts with the *mukhtār*;[6] usually they

[3] For further details, M. Ma'ōz, in *MḤ*, 1962, 235.

[4] Israel, Min. of the Interior, Dept of Minorities, *The Arab local councils in Israel*, xvi (Feb. 1967), 28.

[5] On the *mukhtār* (or headman) in the Middle East, cf. Gabriel Baer, *Population and society in the Arab East* (London, 1964), 165–7.

[6] See Ḥasan 'Abd al-Majīd, in *al-Yawm*, 4 May 1951.

were quite numerous. This is what happened, for example, in Furaydīs, where the Mĕqōrōt Water Company refused to instal running water in the village unless a local council signed a contract with it. So, despite the opposition of many village elders, the inhabitants—tired of hauling the water from a distance—finally won; a local council signed the contract, and soon there was piped water in every home.

Although rival *ḥamūlas* cannot necessarily be expected to favour the institution of a local council (for they prefer to seize control and keep the spoils-system to themselves), the partisans of a local council can generally count on the support of all those who want to participate in ruling and to prevent others from doing so. The *mukhtār* and the village elders who share his power, however, have seldom yielded to pressure, if the envisaged local council seemed like a threat to their own rule. Only when they felt sure that they themselves would be an important factor in the local council have they supported its establishment.

(*c*) *Obstacles to formation of local councils.* Probably the main factor impeding the institution and functioning of local councils among the Arab population in Israel is the social structure of the Arab village itself. Very frequently, the head of a *ḥamūla* fears that the local council, if instituted, will mean a lessening of his own power over the village; so he and the whole of his *ḥamūla* do everything to prevent this innovation. If there is more than one *ḥamūla* in the village, the strongest fears lest the others seize control of the village through the local council; this would mean not only loss of power but loss of face too. For instance, in ʻAyn Māhil two rival *ḥamūlas* could not agree on the chairmanship of the proposed local council; lest the other have it, both *ḥamūlas* agreed to postpone the idea altogether. Only in November 1965, was a local council finally elected. Often enough, a *ḥamūla* boycotts the local council, because the candidate for its chairmanship—or the actual chairman—is a member of a rival *ḥamūla*. Since generally the first step is appointing a local council (which, after some time, organizes elections), such opposition can be a serious impediment. For example, in Kafr Mandā, in Western Galilee, the Ministry of the Interior has been trying, since 1959, to persuade the villagers to agree to the appointment of a local council. The village's 2,000 people simply could not agree among themselves, each *ḥamūla* head claiming the chairmanship. In 1962, after persuasion had failed, the Minister of the Interior decided to decree elections to a local council. The inhabitants of Kafr Mandā did everything imaginable to prevent the elections from being held—

including locking up the registration clerk in his room.[7] In November 1965, when country-wide local elections were held, the villagers of Kafr Mandā again boycotted them.

The strong entrenched power of the *ḥamūlas* receives support from another factor in its opposition to the introduction of local councils. This is the absence of habits of social life within the village unit. For many an Arab villager, the idea that his neighbour holds power equal to his in electing a local council is obnoxious; and the thought that he has to pay money for something that his neighbour, too, is going to enjoy, is absurd.[8] Here we refer to the lack of understanding that any local activity is necessary even if it concerns and benefits someone else, and an unpreparedness to pay taxes. Of these, the second point is the one which causes more active opposition: many villagers refuse to envisage the idea of taxation,[9] even when a local council means collecting funds for their own needs and gaining, in addition, Government grants and loans on easy terms. A local council and tax collection are considered evil, also, because they introduce further Government control and interference in the village's affairs. Suspicion of the central authority, traditionally ingrained, has not totally disappeared. The Israeli authorities have continuously attempted to convince many of those villages of the advantages accruing from elected local government, but apparently they have only partially succeeded in modifying the villagers' resistance, rooted as it is in a different set of values.

(*d*) *Stages in the institution of local councils.* Since a village cannot change suddenly to a new system of local government, to which it is unaccustomed, the introduction of a local council is executed by stages. The time-lag between the stages is dependent on the level of development of the village and its readiness to pass from one stage to the other. Usually, on the initiative of a formal suggestion by the District Commissioner, the Minister of the Interior publishes an order for the institution of a local council in a certain village, specifying its composition, its term of office, its tasks, its powers and duties, and its area of jurisdiction. In general, a fair amount of time lapses from the issuing of the order until the actual nomination of the first local council. During this period, all the local factions favouring or opposing the institution of a local council have a field-day. In some cases, six or seven years have passed from the publication of the order establishing a local council to its actual institution. Even after an

[7] Cf. *ha-Areṣ*, 24 July 1962.

[8] Ma'ōz, in *MḤ*, 1962.

[9] Mansour, 'Birthpangs of Arab municipal government', *NO*, Sept. 1962, 61–63.

appointed local council is set up, the difficulties continue. By this time, however, they have a different character—clashes between the members of the local council. This accounts for the tendency to include sometimes the District Officer or one of his officials in the appointed local council; these can both help to settle differences of opinion and explain the council's rights and duties to its members. When matters are proceeding smoothly, the Minister of the Interior may decree elections to a new local council.[10]

3. *Elections to the Arab Local Councils*

Main characteristics. In Nazareth and in mixed towns with a large Arab population, such as Acre, municipal elections are an occasion for competition between rival national parties. The case is quite different in elections to local councils in smaller Arab localities. The competing lists of candidates in the Arab villages generally belong to one of the following categories: (*a*) local lists based on family ties or membership in the same religious community; (*b*) lists identified with one of the national parties; (*c*) local lists identified with neither a family or religious community, nor with a national party. The general attitude of most villagers to these lists was characteristically expressed by an Arab, who said, 'The *Kneset* is far away, while the local council is very close!'[11]

(*a*) Lists of candidates associated with *ḥamūlas* or religious communities compete for the local council practically in all villages where *ḥamūlas* are in conflict with one another, or where different communities reside side by side. For example, in the local council elections of 3 November 1959, typical lists associated with the religious communities ran against one another in Rāma (a village near the Safad–Acre highway). The list associated with the Greek Orthodox community won four seats on the local council, completely defeating a list of the chief *ḥamūla* of the village. In the same elections, the Greek Catholic and Latin communities in Rāma submitted a joint list of candidates and received three seats. The Druze had four family lists, formed according to the division of *ḥamūlas* within that community; three of these obtained one seat each. MAQĪ gained two seats, partly a result of support by the Greek Orthodox. Yet another list of candidates won a seat thanks to its relationship with the Latin community.[12] To take another instance, in the municipal elections of Shafā 'Amr, held on 2 November 1965, the rivalry between the

[10] Some examples in *ha-Areṣ*, 12 Nov. 1961.
[11] In a personal conversation with me, in Oct. 1965.
[12] Shamīr, in *MḤ*, 1961, 252–4.

Christian, Muslim, and Druze inhabitants came to a head. The list which won most votes was the one headed by Jabbūr Yūsuf Jabbūr, which was connected with the Greek Catholic community.[13] Jabbūr himself is a member of that community, but does not belong to the largest *ḥamūla* in it. Other lists of candidates running for the municipality in Shafā 'Amr, even though associated with various political parties, were basically connected with the various religious communities. The main activity of the *ḥamūlas*, before local elections, is characterized by their common reluctance to share the same list: generally no head of a *ḥamūla* would consider appearing *second* in any list of candidates.

(*b*) In the larger Arab localities, the national parties, too, compete with one another. This is particularly true of MAQĪ (in 1965: RAQAḤ) and MAPAM; the National Religious Party or other Jewish parties only occasionally join the electoral struggle. In such instances, the national parties nearly always win fewer votes in local than in parliamentary elections. The Arab split vote is due not only to the added competition of other lists with local allegiances. Rather it is due to the fact that many of these local lists are sponsored by other parties, such as MAPAI (in 1965: the Alignment). To cite an extreme case, in the November 1965 elections to the local council of Ṭur'ān, 10 out of the 11 competing lists (i.e. all except RAQAḤ's list) were *ḥamūla* lists, and all were connected with the Alignment, in one way or another![14] In frequent instances, local *ḥamūlas* or religious groups vote for a national party in parliamentary elections, in exchange for its financial and administrative support in local elections. It is precisely the large and influential *ḥamūlas* that are interested in enlarging their power by an alliance with a national party; and many national parties, for their part, prefer to ally themselves with these very *ḥamūlas*. To cite one example out of many: in the 1965 elections for the municipal council in Acre, one of the lists of candidates obtained two seats solely on the merit of its alliance with the Alignment. True enough, such local lists seldom stress their ties with a national party, preferring to emphasize their concern with local matters. In very numerous instances, the personal and local interests are more important than the ideological approach—in the eyes of both candidates and voters. In many Arab localities, the coexistence of religious communities is an added factor in the fragmenting of local lists; but the religious element is not an indispensable condition for this fragmentation. Thus in the Little Triangle, which is entirely

[13] Mansour, in *ha-Areṣ*, 24 Dec. 1965.
[14] Mansour, ibid. 22 Apr. 1966.

Muslim, the number of lists for local elections is high, compared to other Arab areas. The cause lies in the relative strength of the *ḥamūla* structure in the Little Triangle and its contentious spirit. For example, in the largest village in the Triangle, Umm al-Faḥm, the whole population is Muslim and consists of about thirty *ḥamūlas*. In the 1965 elections, 23 lists competed for membership in the local council; in several cases families within the *ḥamūlas* rivalled with one another. In Umm al-Faḥm, again, it was difficult to form a local council after the 1965 elections, as a number of persons heading the various lists insisted on retaining for themselves the chairmanship of the local council.[15] This phenomenon may be observed in other Arab villages as well. If anything, the rift within *ḥamūlas* increases between one local election to the next, because of inter-family conflicts, centring on competition for the chairmanship of the local council. Thus in the elections held for the Arab municipal and local councils in 1959, 199 lists of candidates competed; in those of 1965 there were 345 lists.[16] This increase is only partially explained by the rise in the number of Arab local councils. It is related also to personal mobility among the lists and to list mobility among the political parties. In Ṭīra, for instance, a person who had appeared in the 1955 local elections on a local list reappeared in 1959 as connected with MAPAM, and in 1965 as sponsored by the National Religious Party. Another candidate in Ṭīra appeared in 1955 on a list allied with MAPAI, in 1959 with National Religious Party, and in 1965 in the List of Peace sponsored by RAFĪ. Even the order of the candidates' names, including that of its leaders, changes considerably from one local election to the next.

(*c*) Lists which neither belong to *ḥamūlas* and religious communities, nor are identified with any political party, are usually of a personal character, and are often formed as a result of a clash within the locality itself. In most cases, such personal lists do not obtain a seat in the local council, but their presence may raise a storm of debate and thereby cause the vote to be split among more lists than previously. Personal lists are established, usually by families of marginal status in the village, or by groups of youngsters wishing to demonstrate their independence. Infrequently, such a list gains the election of a candidate on a local council, as occurred in Yafī' in the 1964 elections. In this case, the person elected held the casting vote between the adherents of MAPAI and those of MAQĪ in the local council, and his siding with the MAQĪ faction gave it a majority.

[15] Mansour, ibid. 1 Apr. 1965.

[16] Israel, *The Arab local councils*, xvi (Feb. 1967), 10.

Generally, overall Arab participation in local elections was even higher, relatively, than in parliamentary elections, approximating to 90 per cent. Only in rare instances did any village register a lower participation in local than in parliamentary elections; in those cases, the cause appeared to be rivalry between *ḥamūlas*. The following table presents data illustrating participation:

Arab Local Elections, 1959–65

Locality	Council activated on	No. of members in the council		No. of competing lists		No. of lists which won seats		Participation of voters* (per cent)	
		1959	*1965*	*1959*	*1965*	*1959*	*1965*	*1959*	*1965*
Nazareth	1934	15	15	12	10	9	4	84	85
Shafā 'Amr	1934	9	9	8	11	6	7	91	94
Kafr Kamā	7 Sept. 1950	7	7	6	6	5	4	87	94
Abū Ghōsh	27 Dec. 1950	7	7	9	7	6	5	90	87·5
Dāliyat al-Karmil	25 Feb. 1951	9	9	13	8	7	5	94	95·5
'Isfiyya	25 Feb. 1951	9	9	12	9	8	5	89	95·5
Furaydīs	31 Mar. 1952	7	7	4	3	2	3	95	97·5
Bāqa al-Gharbiyya	8 May 1952	11	11	7	15	4	7	94·5	92·5
Ṭaiyyba	8 May 1952	15	13	12	9	8	7	95	91
Ṭīra	8 May 1952	15	11	14	11	9	6	94	92
Kafr Yāṣīf	1 Nov. 1952	9	9	5	8	5	5	96·5	94
Rāma	28 Oct. 1954	13	11	10	8	7	7	74	80
Qalansawa	5 Apr. 1955	9	9	7	10	6	6	97	91
Tamrā	26 May 1955	11	11	4	11	4	6	87	95
Mughār	4 Oct. 1956	9	9	12	19	7	—	89	90
Jaljūliyya	18 Jan. 1957	9	9	5	10	4	6	94	94
Ma'īlyā	12 Dec. 1957	9	9	9	9	4	7	89	94
al-Buqay'a	27 Feb. 1958	13	9	8	11	8	6	90	93·5
Kafr Qara'	1 Sept. 1958	9	9†	13	12	8	8	97	94
Kafr Qāsim	14 May 1959	9	9	7	13	7	6	97	97·5
Jatt	8 Dec. 1959	9	9	11	12	7	6	96	93·5
Ṭur'ān	17 Dec. 1959	9	9	6	11	6	4	93	97
Yirkā	18 Dec. 1959	9	9	3	11	3	3	26	85
Mashhad	12 May 1960	—	7	—	6	—	4	—	95
Umm al-Faḥm	2 June 1960	—	15	—	23	—	13	—	88
Iksāl	1 Aug. 1960	—	7	—	8	—	4	—	86
Yafī'	7 Dec. 1960	—	9	—	5	—	4	—	92
I'blīn	15 Dec. 1960	—	11	—	10	—	5	—	93·5
Dabbūriyya	9 May 1961	—	7	—	9	—	3	—	94
Jisr al-Zarqā'	9 Nov. 1961	—	7	—	2	—	2	—	90
Kafr Bara	3 Jan. 1963	—	5	—	6	—	4	—	98
Jish	26 Mar. 1963	—	7	—	5	—	3	—	89·5
Abū Sinān	16 Feb. 1964	—	7	—	7	—	6	—	93
Beyt-Jān	26 June 1964	—	9‡	—	11	—	9	—	93
Kafr Mandā§	9 Oct. 1964	—	—	—	—	—	—	—	—
Majd al-Kurūm	20 Oct. 1964	—	9	—	8	—	4	—	93
'Ayn Māhil	30 Oct. 1964	—	7	—	5	—	4	—	94
Fassūṭa	25 July 1965	—	9	—	6	—	6	—	94

* In rounded figures.
† Actually the elections were not held in 1965 but on 17 Nov. 1964.
‡ Actually the elections were held on 5 May 1964.
§ Since the inhabitants refused to take part in the local elections and submitted no lists of candidates, no elections could be held; the local council which had been appointed by the Minister of the Interior remained in office.

Source: Based on material in Israel, *The Arab local councils*, xvi (Feb. 1967), 11. At the time there were two other appointed local councils, in 'Arrāba and Sakhnayn, where no elections were held in 1965. Another local council was appointed in Ḥurfaysh later in Feb. 1967.

The table shows the heavy participation of the Arabs in local elections, both in the two municipal and in the thirty-six local councils already activated up to November 1965, as well as the relatively large number of competing lists of candidates. One may add that the electoral campaigns for the Arab local councils are more distinguished by bitter vituperation against opponents than reasoned presentation of the lists' platforms. Personal attacks abound, with defamation the main characteristic.

4. *Some Case Studies of Local Elections*[17]

(*a*) *Bāqa al-Gharbiyya* (Muslims). This is one of the most prosperous villages in the Little Triangle. It has developed considerably since the establishment of the State of Israel. The industrious farmers, assisted by neighbouring Jewish settlements, have visibly improved their agriculture. Bāqa al-Gharbiyya has become the handicrafts manufacturing and commercial centre of its surroundings; the village even has a factory for canned fruit, one of the few industrial enterprises in the Arab villages.[18] Its first local council was appointed by the Minister of the Interior on 8 May 1952. The 11 members of the council were nominated after due consultation with various personalities in the village. Another local council was elected on 26 July 1955, and out of its 15 members, 8 had served in the appointed local council. A new council, elected on 3 November 1959, was composed of 11 members, 4 of whom had already served in the former council. On 2 November 1965, again, an 11-man local council was elected. Remarkably, although personal changes occur in these elections, the lists of candidates represent the same *ḥamūlas*, and usually their leaders remain on the list. Characteristically, none of the national parties participated in the local elections in this village (though they might have supported their local allies). The only exceptions were MAQĪ in 1959 and RAQAḤ in 1965. Both failed to gain even one seat in the local council, more evidence—if this proof be needed—of the strong influence of the *ḥamūlas*.

(*b*) *Ṭīra* (Muslims). Although in Ṭīra, also, the whole population is Muslim, the history of local elections differs from that in Bāqa al-Gharbiyya. Until the six-days' war in 1967, Ṭīra lay right on the border with the Kingdom of Jordan; about 50 per cent of its lands were within Israel, 20 per cent in the no-man's-land, and the rest in Jordan. Some lands belonging to absentee landowners were handed to neighbouring *kibbūtzīm*. In consequence the property of the

[17] Most of the statistical data are based on various publications of the CBS.
[18] Cf. Maḥmūd Bayādse in *al-Mirṣād*, 11 Sept. 1963.

ḥamūlas decreased, and as a result competition between them grew sharper. There are 16 *ḥamūlas* in Ṭīra, with about 100–550 persons in each. In fact, the real competition in local elections takes place between the heads of the more important *ḥamūlas*. In the 1955 local elections all seats were obtained by 3 of the local lists; in 1959 15 local councillors were elected—one on the slate of the National Religious Party, and all others on 8 local lists; in 1965 the candidates of the National Religious Party and RAQAḤ failed, and the 11-member local council went to 6 local lists.

(*c*) *'Isfiyya* (Druzes). The local council of 'Isfiyya was among the first activated in Israel. Its chairman, Labīb Abū Rukn, was later an MK (in the fourth *Kneset*). The local council has jurisdiction over an area of about 2,100 dunams,[19] and in recent years the Minister of the Interior has enlarged this area by adding farming land to it. The residents of 'Isfiyya subsist on farming (including the tobacco crop), or work in Haifa or its neighbourhood; many of them have served in the Israeli army. The first local council was appointed in 1951, and six and a half years later elections were held. Out of the 9 councillors elected in October 1957, only one was connected with a national political party, *Aḥdūt ha-'avōda*, all the other 8 representing local lists. In the 1959 local elections, 12 lists competed; 4 out of the 9-member council had already served in the former. In 1965 9 lists competed; out of the 9 local councillors, only 3 or 4 were identified with the Alignment, which in consequence formed the opposition in the 'Isfiyya local council. This was possibly related to the fact that almost all councillors elected in 'Isfiyya in 1965 were relatively young, born in the 1920s or 1930s—an uncommon feature in Arab local councils.

(*d*) *Dāliyat al-Karmil* (Druzes). This is the largest Druze village in Israel; about 200 Muslims live there, too. Like 'Isfiyya, this is one of the earliest established local councils in Israel. The village numbers approximately 4,000 inhabitants; its area of jurisdiction is about 2,000 dunams, most of it farming land. The villagers have the same sources of livelihood as those in 'Isfiyya. Dāliyat al-Karmil, however, may be considered a model of a well-developed Druze village. It has been connected to the country-wide water system and electricity network, and has prospered economically. The first 5-man local council was appointed in 1951 and another was elected in August 1957. In these elections the most surprising result was that a new local list, the Free Youths, succeeded in obtaining 2 seats on the 9-man council, i.e. half of the 4 new places. The list was led by a young Druze, who

[19] A dunam is slightly less than a quarter of an acre.

had previously served as an officer in the Israeli army. Although the Free Youths claimed an affinity with MAPAI, the latter disowned them and supported another list, which however obtained only 1 seat. Candidates identified with the National Religious Party and *Ḥerūt*, also, gained seats on the local council. In 1959 13 lists competed; 5 former members were elected; among the new members, 1 was identified with MAPAM, another with the National Religious Party, and 2 others with local lists. The situation was completely changed in the 1965 local elections. The number of competing lists fell to 8. Of these only 3 were local, out of which one only obtained a seat. Five others were lists of national parties; of these the National Religious Party failed, but GAḤAL obtained 3 seats on the local council, a list allied with the Alignment 2, MAPAM 2 (possibly thanks to connexions with *kibbūtzīm* in the vicinity), and RAFĪ 1. The large support for the oppositionist GAḤAL was probably a consequence of local resentment at the fact that none of the members of the respected Ḥalabī family had been nominated to the Druze court.

(*e*) *Rāma* (mainly Christians). This village, near the Safad–Acre road, is distinguished by its high level of education and standard of living, expressed in the home, dress, and general behaviour. Although six religious communities live together in Rāma, only the Greek Orthodox and Greek Catholic have a decisive role in local politics, and all other interests veer around them accordingly. This applies to the other, smaller Christian communities; to the few Muslims, chiefly refugees from near-by villages, who have very little influence in Rāma; and to the Druzes, who though not few, are divided into two rival factions. The Greek Orthodox community is the largest in the village; it is still ruled by the older generation, while the 'revolt of the youngsters' is mainly expressed in a tendency towards a communist vote. This community hankers after local leadership, arguing that it is the largest and that it had led the village in the days of British rule in Palestine and that the first chairman of the local council had been Greek Orthodox. Against them, the claim of the Greek Catholic community for leadership is based on the special standing of Eliyās Nakhla, an MK who is also a resident of the village and is, moreover, supported by Archbishop George al-Ḥakīm. In this community, too, a number of youths are striving for power. A local council was appointed in Rāma in 1954. The first elected local council, in 1959, had 13 members. Among the competing lists was one allied with MAPAI (which obtained 3 seats); MAQĪ (2 seats) and MAPAM (none). All others were local lists, characteristically divided on religious lines and the local interests of Rāma's religious communities. This feature also influences the composition of the pro-MAPAI, MAQĪ, and MAPAM slates of candidates. In the newly-elected local council, there were 6 Greek Orthodox, 2 Greek Catholics, 2 Latins, and 3 Druzes. The Greek Catholic councillors refused to co-operate with the chairman of the local council. Bitter conflicts ensued, connected with strife between the religious communities, jealousy between the families, and divergence of opinion about the local budget. Many of these conflicts still continue.

(*f*) *Mughār* (mixed). This appears to be a typical example of a mixed village: about 2,300 Druzes, 1,500 Christians, and 600 Muslims reside together. Unlike many other Arab villages, Mughār has been only partially developed. Since 1948 the inhabitants have been offered such attractive prices for their land that they have sold much of it; nowadays, approximately 90 per cent of the villagers make a living by working outside Mughār. The village has had a local council since 1956, when thirteen of the villagers were appointed. These were *ḥamūla* elders, who probably considered their nomination as a signal honour. The first elected local council, in 1959, included four former councillors; the new ones were from the same social strata. Again, they all saw their new role chiefly as a matter of prestige, not attending the meetings of the local council (which was seldom convened, anyway). Not surprisingly, social and political dissatisfaction among the village youths led to agitation for reform. The common denominator among these youths was opposition to the rule of their elders and a desire for change. Some of them (among the Druzes) had served in the Israeli army; others had graduated from high schools; many had independent views. A number reasoned that since the village elders were the allies of the Government, the youths ought to join the opposition; these drew nearer to the communists, a few even adhering to the local cell of the party. Despite their identical interests, all negotiations for a common electoral campaign by the youths failed. A total of nineteen lists ran in the 1965 elections to the local council. As a result, no list reached the minimum necessary of votes to obtain seats on the local council. New elections were, therefore, held in 1966, with greater co-operation between the candidates. The local council then elected included a communist, the Druze Amīn ʿAsāqila.[20]

(*g*) *Yafīʿ* (Muslims and Christians). Yafīʿ (or Yāfat al-Nāṣira) is a large village on the Nazareth–Haifa road, less than a mile west of Nazareth. Of its population of 3,000, more than 2,000 are Muslims

[20] Sh. Rapapōrt in *Maʿarīv*, 12 Nov. 1965; Dar in *Davar*, 15 July 1966.

and the rest Christians. The sources of livelihood are agriculture and work outside the village. Yafī' has 1 mosque, 3 churches for the 3 Christian denominations—Greek Catholics, Greek Orthodox, and Latins—2 primary schools, piped water, and electricity. In 1960 a local council was appointed, the majority of whose members were politically close to MAPAI. The work of the council was anything but smooth, as its members constantly quarrelled. The villagers did their best to hinder the council's activity, by complaining to various Government offices, disobeying orders, and refusing to pay taxes. The agitation was probably assisted by MAQĪ, on the one hand, and on the other by Arab refugees from two neighbouring villages, Ma'lūl and Majdal, who had moved to Yafī' and now formed about a third of its population. Disorders in the local council, concerning the payment of taxes and the administration of funds,[21] repeatedly brought about its disperal, until the Minister of the Interior called for elections to a nine-man local council, on 24 November 1964. The results were unprecedented. Three lists allied with MAPAI obtained four seats; the Democratic Front (i.e. MAQĪ) also got four seats; while a ninth fell to a list formed by the above refugees. The last mentioned thus held a decisive vote in the Yafī' local council, which they used to elect the head of the Democratic Front to the chairmanship. The chairman, As'ad Yūsuf Kināna, a building worker and a member of MAQĪ's district committee in Nazareth, had studied in the Soviet Union.[22] He was the only communist chairman of a local council in Israel. MAQĪ rejoiced immensely, interpreting this as 'the will of the people'.[23] In fact, there were several contributory causes for the communist victory: from its strong communist organization in adjacent Nazareth, MAQĪ had led a ceaseless propaganda campaign in Yafī'; its representatives had opened a co-operative shop there and a club in which discussions were held. MAPAI, for its part, suffered from the struggle between the three lists allied with it, which frequently attacked one another rather than their rivals. The formation of the Refugee List is noteworthy too. Its main demand was the grant of retroactive building permits for the new homes they had built without any legal authorization, a matter with which MAQĪ could agree more easily than MAPAI: the MAPAI-sponsored Government was reluctant to create a precedent; MAQĪ however was practically sure that it would hardly ever reach a position of authority

[21] As mentioned in the report of the State Comptroller for the years 1960–5, summarized in *ha-Areṣ*, 18 Nov. 1965.

[22] Details in Karmel's article in *Ma'arīv*, 7 Jan. 1966.

[23] The view expressed by Ḥabībī, in *al-Ittiḥād* & *Qōl ha-'am*, both of 27 Nov. 1964.

to grant the permits, anyway.[24] It is interesting to note that the ratio in the Yafī' local council did not change in the November 1965 elections (though the communist chairman of the local council was overthrown later, when one of RAQAḤ's councillors went over to the local lists allied with the Alignment).

(*h*) *Nazareth.* As the largest Arab town in Israel (about 30,000 inhabitants), the centre of Galilee, and the focus of much of the political and cultural life of the Arabs in the State, special significance attaches to Nazareth. Its focal role in Arab politics will be dealt with in a later chapter; at this point discussion is restricted to its place in local government. Since Arab Nazareth has its own electoral polls, completely separate from neighbouring Jewish Nazareth, it is comparatively easy to note the main election trends. The local elections reflect, even more than the parliamentary ones, the socio-political division in Arab Nazareth (designated here simply as Nazareth). Slightly more than half its population is Christian, and the rivalry for local rule in Nazareth dates from the time of the British. The Christians are subdivided into a number of denominations. Practically every political current finds some ripple in Nazareth internal politics. The struggle for the fifteen seats of the municipal council is symptomatic of strong political awareness; the interest in politics is fostered by the relatively high level of education and large number of TV sets. All political parties in Israel are well aware that a majority in Nazareth's municipal council is a position of power in regard to the Arab minority in Israel: the political mood in Nazareth determines, to a large extent, the political behaviour of the Arabs in Israel. Consequently, political strife in Nazareth is partly on ideological lines and partly results from a desire for material benefits. Some of these characteristics are illustrated in municipal elections. Nazareth has had municipal status since 1934. In Israel, the first municipal elections were held on 12 April 1954; the political and religious division is manifest in the results (see p. 171).

Some of the candidates were sponsored by MAPAI. The relatively large communist vote is characteristic of elections in Nazareth, both municipal and parliamentary.[25] This was among the reasons that impelled the nine non-communist local councillors to form a municipal coalition between themselves, to direct Nazareth's affairs, while the six communists formed the opposition in the council. The municipal coalition itself was torn by conflicting views, inspired by

[24] However, see As'ad Yūsuf's interpretation, when interviewed by Mansour, in *ha-Arçș*, 13 May 1966.

[25] As explained above, pp. 83, 87 ff., 141.

the interests of the various religious communities. An added ingredient was the fact that almost every one of these councillors considered himself worthy of being mayor (i.e. chairman of the municipal council).

Nazareth Municipal Elections, 1954

No. and nature of lists	*Valid votes*	*Percentage*	*No. of seats in municipal council*
3 Muslim lists	1,819	23·0	4
2 Greek Orthodox lists	904	11·5	2
1 Greek Catholic list	1,877	23·7	3
1 Communist list	3,034	38·4	6
1 MAPAM list	269	3·4	—
Total: 8 lists	7,903	100·0	15

In the 1959 elections, MAQĪ lost ground in both local and parliamentary elections,[26] and this decline was evident in Nazareth, too. The 15 municipal councillors then elected were divided as follows: 11 allied to MAPAI or sympathetic to it, 1 MAPAM, and 3 communists. MAPAM's propaganda in 1959 was more aggressive, and largely directed against MAQĪ; apparently both MAPAI and MAPAM gained from MAQĪ's losses in Nazareth.

After the 1965 municipal elections,[27] a rather intriguing situation arose. The usual competition of local lists, affiliated to the religious communities, was supplemented by the more active participation of national parties. In addition to local lists allied with the Alignment, and those of MAPAM and RAQAḤ, there were also lists affiliated to the National Religious Party and to RAFĪ. All this brought about an intensification in electoral propaganda. The only differences between the six lists allied with the Alignment were denominational (Muslims versus Christians), or geographical (a list for the Eastern quarter in Nazareth), or social class (a list for rich Christians versus another named the Young Workers). RAQAḤ was led by Fu'ād Jābir Khūrī, one of the first Christian intellectuals in Nazareth to embrace communism, who also belonged to one of the best-liked families in town. RAFĪ supported a list headed by the previously mentioned lawyer Nimr al-Hawārī; initially he acknowledged his connexion with RAFĪ, then claimed his list was independent. The

[26] As explained above, p. 126.

[27] Further details by Mansour, in *ha-Areṣ*, 24 Oct. 1965.

National Religious Party appeared with a list openly bearing the party's name; it was led by members of the Mazzawī and al-Ḥā'ik families, influential within their own Greek Catholic community.

The large number of lists further weakened small groups with no real hold on the voting population in Nazareth. The weaker lists could not get even one seat, and the votes they had received were therefore lost. This played into the hands of the stronger lists, who thus succeeded in placing more candidates on the municipal council. As a result, political polarization in Nazareth's municipal council was almost complete: two lists allied with the Alignment obtained 7 seats, RAQAḤ another 7, and MAPAM 1. The communist success in Nazareth was even more impressive than in 1954. In 1965 RAQAḤ received 4,103, out of a total of 11,096 valid votes. This was an aspect of RAQAḤ's overall success among the Israeli Arabs in the parliamentary and local elections of 2 November 1965, when it succeeded in presenting itself in the image of a nationalist, all-Arab party.[28] Quite possibly, the support of the Egyptian radio for RAQAḤ had had some effect too on Nazareth Arabs. Although MAPAM obtained only one seat on the municipal council, its position was a strong one, as it held a casting vote in any future coalition (for, obviously, the Alignment and RAQAḤ could not work together). The Alignment had been deprived of its majority in the municipal council because of the votes lost by the minor lists allied with it; but its position was still strong. While it was reasonable to expect MAPAM to form a municipal coalition with the Alignment in Nazareth, as it was participating in the national coalition Government,[29] MAPAM had also to take into account *local considerations*. Its whole campaign in Nazareth had been directed against the former mayor and the Alignment's star candidate, Sayf al-Dīn Zu'bī; now it could not agree to enter a municipal coalition headed by the same Sayf al-Dīn Zu'bī. Its condition for a joint municipal coalition with the Alignment was, therefore, that some other Alignment nominee from among the municipal councillors be mayor. To this the Alignment could not agree, as Sayf al-Dīn Zu'bī's list numbered five councillors, and he had been a trusted and reliable ally of the party. To RAQAḤ's offer of a municipal coalition,[30] MAPAM countered by demanding that its own councillor be mayor; and RAQAḤ, naturally, did not at first accept this. Later, however, it agreed, and a MAPAM–RAQAḤ

[28] e.g., *al-Ittiḥād*, 8 Oct. 1965.

[29] Together with other partners, viz. the National Religious Party and the Independent Liberals.

[30] Cf. *al-Ittiḥād*, 12 Nov. 1965.

coalition ruled Nazareth's municipal council from December 1965 to March 1966. The mayor was MAPAM's 'Abd al-'Azīz Zu'bī.[31] The period was one of constant quarrelling in the municipal council, with the new mayor publicly deploring the town's financial situation[32] and calling on the townspeople for support, in a large number of handbills.[33] After 'Abd al-'Azīz Zu'bī's resignation,[34] a stalemate was reached again. With no result in sight, the Minister of the Interior used his authority to disperse the municipal council of Nazareth and to appoint a committee of officials to manage the town's affairs until new elections could be held.[35]

New munipal elections were held in November 1966. There was little difference between the competing groups, except for the fact that the number of lists allied with the Alignment had decreased from six to four.[36] This was a lesson learnt from the 1965 municipal elections; none the less, these four lists constantly attacked one another, attempting to impress the electorate by their independent views.[37] However, unlike those of 1965, the Nazareth municipal elections of 1966 were not held at the same time as the *Kneset* elections. Excitement had decreased, and voter participation fell from 86·4 to 81·4 per cent.[38] Despite RAQAḤ's vocal propaganda[39] and the increase of its support to 4,274 votes, it obtained only 6 seats on the municipal council, compared with the allies of the Alignment, who obtained 7 (and 4,465 votes, instead of 4,477 in 1965), and with MAPAM, which obtained 2 seats (and 1,145 votes, instead of 1 seat and 701 votes in 1965). Thus the main gainer in Nazareth was MAPAM, which doubled its seats on the municipal council at the expense of RAQAḤ. One reason lay in public weariness of the extremist propaganda of both RAQAḤ and the allies of the Alignment, while MAPAM succeeded in presenting itself as a middle-of-the-road political party.[40] Another reason lay in the greater relevance of the employment supplied by MAPAM and its *kibbūtzīm* during the 1966 economic recession. Again, protracted negotiations were held[41] between the Alignment and MAPAM, the latter again agreeing to support any Alignment candidate for mayor except Sayf al-Dīn

[31] Mansour, in *ha-Areṣ*, 7 Jan. 1966.
[32] Details ibid. & 30 Jan. 1966.
[33] Mansour, in *ha-Areṣ*, 25 Mar. 1966.
[34] Cf. ibid. 22 Mar. 1966; and Elgat, in *Ma'arīv*, 25 Mar. 1966.
[35] See Mansour, in *ha-Areṣ*, 28 Sept. 1966.
[36] One of these was allied with both the Alignment and the National Religious Party (see Mansour, ibid. 20 Nov. 1966; cf. Karmel, in *Ma'arīv*, 7 Nov. 1966).
[37] Mansour, in *ha-Areṣ*, 20 Nov. 1966.
[38] Cf. *ha-Areṣ*, 27 Nov. 1966.
[39] Cf. *'Al ha-Mishmar*, 6 Nov. 1966. See also Mansour, in *ha-Areṣ*, 28 Oct. 1966.
[40] Acc. to article on Nazareth in *ha-'Ōlam ha-zeh*, 30 Nov. 1966, 12.
[41] Mansour, in *ha-Areṣ*, 18 Dec. 1966.

Zu'bī. An added reason for MAPAM's opposition to Sayf al-Dīn Zu'bī was the tense relations between him and his relative, MAPAM's 'Abd al-'Azīz Zu'bī, both rivals in Nazareth and in the *Kneset* (both were then MKs).[42] MAPAM again threatened that it would form a municipal coalition with RAQAḤ.[43] At last Sayf al-Dīn Zu'bī withdrew his claims, and the second councillor on his list, Mūsà Kteylī, was elected mayor by the municipal council in mid-January 1967, with 'Abd al-'Azīz Zu'bī from MAPAM his deputy. The new mayor,[44] it should be noted, is an unusual figure among Israeli mayors, Arab or Jewish. He is not a politician, but a retired police officer who became a prosperous grain merchant; his brother is a judge. It is likely that his non-political career has assisted his relative popularity with the Alignment and MAPAM at one and the same time. In 1967 the municipal coalition in Nazareth numbered, however, only eight: one of those elected on a local list, allied with the Alignment, crossed over to join RAQAḤ in the opposition. Such changes of allegiance, though not typical of Arab municipal councillors, do occur and serve to illustrate the superficiality of political loyalties among some of the local representatives.

5. *Political Parties and Local Elections*

The insignificance of the ideological element in the propaganda for local elections in the Arab villages is manifest even in the names of the various slates of candidates: Brotherhood, Co-operation and Brotherhood, Muslim Fraternity, Renaissance, Renaissance and Independence, Reform, Reform and Light, Honesty and Work, Development, Service to the People, Co-operation and Reward, Equality, Union, Peace and Prosperity, Life, Awakening, Hope, and others. While relatively few Arab lists, then generally allied with national Jewish parties ran in parliamentary elections, many more competed in local elections. Only a few of these local lists appeared under the name of a national political party, such as MAPAM, MAQĪ, or RAQAḤ and, in rarer intances, the National Religious Party, MAPAI, or RAFĪ. Even in the latter cases, the participation of a national party in the local electoral contest did not prevent a local list allied to that party from competing too. Fairly often, lists of candidates based on *ḥamūla* connexions campaigned against each other for the local council, even if they were all supported by the same national political party; they obstinately refused, for personal

[42] *Ma'arīv*, 21 Dec. 1966, relates that they were not even on speaking terms.
[43] Ibid. 18 Jan. 1967.
[44] Details on the new mayor in *ha-Areṣ*, 27 Jan. 1967.

reasons, to unite in one list. The pro-Alignment Arabic daily *al-Yawm* (19 Nov. 1965) wrote a few days before the 1965 local elections: 'Negotiations for establishing local councils among the Arabs emphasize family ties, not the general interest.' Although this estimate is mainly applicable to the Arab villages, we have seen that it is at least partially relevant to Nazareth.

The rivalry among the *ḥamūlas* has regularly been exploited by various political parties, which have initiated ties with *ḥamūla* elders. Negotiations have proved fruitful for both sides, particularly in view of the fact that local and parliamentary elections have frequently been held on the same day. This occurred, e.g. in 1955, 1959, and 1965. Political bargaining and friendly horse-trading have led to agreements, the usual pattern of which is as follows: the national party is promised local votes in the parliamentary elections, and in exchange it undertakes to support and finance its friends in their electoral campaign for the local council. In consequence, in almost every single case, the slates of candidates of the national parties have received a larger vote for the *Kneset* elections than for the local ones. These election bargains serve to confuse the real picture of the political alignments in many Arab villages and render difficult the identification and interpretation of various trends. Among the general characteristics are the emphasis on local matters (even more evident in elections to the local councils than to the *Kneset*) and the continuation of *ḥamūla* and personal rivalry, which impedes local factions from making permanent alliances with the national parties. The opportunist and *ad hoc* character of these alliances explains their frailty; the change in the social structure of the village, altering the balance of power among the *ḥamūlas* (some of which are breaking up), ensures the temporariness of such alliances.

(*a*) *The Alignment.* The major characteristic of the Alignment (previously MAPAI) in Arab as well as Jewish localities is its ubiquity. Its presence is expressed by well-planned and adaptable propaganda, both from its headquarters and its numerous representatives. This propaganda varies in emphasis according to area. In small villages and some Bedouin camps where MAPAI prestige is very high, it is regarded as the representative of the traditionally-revered Government; in larger villages and towns, it was to appeal also to the politically conscious, in competition with other parties. Generally, however, the Alignment (and, formerly, MAPAI) has pursued the following line: as it is going to remain the main factor in future Government coalitions, the Alignment will assist those localities which had voted for it in parliamentary and local elections.

The psychological approach of this reasoning is well chosen; it attempts to create an image identifying the Alignment with the Government, hence to be supported, with expectations of recompense. Those *ḥamūla* elders who decide to accept this reasoning maintain that they will be better able to influence the Alignment in the local interest *from within the Alignment* than from without. If they are rewarded for their support, they never mention it (though their opponents do). The Alignment has also been accused of putting indirect pressure on the prospective electorate, but this charge has never been substantiated.

(*b*) *MAQĪ* (*RAQAḤ*). The Communist Party is in a totally different position, often the opposite of the Alignment. Its greatest difficulty is to penetrate into the smaller villages and Bedouin camps, where the Alignment is proportionally strongest and the *ḥamūla* elders hold undisputed sway over the voters. As a result, in the 1965 elections to the local councils RAQAḤ campaigned in only fifteen Arab localities.[45] These were the relatively more developed villages and the two Arab towns, where the communists could hope to appeal to the young and the politically-aware intellectuals. In Nazareth, particularly, the leadership of MAQĪ, later of RAQAḤ, has proved to be dynamic and resourceful. RAQAḤ's branch in Nazareth is led by Fu'ād Khūrī, a veteran communist, and Tawfīq Zayd, who has studied in the Soviet Union. The communist line, in Nazareth and elsewhere, is the oppositionist approach: in man-to-man discussion, in a club if available, otherwise in coffee-houses, to preach the need for radical reforms, decrying the present situation. Written materials are employed less frequently, but *al-Ittiḥād* and other party organs often follow the same violent line, supporting the communist candidates as the only ones sincerely desirous and capable of effecting the expected change.[46] Nevertheless, the communist vote is constantly lower in the Arab local elections than in parliamentary elections—the influence of the *ḥamūlas* often resulting in a split vote.

(*c*) *MAPAM*. The main line of MAPAM in electioneering for the local councils was to present itself in the image of the true friend of the Arabs and, later, as a middle-of-the-road party, between the two extremes—the Alignment and the communists. Party members and sympathizers, arguing in house meetings and via *al-Mirṣād*, extolled MAPAM's day-to-day assistance to the Arab villages and Bedouin tribes. Country-wide results point to the fact that MAPAM's Arab vote was nevertheless noticeably lower in local elections than for the

[45] Acc. to *al-Ittiḥād*, 1 Oct. 1965.

[46] Examples ibid. 14 & 17 Sept., 8 & 12 Oct., & 1 Nov. 1965.

Kneset. This was particularly true of the larger Arab localities, where MAPAM had to deal with strong communist competition. Although MAPAM also campaigned against MAPAI (later the Alignment) its arch-rival remained MAQĪ (in 1965, RAQAḤ). MAPAM worked together with MAPAI (the Alignment) in Government coalitions. Socialist-minded MAPAM could hardly hope for considerable support from *ḥamūla* leaders and their adherents. Therefore, MAPAM directed most of its propaganda, in Arab localities, to intellectual youngsters and to workers—thus colliding with the communists. In electioneering for the *Kneset*, MAPAM always tries to enlist voting in every Arab (as well as Jewish) locality, for all these votes are credited to the party. In local elections, however, MAPAM presents a list of candidates, in its own name, only in those Arab localities where it stands a chance to gain at least one seat in the local council. In other areas the party bargains with one of the local lists for the electoral support in the *Kneset* campaign of that list and its close adherents, in return for which MAPAM assists its *ad hoc* allies in their electoral campaign to the local council. In the 1965 local elections MAPAM appeared (seemingly, for the first time) in family lists. For example, it openly supported the family list of Qāsim Zayd, MAPAM's representative in Umm al-Faḥm (who won a seat on the local council).

(*d*) *The National Religious Party*. It is relatively easy to understand why this party wants the Arab vote for parliamentary elections. It is more difficult to grasp why it should strive for positions of power in the local councils of the minorities; possibly it desires a deeper penetration, to assist it in future electoral contests. The reasons why Arabs themselves support the party, both in parliamentary and local elections, are generally pragmatic rather than ideological. More bluntly, local Arab lists have needed financial help for their contest in the local elections. The fact that, in recent years, the Minister of the Interior has continuously been one of the leaders of the National Religious Party is also of some weight. Voters may have remembered that his office decides most matters connected with municipal and local government. Nevertheless, this party, like others, has received fewer Arab votes in local elections than for the *Kneset*. But it could still point out, in 1962, that its adherents counted the chairman of the local council in Jaljūliyya, two councillors in Ṭīra, and at least one representative each in the municipal council of Shafā 'Amr and the local councils in Kafr Qāsim, Tamrā, and Furaydīs.[47]

[47] Interview with Sam'ān Dā'ūd, a Christian representative of the National Religious Party, published in *ha-Areṣ*, 2 Mar. 1962.

(*e*) *GAḤAL*. This new political bloc, formed in 1965, has continued the policies of its two components, *Ḥerūt* and the Liberals. Therefore, it has addressed itself to the Arabs, in local as well as in parliamentary elections, on economic grounds. In this manner, it has attempted to dispel Arab suspicion of *Ḥerūt*'s militant ideology. In the 1965 local elections GAḤAL ran for election in six Arab villages and obtained seats on two local councils, those of Abū Ghōsh and Dāliyat al-Karmil; in Kafr Qāsim GAḤAL supported a candidate who appeared at the head of a *ḥamūla* list.

(*f*) *RAFĪ*. Similarly to GAḤAL, RAFĪ was a new political force in 1965, and likewise competed for the local councils only in those places where it had some hope of gaining election. In 1965 it generally campaigned through its allied Arab list, the List of Peace. The latter won—thanks to RAFĪ's support—seats on four local councils: Ṭīra, Ṭaiyyba, Dāliyat al-Karmil, and Buqay'a. In many cases RAFĪ and the List of Peace obtained approximately the same number of votes in parliamentary and local elections.

(*g*) *Others*. Other national political parties did not put forward candidates of their own in Arab local elections, but supported local lists in exchange for votes in the parliamentary elections.

THE ARABS IN TRADE UNION ELECTIONS

For a further comparison with parliamentary and local elections, one may refer to the Arab vote in the elections to the tenth congress of the Israeli trade union organization.[48] In Israel the trade union organization, or *Histadrūt*, exceeds the functions usually associated with such institutions: not only does it occupy a central place in the field of professional organization but it has a very important standing in economic life, with definite political implications. In many respects, it is a grey eminence behind the Government.

A few weeks before the 1965 *Kneset* and local elections, the *Histadrūt* held country-wide elections to its tenth national congress. The previous one had been in 1959, when the *Histadrūt* had been almost solely composed of Jews. The only non-Jews who had voted for the *Histadrūt* congress in 1959 were Druzes who had served in the Israeli army. In the intervening years, about 38,000 Arabs had joined the *Histadrūt* (5 per cent of the total membership). Many had voted in their trade unions. However, this was the first time that the Arabs

[48] See Weigert, ibid. 13 Sept. 1965, and Mansour, ibid. 16 Sept. 1965. For an appreciation of the *Histadrūt*'s role and importance in Israel, see Joseph Ben-David, 'Professionals and unions in Israel', *Industrial Relations* (Berkeley, Calif.), Oct. 1965, 48–66.

participated as full members in country-wide *Histadrūt* elections—a noteworthy occasion. The vote was divided among almost the same political parties which took part in the parliamentary contest, including a few with bourgeois orientations. Naturally, the number of voters was smaller than in the *Kneset* or local elections, as only *Histadrūt* members (who had paid their dues for at least three months) could participate, and not the whole adult population. Even so, more than 30,000 Arabs voted in the elections for the *Histadrūt*'s congress in 1965, in the two Arab towns and 100 other Arab localities, including eight Bedouin centres. Arab Nazareth features among the new workers' councils within the framework of the *Histadrūt* elected on that occasion.[49]

The Arab participation in the 1965 elections to the *Histadrūt* congress showed an increase in Arab strength within the trade unions. To a great extent, this was a result of the efforts invested by the *Histadrūt* in the Arab towns and villages: it had opened clinics in them as well as clubs, inaugurated handicrafts courses for Arab women and practical studies for boys and girls, sports, musical and dramatic activities for everyone—in addition to organizing the Arabs professionally, against exploitation.[50] In consequence, Arab membership in the *Histadrūt* grew rapidly after 1960, when they could join as full members.

Arab Membership in the Histadrūt

Date	*Arab members*	*Arabs and their families*	*Percentage of total Arab population in Israel*
Dec. 1960	21,246	49,029	20·5
Dec. 1963	30,900	71,302	26·0
Dec. 1964	34,959	82,054	28·7
Dec. 1965	39,564	93,896	31·3

Source: Shĕnatōn ha-histadrūt, iv: *1964-5*, pt 2, 311, and other *Histadrūt* publications.

All political parties in the *Histadrūt* campaigned energetically, not only because they desired positions of strength within the trade union organizations, but also because this electoral contest was regarded as a dress rehearsal for the November 1965 parliamentary and local elections which were to follow in a few weeks' time.

This applied to the Arab voters, too. Among them, three political

[49] *Shĕnatōn ha-histadrūt* (Histadrūt yearbook), iv: *1964–1965*, part 2, 311.

[50] Compare the articles of M. Bartal of MAPAI and Jamāl Mūsà of RAQAḤ, both in *Davar*, 9 Jan. 1966.

parties almost monopolized the electioneering: the Alignment, MAPAM, and RAQAḤ. All three had platforms emphasizing the equality of the Arab worker in employment, adequate salary and representation in all the *Histadrūt*'s institutions. However, while the Alignment stressed social improvements (such as better housing, education, clinics), MAPAM and RAQAḤ respectively emphasized political subjects (abolition of the military administration, cessation of political dismissals and of land expropriation). The Alignment worked more intensively than the others, largely through personal contacts, while RAQAḤ was least prepared, due to its problems of organization (as it had split from MAQĪ only a few weeks earlier). MAPAM employed a relatively moderate line, apparently preferring not to compete in extremism with RAQAḤ.[51]

In 1965 32,682 Arabs were eligible for the *Histadrūt*'s congress, making up 3·7 per cent of the total number of those entitled to vote.[52] Out of these, 30,288 Arabs, or about 90 per cent, actually voted. This heavy participation (compared with a country-wide average of 77·6 per cent) may be explained as follows: (1) this was the first occasion of Arab participation in country-wide *Histadrūt* elections; (2) Arabs appeared with Jews on the slates of candidates, not on separate ones; (3) appreciation for the *Histadrūt*'s beneficial activities in Arab localities could be expressed by voting; (4) some Arabs had to participate in the elections, since they were employed in the *Histadrūt*'s own enterprises. The votes were divided, regionally, as follows:

Arab Voting for 1965 Elections to Histadrūt *Congress (by regions)*

Region	*Votes cast*
Haifa and western Galilee	14,610
Nazareth and vicinity	7,250
The Little Triangle	5,370
Central region	2,615
The Negev	443
Total	30,288

Out of the above total, the count certified 28,651 valid votes of Arab electors, which had been cast for the following parties:

[51] See Y. Efrat in *'Al ha-Mishmar*, 29 Sept. 1965.

[52] Most statistical data which follow are based on the sources for the table on p. 179.

Arab Valid Votes, 1965 Elections to Histadrūt *Congress (by Parties)*

Party	*No. of votes*	*Percentage of Arab vote*
The Alignment	17,119	60·0
RAQAḤ	5,700	19·8
MAPAM	3,847	13·4
RAFĪ	911	3·1
GAḤAL	622	2·1
Independent Liberals	303	1·1
MAQĪ	149	0·5
Total	28,651	100·0

The distribution of the Arab vote in the *Histadrūt* elections confirms the general trend in the *Kneset* elections, i.e. that the Alignment (formerly MAPAI), the communists, and MAPAM, as political parties permanently active among the Arabs, receive the bulk of their vote. All election-eve parties together receive only the remainder—in the *Histadrūt* elections, a total of only 6·3 per cent of the Arab vote.

(*a*) *The Alignment* obtained 60 per cent of the Arab vote in the *Histadrūt* elections. This was relatively more than among the Jewish voters to the *Histradrūt*, as well as more than it was to receive a few weeks later in *Kneset* elections (together with its Arab allies, 50·1 per cent of the Arab country-wide vote). The reasons are obvious: in the *Kneset* elections, Arabs who were not *Histadrūt* members participated also; parties who had not shared in the *Histadrūt* elections competed for the *Kneset* (e.g. the National Religious Party, and This World) and attracted a portion of the Arab vote. The Alignment's signal success among the Arabs in the *Histadrūt* elections was probably owing to the identification of the *Histadrūt*'s beneficial activities in the Arab localities with MAPAI (the major force in the *Histadrūt*) and to a desire to support a successful alignment of MAPAI and *Aḥdūt ha-'avōda* (the latter also has been an influential factor in the *Histadrūt*). The overall success of the Alignment in these elections was reflected in the results in a number of important Arab localities. In eleven Arab villages in Eastern Galilee, the Alignment received about 61 per cent of the vote; in the Druze villages of

Dāliyat al-Karmil 52 per cent and 'Isfiyya 92 per cent. Most remarkable however were the results in the elections to the Workers' Council of Arab Nazareth. Despite communist strength there, the Alignment gained credit for having established a large '*Histadrūt* house', a well-appointed clinic, and a sports stadium. Out of the 3,896 *Histadrūt* members voting for the Workers' Council in Arab Nazareth, 3,770 votes were valid. Of these, the Alignment received 2,098 votes (55·6 per cent), RAQAḤ 1,105, MAPAM 563, and RAFĪ's List of Peace a mere 4 votes. Therefore, the Alignment had 12 out of 21 representatives on the Nazareth Workers' Council (RAQAḤ 6, MAPAM 3), and its veteran *Histadrūt* worker in Nazareth, George Sa'd, became its secretary.

(*b*) *RAQAḤ* entered the electoral contest to the *Histadrūt* and the various workers' councils without due preparation, since it had hardly reorganized after the 1965 rift in the communist camp in Israel. Nevertheless, RAQAḤ succeeded in maintaining the communist position as second only to the Alignment; despite its relative failure in a number of localities—chiefly, in Arab Nazareth—its overall achievement in the *Histadrūt* elections was impressive. Much of RAQAḤ's electoral support was a protest vote, based on its self-presentation as a nationalist all-Arab party, an image which it developed still further in the subsequent *Kneset* and local elections a few weeks later.

(*c*) *MAPAM*, although only in third place among the Arab voters in the *Histadrūt* elections, was relatively successful, at the expense of the communists and the election-eve parties. Its success was due to the moderate image it had created, between the extremes of the Alignment and RAQAḤ, and to its struggle for better employment conditions, e.g. on behalf of the Arab building workers (persistent demands for a seven-hour workday). Personal relations between MAPAM's *kibbūtzīm* and adjacent Arab localities helped too.

(*d*) *Other parties*, i.e. election-eve, received only marginal votes for the *Histadrūt* elections. For instance, the List of Peace, allied with the newly-formed RAFĪ, received a number of votes in Ṭīra, which was the residence of the list's chief candidate Manṣūr. In the subsequent *Kneset* elections, RAFĪ and the List of Peace improved their electoral support among the Arabs (thanks to connexions with various *ḥamūlas*), as did RAQAḤ and MAPAM. Indeed, the 10 per cent difference between the Alignment's 60 per cent Arab vote for the *Histadrūt* and its 50·1 per cent for the *Kneset* (albeit the latter among a wider Arab electorate) was divided between RAQAḤ, RAFĪ, and the National Religious Party.

Among the most noteworthy feature of the 1965 *Histadrūt* elections is the fact that, despite certain differences in the proportional division of the Arab vote, compared with parliamentary elections, the same sequence in the preferences of the Arab electorate remained unchanged. The relatively large vote for the Alignment and MAPAM in these *Histadrūt* elections seems to indicate a measure of acquiescence in the *status quo*, and that alienation is less widespread among the Arab workers than the Israeli communists have claimed. This has been reflected in the participation of the Arab delegates in the *Histadrūt*'s congress. These took an active share in practically all the debates, expressing considerable satisfaction with *Histadrūt* activities in Arab localities and with their own opportunity to cooperate on equal terms.[53]

[53] Cf. App. G, pp. 249–50 below.

End of Chap 6

p184 Chap

7

LEADERSHIP AND FOCI OF POLITICAL ACTIVITY

ARAB POLITICAL LEADERSHIP IN ISRAEL

ONE of the prominent features in the political life of the Arabs in Israel is the special character of their leadership. It is quite unlike the leadership in the adjacent Arab States. In Egypt and Syria, the ruling élite is in a great measure—perhaps overwhelmingly so—a group originating in the armed forces; but the Arabs in Israel, with the exception of the young Druze, do not serve in the army. In Lebanon, a very considerable share of the Government is in the hands of influential economic and financial circles; but the Arabs in Israel have hardly any similar personalities. In Jordan the king shares some of his power with a group of bureaucrats, some of whom belong to aristocratic families; the Arabs in Israel lack an experienced bureaucracy drawn from the older families, since many experienced officials left in 1948, and those who remained do not penetrate easily into decision-making positions (particularly in sensitive jobs).

Nor does the political leadership of the Arabs in Israel resemble the leadership of the Jewish majority in the same State. The Jewish leadership is composed mainly of veteran workers in the political parties, experienced in politics in which they are generally employed full-time; to these may be added a thin layer from the Israeli professional élite consisting of senior civil servants and generals.[1]

While it is possible to define the main characteristics and describe the major activities of the political leadership both in Israel and in the Arab States, this is not as easy in the case of the Arab minority in Israel.[2] Very few of their leaders, indeed, would call themselves a political élite, continuously working in politics. There appears to be a leadership, whose main criteria are socio-economic, many of whose efforts are concentrated on a local scale and a few only on a national, country-wide level. It seems that there are several causes for these

[1] Cf. S. N. Eisenstadt, 'Patterns of leadership and social homogeneity in Israel', *Internat. Soc. Science B.* viii (1956), 36–54 and his 'Israel', in A. M. Rose, ed., *The institutions of advanced societies* (Minneapolis, 1958), 383–443.

[2] Similar difficulties face the definition of leadership in developing countries. See Y. Dror, 'The improvement of leadership in development countries', *Civilisations* (Brussels), xvii/1–2 (1967), 1–8.

characteristics. (1) As previously stated, in 1948 a considerable number of experienced political Arab leaders did not remain in the area which became Israel; the vacuum has hardly been filled.[3] (2) Among those who stayed behind, there were very few well known to the Arab population and in a position to be considered as its leaders.[4] (3) Although the Arabs in Israel live in large monolithic demographic units, these units are not in one sequence—they are in Galilee, the Little Triangle and the Negev; local particularism still prevents many Israeli Arabs from easily acknowledging political leaders from other parts of the country. (4) The religious division between the Arabs sometimes works against would-be leaders who attempt to enlist support among members of another denomination. (5) The modest number of townspeople among the Israeli Arabs (95,000 at the end of 1965), in comparison with the multitude of villagers (172,800 at the same date) and even the Bedouins (31,500 at the same date),[5] has rendered continuous political work difficult; the most concrete example relates to the Bedouins, sparsely scattered over wide, open spaces. Moreover, even in all six mixed towns, the Arabs reside amidst a much larger Jewish population, among which they are frequently dispersed; even in the cases when Arabs live in the same neighbourhoods in the mixed towns, they still have the feeling of a tiny minority (with the possible exception of Acre, where they form about 25 per cent of the population).

NATIONAL AND LOCAL LEADERSHIP

Despite all the objective difficulties to the rise of an alert political leadership among the Arab minority in Israel, some sort of leadership was bound to spring up, in order to further the interests of this minority; the extreme politicization of Israel made such a development particularly likely. The unflagging activity of the Jewish political parties and other groups, and the absorbing interest in politics could hardly remain unimitated among the Arabs. The latter, in addition, might have remembered the past existence of a veteran political leadership during the years of British rule. None the less, the public activity of Arabs in Israel has only seldom and slightly found expression in formal political organizations, such as membership of national parties; even in MAPAM and MAQĪ (later even in RAQAḤ) the number of registered Arab members has always been modest. Only in 1965 did Arabs participate, for the first time, in country-wide

[3] Asaf, *Hit'ōrĕrūt ha-'Aravīm.*

[4] Cf. Shimoni in *Mōlad,* iii/15. June 1949, 150–6.

[5] *Stat. Ab.* 1966, p. 29, table B/8.

elections to the *Histadrūt*'s congress, so that even in the *Histadrūt* they have not had an opportunity to attain important positions. In the trade unions, also, their number is small, compared with that of Jewish members, and it is as yet impossible to point at an Arab labour leader of national stature. It is true that several Arab trade unionists are capable and devoted,[6] and a few may be of the calibre for leadership—but even these owe their rise in importance mainly to their connexions with Jewish political parties within the *Histadrūt*. Attempts to form all-Arab political groups and organizations have already been described, and their failure analysed. This failure has left MAQĪ, and later RAQAḤ, as the sole political structure, within the framework of which political leaders of national significance have developed. Other personalities, well known to the whole Arab minority in Israel, have been Arab representatives in the *Kneset*.

Much of the Arab political activity is carried on, however, in a local framework and, therefore, the most commonly-found type of leadership may be found among local notables. It is interesting to note that a definite correlation exists between Arab local leadership and the desire for alliances with Jewish parties and groups, on the one hand; and Arab national leadership and the desire to appear independent of non-Arab connections, on the other. Local busybodies from among the Arabs, such as the heads of *ḥamūlas* and others, are often indebted for support (and sometimes financing) to Jewish political organizations. This situation applies, as a rule, to many of those Arab personalities connected with Jewish political parties (mainly with MAPAI) in parliamentary elections. These persons are important only in their local and familial framework, and they are supported by Jewish political parties almost solely for vote-catching purposes. Their significance is far from country-wide. This feature may be easily ascertained from the fact that in all *Kneset* elections the Arab lists allied with Jewish parties obtained practically the whole of their electoral support in certain areas (and only scattered votes elsewhere). The position of those Arabs associated with the leadership of *al-Arḍ*, MAQĪ, or RAQAḤ has been somewhat different. Although they, too, have been particularly popular in a given area—e.g. the leaders of RAQAḤ, in Galilee—they seem to have been fairly well known throughout the State of Israel. Their political supporters among the Arabs have not been among the village *ḥamūlas*, but among inhabitants in the larger villages in the Little Triangle, or (perhaps even more) in the towns, such as Nazareth, Haifa, and Jerusalem. Moreover, among the prominent supporters have been

[6] See Mansour, in *ha-Areṣ*, 11 Feb. 1966.

young Arab intellectuals, whose main arguments and demands are definitely national (rather than local) in scope: complete equality for the whole Arab minority, including equality of opportunities, etc. Many of these, because of personal bitterness, have adopted extreme nationalist attitudes.

Arabs who have been politically active within the ranks of MAPAM, on a country-wide basis, have been placed in an especially difficult position. Theoretically, Jewish-Arab co-operation in MAPAM had ideological premises which might have been expected to elicit wide approval. In practice, Arab members in MAPAM have lost some influence with their potential supporters, because of MAPAM's participation in the Government coalition and in consequence its identification with MAPAI (the Alignment) by many Arabs. This situation has compelled Arab leaders in MAPAM to resort to dialectics: on the one hand, they have had to declare that MAPAM's Government coalition with the Alignment benefits the general interest of the Arabs in Israel; on the other, they have had to gloss over MAPAM's share in the coalition, lest they open themselves to accusations of over-identification with the Alignment. Thus, MAPAM's Arabs have been in not dissimilar straits to those Arabs co-operating with MAPAI (later the Alignment), although the latter were even more frequently exposed to vilification.

In consequence, the struggle for the political leadership of the Arab population in Israel has had a unique character. Instead of being a contest between Arab personalities, it has become, largely, 'a struggle—in the name of the Arabs—between the Jews themselves, for the sake of Jews'.[7] As a result of this peculiar situation, the factors which normally assist the rise of a country-wide leadership for a minority had little effect in Israel; one cannot even point to a political leadership acceptable and acknowledged by a large segment of the Israeli Arabs. Two factors are instrumental in Israel: first, the example of Jewish society, with whom the Arabs have had close contacts, among which there exists an active political leadership; secondly, the evolution of a class of Arab intellectuals, alert to developments both in Israel and in the Arab States; these intellectuals, the majority young people, have the potential to breed political leaders articulate enough to express the desires and hopes of the Arab minority. However, it appears that the division among the religious communities, the jealous competition between the heads of the *ḥamūlas* and, possibly, the parochialism of many Arabs have all combined against the rise of a generally acknowledged Arab leadership.

[7] Palmōn, in *ha-Areṣ*, 14 Jan. 1966.

The character of typical leadership in Arab localities may be better understood if one remembers that the leadership in almost every village has been maintained over generations by the heads of *ḥamūlas*.[8] They have had a greater share in local policy-making than simple heads of families; they have been, in addition, the real intermediaries with elements outside the village. Politically, their power has been bolstered by being part of an unofficial network of *ḥamūlas*, frequently based on kinship. The Ottoman Government maintained this system. The British rule acknowledged it *de facto*, and its tax-collectors and other officials generally worked with the heads of *ḥamūlas*. The State of Israel, too, despite the changes both planned and unintentional in the character of the Arab village, could not disregard the special standing of the heads of *ḥamūlas*. Even though their status has somewhat declined, through their diminished authority over the young intellectuals and the villagers employed in towns, they still possess considerable power over social life and voting in almost every locality. Even the *mukhtār* (in those villages which do not yet have a local council), although still the 'trustee' of the Government, as in Ottoman and British times, is subservient to the heads of *ḥamūlas*. They are supposed to assist him but usually dictate his decisions. This is even more often the case in the villages already endowed with a local council, practically always composed of heads of *ḥamūlas* or their protégés, the only ones who can afford the expense of an electoral contest to the local council. Very frequently the members of the local council, particularly its chairman, are the representatives of the real political forces in village leadership.

In this manner, the youngsters in the Arab village usually have little influence (sometimes none at all) on decisions relating to the affairs of the village—even if these youngsters are educated and have better understanding of national politics. Bitterness and frustration result from this inability to effect any reforms in the *status quo*. Characteristically in almost every Arab village there exists a thin layer of intellectuals and youths (often intellectual youths) who are ardent advocates of reform and potential leaders; their small number serves only to emphasize their inability to achieve their aims. In those infrequent instances when a youth holds a key position in his locality, this is generally not owing to his intellectual abilities or public achievements but rather to the support of his *ḥamūla*. Still, the very advance of youths to such positions is a sign of remarkable progress.

[8] The social role of the *ḥamūla* elders has been discussed above, pp. 21–25. See also Sh. Shamīr, in *NO*, Mar.–Apr. 1962, 93–112.

The process of the slow, gradual change in village leadership is not identical everywhere.[9] One of its manifestations is the increasing number of young people elected in recent years to Arab local councils. We have attempted elsewhere[10] to calculate the relevant figures for the local elections held in November 1959: 221 Arab councillors were then elected, of whom 132, or almost 60 per cent, were aged 21–45 years at the time of election; 69 out of the 221, or more than 31 per cent of this total, were aged 21–35; and only 16 councillors, or about 7 per cent of the total, were over 60 years old.[11] The situation was not markedly altered in the November 1965 local elections, although these were held for the first time in eight additional local councils.[12]

The changes in Bedouin leadership are an interesting case on their own. During the 1948 war a number of Bedouin shaykhs crossed over, with their people, to the Gaza Strip and to Jordan. Only fragments of the original tribes remained in Israel, and—as previously mentioned—everything possible was done to persuade them to settle down. Among the inducements to sedentarization were grants of land, permanent employment, regular education, organized health care, etc. Since progress in sedentarization has necessarily been slow, it was decided to maintain, meanwhile, the socio-political structures of the Bedouins which had already existed under British rule. Therefore the Ministry of the Interior and the military administration worked together to that end: the former shaykhs or their substitutes have been duly recognized as the official tribal chieftains; a Bedouin court was established, to arbitrate between the Bedouins. None the less, parallel with the break-up of the established structure in the Arab village, Bedouin society is undergoing a similar process. In the small tribes particularly the authority of the shaykh is weakening, its place being taken by the State authorities. However, the prestige of the tribal shaykhs among the Bedouins is still sufficient for them to enjoy considerable power; in general, they can influence the political attitudes of their tribe, for instance in voting. In Bedouin society, the youngsters appear to rebel against their elders (and against the 'system') less than in the Arab villages or towns. Most likely these

[9] For examples, about Ṭaiyyba, Rosenfeld in *Mi-bi-Fĕnīm*, Apr. 1956, 458–68. Many of Rosenfeld's conclusions are still valid nowadays.

[10] Landau, 'A note on the leadership of Israeli Arabs', *Il Politico* (Pavia), xxvii/3 (1962), esp. 630–1

[11] See also the official results in *Yalqūṭ ha-Pirsūmīm*, no. 721, 30 Nov. 1959, & no. 723, 4 Dec. 1959.

[12] Detailed information is not yet available. *Yalqūṭ ha-Pirsūmīm*, no. 1232, 17 Nov. 1965, and subsequent numbers, give no particulars about the age of local councillors.

youngsters have had less occasion to come into contact with either urban civilization or with Jewish society.

A somewhat different situation prevails in the Arab towns, especially in Nazareth (for Shafā 'Amr is, actually, a large village; while in the mixed towns the Arabs are submerged among the Jewish majority). True, large and influential families have an impact in Nazareth, too, for example in municipal elections; the Zu'bīs are such a family. The interests of the religious communities also play a significant role in local politics: Christians against Muslims, the Christian denominations against one another, etc. Local patriotism adds its own flavour in influencing politics; the eastern quarter of Nazareth, the residents of which consider themselves poorer and under-privileged, struggle politically against the other quarters. Leaders of families, religious communities, and town quarters fight for positions of strength in Nazareth, sometimes seeking allies in the national political parties. At the same time an increasingly prominent role is played by intellectual youths, many holding extreme nationalist or communist views. Nazareth was one of the early centres of activity of *al-Arḍ* group. It is still the focus of activity for MAQĪ and RAQAḤ, which have in turn gained considerable electoral support. It is probable that these circles alone are providing the breeding grounds for the prototype of national Arab leadership. The political background of these leaders is ideological rather than opportunist, and their orientation is typically one of opposition to the Israeli Government.

THE ARAB MEMBERS OF THE *KNESET*

The tables on p. 191[13] contain some basic data about Arab MKs.

With the exception of the first *Kneset*, when the Israeli Arabs were still dazed by defeat, they have regularly been represented by seven or eight MKs. Half or more of them have repeatedly entered the *Kneset* via Arab lists allied with MAPAI (in 1965, with the Alignment). Personal continuity, however, has been an attribute mainly of the communist Arab MKs: Tawfīq Ṭūbī has sat in all six *Knesets*, Emīl Ḥabībī in four. This is understandable in view of their standing in MAQĪ and, still more, in RAQAḤ since 1965. Among Arab MKs with other political affiliations, continuity has depended on the electoral success of their parties as well as on their loyalty in the *Kneset*. MAPAM has insisted, since the second *Kneset*, on regularly including an Arab in its parliamentary group. The criterion of the

[13] I have had to figure out many of these details by myself, working on election results and parliamentary minutes.

No. of Arab MKs and Party Affiliation

Affiliation	Membership in Kneset No.					
	1st	*2nd*	*3rd*	*4th*	*5th*	*6th*
Allied with MAPAI*	2	5	5	5	4	4
MAQĪ†	1	2	2	1	2	2
MAPAM	—	1	1	1	1	1
Aḥdūt ha-ʿavōda‡	—	—	—	—	1	—
Total	3	8	8	7	8	7

* In the 6th *Kneset* allied with the Alignment.
† In the 6th *Kneset*, RAQAḤ.
‡ Salīm Khalīl Jabbāra, a Muslim journalist from Ṭaiyyba, became a member of the 5th *Kneset* on 5 May 1964, following the resignation of another (Jewish) MK, Y. Ben-Aharōn.

Length of Membership in Kneset *of Arab MKs**

Affiliation	*Membership in*						
	One Kneset	*Two* Knesets	*Three* Knesets	*Four* Knesets	*Five* Knesets	*Six* Knesets	*Total*
Allied with MAPAI†	5	5	2	1	—	—	13
MAQĪ‡	—	—	—	1	—	1	2
MAPAM	2	—	1	—	—	—	3
Aḥdūt ha-ʿavōda	1	—	—	—	—	—	1
Total	8	5	3	2	—	1	19

* Including MKs who served as *Kneset* members only part of the 4-year session.
† In the 6th *Kneset*, the Alignment. ‡ In the 6th *Kneset*, RAQAḤ.

appointment by the party policy-makers has generally been according to party allegiance and loyalty. Thus when its Arab MK, Rustum Bastūnī, left MAPAM during the second *Kneset* (together with a leftist faction led by Moshe Sneh), the party substituted Yūsuf Khamīs[14] for him in its slate of candidates for the third *Kneset*; and in the sixth *Kneset* ʿAbd al-ʿAzīz Zuʿbī was appointed to replace the latter (apparently, in order to introduce a new personality). MAPAI (then the Alignment) seems to have picked its allied MKs according to their vote-catching capabilities; and later changed them according to their party loyalty in parliamentary voting and the need to intro-

[14] On whose views, see *al-Mirṣād*, 6 Nov. 1964.

duce some new blood. In spite of these considerations, MAPAI still tended to hesitate before effecting such changes.[15] Taken as a group, the turnover of Arab MKs in the *Kneset* is fairly low, similar to that of Jewish MKs—so much so that some of them consider being MKs as their profession.[16]

*Age of the Arab MKs**

Kneset	*Number of Arab MKs*		*Average age (years)*	
	Up to 40 yrs old	*More than 40 yrs old*	*Arab MKs*	*The whole* Kneset†
1st	2	1	42	48
2nd	7	1	34	49
3rd	5	3	38	51
4th	2	5	45	52
5th	3	5	45	53
6th	1	6	46	51

* The table refers to the dates of entry into the *Kneset*.

† B. Akzin, 'The Knesset', *Int. Soc. Sci. J.*, xiii/4 (1961), 570, brings data for a *Kneset* cross-section up to the 4th *Kneset*. Later data calculated by me.

In Israel, as in a number of other States, the average age of parliamentary members is quite advanced. The average age of the Arab MKs has been rising fairly steadily, partly because of the continuation of the same people in office. None the less, the average age among Arab MKs has been consistently lower than among Jewish. In comparing ages of the Arab MKs by parliamentary groups, it is interesting to note that the average age of those Arab MKs allied with MAPAI has been consistently higher than those in MAPAM or MAQĪ and RAQAḤ (between which there is no significant difference). This may possibly reflect the tendency for MAPAI (the Alignment) to seek allies among the *ḥamūla* heads and village elders, while MAPAM and MAQĪ (RAQAḤ) attempt to recruit future Arab leaders from among the younger generation.

The religious distribution of the Arab MKs demonstrates the relatively small number of the Muslims among them. Although they

[15] Cf. N. Shṭrasman in *Ma'arīv*, 12 Nov. 1965, 16.

[16] A referendum by the CBS was passed among all 120 MKs at the end of 1965, asking about their professions; 5 members (unnamed) replied that it was membership in the *Kneset*! Cf. CBS, *Results of elections to sixth* Kneset *and local councils* (in Hebrew), i, p. xv.

Religious Affiliation of Arab MKs

Kneset	*Muslims*	*Christians*	*Druzes*	*Total*
1st	2	1	—	3
2nd	2	4	2	8
3rd	3	4	2	8*
4th	4	2	1	7
5th	3	4	1	8
6th	3	3	1	7

* In accordance with a pre-election agreement of these candidates allied with MAPAI, Muslim MK Sayf al-Dīn Zu'bī resigned on 1 Feb. 1956 in favour of the Druze Jabr Mu'addī, who filled his seat; so the total is still 8 MKs.

make up about 70 per cent of the total minorities in Israel, their representation among Arab MKs has rarely been above half and is frequently less. In comparison, the Druze and Christian MKs are fairly numerous. There seem to be two reasons for this distribution. (1) MAPAI (later the Alignment) has consistently striven to secure top candidates on the Arab lists allied with it from all three religious communities; since these lists have normally received 4–5 seats in the *Kneset*, the Druze MK always received more than his community's due share among the minorities (about 10 per cent). (2) The same rule applies, in a lesser measure, to the Christians on the lists allied with MAPAI, the more so since the Christians are often more politically-conscious. The fact that both MAQĪ's (RAQAḤ's) Arab MKs are Christians also contributes to this ratio.

Permanent Residence of Arab MKs

Kneset	*Nazareth*	*Haifa*	*Western Upper Galilee*	*Western Lower Galilee*	*Little Triangle*
1st	2	1	—	—	—
2nd	1	3	1	2	1
3rd	2	3	2	1	1
4th	1	3	—	2	1
5th	1	3	1	1	2
6th	2	2	1	1	1
Total	9	15	5	7	6

All the Arab MKs have come from the following sectors (in this order): Haifa, Western Galilee, Nazareth, and the Little Triangle. Haifa has retained its prominent position because both the two communist Arab MKs live there. The changes from one *Kneset* to another, in this respect, are characteristically insignificant, either because the same MKs have continued in office, or because the policy-makers within the political parties have decided to send, in their stead, personalities from the same areas. It is noteworthy that the southern part of Israel, including the Negev, has consistently been without Arab representation in the *Kneset*, although it continues to be the Bedouin centre.

*Occupational Distribution of Arab MKs**

Farmer	*Journalist & politician*	*Journa-list*	*Lawyer*	*Farmer & lawyer*	*Archi-tect*	*Clerk*	*Land-owner*	*Total*
10	3	1	1	1	1	1	1	19

* According to their own definition.

Most Arab MKs are farmers (including landowners) by occupation and journalists take second place to them. The political significance of the farmers lies in their residence in rural areas and influence in their villages. The political propensity of the journalists (and lawyers too), is easily understandable. Most Arab MKs have attended primary schools and then have added a few years of high school; several have attended university and studied law or architecture. However, as in the case of their Jewish colleagues, there appears to be no definite correlation between the level of education of the Arab MKs and their election to the *Kneset*. It seems that the truly decisive factors, in this respect, were their standing and influence at home, or their political alertness, before their parliamentary career and during its course. Their political interest before entering the *Kneset* tended to be expressed in devoted party work (MAPAM, MAQĪ–RAQAḤ), or at least assistance to the allied party (MAPAI–Alignment). This difference in emphasis between the various groups of MKs has also been carried through into their parliamentary activity.

While serving in the *Kneset*, most Arab MKs have maintained their contact with their electors no less (and apparently more) than their Jewish colleagues. A difference, again, is evident between the various groups of Arab MKs. Those allied with MAPAI (the Alignment) have employed various means of communication, including the daily *al-Yawm*, and many special trips to various localities. As the Arab MK Diyāb 'Ubayd put it, in an interview with *al-Yawm* (20 Oct. 1965), during his *Kneset* days he had written 2,000 letters of recommendation to Government offices, as a result of which 3,233 matters were arranged, among them 214 economic problems of villages and local councils and 723 meetings between Israeli Arabs and their relatives in adjacent countries, etc.[17] Among some local improvements, managed by Arab MKs allied with MAPAI in their own village were: Fāris Ḥamdān sponsored the establishment of a canned fruit factory in Bāqa al-Gharbiyya; Mas'ad Qasīs from Ma'īlyā took care to encourage the tobacco crop in that area; and Eliyās Nakhla from Rāma aided the olive and olive-oil industry in his home environment.

In order to handle all the requests, the Arab MKs allied with MAPAI would be available for personal interviews, and at home during most of the time they were not attending the *Kneset*. Being at home meant, in this instance, incessantly receiving visits of family elders and others. Moreover, their home was changed into a sort of *dīwān*, where the MK would orate on his achievements and his plans for the future, as well as listen to requests, which he would then pass on to the proper quarters with suitable recommendations. The family elders would then repeat his words to the Arab residents in that area.

For their part, the Arab MKs of MAPAM and MAQĪ (RAQAḤ) employed other means of propaganda. They made more extensive use of *al-Mirṣād* and *al-Ittiḥād*, respectively, than the others had made of *al-Yawm*. Apparently less emphasis was put on personal contacts, and more on party meetings, festivals, and (in the case of the communist MKs) mass rallies.

The parliamentary activity of all the Arab MKs may be considered under two headings—the characteristics of this activity and its motives on one hand, and its relationship to the general work in the *Kneset* on the other.

Only in rare instances do the Arab MKs speak up in the *Kneset* on general matters. In parliamentary work they usually concentrate on topics of special interest to the Arab minority in Israel, so that their identification is very apparent. Appeals for peace in the Middle East, constant demands for relaxation of the military administration and of limitations on reunion of Arab families, pressure for raising the standards of living in the Arab minority, requests for larger budgets for roads, clinics, and schools, claims for better opportunities of employment for young Arab intellectuals—all these recur, when-

[17] Cf. two letters written by Diyāb 'Ubayd, ibid. 8 & 14 July 1964.

ever new legislation or the approval of the budget are under consideration.

Understandably, the content and tenor of the requests vary, according to the standing of the initiator within the Government or the opposition ranks. The communist Arab MKs—and sometimes those of MAPAM—touch on general and Jewish subjects as well. What distinguishes them, however, is the extreme character of their demands. As there is very little likelihood (if any) of these being accepted, those MKs may direct their speeches to their potential electors on propaganda lines determined upon by their party. On the opposite side of the *Kneset*, the Arab MKs allied with MAPAI (the Alignment) have concentrated on Israeli Arab affairs, on the lines previously mentioned. In many instances, they probably expect MAPAI approval in advance, at least on general grounds, for their speeches. Hence they face a difficult dilemma. On the one hand, they are well aware that the more moderate their requests, the better chance they have of obtaining Government support. On the other, moderation is not necessarily a virtue in the eyes of the Arab electorate—particularly when compared with communist, or even MAPAM, aggressiveness. Although in a few cases the Arab MKs allied to MAPAI (the Alignment) have attempted to solve this dilemma by temporarily assuming a more independent attitude,[18] usually they have been content to appeal to the electorate in their area of residence and obtain Government support for their intercessions on its behalf. *Ipso facto*, they have renounced the chance of assuming national leadership of the Arab minority.

In the *Kneset*, as in some other parliaments, much of the personal activity and real influence of the MKs is reflected in committee work. The *Kneset* committees do much of the preliminary work in legislation and policy-making. Since their minutes are secret, much useful work is done in them, while the plenary sessions of the *Kneset* are, at least partly, employed for speaking to the people. Committee work, then, is the main opportunity for the Arab MKs to play a more realistic role. Since the smaller parliamentary groups naturally receive limited committee representation, their role is perforce not a decisive one. Nevertheless, the Arab MKs have worked for their voters' interests in these committees, just as they have lobbied the Government and interceded for them before the various offices. All this activity has left them with little time to make speeches in the plenary session. When they do so they frequently employ Arabic (both Hebrew and Arabic are official languages in the *Kneset*), even when

[18] Sh. Segev, in *Ma'arīv*, 22 July 1966, for cases in point during 1966.

they know Hebrew. Examples are Diyāb 'Ubayd (allied with the Alignment), who learnt Hebrew in a Berlitz language school; and Yūsuf Khamīs (MAPAM), who often speaks in the *Kneset* in Hebrew, but at other times in Arabic—to remind his potential electorate of his identification with them.

Most Arab MKs have consistently followed the party line in their *Kneset* voting.[19] An independent vote in accordance with individual conscience, is extremely rare. One of those who flouted his independence in the *Kneset* was MAPAM's Rustum Bastūnī,[20] and retribution soon followed, when his name was dropped from the party's slate of candidates for the next parliamentary elections. Following the party voting line poses problems mainly for the Arab MKs allied with MAPAI (the Alignment). They are already suspected of subservience to the Government,[21] and voting emphasizes this. An extreme case involving their loyalties arose in 1963, in the *Kneset* debate and vote on the military administration. The vote was expected to be so close that the Government coalition needed every single vote in order to defeat the motion for the abolition of the military administration. Hence, on the request of the Government coalition, the Arab MKs allied with MAPAI made a face-saving arrangement: Jabr Mu'addī, Diyāb 'Ubayd, and Eliyās Nakhla, in turn, voted for the Government (that is, against the abolition of the military administration), then abstained—as a gesture towards the Arab electorate.[22] Not surprisingly, their tactics did not fool their rivals, who reproached them with the fickleness of their vote and called them 'traitors' and 'tails of the Government' (*adhnāb al-ḥukūma*).[23]

Such episodes illustrate the difficulties of the Arab MKs, particularly those allied with MAPAI (the Alignment). Their problem has been posed frankly by Sayf al-Dīn Zu'bī, in an interview with a journalist.[24] He complained that the Arab allies of the Alignment in the *Kneset* were hardly ever consulted, though directed as to how to vote. To him, the situation seemed particularly preposterous, since these four MKs were not party members of MAPAI or the Alignment, nor could they join the party, as they were Arabs! Such protests notwithstanding, it appears that all Arab MKs and many others hanker after the prestige and influence that go with a seat in the

[19] See Sh. Avineri in *bĕ-Ṭerem*, 1 Mar. 1953.

[20] For Bastūnī's views, see *JP*, 25 Sept. 1964, and App. A, below pp. 221–4.

[21] For a case involving Mas'ad Qasīs, cf. *Ner*, May–June 1953, 36.

[22] See *Ma'arīv*, 20 Feb. 1963.

[23] Cf. the attack on Diyāb 'Ubayd in *al-Mirṣād*, 2 Aug. 1963; and on Jabr Mu'addī in *al-Ittiḥād*, 23 Oct. 1963.

[24] Shavīṭ, in *Yĕdī'ōt aḥarōnōt*, 14 Oct. 1966.

Kneset. For this signal honour, many of them—particularly the allies of MAPAI—have been content voluntarily to limit the number of their speeches, interpellations, motions for the agenda, etc. Such behaviour is even more conspicuous, when compared with the activity of the fewer communist and MAPAM Arab MKs.

Earlier in this chapter, we have discussed the political impact of

Active Participation of Arab MKs in Kneset *Plenary Sessions**

Kneset	*Type of participation*	*Allies of MAPAI*	*MAPAM*	*MAQI*
1st	General debate	29	—	47
	Interpellations	8	—	36
	Motions for the agenda	3	—	22
	Total	40	—	105
2nd	General debate	57	32	70
	Interpellations	19	82	152
	Motions for the agenda	7	26	24
	Total	83	140	247
3rd	General debate	42	25	27
	Interpellations	16	97	93
	Motions for the agenda	1	11	12
	Total	59	133	132
4th	General debate	29	13	27
	Interpellations	3	31	29
	Motions for the agenda	2	1	17
	Total	34	45	73
5th	General debate	56	30	82
	Interpellations	56	109	112
	Motions for the agenda	4	12	21
	Total	116	151	215

* Based on the indexes of the official *Divrey ha-Kneset*, i–xxxvii. The 6th *Kneset* cannot be included as it was elected in 1965 for a 4-year period, and was still in office at the time of writing. For the first speech in the *Kneset* by an Arab MK, A. S. Jarjūra, see App. H, pp. 251–2 below.

the heads of *ḥamūlas* in local affairs, and noted that through their local influence, some of them have achieved contacts with MAPAI, which enabled them to obtain seats in the *Kneset*. This fact possibly explains their rather passive participation in the *Kneset* debates.

It is worth-while describing the main characteristics of a few Arab MKs, beginning with the two Zu'bīs, Sayf al-Dīn and 'Abd al-'Azīz.

Sayf al-Dīn Zu'bī, born in 1913, has been a political figure in Nazareth since the early days of the State of Israel, when he ran for the first *Kneset* in 1949 at the head of an Arab list allied with MAPAI, called the Democratic List of the Arabs of Israel. He threw in his lot with MAPAI from the first, and this party sponsored his activity; many in Nazareth considered him as their spokesman with the newly established Israeli authorities. Sayf al-Dīn Zu'bī assisted the first military Governor of Galilee to reorganize civil administration in the area ruled by the military administration; he then succeeded in obtaining the co-operation of some Nazareth personalities in re-establishing normal life in Nazareth. It has been in this town that he has based most of his activities—although he was a member of the first and second *Knesets* and is now a member of the sixth. As mayor of Nazareth since 1959, he put to good use his many personal ties with the Establishment; he developed the town and modernized its services. His opponents accused him of spending and dividing spoils among his cronies.[25] None the less, the Alignment supported the candidature of Sayf al-Dīn Zu'bī for mayor in the 1965 local elections, but later could not overcome the opposition of MAPAM and RAQAḤ to him (as described elsewhere). In the 1966 municipal elections the Alignment, hoping for a way out of the stalemate, apparently refused to assist Sayf al-Dīn Zu'bī, whereupon he ran alone and entered the municipal council at the head of a group numbering four, himself included. The group had numbered five in 1965, with the full support of the Alignment, so that the 1966 result was no mean achievement. Only with great difficulty was he persuaded to renounce his claim to the mayoralty.[26]

While Sayf al-Dīn Zu'bī is the type of a successful local leader who thrives on his co-operation with MAPAI (the Alignment), his relative 'Abd al-'Azīz Zu'bī is a dedicated member of MAPAM. Although elected to the sixth *Kneset* in November 1965, 'Abd al-'Azīz Zu'bī's main activity has been in Nazareth affairs, where he

[25] For details see 'Azīz Shihāda, in *Ma'arīv*, 11 Dec. 1967.

[26] Sayf al-Dīn Zu'bī appears to be a prominent MK in the group allied with MAPAI (the Alignment). For the others, cf. 'Alī Muḥammad' Alī, *Fī dākhil Isrā'īl* [1963?], 164–5.

was deputy mayor, and, for a few months in 1965–6, mayor. Born in 1926, he is younger than Sayf al-Dīn Zu'bī and he appears to be the typical local leader who has been very active in party work. The son of a veteran police sergeant, 'Abd al-'Azīz Zu'bī is something of an intellectual. Although an observant Muslim, he had early leftist sympathies, and in 1944 joined the socialist Congress of Arab Workers. He was employed as a junior clerk in Nazareth by the district office of the British authorities up to 1948. After Nazareth had been conquered by the Israeli army 'Abd al-'Azīz Zu'bī learned Hebrew and joined the civil service. He joined MAPAM in 1956 and one of his first successes was in organizing a Jewish-Arab Convention for Peace and Equality in Haifa. Later he resigned from the civil service and became a full-time worker of MAPAM. While still active in municipal affairs in Nazareth, he also directed MAPAM's publishing house in Arabic, and for a time edited an Arabic monthly for the party; he was also a member of the editorial board of the English-language monthly *New Outlook* (appearing in Tel-Aviv), to which he contributed a number of articles.[27] An even more important task fell to him when he was appointed editor of MAPAM's Arabic weekly, *al-Mirṣād*. In it he energetically fought both Arab co-operation with MAPAI and extremist tendencies.[28] He has represented MAPAM in a number of cultural events in Israel[29] and abroad; and is known as an able speaker, in Arabic and Hebrew.[30] He is bound to use these talents in the sixth *Kneset*, in which he has a seat in MAPAM's parliamentary group. 'Abd al-'Azīz Zu'bī, then, is—perhaps even more so than Sayf al-Dīn Zu'bī—a local leader; he is active in municipal affairs, and as an MK, is being groomed by his political party for national leadership among the Arabs in Israel.

The two Arab communist MKs, Tawfīq Ṭūbī and Emīl Ḥabībī, may be considered intellectuals. Both were born in 1922, are residents of Haifa, and distinguished by their fervent activity for their party, MAQĪ, and after the 1965 rift—RAQAḤ.

Tawfīq Ṭūbī,[31] a Greek Orthodox, is the only Arab to have held uninterrupted membership in all six *Knesets*; he may be regarded as the chief Arab communist in Israel. In his youth, he studied at the British missionary school in Jerusalem and later in the American University in Beirut—that breeding ground for so many politicians

[27] e.g., *NO*, July 1957, 14–17; Jan. 1958, 12–17; Oct. 1960, 32–34; June 1964, 32–33, 52.

[28] For instance, see *al-Mirṣād*, 28 Aug. 1963.

[29] Details in *ha-Areṣ*, 6 Jan. 1963.

[30] Acc. to Meysels, in *Ma'arīv*, 6 Sept. 1965. Cf. Sh. Segev, ibid. Dec. 1965.

[31] *Who's who, Israel 1966–67* (Tel-Aviv, Sept. 1966), *s.v.* Toubi.

in the Arab countries. He worked as a supervisor in a labour exchange during British rule in Palestine; at that time he was already participating in strikes, demonstrations, and rallies within the framework of a leftist Palestine Arab Workers' Society. While still relatively young he succeeded in attaining such an influential position with the communists that he was nominated a delegate in the 1949 constituent convention of MAQĪ. He was one of the founders, then leaders, of MAQĪ; later he was one of the prime movers for the break-up in the Israeli communist camp and the establishment of RAQAḤ, in which he is a key figure. Ṭūbī has been very active in a number of front organizations in Israel, e.g. the Israeli Committee for Peace and the Israel–USSR Friendship Association; he has frequently represented his party in meetings and congresses, in Israel and abroad. In the *Kneset* he has repeatedly demanded complete equality for Israel's Arab minority and also taken a stand on problems of internal and foreign policy.

Emīl Ḥabībī,[32] a Protestant, has been a member of the second, third, fifth, and sixth *Knesets*. A teacher by profession, he has also worked as a radio announcer; he is both a prolific journalist and a capable orator. He has worked his way, in the 1940s, through the Arab faction of the Palestinian Communist Party (the League for National Liberation). In MAQĪ Ḥabībī has played a central role, alongside Ṭūbī. In the 1965 rift he stood by Ṭūbī in establishing RAQAḤ. In both his fiery speeches and his frequent editorials in *al-Ittiḥād* (where he sometimes signs the editorials under his pseudonym 'Juhayna'), he has often demonstrated an even more extremist attitude than Ṭūbī's. He has, for example, insistently claimed the right of the Arab minority to self-determination; and has attacked what he considered Israel's ties with world imperialism.[33] His premise is that 'we [i.e. the communist leaders] are men of politics, responsible for the future of a people.'[34] Indeed, it is this sense of leadership, as well as personal ability, which makes of both Ṭūbī and Ḥabībī Arab leaders of national significance.[35]

RELIGIOUS LEADERSHIP

An analysis of leadership in the four main religious communities among Israel's minorities shows that the situation differs from one to the other.

[32] Ibid. *s.v.* Habibi. Also interview with Shavīṭ, in *YA*, 25 Nov. 1966.

[33] Acc. to A. Līn, in *Ma'arīv*, 21 Nov. 1966, Ḥabībī declared that he favoured Syria in the Israeli-Syrian conflict.

[34] Ḥabībī in Kafr Yāṣīf, mentioned in *al-Yawm*, 11 Dec. 1964.

[35] See also, on the Arab MKs in general, Mansour, in *ha-Areṣ*, 29 June 1961.

The Muslims have remained almost leaderless since the 1948 Arab-Israel war; although new appointees have filled religious offices, they have not been ostensibly involved in politics. There appears to be a dual reason for this phenomenon: first since Islam has no religious hierarchy, there exists no framework in which the religious dignitaries might express themselves on any matters except those of faith; second since *qāḍīs* were nominated by the Israeli authorities, perhaps they are identified by some Muslims with their non-Muslim patrons, and hence lack the authority needed for leadership.

The Druzes are divided by the struggle between the community elders and the younger generation. For the time being the prestige of the elders is still high, owing to a number of factors; for example, they know the mysteries of the Druze religion and they keep the *waqf* properties of the community and supervise the use of the income therefrom. Nevertheless, the younger Druze challenge the authority of the elders, and this contest for power weakens the political standing of the Druze religious leadership.

The Greek Orthodox community is passing through a similar crisis, but the authority of its religious leadership has been further weakened. Two causes appear to be responsible. First, the higher religious dignitaries are foreign (Greek), while the priests and most of the flock are natives (mainly, Arab). Secondly, a strong group of Greek Orthodox youth, some with leftist tendencies, have seized power over the community's executive committee and have controlled its internal affairs since 1961.[36]

The Greek Catholics also have their share of foreign dignitaries,[37] but their number is relatively smaller than in the Greek Orthodox community. In addition, the Greek Catholic community is more tightly knit together, thanks to its severely hierarchic structure and to the long tradition of obedience within the Catholic denomination. There is, nevertheless, a certain decline in the standing of the community's leadership, as exemplified in the communist vote of a sizeable section of it, despite the appeal of the community leaders to the contrary. However, the community's head in Israel until 1967, Archbishop al-Ḥakīm, has been very influential. Without doubt, 'among the Christian leaders in Israel, the most powerful voice and influence is that of Archbishop George al-Ḥakīm.'[38]

Al-Ḥakīm may certainly be considered not only a religious leader

[36] Details in *al-Ittiḥād*, 25 Apr. 1961.
[37] M. Gellhorn, 'The Arabs of Palestine', *Atlantic Monthly*, Oct. 1961, esp. 61.
[38] M. S. Lazaron, *Olive trees in storm* (1955), ch. VII ('Minorities in Israel').

but a political one as well—probably the only one among members of the minorities who have served in religious offices in Israel. Not without reason, he has been called 'the political Bishop'.[39] Born in Ṭanṭā (Egypt) in 1908 and becoming a school principal in Cairo, al-Ḥakīm settled in Palestine in 1943, as the Archbishop of Acre and the whole of Galilee.[40] During the 1948 war he was in Lebanon, but returned to Israel later and remained there until he was appointed Patriarch of Damascus, late in 1967. During those years, although he was officially subordinate to the then Patriarch in Damascus, he was practically independent, and his position in Israel was powerful, for several reasons. He headed the largest Christian community in the country and had substantial prestige within it. He directed several economic enterprises, which enabled him to provide employment for his followers, from a position of economic independence. He had considerable personal charm and great talents for persuasion. He derived added strength from his connexions with the Vatican and these ties were rendered particularly significant, by the increasing activity of the Vatican in world affairs, in recent years.

As early as the last years of British rule in Palestine al-Ḥakīm had been active in politics. His attitude at the time was blatantly pro-Arab and anti-Jewish. Nevertheless, the Israeli Government encouraged him to return, after the 1948 war, presumably hoping that he might serve as a link with the Catholic world, and as a leader for Arab anti-communist elements (in view of the growing strength of communist propaganda at the time). Neither expectation has materialized. Soon after his return, al-Ḥakīm started to present to the Israeli authorities demands that were meant (or so it seemed) to increase his popularity with the Arab minority in Israel. His Arabic monthly *al-Rābiṭa*, which had previously been concerned solely with religious and spiritual matters, began publishing political articles, including moderate attacks on the Israeli Government. An example of the sober approach of al-Ḥakīm to Israeli politics may be found in a public letter he wrote in 1955.[41] In it, he refuted the accusation that he was 'anti-Israeli'. He maintained that, on the contrary, he had been working incessantly to bring Jews and Arabs closer, for the sake of developing the whole area. He added that if the term 'anti-Israeli' meant acting to reduce the discrimination against the Arab minority, he was proud of this appellation; his religious and

[39] *Davar*, 3 Feb. 1964. See also Palmōn, 'Maximus V', *ha-Areṣ*, 8 Dec. 1967.

[40] *Who's who, Israel 1966–67*, *s.v.* See 'Archbishop Ḥakīm's view of Israel Arabs' position', *JP*, 12 Jan. 1962 and App. I, below, pp. 253–4.

[41] *Ner*, Feb.–Mar. 1955, 31.

civic duty was to strive towards equality for the Arabs in Israel. He concluded that he considered it essential to let the Israelis know the results of the destructive policy of their Government towards the Arab minority; in so doing, he was working for the interests of the State of Israel.

The Archbishop's opponents among extremist Arabs in Israel claimed that such pronouncements smacked of double-talk. As if to lend force to this accusation, al-Ḥakīm began since the mid-1950s to draw nearer to the views of the Israeli authorities, although never fully identifying with them. That this rapprochement had, among other reasons, a pragmatic basis was indicated by the fact that the Israeli Government returned to the Greek Catholic community some expropriated property, speeded up the payment of compensation for the rest, granted the community exemption from income tax and municipal taxes, and reduction in the custom tariffs. Possibly in connexion with this improvement in relationship, al-Ḥakīm appealed for anti-communist votes and for support to the Arab allies of MAPAI (which always provided a safe seat in the *Kneset* for a Greek Catholic candidate). This co-operation sometimes applied to the Nazareth municipal elections, e.g. in 1954.

When the Popular Front was established in 1958, with MAQĪ's inspiration and sponsorship, al-Ḥakīm called on the organization to purge every single communist and thus open the way to co-operation with all other Arab elements in Israel. In so doing, al-Ḥakīm followed his own anti-communist campaign and approached the attitude of the Israeli authorities. However, his relations with Israeli official circles were in the nature of a continual zigzag, often taking an independent course of action politically, and stressing this fact.[42] In a few rare instances, he made sensational pronouncements, and just as speedily disclaimed them.[43] His general line seems, in recent years, to support MAPAI (the Alignment) and the Government in his pronouncements within Israel; e.g. he called on the Israeli Arabs to vote for the Alignment in the 1965 elections (both to the *Histadrūt* and the *Kneset*), and again to support Israel and keep calm (just before the six-days' war in June 1967).[44] However, in interviews to the foreign press—such as the Italian daily *Oggi*, in 1964,[45] or a BBC correspondent more than two years later[46]—he appears to have complained about the attitude of the Israeli Government to its

[42] e.g., in his article 'The Greek Catholic community', *NO*, Mar.–Apr. 1962, 78–81.

[43] Cf. *Davar*, 3 Jan. 1967.

[44] Mansour, in *ha-Areṣ*, 2 June 1967 and in *NO*, July–Aug. 1967, 26–27.

[45] On 16 Jan. 1964.

[46] See *al-Mirṣād*, 27 May 1966.

Christian citizens, who were allegedly compelled to emigrate. While some Israeli Arabs reacted by accusations of double-dealing (and distributed leaflets decrying it),[47] it seems that Archbishop George al-Ḥakīm has attempted throughout to preserve his freedom of manoeuvre, while at the same time continuing to build up his prestige within the Greek Catholic community. It is this ability for political manoeuvre, together with his religious position, that has given him a special standing of his own in Israeli politics in recent years.

The main characteristic of Arab political leadership in Israel is its fragmentation. The divisions among the communities and within each, indeed, prevented the rise of a joint political leadership for the Arabs in Palestine in previous years, too. However, it appears that within the State of Israel several other variants have been added, which work towards a further split in Arab leadership. Of these variants, the two most important are: (1) rapid change, at a varying tempo, within Arab towns and villages. This change has shaken former socio-political structures, without providing for an alternative, generally acknowledged leadership. (2) The activity of Jewish elements in Arab localities, with varying degrees of intensity. This factor assists the rise of political personalities connected with the Jews who change their allegiance according to opportunist considerations. The only independent political leadership of the Arabs in Israel relevant on the national scale is that of RAQAḤ on the one hand, and Archbishop George al-Ḥakīm on the other, that is, the two political elements possessing ideologies whose sources are outside the State of Israel. In spite of evident rivalry (or perhaps due to it), both have addressed themselves to the nationalist sentiments of the Arab minority—RAQAḤ continuously and loudly, al-Ḥakīm only sporadically and much more moderately.

FOCI OF POLITICAL ACTIVITY

The political activity of the Arabs in Israel is centred, as might be expected, in their main residential areas—Galilee and the Little Triangle. The Bedouin tribes, particularly those in the Negev, are scattered over a relatively large area and their political alertness has constantly been limited (largely because of geographical conditions). The Arabs dwelling in the six mixed towns certainly are politically conscious; but their residence in a preponderantly Jewish environment reduces the practical value of their political activity (with the

[47] Cf. ibid. 2 Aug. 1963, & *ha-Areṣ*, 6 Dec. 1965.

exception of Acre, where the Arabs make up a quarter of the inhabitants, and which has an Arab as deputy mayor).

This section, therefore, attempts to describe Arab politics in Galilee and the Little Triangle, starting with the former, which is larger in population and area, concentrating on Nazareth, the largest Arab town in Israel.

1. *Nazareth*

Nazareth, in the heart of Galilee, determines to a considerable extent the political behaviour of the Arabs in Galilee and, indeed, in the whole of Israel. At the end of 1947 Nazareth[48] had a population of approximately 16,500. Practically all its inhabitants remained in the town during the 1948 war. A number of Arab villagers from the neighbourhood moved there, so that the first population census in Israel, early in 1949, recorded 18,500 inhabitants. At the end of 1966 there were about 30,000 inhabitants,[49] slightly more than half of whom were Muslims. The rise in the number of Muslims in Nazareth, compared with the Christians, may be attributed to several factors: a larger natural increase; the annexation to the jurisdiction of Nazareth of a few adjacent quarters inhabited by Muslims; and emigration trends, operating only among the Christians (who have family connexions abroad and find it easier than the Muslims to acclimatize there).[50] Almost a sixth of the population consider themselves as refugees from various villages, and these generally tend to extremist political views.

The rate of economic progress in Nazareth has been no less rapid. Under British rule, pilgrimage to the town's churches and sites was the main source of its income; the hotel industry, local manufacture, and commerce were pilgrim-oriented. Since 1949 new enterprises (albeit small ones) have been established and the building trade has made marked progress. In addition to the increase in services, food production has risen (chiefly soft drinks, ice-cream, sweets, etc.), stone and wood handicrafts have diversified, and new quarries of stone, chalk, and lime have been opened. Nevertheless, no large industrial plants have been established. While Pinḥas Sapīr was Israel's Minister of Trade and Industry, he repeatedly tried to persuade Arab capitalists to invest in the foundation of new industries, especially in Nazareth, either by themselves or in partnership with

[48] Some of the details are based on a booklet by Ori Stendel, *Noṣrat be-ʻavar w-va-hōveh* (1966).

[49] *Stat. Ab. 1966*, table B/11, mentions 29,100 persons at the end of 1965. The number for the end of 1966 is only an unofficial estimate by the CBS.

[50] Details by Mansour, *ha-Areṣ*, 10 May 1967.

Jewish capital, but they steadfastly refused to do so. Even existing industries, such as the cigarette factory, have hardly renewed their equipment and machinery; as a result, the cigarette industry and others have been operating at a loss.[51]

The development of adjacent Jewish Nazareth has served to spur competition.[52] For instance, a number of workers from Arab Nazareth have found employment in it.[53] The problem of finding employment has remained none the less acute, for although it was reduced in size (many Nazareth workers found employment in near-by *kibbūtzīm*, in Haifa, and even in more remote Tel-Aviv), competition from neighbouring villagers who sought work in Nazareth has continued to be strong.[54] Taken as a whole, the rise in the living standards has been expressed in a threefold increase in the consumption of electricity during 1960–6, in the installation of numerous telephones, in the diversification of home furniture and appliances—including refrigerators, gas, radio, and TV (more than 1,000 TV sets) as well as changes of taste, both in food and clothing. Even the 1966–7 economic recession—which affected Nazareth residents as much as those elsewhere (in particular those who worked out of town)[55]—only slowed down, but did not stop, the development of the town.[56]

Demographic and economic advance in Nazareth have not gone hand in hand with socio-cultural progress. True, the town is the cultural centre of Galilee, but it affords only very limited scope for intellectual activity, nor has it been distinguished by any remarkable literary creativity. Despite the pulse of life in it, it has remained to a large extent bound to traditional social structures. The change in these structures in Nazareth is worthy of a detailed sociological analysis, yet to be undertaken. However, it may be asserted, even in the light of present knowledge, that though members of each local *ḥamūla* no longer live all together in the same neighbourhood, and though the conflicts with the *ḥamūla* have altered in character, its framework is still binding on all its members as the basic social structure. Many of those who refuse to acknowledge the *ḥamūla* ties any more still admit the significance of the religious impact. This

[51] Mansour, ibid. 22 May 1966. [52] Mansour, ibid. 21 & 30 Sept. 1966.

[53] Acc. to 'Abd al-'Azīz Zu'bī, in *al-Mirṣād*, 8 Jan. 1965, about 5 per cent of the workers in Jewish Nazareth were Arabs from neighbouring villages.

[54] Late in 1966 and early in 1967 unemployment in Nazareth increased because of the economic recession in Israel. (Cf. Karmel, *Ma'arīv*, 15 Feb. 1967.)

[55] Margalīt, in *ha-Areṣ*, 23 Apr. 1967.

[56] On unemployment in Nazareth, cf. George Sa'd, in *ba-Histadrūt* (Tel-Aviv), ix, Sept. 1966, 66. There were 1,397 men, 262 women, and 500 youngsters registered as unemployed in the labour exchange in Nazareth at that date.

impact is still so powerful that it frequently obtains priority over nationalist sentiments and political allegiance—when they conflict with the sense of belonging to a religious community. The existence of the *ḥamūlas* and the competition between them is more typical of the Nazareth Muslims (who, incidentally, are all Sunnites) than the Christian communities. Of the latter, the more important ones in the town are: (1) The Greek Catholics, the strongest community in Nazareth, thanks to the able leadership of Archbishop George al-Ḥakīm, its manifold economic enterprises and educational institutions, and its alliance with smaller Catholic denominations in the town (especially with the Latins, well-organized and rich, and with the Maronites).[57] (2) The Greek Orthodox is the most numerous of the Christian communities in Nazareth, but lacking an acknowledged leadership, poor in financial resources, and divided on two levels, by the bitter conflict between the young and the community elders, as well as by rising tension between the Greek religious leadership and the Arab lower-order priests.[58]

The impact of the *ḥamūlas* and religious communities transcends the social sphere and extends into Nazareth's politics. An example may be found in parliamentary and municipal elections, e.g. in November 1959. An examination of the results, by polls,[59] shows that most of MAQĪ's votes derived from the Christian quarters (chiefly the Greek Orthodox)[60] and the refugees (who had moved from adjacent villages to Nazareth). Among the Muslims, the communist vote declined in 1959.[61] The reason seems clear—the rift between 'Abd al-Nāṣir and Qāsim, with the Soviet Union publicly supporting Qāsim. The admirers of 'Abd al-Nāṣir among the Muslims in Nazareth apparently reacted by voting against MAQĪ. The situation was radically altered in the November 1965 parliamentary and municipal elections. Qāsim was no more, the Soviet Union was on excellent terms with 'Abd al-Nāṣir, whose radio in any case called on the Arabs in Israel to vote for RAQAḤ; as for RAQAḤ, it openly campaigned as a nationalist Arab party which praised 'Abd al-Nāṣir. The com-

[57] One of the reasons why the Christian communities in Nazareth have become wealthy is their exemption from municipal and other taxes. See *Ma'arīv*, 15 July & 11 Aug. 1966; cf. Y. Einstein, 'Church property in Nazareth', a reader's letter in *JP*, 28 Nov. 1966.

[58] Saul Colbi, *A short history of Christianity in the Holy Land* (Tel-Aviv, 1965), 62 ff.

[59] The findings are approximate, since most quarters in Nazareth are now inhabited by members of various religious communities; however, almost in every poll there is a preponderant number of electors from one community or the other.

[60] See Kna'an, in *ha-Areṣ*, 1 Apr. 1965.

[61] Acc. to estimates, only about 10 per cent of the Muslim valid votes in Nazareth.

munist vote among the Nazareth Muslims rose accordingly. Indeed, MAQĪ, then RAQAḤ, has constantly expressed itself against the influence of the religious communities in politics; hence their slates of candidates, in Nazareth and elsewhere, have put much less emphasis than other parties on religious affiliation of the candidates.[62] A characteristic example may be taken from the 1966 municipal elections in Nazareth. The third candidate on the RAQAḤ slate was a Muslim who had married a Christian woman; RAQAḤ preferred not to take into consideration the possibility that this might estrange a few voters. So, while MAPAI (the Alignment) and some other parties have been electioneering in Nazareth through the *ḥamūlas* or within the religious communities, it appears that the communists have preferred to campaign according to district, through the party's local committees or cells.

The socio-political fragmentation in Nazareth, mainly due to the ingrained power of the *ḥamūlas* and the religious communities, has in recent years been further aggravated by new loyalties, political or personal. The acuteness of the fragmentation is accentuated by an escalation in personal conflicts—which often prevent political and socio-economic association. The political parties are not alone in finding it difficult to work in such an atmosphere. For instance, even an attempt to establish a local branch of the Merchants' Association failed in Nazareth, because of disagreement over filling the offices of the president and secretary of the branch. The employment situation too, works against political organization: many breadwinners in Nazareth who work out of town form a sort of Arab proletariat, employed by Jewish enterprises; very likely, a number of these is afraid to be openly active in politics lest they displease their employers. This was probably one of the main causes for the successive failures to launch an independent Arab party in Nazareth during the early years of the State. Later, in 1957–8, several Arab teachers in Nazareth tried to form a 'Young Teachers' slate of candidates for the approaching national elections of the Israeli Teachers' Federation. The top candidates were Arab teachers favourable to MAQĪ, but for the sake of prudence, they claimed that they were independents who desired to 'save' education for Arab children. The slate broke down and failed, chiefly due to lack of proper organization. Even the only significant organizational success in Nazareth politics was short-lived: we have

[62] MAPAM, also, does not generally ally itself with religious communities, but in Nazareth it has close connexions with the small Coptic community. It appears that some Copts had been employed as builders by MAPAM's *kibbūtzīm* and later became party workers in Nazareth.

already described[63] how an 'Arab Front', later named the 'Popular Front' was organized with MAQĪ inspiration and sponsorship, in Nazareth and Acre; and how it simply broke down, after a few nationalist politicians (later called *al-Arḍ* group) had left the front.

Had independent association succeeded in Nazareth, perhaps additional means would have been found there to channel political acitivity. However, since all such attempts had failed, the Arabs in Nazareth found themselves faced solely with the extremes. Expressed in practical terms, polarization has meant that any Nazareth Arab who is politically active has to throw in his lot with either 'the Government camp' or 'the camp of the disgruntled'. Each of the two camps is not a unity, but, on the contrary, incorporates varied elements. The Government camp, politically close to MAPAI circles, is supported by the fact that many Government offices (and, until its abolition, those of the military administration) were in Nazareth. This camp is sustained by the institutionalized framework of the *ḥamūlas* and, in some measure, by the leadership of the religious communities; it is supported by all those who have opted for the present situation and therefore oppose any disturbance in Nazareth and the State of Israel. It appears that many officials, teachers and others connected with the Establishment sympathize with this camp and even support it actively. The camp of the disgruntled is headed, on the one hand by the communists, leaders of RAQAḤ (formerly, of MAQĪ), one of whose leading personalities is Fu'ād Khūrī, chief of the communist group in Nazareth's municipal council; and on the other by various alienated, nationalist elements, who have not yet acknowledged (overtly or otherwise) the existence of the State of Israel, and are nourished in their opposition by the extremist propaganda of the radio and television services of the Arab States. RAQAḤ, which employs chauvinistic catchwords in its own propaganda, eagerly competes with the nationalists in Nazareth. MAPAM inaugurated a branch of the party there in 1951, headed by A. Ben-Tzur.[64] It maintains a position between the two camps, representing itself as the party of the golden mean. This is probably the reason for its relatively weak standing, which is handicapped by the political polarization of Nazareth.

The existence of the above political camps is not confined to Nazareth alone, but characterizes the general political disposition of

[63] See above, pp. 93–95.

[64] Who has already been mentioned as an organizer of the Arab Pioneer Youth. He is also the author of a book (in Hebrew) on Arab socialism.

many Arabs in Israel. Nazareth's uniqueness lies in the manner in which political activity is conducted in these camps. The entire town has only one non-political club, the YMCA, which arranges sports and cultural events.[65] Other clubs are the Frank Sinatra *Histadrūt* Club,[66] the activities of which are politically close to MAPAI (the Alignment); MAPAI's own club, inaugurated during 1960–1, for the party's friends in Nazareth (it doubles as a youth centre, mainly attended by the sons of MAPAI's friends); MAPAM's Brotherhood Club, doubling as a kindergarten; and RAQAḤ's own similar club. Because of this situation, anyone who is actively interested in politics is limited to a choice between these clubs. We have previously described MAPAI (the Alignment), MAPAM, and the communists as continuously active among the Arabs in Israel. This is certainly true, if taken to refer to the organization of meetings, rallies, etc., of all three. There is, however, a substantial difference in Nazareth between the parties in the frequency and continuity of their activities among non-party members. Despite the fact that three out of the four political clubs in Nazareth belong to MAPAI (the Alignment) and MAPAM, or are close to them, the political activity of what we have called the Government camp is limited to several house meetings and sporadic rallies, gathering force only on special occasions, such as the First of May, eve of elections, and the like. The activities of those we have named the disgruntled camp are carried on with greater continuity, as well as with greater intensity, in Nazareth: in addition to a flood of written propaganda, personal contacts are consistently maintained and new ones initiated. Active communists, more so than others, have gone out of Nazareth to various villages in Galilee, to campaign in public and private.

A considerable share of communist and nationalist propaganda in Nazareth is directed towards local Arab youth, and some seems to make an impression, despite its exaggerations, or perhaps because of them. The Arab youth in Nazareth seems particularly vulnerable to extremist political propaganda, as it remembers only vaguely the 1948 war—in contrast to the older generation. It is free from the Palestinian type of bitterness, but appears to have adopted a brand of its own, tainted with envy of the successes of Jewish youth and a consequent feeling of frustration. Since Nazareth youth receives few, if any, opportunities for its leisure from municipal resources, it is a relatively easy target for extremist propaganda, ably exploiting its

[65] Actually, the Nazareth municipality, also, runs a club of its own, which keeps out of politics generally; but it appears that it is not used so frequently.

[66] See Mansour, in *ha-Areṣ*, 10 May 1967.

frustrations. The dimensions of the problem may be better grasped, if one notes the young age-structure of the Nazareth population,[67] which is becoming more marked. It is not, then, out of altruism that MAQĪ, then RAQAḤ (which inherited MAQĪ's place in Nazareth, *in toto*) has gone to such trouble to organize the Nazareth youth. With the exception of the scouts, the only youth movement in the town is sponsored by the communists, who have organized it in three groups: (1) Pioneers, up to 14 years of age; (2) an intermediate group, aged 14–16; (3) adolescents, 16 years old and over.[68] For these categories, the Communist Party maintains a youth club in Nazareth, which is quite active. RAQAḤ youth in Nazareth is affiliated to the party's country-wide youth organization. In Nazareth the activities of the communist youth chiefly consist of distribution of handbills, participation in meetings or demonstrations, collection of donations for the party, etc.

The polarization of political activities in Nazareth is noticeable in labour organization also. For a number of years three main organizations have been available to Nazareth's workers. First, the Alliance of Palestinian Workers, affiliated to the *Histadrūt*, with about 10,000 members, in 34 branches, the largest of which was the one in Nazareth. Its secretary was George Sa'd, who is nowadays secretary of the Workers' Council in Nazareth. Within this alliance a number of Arab workers' leaders gradually emerged, but continued to be guided by the Jewish sponsors of the organization, which did not pass unnoticed by the propaganda of the rival Congress of Workers. With the entry of Arab workers into the *Histadrūt*, in 1952, and their acceptance as full members eight years later, the need for this alliance diminished. Secondly, the Congress of Workers, MAQĪ-oriented, has been, in actual political practice, the only independent Arab association in Nazareth whose activity has been continued since before the establishment of the State of Israel. This organization has usually had a membership of about 1,500–2,000, its centre being Nazareth. The Congress of Workers has been working for years independently from the *Histadrūt*, and even in competition with it. For this reason, the congress has developed its own institutions, similar in scope and aims to those of the *Histadrūt*: a sick fund, a provident fund, co-operative services, study courses for workers, etc. Thirdly, the League of Nazareth Workers, an association sponsored by circles of the Christian churches. It was smaller than the other two,

[67] Acc. to the 1961 census, the average number of children for every married woman in Nazareth is 7. See additional details in *ha-Areṣ*, 30 Dec. 1966.

[68] In general, up to 18 years old, when they are recruited into the party.

and its activity was relatively more limited. Its main activities date from 1948 to 1951; later it associated with the Alliance of Palestinian Workers and merged with it. Its secretary was Nadīm Baṭḥīsh, later deputy mayor of Nazareth.

The role of the main political factors in Nazareth was emphasized in the first election to its Workers' Council, during September 1965, already briefly noted.[69] Only three political parties—the Alignment, MAPAM, and RAQAḤ—competed. The total number of those entitled to vote was only a little over 4,000. The Alignment appeared on one list only, because of the paucity of electors and of the fact that this was a vote of *workers*, with little connexion with the notables, whose assistance was required for parliamentary and municipal elections. The Alignment obtained 12 seats on the 21-man Workers' Council, MAPAM 3, and RAQAḤ 6. The latter's relative failure was probably due to its lack of organization (after the 1965 communist rift) and to the fact that it had relatively few members in the *Histadrūt*, the only ones entitled to vote.[70]

2. *The Little Triangle*

The Little Triangle is a narrow strip, 3–6 miles wide, along the border-line of the 1948 armistice agreement between Israel and the Kingdom of Jordan. In this area there are twenty-six villages, from Kafr Qāsim in the south to Umm al-Faḥm (the largest Arab village in Israel)[71] in the north. When the State of Israel was founded, this area had some 35,000 inhabitants; in 1966 over 60,000[72]—i.e. about a fifth of the whole Arab population in Israel and twice as many as in Nazareth. The whole of the Little Triangle, like Nazareth, is inhabited by Arabs. Because of its rural and wholly Muslim character, the Little Triangle tends towards greater homogeneity than internally divided Nazareth, though this is not complete due to different stages of social evolution within it. Religion seems to hold a significant place in public life, especially with the older generation.[73] The promixity to the border appears to affect the Little Triangle in two ways: many inhabitants have part of their family just across the frontier; part of their former land was situated (until the six-days' war, in June 1967) in Jordan.

Many of the socio-economic developments which have occurred

[69] See above, p. 179.
[70] See also Mansour, in *ha-Areṣ*, 16 Sept. 1965.
[71] On this village, cf. ibid. 1 Apr. 1965 & 22 July 1966, suppl.
[72] Acc. to the estimates of the CBS, between 61,000 and 62,000.
[73] Cf. *MḤ*, xv/1–2 (1965), 85.

in Nazareth since 1948 have been paralleled in the villages of the Little Triangle; possibly the jump of the latter into the second half of the twentieth century has been even more spectacular. Because of its proximity to several Jewish towns, the Little Triangle was the first Arab-inhabited area to enjoy rapid progress, encouraged in this by the Israeli Government, the *Histadrūt*, and others. All its villages have piped water, as well as governmental or *Histadrūt* health services; almost all have electricity and convenient new roads; the number of rooms per person has visibly increased.[74] Formerly, farming in the Little Triangle was extensive, and the crops were not sufficiently diversified; more recently, intensive mechanized agriculture has taken its place, with planned crops suited to the needs of the market. During British rule in Palestine, the farm hands, sharecroppers, shepherds, and camel-drivers had formed an average about 80 per cent of the work-force of every village in this area; in 1963 these groups altogether formed only some 20 per cent of the work-force.[75] Many of the others have found profitable employment outside their villages. Hence a sociologist who has investigated the Little Triangle,[76] concludes that

> the Arab villagers have ceased to be farmers and have become a proletariat residing in a rural area. In the village under investigation,[77] salaried workers form about 60 per cent of the male population; most of them are employed outside the village. Their livelihood and economic relations are connected with the labour market.

The comparatively great mobility of Little Triangle Arab workers[78] is, to a large extent, due on the one hand to the loss of their land (which had remained in Jordan), and, on the other, to the attractive remuneration for salaried workers in adjacent Jewish towns. This mobility has contributed to the break-up of the former framework of social institutions in the Arab village. The process has been hastened by the rise in education: elementary education encompasses all villages, while high schools are available in several (e.g. Ṭīra, Ṭaiyyba) or in near-by Jewish towns. The impact of Islam is not so strong among the younger generation, some of whom do not hesitate to declare publicly their non-observance or even their irreligiousness.[79] It is not surprising that the authority of the *ḥamūla* heads (some of

[74] See Mansour, in *ha-Areṣ*, 13 May 1966.

[75] Calculated by Rosenfeld in *Hem hayū*, 172.

[76] Ibid. 182. [77] Ṭaiyyba.

[78] *Moslems, Christians & Druzes*, table 56. This mobility has somewhat lessened during the 1966–7 economic recession (cf. *ha-Areṣ*, 22 July 1966, suppl., 6–7).

[79] Examples in *YA*, 17 Feb. 1967, and *Ma'arīv*, 20 Feb. 1967.

whom in any case had remained in Jordan) has been weakening, although it is still powerful, particularly in those instances when the village elders retain possession of the public property and the means of production. However, even in such villages, they cannot control elections any more (which are secret and equal), or prevent increasing political activity.

The ethnic and religious homogeneity of the Little Triangle population, its proximity to the border as well as to Jewish urban centres, rapid economic advance, a steep rise in the standards of living,[80] progress in education—all have contributed towards a political alertness which seems equal to that in Nazareth. Interest in politics has been fostered by various political parties—chiefly, MAPAI (the Alignment), MAPAM, and MAQĪ (RAQAḤ). All three have carried on active propaganda in the Little Triangle. They have established party branches as well as clubs in the larger villages, intended also to serve smaller localities. In general, the activity of political parties in the Little Triangle resembles that in Nazareth, except that it is more intensive in certain respects. MAPAI (the Alignment) has been even more active in forming political alliances with various *ḥamūla* heads. MAPAM and MAQĪ (then RAQAḤ) pursue an even more aggressive propaganda among the younger generation, but apparently with varying success, because the influence of established social patterns has tended to persist in this Muslim rural environment. Nevertheless, MAQĪ (then RAQAḤ) has been a dangerous rival of MAPAI (the Alignment) in the Little Triangle no less than in Nazareth. The communist vote, for instance, is rising in the Little Triangle, probably owing to its nationalist appeal. The electoral strength of MAQĪ (RAQAḤ) has increased in the larger villages, which have enjoyed a marked economic advance. Remarkably, in those villages, gratitude to MAPAI for economic progress has frequently been a less decisive factor than the fact that development has increased interest in politics (especially among the young), sometimes resulting in a trend towards extremism.

External and internal factors thus combine to alter the character of the disposition of political forces in the villages of the Little Triangle. The *ḥamūla* rivalry and family competition for power still continue; this is particularly true of the periods between elections, when the influence of the younger generation is very limited

[80] *Ma'arīv*, 22 Oct. 1965, suppl., describes Ṭīra as a village of elegant villas, with a new building for the town council, numerous TV antennae, and flourishing schools. Ibid. 26 May 1966, boasts of similar progress in Ṭaiyyba. See, however, the different situation in Umm al-Faḥm, acc. to Mansour, in *ha-Areṣ*, 1 Apr. 1965.

in the decisive affairs of the village. In contrast, as elections draw nearer, the political disposition of forces tends to change, as another factor is added to those formerly mentioned—the contest between the old and the young. This contest does not have quite the same aspect in all villages, nor does it lead to any standard result. Examples of these differences may be drawn from the campaigns and results of the November 1965 local elections in Ṭaiyyba and Jatt. In the former, all the competing lists of candidates loyally belonged to local *ḥamūlas*, with the single exception of RAQAḤ. In the latter, the *ḥamūla* lists were divided among themselves; the largest *ḥamūla*, which forms about half of Jatt's inhabitants, obtained only about 200 votes out of the *ḥamūla*'s 500 (and hence only 3 out of the 9 seats in the local council); or, in other words, a sizeable number of this *ḥamūla*'s members voted for other *ḥamūlas* and lists of candidates. In recent years several of Jatt's teachers have been striving for leadership in local matters, and six of them were candidates for the local council in the 1965 elections: three even headed competing lists. Two teachers obtained seats on the local council of Jatt, one of whom was elected to the chairmanship of the council. Such incidents need not imply that the local *ḥamūlas* have completely lost their power; on the contrary, they usually join forces and redouble their efforts after the elections in order to continue to exert influence behind the scenes in Jatt. In Ṭaiyyba, although three lists of young candidates competed with others for the 1965 local elections, and two of their representatives entered the local council, the real influence of these youths on the council is still very limited, due to the more substantial role of the *ḥamūlas* and village elders in Ṭaiyyba.

An index of political activity in the villages of the Little Triangle is the popularity of the sports clubs.[81] These compete with existing clubs, previously established by the *Histadrūt* and various political parties. The *Histadrūt* strives to make its own clubs into meaningful factors in the socio-cultural scene of the Little Triangle (as elsewhere); it also attempts to use them to promote greater civic pride, and, by extension, adaptation to the State of Israel. The *Histadrūt* clubs are open six days a week; their services include libraries, game-rooms, and conference-halls. MAPAM has instituted clubs of a similar character in Jatt and a few other villages in the Little Triangle, while RAQAḤ has done the same in Umm al-Faḥm and Ṭaiyyba. Some of the sports clubs in the Little Triangle are genuinely intended for sports activities, but others are not; we have already mentioned,

[81] So far as could be ascertained, it appears that similar Arab sports clubs in the villages of Galilee have imitated those in the Little Triangle.

in describing the aftermath of the *al-Arḍ* group,[82] the affair of the sports club in Ṭaiyyba, closed for sedition in September 1966 by order of the authorities.[83] Doubless even sports clubs may well offer occasions, formal or informal, for arguments and debates of a political character. This feature seems to have been in-built, since most have been established by local initiative, with no support from the State authorities, the *Histadrūt*, or the political parties; all these have regarded the sports clubs with some suspicion, as possibly seditious and probable rivals to previously existing clubs. Despite opposition from all these quarters (or most of them), sports clubs have sprung up, especially during 1961–6, in Ṭīra, Kafr Qara', Umm al-Faḥm, Jaljūliyya, Bāqa al-Gharbiyya, Qalansawa, and Ṭaiyyba. In these clubs, sporting activities, chiefly of the local soccer team, take place; in addition, lectures or debates, literary or art circles, as well as language courses are frequently, though not regularly, arranged. Members' fees (generally from £I0·50 to £I1 per month) and periodic collections during the soccer games finance the maintenance of these clubs.[84]

The sports club of Ṭīra, the veteran in the Little Triangle, may serve as a case study. It is highly regarded, and has attempted to be the patron of the sports clubs in Kafr Qara', Qalansawa, and Bāqa al-Gharbiyya.[85] The articles of association of this sports club presented to the District Commissioner and approved by him,[86] specify aims as encouraging sports and education, viz.: to assist in the eradication of illiteracy in Ṭīra; to spread general knowledge; to help the needy; to distribute information about hygiene; and to encourage sports activities among the village youth. These articles of association are innocent and the declared aims of the sports club are legitimate and legal. However, the activities of a local teacher, Ḥusnī 'Irāqī, and others belied the officially presented aims of the Ṭīra sports club and rapidly involved its increasing politicization. The club invited several people to lecture, who were known for their extremist attitudes and their opposition to the State authorities; among the most prominent were Ṣāliḥ Barānsī, one of the ex-leaders of *al-Arḍ* group, and Samīḥ al-Qāsim, an extremist Druze on the staff of the communist bi-weekly *al-Ittiḥād*.[87] Newspaper reports alleged that Egypt's national anthem was played at the end of fes-

[82] See above, pp. 101–2.

[83] Cf. also *Ma'arīv*, 25 Sept., 18 Oct., & 11 Nov. 1966.

[84] I have found no proof concerning the allegations that the sports clubs received financial support from MAQĪ, and later from RAQAḤ.

[85] See also *la-Merḥav*, 27 Apr. 1964.

[86] On 3 Dec. 1961.

[87] The latter lectured about the Druzes in Israel on 12 Sept. 1964.

tivities. These were not confirmed, but the club's organ, *The Message of the Club*, included seditious articles denigrating the State of Israel.[88] On parallel lines, the Ṭīra sports club served practical purposes of political organization. In January 1964 Ḥusnī 'Irāqī and Ḥasan Bishāra, both teachers in Ṭira's high school and promoters of the club, formed an 'initiating committee', the main target of which was to look after village affairs and to found a popular movement, which in time would attain leadership in the village—presumably through the local council—instead of the present leadership.[89]

Similar activities both in sports and in politics, though varying in intensity, are typical also of other sports clubs in the villages of the Little Triangle. For instance, at the end of *'Īd al-aḍḥà* (the feast of the sacrifice), on 22 April 1964, a number of youths met in the sports club of Bāqa al-Gharbiyya, where they organized a public rally, complete with speeches and greetings for 'Abd al-Nāṣir, an act bound to arouse the suspicion of the authorities.[90] Although the sports clubs do not have a national organization for the whole of Israel (there are similar ones in Galilee), or even for the area of the Little Triangle, the ties between them appear to be growing stronger. A typical instance was the soccer games contest initiated by the sports club in Kafr Qara', to which it invited teams and fans from the clubs in Ṭīra, Umm al-Faḥm, Qalansawa, and 'Ar'ara. After the events in Bāqa al-Gharbiyya (which had occurred less than three weeks previously), the military administration intervened and forbade entry to or exit from Kafr Qara'. The Qalansawa soccer team defied the orders and came to play in Kafr Qara', which it did. As a result, a number of the sponsors of the Ṭīra and Qalansawa sports clubs, as well as some of the organizers of the rally in Bāqa al-Gharbiyya were arrested and duly charged. The chairman of the Ṭīra local council, Ibrāhīm Khalīl, requested that the village sports club be closed down 'for encouraging negative activities, opposed to the good of the State'.[91]

Within Arab[92] and Jewish public opinion[93] in Israel, there are conflicting standpoints regarding the activities and role of the sports

[88] See App. J, pp. 255–6 below.

[89] From a manifesto distributed by the committee in Ṭīra during Jan. 1964.

[90] *Ma'arīv*, 23 Apr. 1964.

[91] *'Al ha-Mishmar*, 11 May 1964. One may assume that the chairman of the local council in Ṭīra wanted the sports club closed down, since it served as a meeting place for potential opposition to himself.

[92] e.g. for a different opinion from that held by the chairman of Ṭīra's local council, see Watad, in *al-Mirṣād*, 9 Oct. 1966.

[93] For opposed views, see Sh. Segev in *Ma'arīv*, 3 Oct. 1966, and M. Stein, ibid. 18 Oct. 1966.

clubs; diametrically opposed views have been expressed in the press and elsewhere. What seems to be a fact, amidst conflicting evidence, is that these sports clubs, in addition to various educational and physical-culture activities, serve also as significant foci of political fermentation in the villages in the Little Triangle. They serve as a breeding ground for nuclei of independent political organization, whose ideological basis is Arab nationalism, extremist or moderate (apparently more often the former). It appears that activity in these sports clubs remains local, and that no one club exercises political leadership over the others. Even the sports club in Ṭīra, despite its privileged standing, does not appear to be endowed with sufficient prestige for its political influence to emanate even regionally, let alone on a country-wide basis.

End of Chap 7

8

CONCLUDING REMARKS

An attempt to describe and analyse the political behaviour of the Arabs in Israel does not, at present, lend itself to definite conclusions. The period starting with the foundation of the State of Israel in May 1948 and ending with the abolition of the military administration in December 1966 and the six-days' war in June 1967 is but a chapter in their history. Their dual role as a part of the larger Arab nation and citizens of a State three times at war with it during nineteen years has imposed a tremendous emotional strain on them. The additional pressure to adapt rapidly to twentieth-century government, society, and economics has added to their feelings of alienation.

In consequence, their participation in politics, as expressed in their writings, speeches, and votes has been characterized by a wide range of attitudes, from the most moderate to the extremist.

Not unexpectedly, the younger and better-educated have tended to be more demanding and outspoken. The fact that many of these Arabs who have lived in Israel during the crucial years 1948–67 have accepted the existence of the State of Israel, with themselves as part of it, while some have identified with the State even more fully, strikes a hopeful note. As vigorous activity by the Jewish majority on behalf of the Arab minorities continues, and as the Arab minority increasingly appreciates the positive results of progress achieved and shares in the dynamic activity within Israel, confrontation may well change into co-operation, and thence into integration.

APPENDIX A

RUSTUM BASTŪNĪ ON INTEGRATING THE ARABS IN ISRAEL[1]

A PROGRAMME is needed to improve the present unsatisfactory position of the Arabs in Israel and Arab-Jewish relations within the State. An appropriate atmosphere must be created to form an Arab society capable of integrating itself fully into the modern, dynamic trends of life of this country on the one hand, and to change the Jewish attitude towards anything that is specially Arab on the other.

A new approach is needed, which would separate, first of all, the problems of Israel's Arab community—an internal Israeli problem—from the overall political situation prevailing in the Middle East, the state of 'no peace no war' between Israel and the neighbouring countries—which is an international problem. This aim will succeed only if concentrated efforts are applied to the fields of education and economy, creating through them new structures; and if the Arab community itself will take stock of its present condition and do things instead of waiting for things to be done for them. Any political interference will defeat this aim, as so many past attempts ended in defeat.

Just as the existence of the State of Israel should be recognized by the Arab community, so the Jews must reconcile themselves to the fact that the country belongs to the Middle East . . .

The Israeli Arab has to recognize that he confronts three possibilities:

a. Identification and sympathy with the policies of neighbouring countries that proclaim the destruction of Israel in the near future. Any individual who subscribes to such views must draw the inevitable conclusions and either emigrate or be aware that his continued presence within the State's boundaries is a latent threat to the security of the nation;

b. assimilation into another ethnic group, implying thereby the loss of all distinct cultural and folkloric characteristics:

c. full integration into the social and economic framework of the country, while preserving those historical, cultural and ethnic values that are specific to the Arab community.

We do not subscribe to the belief that the choice is limited to either (*a*) or (*b*). We do not believe in 'double loyalty' since loyalty cannot be divided or split. We do not accept either the view of the majority of Israeli Jews which neglects the problem as such, evading the issue, by pretending that a solution can only be found once peace with the neighbouring countries is made. We also reject another Israeli Jewish view that holds that Arabs are living in this country by grace of charity or tolerance and are

[1] 'Integrating Israel's Arabs', *JP*, 25 Sept. 1964, excerpts.

much better off than, say, Jews would be under Arab domination if Israel were an Arab-ruled country.

The present apathy of the Arab population to general Israeli problems, whether they pertain to the security of the country or to its economic cultural or social life, is primarily due to low morale, lethargy, and lack of that sense of solidarity which forges a nation. All this must change to create a true sense of citizenship which implies sharing responsibilities, duties and rights alike.

The present educational, economic, and social standards of the Arab community in Israel do not permit immediate integration and, therefore, a special crash programme is needed, just as for certain immigrant groups, to enable them to reach the standard of the majority of the population. It is ironical indeed that reforms and evolutionary processes should be rejected by the Arab community in Israel, while these very same measures are being adopted and implemented in the neighbouring countries and hailed there as very progressive.

Sincere and fundamental changes in the fields of education and economics, as outlined in broad terms in the programme we propose, a positive official attitude and an enlightened public opinion would help Israel's Arab citizens to develop their adaptability to a modern technological social structure by making them feel secure.

The concept of an 'Israeli Arab' should not and cannot mean either separatist tendencies (such as the obsolete outdated nationalistic aspirations of a 'Palestinian entity' for example) or what goes by the term of 'assimilation'. It must be a synthesis of Israel's general values and Arab ethnic heritage. This implies that, on the one hand, every Arab in Israel must free himself of the myth of belonging to another territorial unit and that his loyalty to the State of Israel, whose citizen he is, implies betrayal of some vague, undefined, general Arab family. An Arab who feels that his problems cannot be solved and his aspirations cannot be fulfilled within the boundaries of the State of Israel cannot become a responsible citizen; every Arab must sound out his own feelings and decide whether he can accept full responsibility for the existence—present and future—of the State, or, if this is unacceptable to him, leave the country. On the other hand, the Jewish citizens of Israel must realize that their Arab compatriots live here by natural inalienable right, that they are in no way inferior, and that while some of their customs are different, different does not mean inferior.

If the term 'Israeli Arab' is to be a valid description of those to whom it is applied, the Arab community in Israel must cease to be a pawn on the electoral chess-board, a political bargaining counter. It must be able to guide its own social, economic, and educational evolution, so as to be able to contribute fully to the life of the country. It would then produce from within its own ranks the ideology and leadership it now lacks. The efforts of Israel's Arabs should therefore be directed not only towards the political arena, but very much to the educational, economic, and social fields.

The concept of an Israeli Arab as an Israeli citizen belonging to the Arab ethnical group implies that he should be granted the same responsibilities and duties as well as rights—as any other citizen. This attitude, we believe, would be much more effective than the various restrictions imposed at present for so-called 'security reasons'. The question may then be asked whether the Arab citizen of Israel can be loyal to the State and be conscious of its security problems while retaining his specific social and cultural values. We have already said that there can be no divided loyalty and that some mythical belonging to an all-embracing Arab community is a fallacy in the third quarter of the twentieth century, when regional tribal allegiances might be expected to be outmoded. Modern national loyalty, in Israel as everywhere, means spiritual identification with the problems of the State, with its future and its territorial unity.

It must be crystal-clear to every Israeli Arab that modern warfare for all countries is synonymous with annihilation. So much the more so for a tiny country geographically as vulnerable as Israel. It must be quite clear to Israel's Arab community that in the event of a war between Israel and its neighbouring States there would be no safe region, no no-man's land, no rear: the whole of the country and the totality of its population, whether Arabs or Jews, would be in the line of fire. Nuclear weapons do not distinguish between Jews and Arabs. . . .

Here is the programme that the circumstances we have discussed impose on us, if we are to achieve the genuine progress and integration of Israel's Arabs:

A basic revision of the education system with the main stress on:

A drastic raising of teaching and curriculum standards in Arab elementary schools and the planning of some joint activities, sports, and outings with Jewish elementary schools.

Secondary schools with joint Jewish-Arab classes in the exact sciences, sports, etc., while the teaching of literary subjects, the humanities, religious curricula, history, etc., would be separate.

Vocational training to supply the special skills needed in an industrialized society and in modern agriculture.

Training of the youth leaders needed to carry out changes in the Arab social structures.

Long schooldays (Be'er Sheba system) in low-income areas and slum quarters.

A revolutionary approach in the economic field, bringing about:

The inclusion of all Arab areas in general development planning, thereby granting them the same privileges and help as those given to the non-Arab settlements of the same region.

Consolidation of lands, as part of an agrarian reform to be implemented in the rural areas.

The encouragement of light industries to be set up in the Arab sectors as an integral part of Israel's economic development plan: canning and foodstuff industries (table oil refineries, tobacco, etc.); home industries, developing specific local skills such as making carpets, rugs, metal implements, etc.; industries affiliated to the building trade; artisan workshops (spare-parts, garages, service-stations for agricultural machinery); light industry (plastics, chemicals, fertilizers, pharmaceuticals, dye-stuffs, textile finishing, electrical appliances, diamond polishing, etc.).

The resettlement of commuters. Fifty per cent of Arab bread-winners are commuters, people with permanent jobs or occupations in towns. They have to be permanently settled in the immediate vicinity of their place of work.

In order to implement the programme outlined above, it is suggested that the following measures be adopted concurrently:

Setting up specialized committees responsible for studying the different aspects examined here and for submitting concrete working proposals along these lines;

Submitting the findings of these committees to all relevant Government departments with a view to obtaining their opinion, approval and help in the practical implementation of the various measures to be taken.

Setting up a special 'legislation committee' to be responsible for proposing new legislation needed and for enforcing existing legal provisions;

A public information campaign, using all available means, to publicize the aims pursued and to mobilize public opinion, both Jewish and Arab, on their behalf;

The heads of the various committees to form a consultative body serving as a liaison agent between the Arab population and the Government authorities.

End of appendix a

p225
app

APPENDIX B

MANIFESTO OF THE ARAB STUDENTS' COMMITTEE[1]

OH, Arab compatriot!

On behalf of the Arab Students' Committee at the Hebrew University in Jerusalem, we appeal to you to respond to our fund-raising drive. We desire to collect money for our reserve fund, which is earmarked for matters regarding the Arab students and raising their standard.

We are happy to inform you that in so doing, you will be assisting in the foundation of the scholarly and cultural edifice of the Arabs in this country. We require the largest number of educated people and university graduates, to raise the level of their environment, which is, from every point of view, in the direst need of development.

The Arab Students' Committee, representing this year 170 students, has set several aims, the main ones being: a. To defend the rights of the Arabs in this country. b. To work for the equality of our Arab compatriots with the Jews in this country, on all levels. c. To bring about the realization of all liberties of Arabs in this country, including freedom of movement and expression, as well as the removal of all obstacles to their economic and social advancement. d. To encourage Arab students, both boys and girls, to enrol in institutions of higher learning, since education is one of the foundations of every advanced society. e. To raise the level of the Arab village and establish cultural and sports clubs, which will work for the development of Arab mind and body.

The Arab students at the Hebrew University have high hopes of the success of this fund-raising drive, in order to fulfil the above aims.

Your encouragement and help are a lamp to shine on our own road, as well as that of future generations. They will walk, by its light, in the path of a noble life; and we shall increase our diligent activity according to the support we get.

Our confidence in our people is unlimited. Help us so that we may help you in the best way possible! Encourage the Arab students at the Hebrew University! Act to increase their number! Allah assists His servant, as long as the servant assists his brother!

Gratefully,
The Arab Students' Committee
at the Hebrew University, Jerusalem

[1] This manifesto was mimeographed and distributed among the Arab population in Israel; it is undated. Trans. from the Arabic.

End of appendix B

2 2 6
APPENDIX C

TAWFĪQ ṬŪBĪ ON THE ARABS IN ISRAEL[1]

... ISRAEL'S rulers maintain that their hands are stretched forth in peace to the Arab States. But what can be done if this is not apparent even to the Arabs of Israel itself? These rulers refuse to recognize the partnership of the 300,000 Arabs who live in Israel. The military government, emergency regulations, and policy of national suppression carried out by the ruling circles destroy all bridges to understanding.

When Taqfīq Ṭūbī stated in the *Kneset* that the Government neglects this bridge to peace—the Arab population—Levi Eshkol replied that 'Arabs like Tawfīq Ṭūbī cannot be a bridgehead to understanding but to quarrelling and strife'.

I should like to ask the present Prime Minister: is he totally unable to learn from his predecessor anything but the policy of retaliation and raids across the border? Must he be relieved of his job before he learns a simple thing, that he cannot talk to the Arabs without us? Is it not clear to the Prime Minister that he cannot talk to Nazareth without Fu'ād Khūrī, Salīm al-Qāsim, Tawfīq Zayd, and their friends? Eshkol and Amnōn Līn tried twice to storm Nazareth and failed. In spite of terror and pressure, Nazareth gave almost 40 per cent of its vote to the communists and strengthened them. We greet the workers of Nazareth for placing their faith in their communist sons, who will not disappoint them. Nazareth is a symbol to all the Arab inhabitants of Israel. Not only the Arab people in Israel, but also all the Arab peoples withhold their confidence from men like King Ḥusayn and Sayf al-Dīn Zu'bī. The Arab peoples are searching for a way to national and social liberation and therefore they support the communists, anti-imperialists, patriots faithful to the interests of their people. The Eshkol Government is interested in a dialogue with yesmen internally, and with servants of imperialism externally. But through such means it is impossible to speak to the Arabs.

When we say that Israel must follow a different policy towards its Arab population, which can serve as a bridgehead to peace, we are amazed at times at the lack of any desire to understand the importance of the matter. We are astonished that, instead of undertaking such a policy, a foolish approach is gaining ground which views the Arabs as a burden on Israel's security, and thus the Government wastes yet another important chance.

In defending the legitimate rights of the Arab population of Israel, in its struggle for equal rights and against the policy of national suppression and discrimination, our Communist Party has been a faithful servant of the

[1] 'The Arab population—partner and bridge to peace', excerpt from speech to RAQAḤ's central committee, 7–8 Dec. 1966. Trans. from the Hebrew.

democratic cause and of Jewish-Arab friendship. In this struggle our party has won the trust and appreciation of the Arab population and strengthened the respect and confidence in democratic Jewish forces.

Our Communist Party, with its Jewish and Arab members, will continue to fight, to mobilize the Arab population and democratic Jewish forces, for the complete elimination of the military administration, emergency regulations, blacklists and all restrictions on freedom of movement, for an end to confiscation of property of Arab peasants, and for full equal rights for the Arab population—for the sake of democracy in Israel, friendship among our peoples, and for the true interests of the people of Israel . . .

End of appendix C

APPENDIX D

AL-ARḌ'S MEMORANDUM ON THE ARABS IN ISRAEL[1]

ISRAEL, a newly established state, is celebrating this year its 16th anniversary.

Although phenomenal events happened and radical changes swept the map of the world during the last two decades, and in spite of all the tremendous achievements that mankind achieved in recent years, the Arabs in Israel are still far from enjoying their natural rights. They suffer from a dedicated policy of oppression, discrimination and persecution that the Israeli Government wages against them.

The Israeli Government persists in its policy aiming terrific ends apropos the Arab communities; ends that are an affront to international laws of justice and human decency—a policy that contradicts the Government's commitments and its international obligations.

The following are the fundamental factors that are encouraging the Government to pursue its discriminatory policy:

a. The stern and adequate control that the Zionist Organizations exert on the world press. Consequently, all truth is hampered and the difficult situation of the Arab communities, is exposed to the world public opinion, in an erroneous and conflicting picture.

b. The campaign of hatred. The Israeli Government pursues a policy of hatred against the Arabs, encourages that feeling among the Jewish people and spurs on it most eagerly among the new generation, school-boys and students of higher education.

Unfortunately, all endeavours to create a reapproachment between the Arabs and the few democratic Jewish elements, failed and proved fruitless.

c. The stagnant United Nations. In spite of incessant appeals to the UN to deal with, and to investigate, the anomalous situation of the Arabs who suffer oppression and discrimination characteristic of 'occupation periods', so termed by the present Israeli Minister of Justice, the UN remains idle and utterly passive.

The Israeli Government keenly hopes to extinguish the Arab national feelings and to liquidate completely the Arab national entity in Israel. The Zionist plans, even before the establishment of the State of Israel, conceived an 'état' solely Jewish in all aspects. Reuven Barqat, the outgoing political secretary of the *Histradrūt* and the present secretary-general of

[1] Excerpts from *al-Arḍ*'s memo. sent to the Secretary-General of the UN, July 1964. Style and punctuation are those of the English original. A Hebrew translation was published in the monthly *Maṣpen*, Aug.–Sept. 1964, 2–5, and a French one in *Les Temps Modernes* (Paris), xxii/253 *bis* (1967), 792–810.

MAPAI, the ruling party, declared, in 1955: 'We thought of a State solely Jewish, without minorities.'

Faithful to achieve the maximum of those directives, the Government adopted sinister laws and harsh measures against the Arabs who preferred to remain in Israel after 1948, in the hope that the avengeful methods would be used against them. Unfortunately, all good hopes vanished in the face of tyranny, abuse and discrimination—sorrowful facts that are endlessly keeping the Arabs in a constant state of uneasiness. . . .

The *al-Arḍ* Group believes that the Arabs in Israel are part of the Palestinian Arabs who are an integral part of the whole Arab Nation.

The following are their aspirations:

a. Total equality for all citizens with full right to the basic natural freedoms; and an end to discrimination and oppression.

b. The acceptance on the part of Israel of the UN Resolutions of 29 November 1947 on the Partition of Palestine—a just solution which safeguards the interests of the Arab and Jewish people and affirms stability and peace in the Middle East.

c. The adoption, by Israel, of a policy of non-alignment, positive neutralism, and peaceful coexistence.

d. Israel's recognition of the Arab national movement, which calls for unity and socialism, as the most progressive and reliable force on which the future of this region depends—an outlook on which the future of Israel herself depends.

e. Co-operation with all bodies in Israel, that profess the realization of the above-mentioned ideals, or some of them. . . .

Unashamed of their most ridiculous stand, the Zionist press and the official propaganda apparatus in Israel dare criticize the internal situation in some other countries, while the situation in Israel herself is utterly lamentable. The authorities are waging an incomparably mean and violent campaign of terror, persecution, and discrimination against the Arabs who are, in spite of all false allegations, the first legitimate owners of the country.

The slight hope which cherished our minds and faith in the courts of justice vanished just after the High Court of Justice gave its judgement against the cause of *al-Arḍ* Co. Ltd. That judgement, which aroused the indignation of all free-conscious citizens, was a deadly blow to the freedom of the individual and of the press. The indifference of the Jews to the plight of the Arab citizens who alone suffer the consequences of the Emergency Regulations and the Military Rule, emphatically urge the effective interference of the United Nations. The UN is urgently requested to take into good consideration the complaints of the Israeli Arab citizens and to safeguard their rights.

The Israeli Government hopes, by exerting pressure and practising terror, to create among the ranks of the 'Israeli' Arabs a state of fear, despair, and submission. We declare that this will never happen. We are well determined to resist oppression and fight fiercely for our rights—and it must be remembered that such outrageous acts lead only to hatred and animosity. The government also hoped for an explosion of bloody riots on the part of the Arabs, which might be used vis-à-vis the world public opinion as an excuse to inflict a deadly blow to the minorities. Once more we say that this Machiavellian scheme will have widespread repercussions even beyond the boundaries of Israel, and will certainly affect the whole Arab World and all free-conscious people.

We hereby indict Israel for all her unlawful policies. She should bear all the responsibilities and consequences, which are also shared by the United Nations if it shall remain idle and stagnant. The destiny of 262,000 Arabs in Israel is not a trifle, but it is an issue that urges justice, understanding, and reason. What was good for Israel after World War II and now, is also good for the minorities living inside her boundaries.

The peace and stability of the region, as well as the enigmatic future of Israel, depend on the behaviour of the Israeli leaders alone.

End of Appendix D

APPENDIX E

EXCERPTS FROM *THE ISRAELI ARAB AWARENESS*[1]

Preface to the pamphlet

Dear Brother!

I have read this pamphlet and was pleased to find in it an expression of the same thoughts and opinions which I hold, and which I have striven consistently to realize.

Therefore I wish to stress with much satisfaction my full appreciation for those who have written *The Israeli Arab Awareness* for the frankness of their sincere words. They were right to call daringly to our public to fulfil the obligation of allegiance which falls upon every citizen of our country. They are worthy of admiration for their battle against perverted thoughts and extremist, distorted slogans which are circulated among our public.

I view this pamphlet and the lofty ideas contained in it as a guide to the Arab citizen of Israel in the path of stability, security and peace.

Sayf al-Dīn Zu'bī
Mayor of Nazareth

Remarks of the writer of the Pamphlet

We have always believed that we are Israeli Arabs, proud of our Arab nature and faithful to Israel at the same time.

We feel it our duty to explain this pamphlet *The Israeli Arab Awareness* in which we believe. We are convinced that this awareness is the only path open to the Arab citizen of Israel, through which he can feel himself an integral part of the State with whose fate he is bound up.

We hope that this work of ours will contribute to a solution of the problems facing us for greater understanding and better prospects of peace between Israel and its neighbours.

Introduction

Many are the problems on the State of Israel's agenda, including security, economics, immigrant absorption, conquest of the desert, and others . . .

This pamphlet does not pretend to deal with all these problems. We shall confine ourselves to everything which concerns Israel's Arab citizens, since, as Arab citizens, we see the Arab problem as ours, in whose solution our fate is involved.

[1] Pamphlet (1962). Trans. from the Arabic.

Despair and disappointment with the Arab leadership of 1948 gripped the Arabs of Israel when the State was established. From the psychological point of view there was full readiness then to recognize the principle of brotherhood among peoples and the right to full integration in the life of the State of Israel and in determining its nature.

This opportunity was not grasped by the powers and institutions dealing with these matters, and this is to be regretted.

Meanwhile circumstances changed with the revolt of the Free Officers in Egypt in 1952. This revolt awoke perverse hopes in certain circles among us. The idea crystallized that this new Arab leadership would be able to accomplish what its predecessors could not.

With the assistance of external propaganda media, the waves of enmity spread, carried by destructive groups among us. This hatred endangers our future, in general, and complicates and puts off a solution to the problem, specifically. This is in spite of the tremendous progress in all aspects of life in the Arab sector, since nothing is done by institutions and their heads to encourage an Israeli Arab awareness, which was beginning to take hold among us as a result of the great progress in the economic sphere and others.

As in the first years of Statehood, so too thereafter: the Israeli authorities did not know how to make the most of our progress in order to direct the public in Arab areas towards loyal citizenship. Not only did they not encourage Israeli Arab consciousness but in certain instances even fought this tendency for reasons which are not clear to us. . . . Perhaps the picture is clearer to those responsible, and perhaps there is not a complex of causes here, but simply an absence of belief in the possibility of loyalty on the part of Israeli Arabs to the State of Israel.

In any event the result was that the debates on this subject did not remain within the framework of these institutions alone. The matter became known to the Arab public at large. It is this fact which has spurred us to present the question in all its starkness:

Can an Arab citizen be loyal to the State of Israel and proud of his Arab heritage at one and the same time?

As for us, we are convinced that this is possible. Therefore it seems to us natural and beyond question to express an opinion on this subject in public and to arouse both Arab and Jewish public opinion.

In expressing our stand openly and without sentiment, we do not deny that we, Israeli Arabs, have within us a residue of complaints against events in the past until the tragedy of 1948.

These accusations are two-fold. On the one hand, they are directed against the reactionary and bourgeois Arab leadership headed by Ḥājj Amīn al-Ḥusaynī, and, on the other, against the British Mandatory authorities. But whom shall we accuse if a new hatred will develop at the instigation of external means of propaganda, with which inciting elements internally work hand in hand, in order to cultivate and spread new waves of animosity?

One thing is clear to us. These waves of enmity do not deposit their bearers on safe shores, and the consequences will be on our heads. In anticipation of what might result, we feel it a sacred obligation to strive in time to prevent occurrences which would be a calamity to all of us.

Our purpose therefore is to expose this problem at its roots. For we believe that in so doing we can erect a preventive dam against the rising stream of hatred which has begun to spread in certain circles among us.

We wish to replace this hatred with the spirit of true brotherhood which will lead all of us to a better future. . . . It is therefore superfluous to add that the Arabs of Palestine were not allowed to express their opinion on anything which happened or which was to be. These things were dictated from above by force. Doubts concerning matters so decided, or opposition to them, resulted in sanctions. Therefore we find that everything which occurred in the tragic past of this land, everything concerning us and the Jews, is attributable to the leadership of those who appointed themselves as our heads. They alone are responsible. They took an active part in the avowed policy of the Mandatory: a policy of divide and rule, knowingly or unknowingly. They were the ones who rejected the British suggestion concerning the immigration of 100,000 Jews from among the victims of Nazism. Likewise the idea of a bi-national state was rejected and opposed by them. Their policy was one of refusal. They refused and refused . . . and said no also to the partition resolution which was adopted by the UN General Assembly. This resolution saw the solution for the lives of the peoples in this land in the creation of two states, a Jewish and an Arab State.

Opinions on the Arab Refugees

a. Treacherous leadership internally and externally. b. The absence of preparation for civil war on the part of the Palestinian Arabs as a body. c. Terror in the Arab area—and the confusion in 1948. d. Atrocity propaganda.

These four factors were the main elements in the flight which created the problem of the refugees.

A solution for the refugee problem is possible today. It can be accomplished in part if flexibility and understanding are used, for it must always be remembered: 'If you overreach yourself, you end up with nothing'. Without concessions on both sides, it will be impossible to attain the desired compromise.

On the other hand, the other and more difficult path to a solution is to find one within the framework of clarifying the whole range of problems confronting Israel and its neighbours. To be sure, such a solution would be more radical. On this basis we call upon the leaders of the Arab states to meet with the representatives of Israel in order to discuss the complex of problems—only then will the problem of the refugees find its solution.

We and reality

During these years, thanks to constructive government and *Histadrūt* planning, the standard of living of Israel's Arabs has risen, having long surpassed that of the population of other States in the region. In spite of this, certain circles among us still refuse to view Israel as their State and are not ready to admit the right of the Jewish people to return to the land of its fathers.

These groups view the State of Israel as a temporary phenomenon. They fervently hope for the day when the Arabs will be able to obliterate it. This truth has not escaped the attention of the Jewish citizen, who is ready to give his life for his country. This is the root of the mutual distrust; this is the origin of the instability and lack of certainty which characterise so many of the Arab citizens of Israel.

The absence of peace between Israel and its Arab neighbours gives Israel today a legitimate right to defend itself against its enemies, like all other nations of the world. As for enemies—it is all the same whether they are internal or external.

The antipathy which is cultivated by certain circles among us is a sufficient cause for the authorities to take severe precautionary measures against us. Against this, we receive no benefit from the neighbouring countries, in whose eyes we are worthless. They are ready to sacrifice us on the altar of their ambitions and desires without blinking an eye.

. . . The results of this conflict among extremist factions which are developing among the inhabitants of this country are clear to us. We shall sin against ourselves and those who will come after us if we allow the current situation to continue to develop.

. . . Therefore, fellow reader, if your life and peace are dear to you, if the future of your offspring is important to you, raise the flag of peace. There is no future in war and especially not for us, the Arabs of Israel.

Our Clear Belief

In order to prevent any misunderstanding in advance, we wish to emphasize at the outset our view, according to which—in opposition to the minority which incites in our midst—there are two other camps. One, and it is not insignificant, is loyal to the State. The other, which is the clear majority, is indifferent to what is going on around it. We have risen to sound an alarm against this indifference, since it is interpreted otherwise externally. The expansion of the disloyal minority is not refuted by indifference. The opposite holds: the imprint of this minority gives the impression that the entire public, including the indifferent ones, share the same tendency.

. . . In our opinion there is no avoiding the expression of allegiance and loyalty to our State. This assumption is beyond all argument, we think. For the cause of all our problems lies in the lack of trust in us on the part of the Jewish citizens of the State of Israel.

. . . As for ourselves, we would not have made this statement had we not ourselves delved into the roots of the problem. It seems to us not only that there exists the possibility of integrating proud Arabism with loyalty to Israel, but that we have an obligation to take steps in this direction.

. . . No one disagrees that today we feel ourselves free men, living in an independent, democratic State whose Government excels in its efficiency—the only one like this in the Middle East.

. . . Common sense, logic, and decency show but one way for us: to hold on to the State and the government which enables us to make such progress, and to aim for additional accomplishments for our children's sakes!

. . . We who stand for true democratic socialism which inspires neighbouring Arabs as well, we who aspire to the elimination of poverty, disease, illiteracy, social deprivation and authoritarian government, see in national socialism a distortion of socialism. For do not several of the leaders of the Arab States adhere to national socialism?

. . . Again, concerning relations between the Arab peoples and Israel. We believe in the historic right of the Jewish people to its State. Israeli socialism is a shining example to the Arab peoples, in our opinion, since it aspires to the same goals through democratic means—which is the primary condition for social justice.

The balance of ideas set forth herein is in one direction only. It should be clear that there is no contradiction between our being Arabs, as our neighbours outside, and Israelis like our neighbours at home.

Conclusions

a. The policy of threats on the part of our neighbours foresees destruction for all, and above all for us, . . . we must oppose this policy . . .

b. Peace is the foundation of our existence . . . mediation for peace is a goal for us, which we must work towards as pioneers.

c. Social justice and democratic socialism mean progress for the Middle East. Our first act must be to struggle to realize this at home and for our neighbours.

d. As democratic socialists we see Israel in the forefront of the nations which represent such a regime . . . our conclusion is that we must view our country as a guide for socialist democracy in the Middle East.

e. A condition for stability in our lives and elimination of the crisis of distrust which exists today is the clarification of problems.

f. We must set forth the above-mentioned matters as a goal before our younger generation.

g. . . . We must take upon ourselves all the obligations which fall upon every citizen in every country.

h. We must unite behind all the lofty goals set forth above . . .

Let us be the pioneers of peace and work together with our brothers in the Israel labour movement, which can be the harbinger of social justice.

Let Our Voice be Heard

Let our voice be heard by the Jewish public—let our voice be heard as the voice of Israeli Arab public opinion. . . . Our call therefore is to every Israeli Arab who esteems himself and understands the situation . . . Our call is directed also to the Jewish public which doubts our loyalty. We turn by means of this pamphlet to the neighbouring Arab masses . . . and we turn to world public opinion to do whatever is possible for peace between Israel and its neighbours—for the good of the region and its inhabitants.

End of appendix E

APPENDIX F

AMNŌN LĪN ON THE ARABS AND THE SIXTH *KNESET* ELECTIONS[1]

Introduction

This report is submitted to the election headquarters of the Alignment in order to enable study of the background of our work and the circumstances which influenced our activities among the Arab and Druze population. In the light of the report, we shall find it easier to inspect our work, its failures and successes, in order to reach conclusions and lessons for the future.

a. *Evaluation of Public Opinion without Illusions*

i. *Development and progress are not a guarantee that the Arabs will vote for us*

In all the election campaigns that have taken place to date, MAPAI has succeeded in concentrating around itself and its allied Arab lists about 50 per cent of the Arab and Druze vote. This fact raises the question, what was the reason which led the Arabs to give such a high percentage of their votes to MAPAI—and in any event—far higher than the percentage of votes which MAPAI obtained among the Jewish public.

Are the ideas of MAPAI really accepted by the tens of thousands of Arabs who voted for it? Was MAPAI's activity among the Arabs more effective than it was among Jews? Do the aims of MAPAI fit the interests of the Arabs more than that of the Jewish voters?

It is not simple to give a full and cogent answer in this survey, lest too frank a discussion harm in no small measure the very matter for which we are working. Therefore we shall content ourselves with general comments which have in them enough hints for those who know what is going on amidst the Arab and Druze population.

The most important fact, which even the country's enemies within and without cannot ignore, is the widespread development activity undertaken by the Government under MAPAI's leadership from the day the State was founded until the present. At first glance one could assume with a certain degree of correctness that the development and progress which we have brought the Arab community in Israel explain the high percentage of Arab and Druze votes for us. But if we accept this assumption, how can we

[1] Mimeo. report by Amnōn Līn, Director of the Alignment headquarters, Arab Dept, on the election campaign for the 6th *Kneset* among the Arabs in Israel. Probably presented to the Alignment's chiefs. Undated (early 1966). Trans. from the Hebrew.

explain the fact that in the very Arab villages where the Government, through its own and *Histadrūt* organs, has not yet managed to carry out development projects, we have received in election campaigns in the past, as well as now, about 80 per cent of the votes? On the other hand, to our astonishment, it appears that in large villages where we invested tremendous resources over a number of years and built outstanding development projects, we have not succeeded in obtaining more than 40 per cent of the vote. In connexion with this, how can we explain that in villages where nothing has been done, the Communist Party has only been able to get a tiny fraction of the vote, whereas in prosperous villages, flourishing as the result of the influence of development, it has obtained worrying results?

Therefore it would seem that the secret of our success in election campaigns is not the direct result of our consistent work for the development and prosperity of the Arab village.

ii. *The split personality of the Israeli Arabs*

The Arabs constitute a minority in our country, but it is worth remembering that only eighteen years ago they were the majority and we the minority. The Arab minority in the State of Israel, which is the product of the struggle between the two peoples, carries a different stamp than any minority in any other country. Around our land there are Arab States which day and night proclaim that their chief aim is to wipe out our State; it is understandable that in such circumstances the Arab States do not recognize the State or its existence.

The emergence of 'Abd al-Nāṣir in the Eastern sky and the Arab nationalist awakening in the surrounding countries created a new situation in our region. The Arab States have set up powerful propaganda organizations, which bring their word through radio and television to every corner and every house in our land. Thus the propaganda reaches in its full extent the Arab minority in Israel, a minority which constitutes a body inseparable from its brothers in the neighbouring countries.

Since our country is one of justice and ethics, and out of loyalty to our social ideals, we have worked hard to give the Arabs a part in most of the progress and development projects from which the Jewish public benefits. We have developed an educational network which has no parallel in any one of the Arab States, and we have developed a generation of educated Arabs who have learned to listen and ask and be aware of what is going on in the country and the world. We have done much towards helping this educated generation to fit into political life out of a feeling of partnership and responsibility. We cannot ignore the fact that the very prosperity which we have brought to the Arab sector made it possible for every Arab citizen to listen day and night to the propaganda beamed at him by his brothers across the border. It is therefore understandable that this propaganda has penetrated and conquered the hearts of many of the young

Arabs, and influenced them to a considerable degree. These circumstances make it easier for extremist groups to work in their midst, calling on these young people to struggle against the Government and raise their voices against the leading party of the country.

Therefore it is no wonder that in the villages which benefited most from Government development, MAQI received many votes from these same youths who were educated and became aware of what was going on around them, while in their hearts fermented the hope influenced by the poisonous propaganda coming from over the border. Against this, in villages where there is not yet a generation of restless and aware youth, there is no internal conflict in the minds of the Arabs.

To our great regret, the Government has not devoted enough thought to the situation in the Arab sector. It can be assumed with a high degree of certainty that if the supreme elected bodies of the party had given the time deserved by these discussions, it would have been possible to find ways to a solution of the problem.

We should have grasped that, alongside the great things which the State has done for the progress of the Arab sector, we should have made a supreme effort through information and educational activities to inculcate an 'Israeli Arab awareness' in the hearts of young Arabs. We have made a grave mistake in leaving the education of the younger Arab generation in the hands of the radio and TV stations which are run by the propaganda machine of the Arab States. If we had invested efforts in inculcating the 'Israeli awareness' we would have supplied the youth with a logical consciousness which would have immunised them against extremist influences. Perhaps we would have succeeded in creating cadres of active workers who sincerely believe in the rightness of such an awareness. We could have set up this theoretical concept with which to fight the idea whose source is the other side of the border.

The significance of *The Israeli Arab Awareness* is that it is both possible and natural for an Israeli Arab to be a faithful citizen of the State and proud of being an Arab. This concept in a way is an answer to his doubts and fears that his soul must be split between his duty to remain loyal to the State in which he lives while his heart is drawn to his brothers in Arab countries.

To our regret we have not worked in this direction and therefore, when we came to plan our information campaign among the Arabs, we knew that we could not succeed in creating a wave of support if our chief theme were to be emphasis on economic prosperity or the achievements of the Arab labourer in comparison to that of the Arab labourer in neighbouring lands. It is interesting to note that the Arabs see all the progress and development projects we undertake as a natural process in a democratic state, rather than as evidence of good will on our part towards them.

We were confronted by the necessity to find other ways of creating public support and identification with us, as against the strong inimical currents at work among the Arabs.

b. *The secret of success is a display of strength*

From the experience of minorities in all countries we have learned that it is the natural and rational interest of every minority in the world to aim at identification with the strong, stabilizing factor which rules the country and not with the groups battling against it.

This does not mean fear of the law, but rather fear of any political shock on whose heels the minority is liable to be hurt more than any other group in the country. Therefore it is clear that MAPAI (before the creation of the Alignment), from the day the State was established, has been the largest and strongest party, whose chances seemed best to put together the future Government. As such, MAPAI was a shield to the minorities in Israel against political upheavals and a guarantee for the prevention of retribution.

This was the main reason explaining the fact of the high vote for MAPAI among Israeli Arabs in all election campaigns since the creation of the State. If we wish to answer the question raised at the outset of this survey as to why the Arabs voted so overwhelmingly for MAPAI we can sum up in the definition:

The Arab vote for MAPAI was always a function of their recognition and proper evaluation that MAPAI was the strongest and most stable element with the best prospects of controlling the Government of tomorrow.

Our success in the election campaign depended on our ability to infuse into the Arab residents the confidence that we had the best prospects of controlling the future Government.

This was the chief theme on which our information was based among the Arabs of Israel.

When we came to plan our plan of action among the Arabs in the last election campaign (for the sixth *Kneset*) we had to make a 'situation appraisal' of the circumstances in the Arab sector:

i. To test our strength and position.
ii. To test the strength of elements fighting against us.
iii. In the light of these—to decide whether to appear again this time with Arab lists, and with how many? (Or perhaps it would be preferable to add Arab candidates to the Alignment's list—and to call upon the Arabs to vote for the mixed list.)

c. *Evaluation of our strength and position—on the eve of elections*

i. As explained above we always drew our strength on the Arab 'street' from our stable strength among the Jewish public. But this time MAPAI had suffered severe shocks in the last two years, and as a result of these shocks some of MAPAI's outstanding figures left the party to form RAFI. The echoes of this upheaval reached the Arab public with full force, as a result of the fact that thousands of young Arabs learned over the years to read Hebrew, and they usually read the Hebrew evening papers daily (a phenomenon which was not so apparent in former years). It is not difficult for us to explain to readers of this survey that these shocks and the founding of RAFĪ by Ben-Gurion and other outstanding personalities, considerably diminished the belief and confidence of Arab residents in the stability of our strength. In their hearts a doubt was created whether we still constitute the sole force which has the prospects for rule tomorrow. And we must realize that the moment that confidence in our strength was shattered and the doubt arose whether we really will rule tomorrow—then the groundwork was laid to wreck us, and we were likely to lose the background out of which grew our achievements and victories of the past.

This was our situation among the Arabs on the eve of the election campaign for the Sixth *Kneset*.

ii. In view of MAPAI's difficult position on the Arab street, we had but one possibility in order to restore the belief of the Arab masses in our strength, and it was: the inculcation of a new belief—in the alignment of MAPAI with *Aḥdūt ha-'avōda*. The latter in the past had not had much success among the Arabs, when it was one of the small parties fighting against the dominant one. It is worth noting that in the elections to the fourth *Kneset*, *Aḥdūt ha-'avōda* received 4,179 votes in all; in the elections to the fifth *Kneset*, this declined to 3,692 votes. But one should not depend solely on these figures and conclude that our appearance together with *Aḥdūt ha-'avōda* in a joint alignment did not add votes; on the contrary: today it is clear that as a result of the shocks which affected MAPAI, especially after RAFĪs foundation, our appearance in a joint alignment with *Aḥdūt ha-'avōda* was of considerable benefit, and perhaps even saved us from a great defeat, since our appearance in this strengthened line-up made it possible to create confidence anew in our strength, which was hurt by RAFĪ's creation and its appearance in the Arab street.

Again we used the tried and true theme but this time it was not the strong and stable MAPAI, but the Alignment, strong as the new rising power, with the best prospects of ruling tomorrow.

d. *Evaluation of the strength of rival parties*

1. In all past election campaigns MAQĪ was our most difficult rival among the Arab population. We had no illusions that every Arab who voted for MAQĪ was a communist who really believed in the principles of communism. We knew that MAQĪ's strength among the Arabs arose from the fact that it was a substitute for a nationalist Arab party which until now had not succeeded in forming in order to challenge us at the polls. MAQĪ for the Arabs was a legitimate address for all those who wanted to vote for a party which identified with the aims of the extremist circles active in their midst. (Without a doubt there was tremendous significance in the agreement between 'Abd al-Nāṣir and the communist world for the identification of Arab residents with MAQĪ.) The split in MAQĪ between the Sneh faction and the Ṭūbī–Ḥabībī faction created a new situation for us to consider seriously. If in the past MAQĪ was but a

substitute for Arab nationalism, with the founding of the New Communist Party of Ṭūbī and Ḥabībī, this became an Arab party much closer than any other to extremist nationalist circles with influence in the Arab street.

'The Voice of Cairo' served the New Communist Party in unprecedented fashion. The radio broadcasts of Cairo called upon the Arabs of Israel to vote for this list since it was nearest to the aims of the 'Arab Liberation Movement'. (This was after the banning of *al-Arḍ* list by the Central Election Commission and the confirmation of the ban by the Supreme Court.)

In elections to the fourth *Kneset* MAQĪ received 8,813 votes among the Arab population. In elections to the fifth *Kneset* MAQĪ received 19,308 votes, constituting a steep rise of 10,495 votes.

This rise of MAQĪ in the Arab street was a realistic reflection of the trend of thought among Arab youth, educated by the TV and Arab radio stations. We should have assumed that with the rise in the number of Arab voters, mainly of youth who had just reached voting age, a steep rise would occur in the number of votes for the Ṭūbī–Ḥabībī faction.

Qualified Arab voters for the fifth *Kneset* numbered 105,000. Qualified Arab voters for the sixth *Kneset* numbered 130,000, that is, there was an addition of 25,000 young voters.

If MAQĪ had received 19,300 votes in the election to the fifth *Kneset*, we could reasonably assume that with the addition of 25,000 young voters and in the wake of the weakened confidence in our strength in the Arab street, the New Communist list would obtain about 40,000 votes, taking into consideration that the young people have a growing influence on their families and clans in the villages and towns.

2. We assumed that MAPAM would retain its strength in the Arab street thanks to its consistent work among the Arabs, especially because of the employment of many hundreds of Arab workers in its *kibbūtzīm*. We estimated that MAPAM would be able to increase its strength somewhat by dint of serious work.

MAPAM received 10,214 votes in the elections to the fourth *Kneset*. MAPAM received 9,322 votes in the elections to the fifth *Kneset*, thus retaining its votes more or less. On this basis and in view of MAPAM's activities, we felt that this party would receive 13,000 Arab votes.

3. Our calculation concerning RAFĪ was different from that made by us concerning any of the other parties competing with us in the Arab street. Despite the poison and hate which characterized RAFĪ's appearance and struggle against us in the Jewish street, we could justifiably hope that, of all people, RAFĪ's leaders, many of whom had held posts in the defence sphere, would take care not to incite the Arab public against us—that is, against the Government. We deceived ourselves with the hope that, in spite of everything, RAFĪ's people would not carry over the internal struggle to the Arab street as well.

We believed that RAFĪ would take into consideration the fact that only we, as the central force ruling the country, were capable of leading a successful struggle against extremist elements in the Arab street, and we hoped that they would enable us to concentrate on this difficult struggle without being distracted by RAFĪ in the Arab street as well, but, as has been noted, this was a false hope.

RAFĪ's workers, who only yesterday were our partners in the election campaigns, and knew very well that the secret of our success lay in the *legend of our unconquerable strength*, did not refrain from fighting against us in a most negative fashion. Completely ignoring the danger of blasting confidence in our stable power, RAFĪ began to break down that wall which in the past had prevented a mass Arab vote for the extremist factions (and this time the threat was the Ṭūbī–Ḥabībī faction). Without any pangs of conscience, the chief theme of their information to the Arabs was the weakening of confidence in the Alignment's strength and in introducing a doubt into the hearts of the Arabs whether the Alignment really had any prospects of ruling after the elections. In any event we knew that RAFĪ would try to win over in every village the very families which had been connected to us in the past and it was clear to us that RAFĪ's workers would not pit their strength against MAQĪ and MAPAM to win supporters to their side. Therefore we had to consider RAFĪ's activities in the Arab street very seriously, especially after the creation of RAFĪ's Arab list, headed by Ṣuwayliḥ Manṣūr of Ṭīra in the Little Triangle.

4. We estimated that the National Religious Party, GAḤAL, and other lists would retain their strength more or less. According to our estimate of the situation, we assumed that of the 130,000 Arab votes, all the competing parties including the New Communists would get about 60–65,000 votes, and therefore about 49,000 votes would go to the Alignment and its Arab lists. This estimate was made on the assumption that voting among the Arabs would not exceed 80 per cent of those eligible.

In view of this prediction, we had to plan our steps and our evaluations in the struggle for Arab and Druze votes.

e. *The Struggle by means of Arab Lists—or Integrating Arabs into the Alignment List*

In the past MAPAI had competed for votes among the Arabs through the Arab lists allied with it.

The basis for creating three lists for the third and fourth *Knesets*, and two lists for the fifth, lay in the family splits in the Arab villages and in the family competition and rivalry which prevented unifying in order to vote for one list.

The results of voting in all past election campaigns showed that this approach justified itself. The Arab lists linked to MAPAI together amassed 45 per cent of all the Arab vote and together with votes given directly to MAPAI about 50 per cent of all the votes of the Arabs.

With the opening of the election campaign to the sixth *Kneset* and after the creation of the Alignment, a suggestion was made by *Aḥdūt ha-'avōda* to eliminate separate Arab lists and in their place to incorporate Arab candidates in the Alignment list, and to call upon Arab voters to vote directly for the Alignment ticket.

We had to examine and weigh this suggestion for its advantages and disadvantages.

i. *Advantages*

a. *The Difficult Position of the Arab Lists.* The initiators of the idea of scrapping the Arab lists were right, in that their situation in the Arab street was extremely difficult. The Arab public was tired of the existence of two Arab lists. They were no longer interested in continuing to be tied to Arab lists when they had the possibility to associate directly with our party or with the Alignment. The Arab public in the country had matured politically, and most of the Arab residents knew for certain that Arab lists had no chance of changing or setting policy which would answer Arab needs. The Arab voters knew that only the Jewish parties and especially the ruling party (MAPAI or Alignment) have the power to solve the problems of the Arab sector. Thus the opinion grew among Arabs to ask us to eliminate Arab lists and enable them to vote directly for the Alignment ticket.

b. *The Difficult Position of Arab* Kneset *Members.* Those who recommended dropping the Arab lists also based themselves on the difficult position of Arab *Kneset* members who stood at the head of the separate lists, partly because of their personal conduct and partly because of the fact that MAPAI obliged them to vote for the continuation of the military administration. Putting them up again as candidates for the *Kneset* would create difficulties for us in concentrating around the Arab lists those Arab voters who would prefer to vote directly for the Alignment list. With the elimination of the Arab lists, we would be able to change the candidates who were no longer viewed by the public as their representatives by introducing new, young representatives in the Alignment list, a move which would create a positive awakening and renewed confidence in us.

c. *Splitting strength and effort instead of concentrating it.* From the experience of previous election campaigns, MAPAI learned that two lists competing for votes on the Arab street meant neglect of the struggle against the real rivals, MAQĪ and the other parties. Instead of concentrating their joint strength in order to weaken rival parties, they fought each other. Thus it can be understood that the advocates of dropping the Arab lists insisted on the need to concentrate strength in order to weaken the rival parties, especially the New Communist Party.

ii. *Disadvantages*

a. *General.* There were not many among us who disagreed with the assumptions and description of the difficult condition of the Arab lists. Most of those knowledgeable in Arab affairs preferred personally to work for the Alignment list rather than for independent Arab lists. But we had to be open-eyed about the disadvantages of the suggestion. The greatest drawback seemed to us the negative effect which coopting Arab candidates to the Alignment list would have among the Jewish public. We feared that RAFI and GAḤAL would exploit this deed in order to incite communities and various groups against us. As is well known, putting together a list for the *Kneset* is the most difficult of tasks. It is not hard to imagine that certain people among the Alignment's supporters who would be personally offended by being put far down on the list would use the fact that Arab candidates were in safe places ahead of them, as a justification for leaving, and even for inciting their supporters against us. We had to place the strong *prospect* which we might have among the Arabs by incorporating Arabs into the Alignment ticket against the certain *danger* that such an act would cause us untold damage among the Jewish public.

b. *Cut-off Percentages and Appearance of Independent Extremist Arab Lists.* If we were to eliminate the Arab lists and incorporate three or four Arabs in the Alignment list in secure places without raising the qualifying percentage to at least 3 per cent (30,000 votes), then we could anticipate a most dangerous phenomenon: extremist Arab circles would appear among the Arabs and explain to their supporters that their hour had come. The Alignment would put three or four Arabs in good places and their election would be assured by Jewish votes. These groups would then call upon the Arabs to work to get another two or three Arab representatives by setting up an independent, non-party list. This danger seemed extremely serious to us in view of the very low qualifying percentages, which this time required no more than 13,000 votes in order to insure the success of a list. This small percentage was a temptation to extremist elements to try to compete with us in the Arab street, even without elimination of our Arab lists. How much greater would this temptation be if we cancelled the Arab lists without raising the qualifying percentage, and thus leave the Arab sector open and free for the appearance of an independent Arab list? Without a doubt, if we had eliminated the Arab lists and put Arab candidates on our ticket, many Arabs who formerly had voted for these lists would have been drawn away by the propagandists of the independent Arab list. A vote for such an Arab list would come out of a desire to get as many Arab representatives as possible into the *Kneset*, in the certainty that the Alignment would guarantee the entry of the Arab candidates on its ticket by means of Jewish votes. Therefore the important principle was set in this discussion that, as long as the qualifying percentage is not raised by act of *Kneset*, there is no possibility of eliminating the Arab lists.

iii. *Conclusions*

We chose the most difficult path because of the great risks which we saw in choosing the path which seemed easy. We decided to retain the Arab lists despite our knowledge of their weaknesses and the difficulties in store for us to mobilize votes around them.

f. *Results of the Elections to the Sixth* Kneset

i. Comparing the results of the elections to the sixth *Kneset* with that of the fifth, we feel that we have retained our strength in the Arab street:

One Arab list received	23,430 votes
Another Arab list received	16,464 votes
The Alignment received	13,353 votes
Total	53,247 votes for the Alignment lists

This result gave the Alignment four Arab mandates and two Jewish mandates in the *Kneset*, which are 50·1 per cent of all the Arab votes.

In elections to the fifth *Kneset*, MAPAI had received 43,934 votes which were 50·5 per cent of all the Arab votes at the time.

ii. *RAFĪ's Appearance Prevented a Greater Victory Among the Arabs*

RAFĪ set up an Arab list identified with it, headed by Ṣuwayliḥ Manṣūr of the Triangle. The basis of this list were votes of elements opposed to *Kneset* member Diyāb 'Ubayd of the Triangle and to Shaykh Jabr Mu'addī of Galilee, both of them candidates on our list.

In elections to the fifth *Kneset*, Ṣāliḥ Khneyfeṣ (formerly MK) appeared at the head of an independent list of his own, with Liberal Party support, and his list obtained 3,561 votes.

By creating an alliance between Ṣuwayliḥ Manṣūr of the Triangle and Shaykh Ṣāliḥ Khneyfeṣ of Galilee, RAFĪ hoped to obtain a sufficient amount of votes in order to exceed the qualifying percentage requirement and put one Arab representative of its own into the *Kneset*. During the course of the election campaign it became clear to the RAFĪ people that Ṣāliḥ Khneyfeṣ' backers were not ready to vote for Ṣuwayliḥ Manṣūr's list and therefore they preferred to give them the possibility of voting directly for RAFĪ.

Arab list of RAFĪ received	5,536 votes
RAFĪ itself received	2,568 votes
Total RAFĪ vote in Arab sector	8,104 votes

There is no doubt that these 8,000 votes could have been added to our list if there had been no RAFĪ activity among the Arabs. It is clear that RAFĪ itself erred seriously in creating an Arab list. If it had worked among the Arabs to convince them to vote directly for its ticket then it certainly would not have lost the 5,536 votes of Ṣ. Manṣūr's list, which did not reach the minimum qualifying percentage.

In any event RAFĪ's appearance among the Arabs caused us a loss of more than 6,000 votes which no doubt would have been given to us by one means or another.

iii. *MAPAM*

In complete contradiction of our estimates, MAPAM did not succeed in retaining its strength in the Arab street. In the elections to the Fifth *Kneset* MAPAM had received 9,332 votes. This time, it received 9,766.

Taking into consideration the increase in the number of voters, the considerable investment and consistent activity of MAPAM among the Arabs, this result does not represent retention of strength by MAPAM but rather a decrease.

iv. *The National Religious Party*

In these elections the National Religious Party received 4,794 votes. In the elections to the Fifth *Kneset* it had received 2,673 votes. This consistent rise, albeit slow, of the party among the Arab public arises from the fact of its constant presence in the Government, and thanks to the fact that three important ministries are in the hands of its Ministers in the Government: the *Interior Ministry*, which has great influence on local councils and *mukhtārs* in the villages; the *Ministry of Religions*, which has considerable influence on religious judges and on circles connected with the Ministry in the field of religious activity; the *Welfare Ministry*, which has direct contact with many of the needy.

All the remaining parties gathered only a few hundred votes apiece, but this does not require a separate analysis.

v. *New Communist List*

The elections to the sixth *Kneset* caused us a positive, significant and unexpected surprise. In contradiction to all predictions, the New Communist list did not succeed in mobilizing the number of votes around it which we feared.

In line with what we wrote above (evaluation of the strength of rival parties), we estimated the strength of this party in these elections at between 30,000–40,000 votes. The election results reveal that we were able to deal the New Communist Party a strong blow, if not a defeat, in that it received only 24,000 votes.

Perhaps this is the place to note the secret of our success.

g. *The Secret of our Success was our Appearance as the New Force bringing Tidings of a new Approach to Solutions requiring Daring*

In contrast to all the gloomy predictions based on a rise of inimical extremism among the Arabs of Israel, and despite the injury to our authority as the central force through the appearance of RAFI, and the weakness of the Arab lists, we were able to mobilize around the Alignment lists 53,247 votes, which were 50·1 per cent of the total Arab vote. We thereby guaranteed the growth of the Alignment's strength in the *Kneset* by six members: 4 Arabs and 2 Jews who were chosen by Arab votes.

h. *Conclusion*

How can this victory be explained?

i. We succeeded in creating a positive public following for the Alignment and for the central personalities at its head.
ii. We were able to inculcate a belief in the hearts of Arab residents in the sincerity of our intentions to find logical solutions to the complex of problems with which the Arab citizens contend.
iii. We did not flatter the Arabs nor did we make promises which we cannot keep.
iv. We were wise to appear as a responsible force which united in the Alignment the essential groups interested in guarding the democratic nature of the Israeli Government.
v. We were able to inculcate into the Arab consciousness a feeling for our strength and certain prospects, for we were the most likely ones to put together the future Government of Israel.

249

APPENDIX G

SOME RESOLUTIONS OF THE TENTH CONGRESS OF THE *HISTADRŪT*[1]

THE Congress welcomes the representatives of the Arab workers from all the various parties, who are taking part in the Conference for the first time as elected representatives, and views this as an expression of the fulfilment of the decisions of the Ninth Congress concerning the acceptance of Arab workers and their incorporation into its elected bodies.

The Congress notes with satisfaction the entry of tens of thousands of Arab workers into the *Histadrūt* and calls upon those who have not yet done so to organize in it as members having equal rights and obligations.

The Congress sees the work of the *Histadrūt* among the Arab population as an important factor in fostering co-operation towards increased understanding between Jews and Arabs and calls for the broadening and intensification of activities in this sphere.

The Tenth Congress sends greetings to the Workers' Council of Nazareth, which has been elected for the first time in that city. The Conference wishes the Council fruitful activity, and calls upon it and the Workers' Council of Upper Nazareth to work together for the good of the labourers in both parts of the city in the framework of an overall joint council.

The *Histadrūt* will set up local committees in the larger Arab and Druze villages, in order to prepare them for manifold and fruitful activity in the *Histadrūt*.

The Congress calls upon councils in mixed towns to integrate into their institutions elected Arab representatives who will serve as a bridge between them and the Arab *Histadrūt* members in these towns.

Culture and Information

The *Histadrūt* will continue to work to strengthen understanding and friendship between the Jewish worker and the Arab worker, and among Jewish and Arab residents of the country in general, by initiating joint meetings, mutual visits, and joint activities between Jewish and Arab youth.

In co-operation with the Workers' Council and local authorities, the *Histadrūt* will see to the expansion of the nursery school network for young children in Arab villages where the Arab woman goes to work outside the home.

The *Histadrūt* will continue to set up appropriate facilities in the Arab

[1] Excerpts relating to the Arabs from resolutions of the 10th *Histadrūt* Congress, 1965. Trans. from the Hebrew.

villages, will strengthen education by expanding the network of ' 'Amal' schools in the Arab area, and will encourage students from the villages to continue their studies in the ' 'Amal' schools in neighbouring Jewish settlements.

The *Histadrūt* will add stipends for students in these schools, both elementary and secondary, in order to encourage the continued education of the younger generation.

The *ha-Pō'el* Centre will continue to develop the various branches of sport, set up sport facilities and encourage every local initiative in this sphere.

The Executive Committee of the *Histadrūt* and the Workers' Councils will continue to emphasize cultural and educational activities in Arab settlements, extension of the network of clubs and an increase in their activities, —art, dance, drama, music—as well as stepping up the publication of books in Arabic.

Mutual Aid

The Sick Fund, with the aid of various insurance funds, will continue to set up clinics in Arab villages and see to proper medical service. The Central Committee of the Sick Fund will expand the network of special courses for training Arab nurses and will encourage Arab students, through the giving of stipends, to study medicine with the intention of filling the gap in this area in clinics located in Arab settlements.

APPENDIX H

FIRST SPEECH BY AN ARAB MEMBER OF THE *KNESET*[1]

THIS is a great and highly important day, on which the whole population celebrates the opening of the *Kneset*, which will undertake to legislate the laws and regulations of the country. I wish to avail myself of the opportunity to exchange faithful greetings with you, on this great day, together with my colleague, the second Arab *Kneset* member. The Lord on High has bestowed on us the representation of a considerable part of the Arab citizens, and I pray that we shall succeed in this for the sake of all citizens without distinction. It is to be regretted that Arab representation in the Constituent Assembly has not found its full expression. This fact places upon us a dual responsibility concerning the realization of the tasks devolving upon us towards the Arabs of the State of Israel. We would not want to shoulder this great responsibility if we were not certain that the Members of the *Kneset* would support and encourage us and co-operate with us, since they themselves, as men whose path is guided by uprightness, know that the eyes of the Arab citizens of Israel are turned to this Constituent Assembly, the advocate of justice and the good of all.

Honourable gentlemen! Even though the parties and institutions are many and although outlooks and opinions vary, most elements in the population agree unanimously on the basic principles whose crux is: 'the young State of Israel will be established on foundations of freedom, justice, and peace. It will grant social and political rights equally to all its citizens irrespective of religion, race, or sex.' This was proclaimed by the Provisional Council of State on Friday, the Fifth of Iyyar, 5708—14 May 1948.

Justice, worthy gentlemen, is the chief foundation of government. It can be attained through daily deeds of upholding justice and righteousness in the country. It would be beneficial, therefore, if we were to make our way with energy and determination despite the obstacles which will stand in our path. It would be worth-while to choose for ourselves a policy of understanding. Let us refrain from dubious traditions and avoid following the precedent of others. It is preferable to preserve a completely neutral independence. Let us be diligent in seeking the truth wherever it may be found. Let us guard the justice of everything we do, so that no evil come to all seekers of justice.

We view with joy the first buds heralding the end of the struggle in the Holy Land, an end which will be followed by treaties of good neigh-

[1] Speech by Amīn Salīm Jarjūra, 15 Feb. 1949. Text from the official *Divrey ha-Kneset*. Trans. from the Hebrew.

bourliness between Israel and the neighbouring Arab States, the recognition by the nations of the world of the young State of Israel, one after another, giving us honour and glory. From day to day the number of our supporters grows. Our State must demonstrate in all its deeds that it seeks justice and righteousness, and hopes for freedom, tranquillity and the establishment of peace, and that it will serve as an example of truth and a great force for the good of mankind.

End of Appendix H

2251

APPENDIX I

AL-RĀBIṬA ASKS THE ARAB MINORITY: 'QUO VADIS?'[1]

'. . . QUO vadis?' is our final question to our Arab readers in Israel or, more appropriately, to all the Arab inhabitants of Israel. Where is fate leading us? Whither should we direct our gaze?

Doubtless, many of us, these recent years, have been drinking the heady wine of Arab nationalism. Doubtless, some of the extremists have set their hopes on their present problems ending through the intervention of a victorious saviour, who would come from outside Israel and would redirect the flow of water into a course favourable to them.

Most of us have been living in this drunken state and with these patriotic ideals; revolutionary thoughts and enthusiastic sentiments have overwhelmed the thinking of most of our youth. We have been living, as we still do, abroad—in spirit and thought—even if our bodies are within Israel and are tied up with our vital interests, daily livelihood, and real problems.

Now we awake and see that all these hopes are dashed one after the other, for reasons which space does not allow mention. External conditions do not assist the realization of our hopes. We awake and see that reality demands that we work out our internal matters rather than live in the clouds, fog, and mirage which have continually grown more remote from us in the desert of world and Arab affairs. We awake and see, for instance, how the threads of unity among the Arab States have been snapping, thus weakening it both internally and externally. We awake and see that all the hopes we have pinned on the United Nations for the solution of the Palestine problem, the refugee problem and most of our own problems, have faded: the last session has been like the preceding ones, with orators pleading for or against, while the problem is being deferred for another year; so that we come out saying: nothing doing!

Having awakened from a deep sleep of several years, we perceive the political parties around us, fighting for us—not for our interest, despite everything they say, write and publish, but for their own. We perceive a new Government being formed and starting its activities, without a single representative of those leftist parties for whom most of us voted despite the warnings we had published in this journal. So what can they do now,

[1] *Al-Rābiṭa*, Nov.–Dec. 1961, 14–16. Trans. from the Arabic. This monthly is read not only among the Greek Catholic community, which publishes it, but by other Arabs too. According to *JP*, 12 Jan. 1962, suppl., p. 11, this anonymous article was written by Archbishop George al-Ḥakīm himself. True or not, like the rest of this journal, it certainly represents his views.

these leftist parties into whose lap we have jumped and which had promised us that they would gain us our rights? There is a big difference between what they say and promise, and between what their real possibilities of action are.

We behold, also, several Arab members of the *Kneset*, whom we have supported and who are now supporting the present Government. We hope that this Government will enable them to solve at least a few of our problems.

Above all, we awake and notice that we have to continue living in Israel, with the people of Israel, among whom we constitute a minority. We have to demand our rights in full, but at the same time be prepared to fulfil the obligations imposed by our country. Upon awakening, we look around and see in this country friendship societies: some are for Russian-Israeli friendship, others for American-Israeli friendship, etc. However, we cannot find a society working for true friendship between the Arab and Jewish peoples, not on the basis of party interests, but on the truer grounds of reciprocal respect and the frank struggle for injured rights, loyally and mutually-assisting. Should not some of those youngsters, whose senses have not been deadened by empty propaganda and vain enmity, come and fight, instead of hiding in the shelter of their home? Should they not share in serious, realistic work, to improve the lot of the Arabs in this country in a pure respectable manner, unmoved by the search for honours and benefits, but striving for the public interest? We are certain that there are many such people among us, but they do not come to the fore, since they shirk responsibility or fear the biting words which the mouthpieces of false propaganda may write about them in the extremist weeklies of the political parties. We, however, consider the present situation as a crossroads, which does not allow them or other truly noble persons to stand aside. On the contrary, they have to sacrifice all they can for the sake of their brethren and their people . . .

End of Appendix I

APPENDIX J

EDITORIAL IN *THE MESSAGE OF THE CLUB* IN ṬĪRA[1]

THIS greeting will be on the lips of all throughout my village, will serve as the introduction to every conversation and the heading for every word of praise tomorrow, on the Holiday of Sacrifice.

In it we greet, justly, the giants who glory in the virtues of sacrifice and loyalty, and greet, unjustly, those midgets who abase their heads in the mud of treachery and egoism.

We greet, justly, the pioneers who vowed to serve the rights of the Arab people in this land and went to defend it stubbornly during 16 years without let-up or weakening.

We greet, unjustly, those who vowed to serve Satan and used the simple pioneers of their people as material to bargain with in order to advance their own interests at their expense.

We greet, justly, every honourable Arab youth who has spent this entire lengthy period in the land, and who believes that justice which springs from conscience is the main thing and that justice which comes from private interest is secondary; the youth who, in order to carry out this principle, was ever diligent to make his behaviour a surrender to the rule of conscience, to be ready to sacrifice the less important if he sees a need to serve the principle.

We greet, unjustly, people found in our midst who preferred to sacrifice their clean conscience one hundred times daily on the altar of private profit and egotistic peace.

We greet, justly, all those notables who have been alert to the evil which has afflicted their minority and to every pressure and improvement which the Arab people has suffered, and who determined to be as burnt-out candles in order to light the way for this defeated people who are sinking in waves of darkness.

We greet, unjustly, all the opportunists whose sensitivities have not been touched by this evil, but, on the contrary, have used it in order to draw from the filthy waters, as an opportunity to hunt the souls of their people on the altar of their interests.

We greet, justly, all those heroes who have fought stubbornly in every sphere, and withstood terror and the conspiracy of darkness closing in on them from the outside, who stood sturdily together in order to fight the black hate which was revealed towards them by shadows of men and non-

[1] 'Holiday Greetings', editorial by Ḥusnī 'Irāqī in the organ of the Ṭīra sports club, 22 Apr. 1964. Trans. from the Arabic.

men, like flintstone which endures despite all the tempests which rage around it.

We greet, unjustly, all those miserable ones with lowly souls, people who are our brothers by blood alone, but in actuality are far distant from us. Those who are not satisfied with the sword of terror from outside, who have cut off from the honourable man every means of making a livelihood, but have competed with this sword with one of their own making, the product of their revenge and wicked souls, in order to banish their sons from their homes, a warning to ostracize them and threat to dismiss them—in order to save their own souls.

We greet, justly, those who knew that if they were to choose the road to peace, riches and fame, the road of flowers, they would have attained its benefits ahead of others but, in spite of this, chose to go in the path of thorns, the way of struggle and sacrifice, chose it in order to quiet their conscience and not to enrich themselves—and gained fame only from the glory of their struggle.

We greet, unjustly, those who preferred quiet, riches and fame, and therefore prostrated themselves to all those who were of use to them and flattered all those in power.

This greeting is a just compliment from the heart to all the noble souls, a sincere compliment which is not meant to win honour and has in it no hypocrisy.

I send it to all the heroes of sacrifice on the Holiday of Sacrifice.

End of appendix J

2257 Ишр

APPENDIX K

THE QUESTIONNAIRE[1]

a. *First part. We would like to start by asking you a few personal questions:*

1. Date of birth........ Place of birth (locality)........

2. Residence (locality)........

3. Occupation........

4. Are you satisfied with your work?—
i. Yes. ii. No. iii. Another reply........

5. Are you a member of the *Histadrūt*?
i. Yes. ii. No. iii. Another reply........

6. Do you participate in *Histadrūt* activities?
i. Yes........ which activities?........
ii. No........ why not?........
iii. Another reply ....

7. Do you read Arabic newspapers?
i. Yes........ which ones?........
ii. No........ why not? ....
iii. Another reply........

8. Do you read newspapers in Hebrew or other languages?
i. Yes........ which ones?........
ii. No........ why?........
iii. Another reply........

9. Which newspaper do you prefer to read?........ why?........

10. Do you listen in to Israeli broadcasts?
i. Yes........ in which language?........
ii. No....... why not?........
iii. Another reply........

11. Which Israeli programme(s) do you prefer to listen to?
i. .... ii. .... iii. ....

[1] This is the final form of the questionnaire used for interviewing. Only 112 people agreed to be interviewed. It is partly an 'open' questionnaire and partly a 'closed' one. Several queries are intended to determine the interviewee's political alertness and his general knowledge of what goes on in Israel; others to sound out his opinions. In a covering letter anonymity was promised and fully implemented; no questionnaire bore the interviewee's name. Trans. from the Arabic.

12. Do you tune in to other broadcasting stations?
    i. Yes........ which ones?........
    ii. No........ why not?........
    iii. Another reply........

13. To which broadcasting station do you prefer to listen?........ why?........

14. To which programmes do you prefer to listen?........

15. Which station is distinguished by good radio commentators?......

16. Do you listen regularly to radio commentators?
    i. Yes........ why?........
    ii. No........ why?........
    iii. Another reply........

17. Do you watch television?
    i. Yes........ which channels?........
    ii. No........ why not?........
    iii. Another reply........

18. Which TV programmes do you like in particular?........

19. Do you prefer the radio or TV?........ why?........

b. *Second part. Here are a few general questions about the State of Israel.*

20. Who is the President of the State?........

21. Which names of Government Ministers do you remember?......

22. Which political parties can you name?........

23. Which party is most capable of representing the interests of the Arabs in Israel?........ why?........

24. Which party do you consider least suitable to do this?........ why?........

25. What do you think are the most pressing problems facing the State of Israel?
    i. .... ii. .... iii. .... iv.........
    v. .... vi. ....

26. What do you think are the most pressing problems facing the Arab States?
    i. .... ii. .... iii. .... iv. ....
    v. .... vi.........

27. Do you, as an Israeli citizen, feel that the régime in the State of Israel is democratic?
    i. Yes........ ii. No........ iii. Another reply........

28. What indications are there that the régime in Israel is democratic? ....

29. What indications are there that it is not?........

c. *Third part. We would now like to know your views about the problems facing your environment. You are certainly aware that every society has its own characteristics and problems. So let us ask you:*

30. What are the problems facing your village/town?........

31. What solutions for these problems would you suggest?........

32. What general problems does the Arab citizen in Israel have? ....

33. What solution for these problems would you suggest?........

34. What do you consider the best solution for the problems pending between Israel and the Arab States?........

35. The Arabs in Israel, like others in that country, have a number of desires and interests.
    i. How do they voice these desires and interests?........
    ii. How should they voice them?........

36. What is the role of the following parties and groups, among the Arab population in Israel:
    i. MAPAI........
    ii. The Alignment........
    iii. *Aḥdūt ha-'avōda*........
    iv. MAPAM........
    v. MAQĪ........
    vi. RAQAḤ........
    vii. *Al-Arḍ*........
    viii. The National Religious Party........
    ix. The Independent Liberals........
    x. RAFĪ........
    xi. GAḤAL........
    xii. Co-operation and Brotherhood.
    xiii. Progress and Development.
    xiv. This World........
    xv. The List of Peace........

37. What should be the attitude of the Arabs in Israel towards parties and groups? Do you suggest:
    i. That the Arabs join them........
    ii. That they form an independent Arab party........
    iii. Another reply........

38. How have you reached this conclusion?........

39. Whom do you consider as prominent Arab personalities in Israel? ....

40. Whom do you consider as the foremost leader in the Arab world nowadays?
    i. King Ḥusayn........
    ii. Amīn al-Ḥāfiẓ........
    iii. Jamāl 'Abd al-Nāṣir........
    iv. Ḥabīb Būrgība........
    v. King Fayṣal........
    vi. Another reply........

41. Why?........

d. *Fourth part. To conclude, we would be grateful for your opinion concerning the development of the Arab environment in Israel:*

42. What do you consider as the main achievements to date in developing the Arab environment in Israel:
    i. In the cultural field........
    ii. In the economic field........
    iii. In the social field........

43. What steps are necessary, in your opinion, for raising further the level of the Arab village or town in Israel?........

44. What ought to be done in order to bring Arab and Jew closer to one another in this country?........

End of Appendix K

APPENDIX L

INTERVIEWING THE ARABS—SOME CONCLUSIONS

PREPARATION OF THE QUESTIONNAIRE

AT an early stage of this study it was felt that it would be useful to conduct interviews in an attempt to verify several hypotheses concerning the political behaviour of the Arabs in Israel. Sociologists, such as Professors Morroe Berger in his *Bureaucracy and Society in Modern Egypt*, and Daniel Lerner in *The Passing of Traditional Society* have already pointed out the difficulties of conducting interviews in countries of the Middle East. Their projects, however, seem not to compare in difficulty with the prospect confronting the student of politics attempting to interview Arabs in Israel.

An initial step was to employ pilot-questionnaires interviewing a sample of Israeli Arabs, with extremely disappointing results, or rather a lack of results. At this stage most of those interviewed refused point-blank to co-operate; this applied to practically all the farmers (who, when they agreed to answer, were obviously insincere, giving standard replies expressing loyalty to the State, etc.), as well as many of the townspeople. Those who agreed to reply were highly suspicious, despite the fact that the interviewing was manifestly sponsored by the Hebrew University in Jerusalem and that the interviewers were students—Jews and Arabs alike. If anything, those interviewed were more suspicious of the *Arab* students, whom they sometimes regarded as agents of the Israeli security services! It is possible that the attitude of those Arabs who were interviewed might be partially explained by lack of familiarity with interviewing and by aversion to any intrusion into their private views and affairs; even the 1961 population and housing census of the Israeli CBS ran into several difficulties among the Arabs, despite capable pre-census propaganda on a country-wide basis.[1] The fact that 1965 was an election year (on November 1965 both parliamentary and local elections were held) must have been an added factor: many suspected the interviewers of being the agents of political parties trying to ferret out their political inclinations before the elections. This setback may in itself be considered as another indication of substantial alienation on the part of the Arab population in Israel.

As a result of this experience, three main decisions were made regarding the preparation and application of a final questionnaire: (1) to formulate all queries with even greater caution than previously. (2) To postpone all interviews until after the elections, i.e. to 1966. (3) To give up the original plan to interview a statistically representative section of the Arabs, including semi-literate or illiterate farmers; instead, a more profitable approach appeared to be to sound the opinions of a section of the more literate and articulate—what might be termed interviewing a 'reputationist' section of the Arabs in Israel. Out of the 250 approached only 112, or less than half, agreed to answer, so that the sampling proved less reliable than originally intended. However, as interviewing proceeded, we succeeded in correcting this, at least in part. Though the results of the interviewing do not therefore represent a statistically exact cross-section of 'reputationist' opinion among the Arabs in Israel, they nevertheless present an articulate impression of this opinion, not infrequently accompanied by revealing sidelights. As such, the results of these interviews merit a rather detailed account.

THE INTERVIEWEES

The religious community, locality, occupation, and age distributions of the 112 Arabs who agreed to be interviewed are shown in the following tables:

Distribution according to religious affiliation

Muslims	49
Druzes	16
Greek Orthodox	17
Greek Catholics	12
Latins	3
Protestants	2
Baptists	1
Armenians	1
Christians (community unspecified)	10
Aḥmadīs	1
Total	112

*Distribution according to locality**

Nazareth	28	Yamma	4
'Isfiyya	15	Rāma	2
Jerusalem	14	Acre	1
Haifa	13	Shafā 'Amr	1
Ṭīra	10	Ma'īlyā	1
'Ar'ara	8	'Ayn Māhil	1
Jaffa	6	Kabābīr	1
Ṭaiyyba	5	Unspecified	2†
		Total	112

* Refers to present residence.

† One of those did not specify, the other replied just 'Galilee'.

Distribution according to occupation

Teacher	27 (including 3 women)	Pharmacist	1
Official and clerk	24 (including 3 women)	Bookkeeper	1
Worker	13	Grocer	1
Farmer	6	Owner of filling-station	1
Party and communal worker	6	Salesgirl	1
Part-time student	6 (including 1 woman)	Carpenter	1
Student	4	Electrician	1
Lawyer	4	Mechanic	1
School-principal	3 (including 1 woman)	Housewife	1
Journalist	2	Retired clerk	1
Tailor	2	Unemployed	1
Priest	1	Unspecified	2
Construction engineer (self-employed)	1	Total	112

Distribution according to age

Date of birth	*number*	*Date of birth*	*number*
1890	1	1932	2
1898	1	1933	3
1900	3	1934	5
1910	1	1935	2
1912	1	1936	5
1914	1	1937	4
1915	1	1938	7
1916	1	1939	3
1917	1	1940	3
1919	1	1941	2
1920	1	1942	9
1922	3	1943	5
1923	2	1944	3
1924	4	1945	7
1925	5	1946	2
1926	2	1947	3
1927	3	1948	2
1928	2	Unspecified	3
1929	4		
1930	2	Total	112
1931	2		

The religious affiliations of those interviewed roughly correspond to their relative proportions among the minorities in Israel (e.g. the Druzes about 10 per cent, the Aḥmadīs about 1 per cent, etc.), with one important exception: the Christians were over-represented among the interviewees (at the expense of the Muslims), for two reasons—their greater articulateness and their division into several denominations, which it was felt should be represented.

The distribution by localities takes into account the main residence centres of the Arab population, with an emphasis on urban concentrations—both wholly Arab (Nazareth, Shafā 'Amr) and mixed (Haifa, Jaffa, Acre). The villagers are from Galilee (20) and the Little Triangle (28), slightly more from the latter to compensate for the stress put on Galilee by the large number of interviewees in Nazareth (a quarter of the total). In the Little Triangle, preference is given to the larger villages, such as Ṭīra and Ṭaiyyba. These are more politically conscious and their inhabitants showed greater readiness to co-operate with the interviewers. In the smaller localities, people were wary of being interviewed, while the Bedouins formed an extreme case, refusing point-blank.

The 102 men and 10 women who were interviewed occupationally tend to the teaching and white-collar professions, more articulate than others, as a rule. They include 10 students, 6 of whom study only part-time, earning a living the rest of their time. Among the others, workers (13) and farmers (6) are the only comparatively large groups, the remainder being scattered at random among various occupations and covering a fairly wide range of interests and opinions.

As to the age of those interviewed, only 13 were born in 1920 or earlier, while the other 99 were born in or after 1922, i.e. were 44 years old or younger at the time of the interview; 58 interviewees (or more than half of the total) were 30 years old or less at the time they were approached for interviews. This concentration on the young was intentional, as not only did they seem readier to reply candidly and fully to the interviewers, but their views seem particularly relevant for an understanding of the present and evaluation of the future, when these young people, or others of their generation, will be the leaders.

RESULTS

Questions 4–6 represented an attempt to discover the attitudes of the interviewees to their work and to the *Histadrūt*;[1] 81 were satisfied with their work, 22 were not, 5 gave other replies (of these, 3 maintained they could find no other work—which places them close to the category of those dissatisfied with their work), and 4 did not reply. This seems to indicate a rather positive attitude, if one considers that these answers were given in 1966, a year of economic recession and growing unemploy-

[1] Since there are no up-to-date statistics of Arab, as distinct from Jewish, employment, it was considered of some interest to elicit attitudes towards employment and the *Histadrūt*.

ment. Perhaps one reason was the relatively large number of interviewees (84), or almost three-quarters, who were members of the *Histadrūt*, and reported satisfaction with their work; probably this is a result of the better employment conditions secured by the *Histadrūt* for both Jews and Arabs. None the less, only 42 of the interviewees replied that they had been participating in *Histadrūt* activities, with another 7 claiming sporadic participation. The types of participation, in this order, were: lectures, professional activity, trips, courses for women. Those unresponsive to *Histadrūt* activities claimed as reasons, in this order: lack of time, lack of interest, unawareness of such activity (1), the political character of the *Histadrūt* (1). These figures suggest low participation in *Histadrūt* activities by those enjoying the benefits of its professional support.

Another group of questions (7–9) referred to the exposure of the interviewees to such media of mass communication as the press, radio, and television. Only 99 out of the 112 claimed to read Arabic newspapers or journals; of the others 8, mostly villagers, maintained that they were a-political and hence found little of interest in the Arabic press. It is interesting that three others claimed that they had been reading the press in other languages and therefore found little to stimulate them in the Arabic newspaper. However, of those who did peruse the Arab press, several read more than one newspaper or journal. Thus 77 read *al-Yawm*, 40 *al-Mirṣād*, 33 *al-Ittiḥād*, 12 *Hādhā'l-'ālam*, 8 *al-Jadīd*, 8 *al-Muṣawwar*, 1 *al-Salām wa'l-khayr* (a religious publication), 1 *Ṣadā'l-tarbiya* (an educational journal). Newspaper reading in such a high degree seems hardly representative of the whole Arab population, if one takes into account the low circulation figures, previously mentioned; it is however characteristic of a 'reputationist' cross-section. This is manifest from the fact that 93 read newspapers and journals in other languages too (those who did not, usually claimed that they possessed no reading fluency in other languages). Those who read the non-Arabic press, preferred Hebrew evening papers—*Ma'arīv* 53, *Yĕdī'ōt aḥarōnōt* 21—or morning papers: *ha-Areṣ* 30, *Davar* 16, and a sprinkling most of the others. 26 read *The Jerusalem Post*, 17 the Hebrew weekly *ha-'Ō̱lam ha-zeh*. Remarkably, some read foreign periodicals, also: *Time* 5, *Newsweek* 1, *The Economist* 1, *Herald Tribune* 1.

All this appears to indicate that these interviewees are an intellectually alert group—provided the information is correct; it is possible that in some cases names of additional journals have been cited in an effort to impress. Some evidence in this direction may be deduced from the hesitation felt by many in indicating which newspaper or journal they preferred and why: 15 did not reply, 14 others maintained that they had no preference, and yet another 3 that all newspapers were equally good. Of those who indicated preferences, most chose Hebrew publications; among the reasons most frequently mentioned: wide coverage, able analysis, independence, and objectivity. Of those preferring Arab newspapers, 17 indicated *al-Yawm* ('the only Arabic daily', 'suited to Arab readers'), 4 *al-Ittīḥad* ('generally truthful', 'treats the problems of the Arab minority'), and 2 *al-Mirṣād* ('reflects various opinions concerning the Arabs in Israel'). Interestingly, the order of preference roughtly reflects the support for various political forces in Israel.

Questions 10–16 attempted to determine radio-listening habits and preferences. Radio listening is very widespread: only 6 were not in the habit of listening (although 20 did not reply). Practically all those listening (86) have been tuning to Israeli broadcasts in Arabic; and many (76) to those in Hebrew, apparently in addition to Arabic broadcasts; a few tuned in to Israeli broadcasts in English (8) or French (3), that is less than those who claimed to be reading *The Jerusalem Post* or foreign press in English. As to their preferences in the Israeli broadcasts, 12 replied they had none. The others however often chose several preferences, apparently indicating regular habits. The most-favoured Israeli radio programmes were: news (68), music (36), news commentaries (25), selected law reports (14), and literary criticism (13), with others divided among various features. This, again, suggests considerable interest in current events and their interpretation.

Only 7 interviewees answered that they were not in the habit of listening to other Arabic broadcasts, beamed from abroad. All others cited at least one Arab radio station they had been tuning in to, and many cited several. While 28 replied that they had been listening to most Arab stations, giving no particulars, others gave full details: 65 to Cairo and the Voice of the Arabs (Egypt), 48 BBC, 47 Jordan, 26 Lebanon, 9 Middle East (Cyprus), 8 Damascus, 6 the Voice of America, 3 Moscow, 1 Iraq. Although the sum-total of listening hours had not been requested (for it was doubtful whether any accurate calculations could be arrived at), it seems likely that the potential impact of radio stations on the political attitudes of their listeners would be marked. One might relate this to the replies on the preference for various broadcasting stations. 29 gave no specific reply (of these 16 answered 'all stations'), some of whom very possibly hesitated to show, even anonymously, a preference for a foreign station. Of those more specific, a few were still cautious enough to give more than one answer. 31 maintained they preferred Israeli broadcasts ('objective', 'exact'), 27 Cairo and the Voice of the Arabs ('varied', 'work for national liberation'), 25 BBC ('high quality', 'neutral'), 9 the Middle East ('varied'), 7 Jordan ('varied'), 5 Lebanon ('high quality'), 2 Damascus. Preference for types of foreign programmes was in the same order as for local ones: news, music, comment. A question about which station supplied the best political commentaries was apparently considered loaded, for 47 avoided answering it. Some of those who did gave more than one reply—perhaps to cover themselves—the final order however being: Israel 32, Cairo and the Voice of the Arabs 26, BBC 25, Jordan 4, Moscow 3, Lebanon 1, Damascus 1; that is the same order of preference as for listening to the stations in general. One may assume, in the light of this and previous replies, that listening to Arabic news and comments is one of the main reasons for tuning in, generally, among the interviewees. This impression is confirmed by those stating that they listen regularly to comment: 52, as against 49 (11 did not reply). Since the radio stations of Egypt are second in popularity only to Israel's, on all the above counts, their effect can be easily gauged.

Enquiries regarding television viewing and its relation to listening to the radio were embodied in questions 17–19. The size of the television audience is, naturally, smaller: 35 do not watch it at all, the main reasons being the absence of TV sets as well as lack of time. Of the others, viewing is mainly of Lebanon 58, Cairo 48, Syria 9, Israel 4, Cyprus 4, Italy 1. Since Israel, in 1966, had only educational television, the small number of Arabs watching it is easily explained. The preponderance of Lebanon is probably thanks to the fact that it successfully presents entertainment, clearly received on television screens in Galilee. More striking is the popularity of Egyptian television, whose programmes are largely politically oriented. The order of preference is different from that of radio listeners. Very possibly due to the high quality entertainment value of Lebanese television, films come first, followed by plays, sports events, and only then newscasts. The replies as to TV-radio preference are instructive: 8 did not reply, and 17 could not make up their minds. Those who decided were almost equally divided: 43 preferred radio ('varied programmes', 'may be watched while working at something else', 'does not harm the eyes'), while 44 preferred television ('one can both watch and listen', 'it is more lively', 'more enjoyable', 'more instructive'). To sum up, on the evidence of these responses, television has as yet made more limited inroads than the radio among the Arabs in Israel. Nevertheless, its impact is not necessarily smaller, due to its forceful visual presentation and to the absence of competition by Israeli television.

Knowledge of important political facts was tested by questions 20–22. These started with a relatively simple query, as to who is the President of the State. Out of the 112 interviewees 107 answered correctly: Mr Zalman Shazar; only 4 indicated Mr Eshkol, the Prime Minister, and 1 alone could not reply. Different results are noticeable in the replies on names of Government Ministers they remember. Significantly, 8 interviewees could not remember any. Most of the others, 92, identified Mr Eshkol, but only 82 A. Even, 74 P. Sapīr, 72 Y. Allōn, 58 E. Sasōn, 38 B. Shīṭrīṭ; it is revealing that, in addition to the Prime Minister, the best known Ministers are for foreign affairs, finance, labour, posts, and police. All other Ministers obtained only 35 votes or less. Several considered that Messrs D. Ben-Gurion and M. Dayyan were still Ministers (6 replies each) and others bestowed this distinction on several MKs, chief rabbis, and the chief of staff. The several odd replies do not detract from the general knowledge shown by most.

It is more surprising that, so soon after the *Kneset* elections, 5 interviewees could remember the name of no political party, two of whom frankly confessed they did not know. Of the others, 96 remembered the Alignment of MAPAI and *Aḥdūt ha-'avōda*, 94 MAPAM, 84 the National

Religious Party, 62 GAḤAL, 61 RAFĪ, 41 This World, and 39 the Independent Liberals; 37 mentioned 'communists' in general, but 56 specified MAQĪ and 54 RAQAḤ. Other parties and groups were mentioned 31 times or less (the Arab lists allied to the Alignment 14 only, probably because they were not considered a party). So, although one might perhaps have expected better knowledge of various party names, still the response was quite satisfactory in this respect.

Questions 23 and 24 took up from here and led, hopefully not too obviously, to the interviewee's opinion as to which parties were most and least suitable to represent the interests of the Arabs in Israel. This was intended, at least in part, to reveal the political leanings of the interviewees. To the query as to which party was most favoured for the above purpose, 22 abstained completely and another 25 avoided the issue, by maintaining there was no such party at all, or similar reasoning. Of the remaining 65, the replies were distributed as follows: the Alignment 43 ('balanced and realistic', 'has proven itself as encouraging Arab workers'), MAPAM 7 ('a socialist party', 'works for the equality of the Arabs'), RAQAḤ 7 ('represents Arab workers', 'protects Arab rights'), This World 7 ('protects Arab rights', 'strives for peace with the Arabs'), an independent Arab party 1. Surprisingly, however, to the next question, on the least favoured party, although a somewhat larger number (50) abstained, replies were broken up into more categories. One naturally wonders why a question about disliking political parties should have evoked a greater response than that favouring parties, were there not a solid foundation for suspicion and disenchantment. The party most objected to for representing Arabs was *Ḥerūt* with 22 ('extremist', 'anti-Arab') followed by the communists with 19 ('undemocratic and dependent on Moscow', 'double-faced'), This World 5 ('falsifiers'), the National Religious Party 3 ('inactive'), the Alignment 3 ('has not convinced us of assisting the Arabs'), MAPAM 1 ('double-faced'), RAFĪ 1 ('has not assisted the Arabs'), all Zionist parties 1 ('Zionism is against Arab nationalism').

Questions 25 onwards were mainly intended to obtain some idea of the problems which the interviewees considered as more immediately pressing. It was considered advisable to investigate this in an indirect manner, by asking about the problems facing the State of Israel and the Arab States and the interviewee's own opinion as to solutions; and revert to the point in later questions, centring on local problems.

Only 7 interviewees did not reply to the question on the problems facing the State of Israel. The others gave full vent to their views, replying in considerable detail. Reclassified by subject, these are as follows: (1) *Politics*. Israel's peacemaking with the Arab States 53; the Palestine problem and the refugees 13; party rivalry between various interests 6; policy making 5; political stability 2; Israel's becoming an established State 2; improvement of the struggle for civil rights 1; relations with Germany 1. (2) *Defence*. Security from day to day 49; disarmament in the Middle East 2. (3) *Economics and finance*. Employment and economic stability 61;

unemployment 34; joining the European common market 10; rising prices 8; the need for capital 3; trade deficits 2; taxation 2; the import-export balance 1; finding new markets for Israeli products 1; the need to raise salaries 1; striking for better wages 1. (4) *Development.* Water problems, e.g. desalinization 10; development 6; the building trade 2; industrialization 2; using development for reducing foreign assistance 1. (5) *Social problems.* Jewish-Arab relations 19; Jewish immigration 10; discrimination 7; the merger of Jews of various origins 7; the class struggle 6; equality 4; youth problems 3; Arab feelings of being a second-class citizen 2; the shortage of physicians in the villages 2; settlement in the Negev 2; the disrespectful attitude of the new Arab generation towards tradition 2; demographic problems 2; imperialism 1; emigration from Israel 1; the *Histadrūt* 1; problems of workers 1; religion 1. (6) *Various.* Nationalism in the area 1; freedom from chauvinism 1; the loss of hope for a better future 1.

The same interviewees proved somewhat less talkative when asked about the problems facing the Arab States; 15 preferred to voice no opinion. Those who aired their views emphasized economic problems 35; political instability 33; union and disruption 30; socialism against imperialism 19; the Palestine problem and the refugees 15; the problem of Arab leadership 13; peace with Israel 9; raising the standards of living 8; relations with Israel 6; fighting poverty and disease 6; education 6 (other points receive a passing mention only). Characteristically, the concern of the Arabs in Israel with their status and problems, so evident in the previous questions, is also manifest in this one, in a more oblique way.

In an attempt to pinpoint some of the main Arab grievances about their actual situation in Israel, questions 27–29 asked their views as to whether this State was democratic; 4 did not reply. Of the 108 others, 68 replied affirmatively, 40 replied negatively: the bulk, or 28, of these argued that the State was undemocratic because of the unequal treatment of its Arab minority; the other 12 gave no reason. Remarkably, the interviewees then considered their own situation (as they saw it) the only hindrance to complete democracy in Israel! This attitude was reiterated in their answers to the two subsequent questions.

To the query asking them to indicate evidence of democracy in the State of Israel, 30 chose not to answer; they were among those who had replied negatively to the previous question. The others gave a variety of replies including: the existence of a free press and freedom of expression 56; the functioning of a *Kneset* elected by free and secret elections 49; social justice 43; political and civil equality 25; freedom of political organization and activity 19; the division of power 12; freedom of travel 12; freedom of the individual 8; independence of the judiciary 7; national insurance 4; projects of development 4; freedom of religion 4; supervision of the executive 3; sovereignty of the people 3; free, compulsory education 3; equal opportunity 2; the rule of law 2; the existence of an opposition 2;

the election of Arabs to the *Kneset* 1; the protection of Arabs by the judiciary 1; equality between men and women 1.

More revealing are the replies which maintain the absence of democracy in the State of Israel; 59 among those who thought that Israel was a democracy did not reply to this point. Those who did argued that there was no democracy in Israel, on the following grounds: the military administration 25; discrimination 20; expropriation of land 17; restrictions on freedom of expression 14; absence of suitable Arab representation in the *Kneset* and larger municipal councils 5; inequality of the Arab minority 4; defence regulations 4; the requirement of travel permits 3; the general official attitude towards the Arab minority 3; the absence of Arabs in Government offices 3; the non-existence of a constitution 3; religious compulsion 2; the selfish character of political parties 2; the activity of the security services 2; preference for the Jewish citizen over the Arab 2; preference for Jewish education 2.

Question 30 and subsequent questions were intended to probe a little deeper and find out about the more particular grievances of the Israeli Arab—by asking him about *local* problems he might have been facing. Only 3 interviewees did not want to commit themselves, while all others answered in detail. In this connexion, significantly, less consensus was evident, as each interviewee was encouraged to present what *he* considered meaningful. Hence a greater variety of opinions were expressed with a proportionately smaller number of answers to support each, usually one or two only. They refer to education (for or against co-education); health (night service of physicians); work (fear of unemployment); social relations (complaints against constant conflicts, or the rule of *ḥamūlas*); lodgings (insufficient building activity); communications (the need for road repairs); agriculture (problems of irrigation, the need for modernization); village development (public gardens); and the looseness of teenage morals (mainly in Jaffa).

Although 18 interviewees abstained from replying to question 31, requesting solutions to the above, many of the others answered fully and constructively. Here a somewhat larger consensus of opinion found expression in a number of apparently popular solutions: the establishment of local councils 14, financial assistance by the Government 13, foundation of clubs 10 and the institution of courses in them 9, broadening the school network 9, support for a new, younger leadership 7, industrialization 6, adult education 6, provision of Government employment for Arab intellectuals 5, abolition of the military administration 4, introduction of electricity 4, enlargement of the area designed for building 4. Many more, however, indicated their personal solutions to local problems of their own which, though not generally applicable, are equally revealing. Among these, may be mentioned the following: equalization of the status of girls to that of boys, improvements in the lot of the Arab woman, provision of employment for everybody, institution of a five-day working week, separation of local development from politics, establishment of light industries, co-education of Arabs and Jews, greater public mindedness, military service for all young Arab males, education for co-operation, and a privileged standing for the Arabic language.

The above local grievances (some of which were no doubt common to Israeli Jews, too) reflected personal ones as well. Question 32 was intended, more directly, to try and elucidate these, at the risk of repetitiveness. The interviewee was asked about the general problems of the Arab in Israel, on the assumption that his reply would reflect his own complaints and hopes; 15 did not answer. Among the others there seems to have been substantial consensus on some points: unemployment 33, the military administration 23, expropriation of land 19, discrimination in employment (mainly against intellectuals) 17, second-class citizenship 12, improvement of education 10, mutual suspicion between Arabs and Jews 9, freedom of movement 8, village development 6, altering the local leadership 5. Others individually inveighed against the cost of living, the tactics of political parties, the slow pace of modernization, polygamy, the *mahr*, and—conversely—the shiftiness of Arab youth. Yet others deplored what they considered the absence of a firm policy regarding the Arab minority and Jewish lack of confidence in the Arabs, both features obstructing integration in the State of Israel.

That it is easier to deplore a situation, real or imaginary, than to offer practical suggestions for change was proved by the replies to question 33. Of the interviewees 17 did not reply at all, and among the others relative consensus was achieved on few solutions, such as the abolition of the military administration (however, only 7 mentioned this) or speedier development of the Arab village (8). Several evaded the issue, maintaining that 'the State should solve this'. Others suggested the grievances of the Arab in Israel should be redressed in the following manner: employment (for Arab intellectuals and others), education (co-education), planned industrialization (in the villages), co-operation with the Jews (encouraging it by joint activities, as well as lectures), achievement of peace with the Arab States (solving the problem of the Arab refugees), replacement of Arab leadership (by a younger one).

Many of the interviewees had evaded the issue of the relations between Israel and the Arab States, or their answers were almost lost in a multitude of detail. Question 34 focused on this point, which was one of urgent concern to them; 13 had no opinion to offer, but the others compensated by their rather interesting replies—definitely political in outlook. An impressive number of interviewees, 56, thought that everything depended on the solution of the Arab refugee problem, while 19 proposed talks between Israel and the Arab States, and 11 affirmed that peace ought to be based on right and justice. Six opted for the recognition of Israel by the Arab States, while 5 attached importance to the co-option of more Israeli Arabs in policy-making. Other views were as follows: time would provide a solution; coexistence between the world blocs would help; Israel should persuade other States that it is here to stay—and the Israeli Arabs could help in explaining the truth about life in Israel; disarmament was necessary; a federal union between Israel and the Arab part of Palestine, a union of the whole Middle East or a common market within it, would solve the conflct.

The next step was to find out what the interviewees thought about the ways in which the Arabs in Israel expressed their opinions and defended their interests and the best means of doing so open to them. As to the first, 34 did not reply (possibly the query was not sufficiently clear). Those who did indicated—in this sequence—the following: the press, mass communication (radio, etc.), the *Kneset*, the political parties, personal contacts, meeting with Jews, demonstrations, work within the framework of the *Histadrūt*. Some interviewees stressed personal contact, probably a new version of the *wāsṭa*—although several frowned on this. Indeed, a few replied that the Arabs in Israel do not express themselves at all, because of their lack of understanding in politics.

Greater interest attaches to the suggestions of the interviewees for more suitable means of expression. A wide range of opinions was presented (with little consensus): the local and foreign press, an independent Arab press, an independent Arab party, the *Kneset*, the United Nations, complaints to the authorities, committees to advise the Government, the radio, democratic means—such as elected representatives (not the established leadership)—popular rallies, personal contacts, visiting, letters. A single interviewee favoured violence.

The next question reverted to political attitudes, referring to the parties. While previous queries had concentrated on the most and the least favoured parties, this one listed each party or political group separately, and generally received, as expected, mixed reactions. The replies combine into the image held by the interviewees of each group. Several noted that most Israeli parties put party interest before national interest, were Zionist and 'anti-Arab', divisive in effect, and motivated chiefly by vote-catching. Many interviewees were, however, more specific.

1. MAPAI had achieved much for the Arabs in Israel, particularly in education, village development and providing work; but did not accept Arab members, was responsible for the military administration and for spreading discord among the *ḥamūlas*, for the sole purpose of vote-catching.

2. The Alignment was seen as a continuation of MAPAI, but stronger—hence the only vehicle for achieving the integration of the Arabs in Israel; however some suspected it of considering only its own interests.

3. *Aḥdūt ha-'avōda* was appreciated for sometimes supplying employment, but was otherwise considered simply as the junior partner of MAPAI in the Alignment; a vote-catching party, with no real interest in the Arabs (a 'tongue without a heart').

4. MAPAM was highly praised for providing Arabs with paid work in its *kibbūtzīm*, including an Arab in its parliamentary group, fostering Arabic culture, and working for peace in the Middle East and better

Arab-Jewish understanding in Israel. However, others could not forgive its Zionist character and considered it double-faced, misleading the Arab youth with vain promises.

5. MAQĪ was generally considered as a weak party, unable to play any decisive role, and compensating by loud talk and appeal to feelings. Worse still from the point of view of many interviewees, it had recently become pro-Zionist and hence was misleading the Arabs.

6. RAQAḤ received a much more divided evaluation. It was considered by some as a courageous party, the only one truly watching over the rights of the Arabs in Israel ('a crystallization of Arab nationalism'), and publishing a very readable press. Others saw it as an opposition group inciting simple folk by playing on their feelings ('drum-beating'), hence a destructive association with no solution to offer.

7. *al-Arḍ* was labelled by many as inactive, a thing of the past, which had appealed solely to a few intellectuals. Those who described it characterized it as more damaging than helpful, an extremist group which had injured the interests of the Arabs in Israel by presenting them to public opinion as hostile to the State.

8. The National Religious Party was considered by a few as favouring religion and the building of mosques, but most considered it as an oddity in politics ('a revival of the Pharaonic times'), of little importance among the Arabs and mainly interested in vote-catching.

9. The Independent Liberals were seen to include 'positive intellectuals' and 'men of ideals' but more generally were accused of being an impotent party ('its smoke does not blind') and quite inactive among the Arab population, except on election-eve.

10. RAFĪ was suspected by several as still being close to MAPAI, while many more considered it as anti-Arab and responsible for the military administration and a warlike attitude ('come, oh Arab, to fight the Arabs!').

11. GAḤAL was seen by many as an even more warlike party ('Mr Begīn is equal to war'), a continuous opposition party which denied Arab rights within Israel.

12. Co-operation and Brotherhood was praised for watching over Arab interests but most blamed its representatives for serving MAPAI interests in order to keep their *Kneset* membership ('representatives of seats') and for fostering discord among the *ḥamūlas*.

13. Progress and Development received very much the same reaction ('both lists are not what their names indicate'), while one interviewee considered them both as a joke.

14. This World, as a new party, provoked a mixed reaction, for some interviewees claimed they did not know enough about it. Several praised its defence of Arab interests and its stand for peace ('with more courage than skill'); others suspected it of 'trading in Arab votes' and inciting the Arabs to chauvinism.

15. The List of Peace, allied with RAFĪ, was defined as a vote-catching

group of notables, opportunist and too small to have any real influence. Others considered it as stillborn and totally insignificant among the Arab population.

Since it had been foreseen that many interviewees would criticize the existing political parties, the next two questions (37–38) were designed to determine their attitude towards Arab political activity within the existing parties as opposed to the establishment of an independent Arab party; 22 did not reply, while 50 favoured Arab integration in, or alliances with, the existing parties, and 40 a new, independent Arab party. The reasons they advanced were many and—considering the fact that 34 abstained—quite varied. Those who favoured integrating into the existing parties argued as follows: experience showed that this had worked out; integration would progress in this way; loyal Arabs had no need for a separate political organization; a joint struggle for equal rights stood a better chance for success; an independent Arab party would be too small to be effective. Those who favoured the opposite viewpoint argued that experience showed little to have been achieved by the present course of action; mixed parties would still remain Jewish in outlook; each political party watched over its own interests and would not assist the Arabs; alliances with Jewish parties, such as the Alignment, had already shown that the Arabs were subordinate in a Jewish party; an independent Arab party would be able to collect Arab votes dispersed among the Jewish parties; only an Arab party would have Arab interests at heart and, if sufficiently strong, would be able to achieve results.

Questions 39–41 attempted to sound the opinions of the interviewees on Arab political leadership, both in Israel and abroad; 89 of the interviewees, or about 80 per cent of the total, replied that there were no leaders, but nevertheless several of these, as well as the others, indicated one or more names—usually several. Archbishop al-Ḥakīm was considered as a leader by 11 (mainly within his flock), Sayf al-Dīn Zu'bī 8, Eliyās Nakhla 4, Jabr Mu'addī 4, Tawfīq Ṭūbī 4, Emīl Ḥabībī 3, 'Abd al-'Azīz Zu'bī 3, Labīb Abū Rūkn 2, Rustum Bastūnī 2, Fāris Ḥamdān 2, Yūsuf Khamīs 2, Jabbūr Yūsuf Jabbūr 2, Shaykh Amīn Ṭarīf 2, Kamāl Manṣūr 2, Ṣāliḥ Barānsī 2, Rāshid Ḥusayn 2. It is noteworthy that apart from al-Ḥakīm and Ṭarīf, the leaders of the Greek Catholic and Druze communities, respectively, responses cited mainly Arab MKs. Others were Jabbūr, mayor of Shafā 'Amr; K. Manṣūr, a Druze active in public affairs; the ex-*al-Arḍ* leader, Ṣ. Barānsī; and the poet R. Ḥusayn. Other candidates were mentioned once only, among them Ṣabrī Jiryis and Ḥabīb al-Qahwajī, ex-*al-Arḍ* activists. This diversity of opinion tends to show that not only could the interviewees not agree on leading political figures among the Arab population in Israel; with few exceptions, they seem to have interpreted the question formally, to mean leaders of religious communities and MKs.

The above choice, it should be remembered, was open. In the question on Arab leadership outside Israel, six possibilities were offered—King

Ḥusayn of Jordan, Amīn al-Ḥāfiẓ of Syria, ʿAbd al-Nāṣir, President Būrgība, King Fayṣal of Saudi Arabia, and any other reply. Though 24 chose not to answer, those who did frequently suggested more than one name and added reasons for their choice. ʿAbd al-Nāṣir came first, mentioned 69 times, or almost 80 per cent of all those who replied (reasons: progressive, socialist, devoted to the Arab cause, fighter against imperialism, an international figure, reform-minded). Būrgība was mentioned 20 times (a realist, balanced leader, serving his people well, interested in peace). Ḥusayn 4 times (a leader of his State in arduous times, is no extremist). Amīn al-Ḥāfiẓ twice (a man of action). King Fayṣal once (a religious person). The 'other' answers mentioned, once each, al-Atāsī of Syria (no reason given); al-Ḥilū of Lebanon (works for his country's future); and Aḥmad al-Shuqayrī, of the Palestine Liberation Organization (a Palestinian who has succeeded in obtaining Chinese support for his cause).

Many questions had been so phrased that they openly invited critical comment. Towards the end, an opportunity was therefore given the interviewees to express their opinions (43–44) on what had been done for the Arab population, in the cultural, economic, and social fields. All except 23 interviewees responded in some detail, which may be summarized as follows:

1. The cultural field. Enlargement of the scope and improvement in the quality of education (free, compulsory education; new schools; teachers' courses; acceptance of Arab students at the universities; instruction for girls at all levels; the rise of educational standards) and the spread of culture (adult education; clubs and courses; publication of books). The very few objectors claimed that more ought to have been achieved, and that political considerations lay behind the overall rate of progress.

2. The economic field. A rise in the standard of living (more money; better homes; running water; electricity), rapid development (new roads; building), advance in agriculture (better crops; planned marketing), progress in production (thanks to credit and loans) and employment (good pay for workers; entry of Arabs into the *Histadrūt*). Those few who took a pessimistic view of the situation pointed to the absence of industrialization and to the change in character of some villages, now resembling hotels for residents employed elsewhere, in the towns.

3. The social field. Most interviewees indicated a change for the better —in health and welfare (improvement in health and hygiene; establishment of clinics; national insurance; social welfare), the social standing of women (equality; integration through courses and women's clubs), advances in social relations (new clubs, several cinema halls) and the development of local government. The interviewees who took a negative attitude claimed, however, that the penetration of modernization into the Arab village was no more than skin-deep, that there was no social life worth the name, and that the old family traditions reigned supreme.

Many suggestions regarding steps to improve the situation of the Arab population, in village and town, were forthcoming. Their general theme appears to have been the desire for intensification of village development, industrialization, modernization of agriculture, further progress in education, planned social activities, full employment (including more Arabs in the civil service), substitution of the traditional leadership by a younger one, larger co-operation between Arabs and Jews (reside together, trust one another).

In the above replies, as in many previous ones, Arab-Jewish confrontation appeared to be of immediate concern to many interviewees. The last question (44) examined this confrontation by inquiring into ways whereby the two groups could draw closer together. Only 12 did not answer; again, the answers were quite diverse, several of them repeating previous suggestions. In order of frequency responses were as follows: full equality for the Arabs, frequent contact between the two peoples, Arab participation in the economy, a press campaign for rapprochement, joint activities in all fields, lectures, integration of Arabs into the State, compulsory teaching of Arabic to Jewish school-children, establishment of committees to foster goodwill, appointment of an objective commission of inquiry made up of University professors, mutual esteem, a joint effort for bringing peace to the Middle East, translations, and preparation of a school textbook in Hebrew on *Our brethren the Arabs*, whose use would be compulsory.

TENTATIVE CONCLUSIONS

Where relevant, material from the replies to the questionnaire has been drawn upon in writing the preceding chapters of this book and, therefore, need not be repeated. However, the foregoing analysis of the replies has revealed several major trends which would repay attention.

Among the more remarkable features is the wide range of the opinions expressed. While general consensus could hardly have been expected on any one point, the diversity of replies might indicate a larger diffusion of views than is generally the case in 'reputationist' circles. Many of the interviewees were politically alert and quite willing to discuss their views. Listening to the local and foreign (mainly Egyptian) radio, and watching foreign television (chiefly Lebanese and Egyptian) were extremely widespread; newscasts and political comment were frequently favoured. They were fairly well-acquainted with the names of the more important Government Ministers, particularly with those having a decisive say in Arab affairs, as well as with the names of major political parties, especially if active among the Arabs.

When it came to expressing their personal opinions on sensitive political matters, not a few interviewees sometimes showed caution, despite the promised anonymity, and therefore chose to remain silent. However, a majority—generally a large one—aired their views freely. In expressing attitudes towards the various political parties, for instance, their general attitude has provided no surprises statistically. Their political judgement, however, was on preponderantly pragmatic lines, that is, political parties were favoured by most interviewees subject to their positive activity in the interests of the Arabs in Israel. In this approach the interviewees appear to have reflected the attitude of the Arab minority.

No less characteristic are the grievances voiced and the suggestions put forward. While considerable, if not total, consensus exists on national matters—such as the need for complete civil equality, economic progress, or solving the Arab refugee problem, most interviewees concentrated on local and personal affairs. This conclusion may be drawn from the emphasis of the various solutions they put forward. While in national matters these were formulated in a rather general, almost stereotyped, manner, more practical suggestions were brought forward for local and personal grievances, indicating greater concern. Overwhelmingly, solutions are on a socio-economic level, with politics often mirroring socio-economic problems. The disillusionment of many interviewees with all political parties stemmed from neglect of local interests by most parties. The interviewees' preference for local leaders, when indicating Arab political leaders in Israel, further tends to bear out paramount concern with communal and economic problems. The lack of a national political figure among the Arabs in Israel, while obviously limiting replies, itself indicates the emphasis on local issues.

The younger interviewees, however, showed themselves more politically conscious. They formed the bulk of those supporting the establishment of an independent Arab party. No doubt, in addition to national (or nationalist) considerations, personal ambition helped condition their choice, as the younger people stand little chance of speedily advancing within the existing parties. That their rise to prominence has been blocked by the older, traditional leadership was apparent from many of their replies. Not infrequently, they grumbled that the State authorities supported the traditional leadership in its contest for power with the younger generation.

End of appendix L

Pages 278-279 contain the glossary which has been read.

(now turn to page 280

D.P.P.
Page 278

Read on page 1

GLOSSARY

(A = Arabic; H = Hebrew; T = Turkish)

Aḥdūt ha-‘avōda (H)—‘Union of Labour’, Israeli political party (left of centre). Affiliated with MAPAI in an ‘Alignment’, later united with it and RAFĪ in the Israeli Labour Party.

al-‘Amal (A)—Israeli Arab Labour Party.

al-Arḍ (A)—‘The Earth’, a nationalist Arab group, active during the years 1959–64.

GAḤAL (H)—Gūsh Ḥerūt—Līberalīm, ‘Ḥerūt-Liberals Bloc’, a political alliance of these two parties, formed before the 1965 elections.

Ḥamūla (A)—Patrilineal association, on which social cleavage in the Arab village is based.

Ḥerūt (H)—‘Freedom’, Israeli political party, right of centre and militant; allied with the Liberals in GAḤAL before the 1965 *Kneset* elections.

Histadrūt (H)—General Federation of Labour.

Kibbūtz, pl. *kibbūtzīm* (H)—Jewish collective settlement.

Kneset (H)—Israel’s one-chamber, 120-member Parliament.

MAPAI (H)—*Mifleget Pō‘aley Yisra’el*, ‘The Party of the Workers of Israel’, largest Israeli political party. Entered into an Alignment with *Aḥdūt ha-‘avōda* before the 1965 *Kneset* elections and fused with it and RAFĪ, in 1968, into the Israeli Labour Party.

MAPAM (H)—*Mifleget Pō‘alīm Mĕ’ūḥedet*, ‘United Workers Party’, left-of-centre Israeli political party.

MAQĪ (H)—*Miflaga Qōmūnīsṭīt Yisrĕ’elīt*, ‘Israeli Communist Party’.

Millet (T)—‘community’, refers to non-Sunnite recognized communities in the Ottoman Empire.

Muftī (A)—Muslim legal scholar.

Mukhtār (A)—‘elected’, village-headman, elected during Ottoman and British rule by the village elders, then appointed by the authorities.

Muthaqqafīn (A)—‘educated’, the Arab intelligentsia.

Ha-‘Ōlam ha-zeh Movement—This World—a New Force.

Qāḍī (A)—Muslim judge of the religious courts.

RAFĪ (H)—*Rĕshīmat Pō‘aley Yisra’el*, ‘List of the Workers of Israel’, the group which broke away from MAPAI in 1965 and rejoined it, in 1968, within the Israeli Labour Party.

RAQAḤ (H)—*Rĕshīma Qōmūnīsṭīt Ḥadasha*, ‘New Communist List’, the group which broke away from MAQĪ in 1965.

Samne (A)—milk-fat, a staple Bedouin food.

Sharī'a courts—Religious courts of the Muslim community.

ha-Shōmer ha-ṣa'īr (H)—Jewish youth organization of MAPAM.

Waqf (A)—Immovable property, whose revenue has been earmarked for some philanthropic purpose (generally, religious or educational).

Wāsta (A)—'mediation', intervention with the authorities on behalf of an interested person.

End of Glossary ✓

SELECT BIBLIOGRAPHY

THIS select bibliography does not include the daily press. Authors' names have been transliterated as consistently as possible, except in those cases where they have their own, frequently employed, form. For periodicals, the date only has been given, except in cases where a mention of the volume was necessary in order to avoid confusion.

A. ARABIC

1. *Books*

'Alī, 'Alī Muḥammad. *Fī dākhil Isrā'īl: dirāsat kiyānihā'l-siyāsī wa'l-iqitiṣādī* (Inside Israel: a study of its political and economic nature). [Cairo], al-Dār al-qawmiyya li'l-ṭibā'a wa'l-nashr, n.d. (1963?). 368 pp.

al-Fikra al-'arabiyya al-isrā'īliyya (The Israeli Arab idea). Haifa, Maṭba'at Jarjūra, 1964. 28 pp. (Arabic and Hebrew.)

Jam'iyyat al-duwal al-'arabiyya—al-amāna al-'āmma. *Al-Aqalliyya al-'arabiyya fī ẓalām Isrā'īl* (The Arab minority in the darkness of Israel). Cairo, Lajnat al-ta'līf wa'l-tarjama wa'l-nashr, 1960. 72 pp.

Jiryis, Ṣabrī. *Al-Muwāṭinūn al-'arab fī jaḥīm Isrā'īl* (The Arab compatriots in the hell of Israel). Jerusalem, Maktab jam'iyyat al-duwal al-'arabiyya, 1967. 132 pp.

Kanafānī, Ghassān. *Adab al-muqāwama fī Filasṭīn al-muḥtalla, 1948–66* (The literature of resistance in occupied Palestine). Beirut, Dār al-ādāb, [1966]. 144 pp.

al-Kīlānī, Mūsà Zayd. *Sanawāt al-ightiṣāb: Isrā'īl 1948–65* (The years of violence: Israel 1948–65). N.p., [1966?]. 119 pp.

Al-Ufq al-jadīd: majallat al-adab wa'l-thaqāfa wa'l-fikr, Jan. 1965. Special issue on *Adab al-nakba* (Arab literature on the tragedy of Palestine). 80 pp.

Yōm Ṭōv, Simḥa. *Qaryat Ṭur'ān* (The village of Ṭur'ān). Jerusalem, Min. of Interior, Dept of Minorities, n.d. 94 pp.

2. *Articles in* al-Jadīd

Ḥadīth al-shahr: al-ḍaḥāyā sataṣrakh ḥattà yantahī'l-iḍṭihād (Monthly report: the victims will scream until oppression ends). Sept. 1958, 4–6, 57.

Ḥadīth al-shahr: ilà'l-ma'raka (Monthly report: let us struggle!). Aug. 1955, 4–7.

Ḥadīth al-shahr: khātimat Ibn Ghūriyōn wa'l-mashrū' al-shāmil (Monthly report: Ben-Gurion's signature and the 'final solution'). Dec. 1953, 4–6, 45.

Ḥadīth al-shahr: khuṭwa hāmma 'alà ṭarīq ṭawīl (Monthly report: an important step on a long road). Jan. 1965, 3–4.

Ḥusayn, Rāshid. Ṣawt al-muḍṭahadīn (The voice of the oppressed). June 1965, 11–14.

Ibn Khaldūn (pseud.). Ḥawl kitāb 'kayfa tuḥkam Isrā'īl': man yaḥkum Isrā'īl (About the book 'How Israel is governed': who governs in Israel?). Apr. 1954, 13–20.

Khamīs, Ṣalībā, Ḥadīth al-shahr: marḥala ḥāsima fī niḍāl 'arab Isrā'īl' (Monthly report: a decisive stage in the struggle of the Arabs of Israel), Oct. 1963, 3–4.

—— Ḥadīth al-shahr: waḥdat al-maṣīr (Monthly report: the unity of destiny). Mar. 1962, 3–5.

Nīqūlā, Jabrā. Aḍwā' wa-ẓilāl: ḥawl ta'līm al-adab al-'arabī fī Isrā'īl (Lights and shadows: about the teaching of Arabic literature in Israel). Nov. 1959, 48–49.

B. HEBREW

1. *Books*

Encyclopaedia Hebraica, vol. vi (=Palestine and Israel). Ramat Gan, Massada, 1957.

Har'el, M. *Yānūḥ: kĕfar dĕrūzī ba-Galīl* (Yānūḥ: a Druze village in Galilee). Jerusalem, Prime Minister's Office, Adviser on Arab affairs, 1959. 54 pp., map. Mimeo.

Jiryis, Ṣabrī. *Ha-'Aravīm bĕ-Yisra'el* (The Arabs in Israel). Haifa, al-Ittiḥād Press, 1966. 173 pp.

Ha-Mizraḥ he-Ḥadash, xv (1–2): 1965. Special issue on the Arabs in Israel. xvii, 195 pp.

Rosenfeld, Henry. *Hem hayū fallaḥīm: 'iyyūnīm ba-hitpattĕḥūt ha-ḥevratīt shel ha-kĕfar ha-'aravī bĕ-Yisra'el* (They were fellaheen: studies in the social development of the Arab village in Israel). N.p., ha-Kībbūtz ha-me'ūḥad, 1964. 223 pp.

Segal, Yōram. *Ha-Bĕniyya ba-kĕfarīm ha-'araviyyīm ba-Galīl wĕ-hitpattĕḥūta* (Building and its development in Arab villages in Galilee). Jerusalem, Ministry of the Interior, 1967. vi, 64, xiv pp.

Stendel, Ori. *Ha-Mī'ūṭīm bĕ-Yisra'el* (Minorities in Israel). Jerusalem, Prime Minister's Office, Information Centre, Mar. 1965. 55 pp. Mimeo.

—— *Noṣrat be-'avar w-va-hōwe* (Nazareth in past and present). Jerusalem, School for Tourism, 1966. vi, 57 pp. Mimeo.

Vilnay, Zev. *Ha-Mī'ūṭīm bĕ-Yisra'el: Mūslĕmīm, nōṣĕrīm, dĕrūzīm w-beha'īm* (Minorities in Israel: Muslims, Christians, Druzes and Baha'is). Jerusalem, Mass., 1959. 270 pp.

Ha-Yōm ha-ri'shōn: dīn wĕ-ḥeshbōn tamṣītī mi-yōm ha-'iyyūn ha-yĕhūdī—ha-'aravī she-ne'erakh bĕ-veyt Dī-Nūr: 19.3.64 (The first day: a summarized report of the first Jewish-Arab study-day in the Dī-Nūr home: 19 March 1964). N.p. (Tel-Aviv), n.d. (1964). 30 pp. Mimeo.

2. *Articles*

Aḥīsar, A. Tazkīrō shel Sheykh Ṭāhir al-Ṭabarī (The memorandum of Shaykh Ṭāhir al-Ṭabarī). *Ner*, Aug. 1953, 19–20.

Amīttay, Y. Be'ayōt ḥīnnūkh wĕ-tarbūt shel 'araviyyey Yisra'el (Problems of the Arabs of Israel in education and culture). *Ba-Sha'ar*, May 1960, 13–20.

'Aravīm bĕ-Yisra'el (Arabs in Israel), *in* Ha-Mō'adōn la-maḥshava ha-'ivrīt, *Ṣĕvat ri'shōna: Diyyūnīm w-khĕtavīm: 1966*. Tel-Aviv, 1966, 62–69. Mimeo.

Argōv, Me'īr. Ha-Mĕdīna w-mī'ūṭeyha (The State and its minorities). *Gesher*, Dec. 1959, 24–38.

Asaf, Michael. Ha-Īnṭelīgenṣiyya ha-'aravīt bĕ-Yisra'el (The Arab intelligentsia in Israel). *Ammōt*, June–July 1965, 51–59.

——Tahalīkh hishtallĕvūtam shel ha-'aravīm bĕ-Yisra'el: nisyōn sīkkūm ri'shōn (The integration-process of the Arabs in Israel: a first attempt at summing-up). *MḤ*, Oct. 1949, 2–7.

Avineri, Shlomo. Yiṣṣūgō shel ha-mī'ūṭ ha-'aravī (The representation of the Arab minority). *Bĕ-Ṭerem*, 1 Mar. 1953, 32–34.

Ben-Ḥananya, Yĕhōshū'a (pseud. of Y. Yĕhōshū'a). Ha-'Ittōnūt ha-'adatīt ha-nōṣĕrīt bĕ-Yisra'el (The press of the Christian communities in Israel). *MḤ*, 1959, 24–28.

Ben-Tzur, Avraham. Tahalīkhīm ba-ṣibbūr ha-'aravī wĕ-tafqīdey ha-nō'ar ha-'aravī ha-ḥalūṣī (Processes among the Arab public and the role of the Pioneer Arab Youth). *Ba-Sha'ar*, Dec. 1959, 7–10.

Benor, J. L. Ha-Ḥīnnūkh ha-'aravī bĕ-Yisra'el (Arab education in Israel), *MḤ*, Autumn 1951, 1–8.

——Kamma mi-be'ayōt ḥīnnūkh ha-'aravīm bĕ-Yisra'el (Some of the problems of Arab education in Israel). *Mĕgammōt*, Jan. 1957, 90–93.

Eliad, Nissim. Ha-Ezraḥīm ha-'araviyyīm wĕ-ha-mĕdīna (The Arab citizens and the State). *Tĕmūrōt*, Nov. 1966, 10–12.

Herden (Halpern), David. Pĕgīshōt 'im ṣĕ'īrīm 'araviyyīm (Encounters with Arab youths). *Ammōt*, Oct.–Nov. 1964, 29–41.

Hirschberg, H. Z. Be'ayōt ha-sharī'a bi-mĕdīnat Yisra'el (The problems of the *Sharī'a* in the State of Israel). *MḤ*, Jan. 1950, 97–108.

—— Ha-Ōkhlūṣiyya ha-'aravīt bi-mĕdīnat Yisra'el (The Arab population in the State of Israel). *Qama*, iii: 1949–50, 213–22.

Layish, Aharon. Ha-Shīppūṭ ha-'adatī shel ha-dĕrūzīm bĕ-Yisra'el (Community jurisdiction of the Druzes in Israel). *MḤ*, 1961, 258–62.

Ma'oz, Moshe. Ha-Minhal ha-mĕqōmī ba-yishshūvīm ha-'araviyyīm. *MḤ*, 1962, 233–40.

Qāsim, K. Ha-Īnṭelīgenṣiyya ha-'aravīt bi-mĕdīnat Yisra'el (The Arab intelligentsia in the State of Israel). *Ner*, Feb. 1953, 14–15.

Rubinstein, A. 'Aravey Yisra'el: gīsha mĕṣī'ūtīt (The Arabs of Israel: a realistic approach). *Kalkala wĕ-ḥevra*, June 1966, 29–31.

Salmōn, S. Hōra'at ha-'ivrīt wĕ-ha-'aravīt bĕ-veyt ha-sefer ha-'aravī ha-yĕsōdī (The teaching of Hebrew and Arabic in the elementary Arab school). *Mĕgammot*, Jan. 1957, 93–97.

Sarṣūr, Sa'd. Pĕ'ūlōt ha-ḥīnnūkh ha-mashlīm bĕ-qerev ha-yishshūv ha-'aravī ba-Areṣ (The activities of complementary education among the Arab population in Israel). *Ha-Ḥīnnūkh*, Jan. 1967, 53–57.

Shimoni, Y. 'Araviyyey Ereṣ Yisra'el: ga'ōn wa-shever (The Arabs of Palestine: pride and catastrophe). *Mōlad*, June 1949, 150–6.

Simon, E. A. Ha-Mi'ūṭ ha-'aravī bĕ-Yisra'el bi-shĕnat he-'asōr (The Arab minority in Israel in its tenth year). *Ba-Sha'ar*, May 1958, 34–35.

Stendel, Ori. Ha-'Aravīm wĕ-ha-dĕrūzīm bi-mĕdīnat Yisra'el (The Arabs and Druzes in the State of Israel), *in* M. Ziv, ed., *Mĕdīnat Yisra'el w-tĕfūṣōt Yisra'el bĕ-dōrenū*. Haifa, Yūval, 1964, 95–114.

Ṭōmā, E. Ḥīnnūkh yĕladīm ba-kĕfar ha-'aravī (The education of children in the Arab village). *Mĕgammōt*, Apr. 1955, 130–8.

Waschitz, Y. Ma'amad ha-pō'alīm: hitpattĕḥūyōt wĕ-gōrĕmīm (The workers' class: developments and factors). *Ba-Sha'ar*, Apr. 1960, 18–22.

—— Tĕmūrōt bĕ-ḥayyeyhem shel 'Aravey Yisra'el (Changes in the life of the Arabs of Israel). *MḤ*, July 1950, 257–64.

Weigert, G. Sōfĕrīm 'araviyyim bi-mĕdīnat Yisra'el (Arab writers in the State of Israel). *Mōlad*, Nov. 1959, 577–9.

Yinon, Avraham. Nōs'īm ḥevratiyyim bĕ-sifrūt 'araviyyey Yisra'el (Social topics in the literature of the Arabs of Israel). *MḤ*, 1966, 349–73.

Zīper, Y. Ha-'edōt ha-nōsĕriyyōt bi-mĕdīnat Yisra'el (The Christian communities in the State of Israel). *MḤ*, Apr. 1951, 197–208.

Zu'bī, 'Abd al-'Azīz. 'Al be'ayōt ha-mī'ūṭ, ha-'aravī bĕ-Yisra'el (About the problems of the Arab minority in Israel), *in Sefer ha-shana shel ha-'ittōna'īm*, xxii, 1963, 159–61.

—— Ha-Mī'ūṭ ha-'aravī bĕ-Yisra'el (The Arab minority in Israel). *Ba-Sha'ar*, Feb. 1958, 17–19.

C. OTHER LANGUAGES

1. *Books*

Arabs in Israel. Special issue of *NO*, Mar.–Apr. 1962. 112 pp.

The Arabs of Israel. N.p. (Jerusalem?): n.d. (prob. 1955). 30 pp.

Ben-Porat, Yoram. *The Arab labor force in Israel*. Jerusalem, Falk Inst. for Economic Research, 1966. xii, 99 pp.

Bentwich, J. S. *Education in Israel*. London, Routledge, 1965. xiv, 204 pp.

Centro Arabo di informazioni, Rome. *La minoranza araba nella Palestina occupata*. Rome, n.d. 55 pp.

Cohen, Abner. *Arab border-villages in Israel: a study of continuity and change in social organization*. Manchester University Press, 1965. xiv, 194 pp.

Colbi, Saul. *A short history of Christianity in the Holy Land*. Tel-Aviv, Am Hassefer, 1965. 75 pp.

Czudnowski, Moshe M. & Landau, Jacob M. *The Israeli communist party and the elections to the fifth Knesset, 1961*. Stanford, Calif., Hoover Inst. on War, Revolution, & Peace, 1965. vi, 101 pp.

Eisenstadt, S. N. *Israeli society*. London, Weidenfeld, 1967. ix, 451 pp.

Frei, Bruno. *Israel zwischen den Fronten, Utopie und Wirklichkeit*. Vienna, Europa Verlag, 1965. 200 pp.

Golany, Gideon. *Beduin settlement in the Alonim-Shfar'am hill region.* Hebrew & Engl. Jerusalem, Min. of Interior, Dept of Minorities, & Hebrew Univ., Dept of Geography. N.d. (1967). xxiv, 60 pp. Mimeo.

Hadawi, Sami. *Israel and the Arab minority.* NY, Arab Information Center, 1959. iv, 40 pp.

—— *La minorité arabe en Palestine occupée.* Cairo, Le Séminaire international de Palestine, 1965. 76 pp.

—— *Palestine: questions and answers.* NY, Arab Information Center, 1961. x, 86 pp.

Israel, Ministry for Foreign Affairs, Information Dept. *The Arabs in Israel.* 1st ed. Jerusalem, 1958. 87 pp. 2nd ed., Jerusalem, 1961, 51 pp.

Lazaron, Morris S. *Olive trees in storm.* NY, American friends of the Middle East, 1955. viii, 111 pp.

Marx, Emmanuel. *Bedouin of the Negev.* Manchester University Press, 1967. 251 pp.

Nasser, Jamal A. *The resentful Arab, the truth about the Palestine question.* 2nd ed. Amsterdam, Holland NV. Publishers, 1964. 160 pp.

Peretz, Don. *Israel and the Palestine Arabs.* Washington, DC, The Middle East Institute, 1958. xiv, 264 pp.

Sayegh, Fayez A. *Discrimination in education against Arabs in Israel.* Beirut, Palestine Liberation Organization, 1966. 32 pp.

Schwarz, Walter. *The Arabs in Israel.* London, Faber, 1959. 172 pp.

Zarhi, S. & Achiezra, A. *The economic conditions of the Arab minority in Israel.* Givat Haviva, Center for Arab and Afro-Asian Studies, 1966. 24 pp.

2. *Articles*

A.M. Coexistence in Galilee. *NO*, July–Aug. 1964, 39–42.

Abu Hana, Anis Rashid. Arabs at the Hebrew University. *NO*, July–Aug. 1958, 54–56.

Abu Muna, Butrus. Spotlight on Arab students. *NO*, Mar. 1965, 45–48.

Arab intellectuals on Israel. *NO*, Nov.–Dec. 1962, 55–64.

al-Atawna, Musa. What the Bedouin want. *NO*, Sept. 1960, 15–18.

Bayadsi, Mahmud. Land reform and the Israeli Arabs. *NO*, Feb. 1961, 18–22.

Benor, J. L. Arab education in Israel. *Middle Eastern Affairs*, Aug.–Sept. 1950, 224–9.

—— Christian education in Israel. *Christian News from Israel*, June 1958, 39–43.

—— Some problems of Arab education. *NO*, Oct. 1957, 24–27.

Berck, M. G. Can Israel handle its growing Arab minority? *The Reporter* (NY), 12 Dec. 1957, 30–35.

Chelhod, Joseph. L'organisation judiciaire chez les Bédouins du Négueb. *Anthropos*, lx (1965), 625–45.

Efrat, Arie. The Bedouin in the Negev. *NO*, July–Aug. 1960, 37–40.

Eliad, Nissim. Can Arabs identify with Israel? *NO*, Jan. 1967, 21–24.

Falah, Salman A. Druze children go to school. *NO*, Feb. 1966, 36–39.
—— Druze communal organization in Israel. *NO*, Mar.–Apr. 1967, 40–44.
—— The Druze community in Israel. *NO*, June 1962, 30–35, 53.
Flapan, Simha. Les arabes en Israël. *Esprit* (Paris), Sept. 1966, 232–46.
—— National inequality in Israel. *NO*, Nov.–Dec. 1964, 24–36.
—— Planning for the Arab village. *NO*, Oct. 1963, 23–31; Nov.–Dec. 1963, 65–73.
Future of the Arab minority in Israel. *NO*, June 1960, 40–45.
Gavron, Daniel. Education for the Bedouin. *NO*, Sept. 1965, 24–28.
Gellhorn, Martha. The Arabs of Palestine. *Atlantic Monthly*, Oct. 1961, 45–65.
Goitein, S. D. The Arab schools in Israel revisited. *Middle Eastern Affairs*, Oct. 1952, 272–5.
Hertz, Israel. The Bedouin of the Negev. *NO*, June 1960, 28–31.
Hussein, Rashid. The Arab school in Israel. *NO*, Nov.–Dec. 1957, 44–48.
In Israel, racial deiscrimination and spoliation of the Arab minority. *The Scribe, the Arab Review* (Cairo), Dec. 1963, 18–21.
Jews and Arabs in Israel. *NO*, Dec. 1966, 46–79.
Kardosh, Mansour. For a Palestinian Arab state. *NO*, May 1966, 43–44.
Katan, Victoria. A silent revolution. *NO*, Jan. 1960, 47–49.
Landau, Jacob M. Les Arabes israéliens et les élections à la quatrième Knesset. *Intern. R. of Soc. History* (Amsterdam), vii (1962), 1–32.
—— Die arabische Minorität in Israel. In Jacob M. Landau, ed. *Israel.* Nürnberg, Glock & Lutz, 1964, 133–61.
—— Jewish-Christian-Moslem relations in the State of Israel—problems and perspectives. *Perspectives in Jewish Learning* (Chicago), iii (1967), 1-8.
—— A note on the leadership of Israeli Arabs, *Il Politico, Revista di Scienze Politiche* (Pavia), Sept. 1962, 625–32.
Landman, S. Local government for Arab centres in Israel. *Christian News from Israel*, Aug. 1954, 31–32.
Layish, Aharon. Muslim religious jurisdiction in Israel. *Asian & African Studies* (Jerusalem), i (1965), 49–79.
—— The Muslim waqf in Israel. *Asian & African Studies*, ii (1966), 41–76.
Livne, Eliezer. Israeli democracy and the Arabs. *NO*, June 1960, 45–48.
Mansour, Atallah. Arab intellectuals not integrated. *NO*, June 1964, 26–31.
—— Arab land: sale or requisition? *NO*, Mar.–Apr. 1964, 82–84.
—— Arab literature and writers in Israel. *NO*, May 1964, 54–56.
—— Fear of war and faith in peace. *NO*, July–Aug. 1967, 27–30.
—— How the Arabs voted. *NO*, Nov.–Dec. 1965, 22–25.
—— Israel's Arabs go to the polls. *NO*, Jan. 1960, 23–26.
—— Juvenile delinquency among Arab youth. *NO*, July–Aug. 1964, 33–35, 59.
—— Leisure time for young Arabs. *NO*, Apr.–May 1965, 51–54.

Marinoff, I. Christian minorities in Israel. *Contemporary Review* (London), Jan. 1956, 20–24.

Marmorstein, Emile. Rāshid Ḥusain: portrait of an angry young Arab. *Middle Eastern Studies*, Oct. 1964, 3–20.

Militsky, D. Emancipation of Arab women in Israel. *Christian News from Israel*, Sept. 1953, 22–23.

Moreh, S. Arabic literature in Israel. *Middle Eastern Studies*, Apr. 1967, 283–94.

Oded, Yitzhak. Land losses among Israel's Arab villagers. *NO*, Sept. 1964, 10–25.

Ofner, Francis. Resettlement of Arab refugees in Israel. *Christian News from Israel*, Sept. 1953, 22–23.

Party programs on the Middle East and foreign policy, on the Arab minority in Israel. *NO*, Nov.–Dec. 1959, 59–63.

Peretz, Don. The Arab minority of Israel, *Middle East Journal*, Spring 1954, 139–54.

Rejwan, Nissim. Military government—the real issue. *NO*, Jan. 1967, 25–27.

Rosenfeld, Henry. A cultural program for the Arab villages. *NO*, Jan. 1961, 36–49.

—— Social changes in an Arab village. *NO*, Feb. 1959, 37–42; Mar.–Apr. 1959, 14–23.

—— Wage labor and status in an Arab village. *NO*, Jan. 1963, 5–9, 18.

Schiff, Ze'ev. Arab secondary education in Israel. *NO*, May 1960, 32–34.

Shamir, Shimon. Changes in village leadership. *NO*, Mar.–Apr. 1962, 93–112.

Shbat, Ibrahim. Co-existence and not emigration. *NO*, Mar.–Apr. 1966, 47–50.

Solente, Christiane. Attitudes israéliennes à l'égard du probème de la minorité arabe. *L'Afrique et l'Asie* (Paris), lii (1960), 29–43.

Stan, Aviva. 'Landed gentry' in an Arab village. *NO*, Feb. 1964, 54–58.

Tuma, Elias H. The Arabs in Israel: an impasse. *NO*, Mar.–Apr. 1966, 39–46.

Watad, Muhammed. Arab youth in Israel—today and tomorrow. *NO*, June 1964, 22–25.

—— Combatting unemployment in the Arab village. *NO*, May 1967, 52–54.

—— Is it a crime to meet Jews? *NO*, July–Aug. 1964, 36–38, 45.

—— Unemployment haunts the Arab Village. *NO*, Sept. 1966, 29–32.

—— The war of generations in the Arab village. *NO*, Oct. 1964, 29–32, 50.

—— Why was El-Arḍ banned? *NO*, Sept. 1964, 44–48.

Weigert, Gideon. Arab Jewish economic cooperation in Israel. *Welt des Islams* (Leiden), n.s., viii/4 (1963), 243–51.
—— Cooperative movement in Israel—lessons for India. *Indian Co-operative Review* (New Delhi), July–Sept. 1965, 589–605.
—— Kafr Kassem revisited. *Welt des Islams*, n.s., viii/4 (1963), 259–61.
Zu'bi, Abdul Aziz. The Arab minority in Israel. *NO*, July 1957, 14–17.
—— Discontent of Arab youth. *NO*, Jan. 1958, 12–17.
—— Nazareth looks for the future. *NO*, Oct. 1960, 32–34.
—— Talking frankly and facing facts. *NO*, June 1964, 32–33, 52.

End of Select Bibliography
End of Book – The Arabs in Israel

GENERAL INDEX

'Abd Allah (King), 2
'Abd al-Nāṣir, Jamāl, 32, 52, 83, 90–91, 94–95, 103, 106, 123–4, 128, 134, 208, 218, 238, 241, 260, 275
Abū Ghōsh (village), 119, 126, 141, 158, 164, 178
Abu Ghosh, Subhi, xi
Abū Laban, 72
Abū Manna, B., 49 n., 50 n.
Abū Mu'ammar, 'Awda, 139, 140
Abū Ra's, 'Uthmān, 88
Abū Rukn, Labīb, 166, 274
Abū Sinān, 164
Acre, 5, 6, 11, 83, 85, 105–6, 119, 126, 145, 161–2, 167, 185, 203, 210, 262, 264
Adaptation: Bedouins, 25 ff.; effects of mass communication, 31–32; expression of, 35–37, 67–68, 222, 232; *Histadrūt* as agent of, 216–17; intellectuals as carriers, 48–49; politics as a meeting-ground, 71 ff., 76, 130, 157, 210; problems, 28 ff., 76, 130, 157, 210; social factors, 19 ff.
Adhnāb al-ḥukūma, 37
Adviser for Arab Affairs, 106 n., 137, 156–7
Africa, 42
Agitation, *see* Extremism
Agranat, 100
Agriculture, 6, 12, 23–24, 80, 114, 129, 132, 138, 151, 165–6, 169, 214, 223, 270, 275–6
Agriculture and Development (electoral slate), 75, 113, 115, 118, 121, 127
Aḥdūt ha-'avōda: Arab MKs, 191, 243; foundation of an Arab group, 78; image among Arabs, 259, 267, 272; local elections, 166; parliamentary elections, 119, 121, 125, 127–8, 132–3, 135, 146, 152, 241; trade union elections, 181
Aḥmadīs, 4 n., 262, 264
al-Akhbār al-kanā'isiyya, 62
al-'Ālam al-muṣawwar, 62
Alienation: confrontation with Jews, 66 ff., 104, 226–7, 234, 239; expression of, 29 ff., 37–38, 96 ff., 129, 151, 183, 219, 261; intellectuals as carriers, 43, 49, 59; polarization, 210 ff.; political activism, 96 ff., 117, 119, 129, 255–6; sources of, 19 ff., 43, 104, 135 ff. *See also* Extremism; Opposition
Alignment: Arab leadership, 187; Arab MKs, 137 ff., 190–4, 196–7, 199; image among Arabs, 237, 240–1, 243–5, 259, 267–8, 272–4; local elections, 157, 162, 166–7, 170 ff.; local politics, 209, 211, 213, 215; parliamentary elections, 135, 137–44, 146–9, 152, 247–8; trade union elections, 78, 180–3, 213
Alliance of Palestinian Workers, 109, 111, 212–13
Allōn, Yig'al, 91, 137, 267
al-'Amal (newspaper), 78, 125
al-'Amal (party), *see* Israeli Arab Labour Party
American University in Beirut, 200
'Arab al-'Arāmsha, 40 n.
Arab candidates, *see* Lists of Arab candidates
Arab Committee for Israel, 38
Arab Front, *see* Popular Front
Arab-Israeli war (1948), 2, 10, 20–21, 31, 36, 43, 59, 66, 72–73, 108–9, 139, 189, 202–3, 206, 211, 233
Arab-Jewish confrontation: expressions of, 66 ff.; in *Histadrūt*, 183, 249–50; in *kibbūtzīm*, 81; in literature, 66–68; in politics, 66, 73, 85 ff., 94–95, 103, 187, 227 ff., 253 ff.; in voting, 108 ff., 135; social, 221 ff., 227 ff., 231 ff., 253–4; versus co-operation, 220, 276. *See also* Minority-majority relations
Arab-Jewish social contacts, 2, 33, 37–38, 41, 47, 52, 55–56, 58, 136, 187, 223, 276
Arab List—the Centre, 120–1
Arab minority in Israel, *see* Minority *and other headings*
Arab nationalism, *see* Nationalists, Arab
Arab Pioneer Youth, 80–81, 119, 210 n.
Arab politicians, ix, 66, 109, 185
Arab Popular Bloc, 78
Arab Public Committee, 93
Arab refugees: allowed to stay in Israel, 112; flight of, 36; in literature, 66–67; inside Israel, 104, 169, 208; representatives of, 73; return of, 59, 64, 109,

Arab refugees—*contd.*
124, 135, 142; solutions for, 233, 253, 271, 277
Arab Socialist List, 100–1, 136
Arab States, 4, 5, 16, 18, 35, 37–38, 44, 46, 48, 51–53, 55, 60–61, 63, 65, 68, 76, 82–84, 86, 109, 117, 184, 201, 226, 233, 238–9, 252–3, 258–9, 268–9, 271
Arab Students' Committee, 54–57, 92, 225
Arab teachers' seminar, 39
Arabic, x, 40, 57 ff., 67, 110, 114, 196–7, 200, 257, 265–6, 271, 276, 278
Arabic literature in Israel, *see* Literature, Arabic (in Israel)
Arabs in Israel, *see* under various headings
'Arad, 25–26
'Ar'ara, 81, 218, 262
al-Arḍ (group): articles of association, 102–3; centres, 190; electioneering, 100–1, 125–6, 136, 242; failure, 74, 99, 101; foundation, 92 ff., 123, 210; ideology, 106; image among Arabs, 259, 273; influence, 104–5, 107; litigation, 96 ff.; membership, 98–99, 105–6, 186, 217, 274; opposition to, 75; period of activity, 278; publications, 95–98, 103, 228 ff.; tactics, 97 ff., 102–4; ties with sports clubs, 101 ff.
al-Arḍ (weekly), 96, 103, 107, 217
ha-Areṣ, 67, 265
Armenians, 4 n., 8, 262
Armistice Agreements, 32, 73, 112, 213
Army, *see* Military service
'Arrāba, 164
Asaf, Michael, 40 n., 45
'Asāqila, Amīn, 168
Asia, 42
Assimilation, 221
al-Atāsī (President), 275
Autonomy, 7 ff., 10, 13
Avnerī, Ūrī, 64 n., 145
Awakening (electoral slate), 174
'Awda, Sulaymān, 105
'Awja al-Ḥafīr, 26
'Ayn Māhil, 159, 164, 262
'Azāzma Bedouins, 139

Balfour Declaration, 1
Baptists, 262
Bāqa al-Gharbiyya, 43, 129, 164–5, 195, 217–18
Bar-Ilan University, 49
Barānsī, Ṣāliḥ, 100–5, 217, 274
Barānsī, 'Uthmān, 63
Barqat, R., 137, 228
Barṭa'a, 30, 87
Bastūnī, Rustum, vi, 38, 80, 119, 197, 221, 274
Baṭhīsh, Nadīm, 213
BBC, 204, 266
Bedouin courts, 189
Bedouins: camps, 6, 26, 39, 143, 153, 175; centres, 194; leadership, 189; political demands, 130, 185; sedentarization, 7, 123, 138; services, 7, 26–27, 39, 40, 138; social change, 25 ff.; voting, 115–16, 121, 127, 133, 139–40, 146–7, 153, 179
Be'er Sheba, 5, 25–26, 80, 223
Begīn, M., 273
Beirut, 57, 200
Belgrade, 35
Ben-Aharōn, Y., 191
Ben-Gurion, David, 87, 135, 139, 241, 267
Ben-Tzur, A., 210
Berger, Morroe, 261
Beyt-Hillel students' club, 56
Beyt Jān, 22, 164
Bible, 143
Bilād, 55
Bi'na, 93
Bi-national State, 2, 119, 233
bi-Ṣarāḥa, 131
Binya, Joseph, xi
Birth-rate, 4, 16
Bishāra, Ḥasan, 218
British Emergency Regulations, 3, 97, 226, 229
British Mandate in Palestine, ix, 1, 4, 5, 8, 9, 20–21, 71, 232–3
British rule, 7, 36, 39, 44, 61, 65, 69, 72–73, 81, 156, 167, 170, 185, 188–9, 200–1, 203, 206, 214, 278
Brotherhood (electoral slate), 174
Brotherhood Club, 211
Buber, Martin, 38, 117
Buqay'a, 164, 178
Būrgība, Ḥabīb, 260, 275

Cairo, 106, 148, 203, 242, 266–7
Carmel (mountain), 12, 14
Carmiel, 6
Censuses, 4 n., 7, 9, 44, 206, 212 n., 261
Central Elections Commission, 100–1, 136, 242
China, 61, 275
Christian courts, 10, 17

Christians: centres, 16–18; churches, 212; education, 39 n.; emigration, 4, 206; judicial autonomy, 8–9, 17; leadership, 24, 202–5, 208; MKs, 75 n., 193; political attitudes, 8–9, 16, 60, 73, 75, 80, 262–4; priests, 45; publications, 62, 65, 67; relations with religious parties, 143; rivalry with other communities, 162, 167 ff., 190; statistics, 7–8, 16; support for Communists, 83, 91, 123, 148, 208–9
Cinema, 20 n., 55, 136 n.
Circassians, 4 n., 13
Citizenship Law, 116
City College in Haifa, 49
Cohen, Abner, 8 n., 46 n.
Cohen, Aharon, 2 n.
Cohen, Eli, 34
Cohen, J. J., 56
Communists: activity, 81 ff., 204; Arab MKs, 190, 194–6, 198, 200–1, 226; break-up, 87; image among Arabs, 79, 84, 87 ff., 268; influence, 20, 44, 69; leadership, 190, 194 ff.; local elections, 167 ff., 176–7; local politics, 208 ff., 215; membership, 72, 78, 82–88; parliamentary elections, 135, 141–2, 146–8, 154, 238, 241; premises, 43; propaganda, 22, 82, 91–92, 226–7; publications, 38, 61 ff., 86, 89–90; students, 56, 92; tactics 11, 90 ff.; trade union elections, 182–3; versus Zionism, 71, 79; voting, 70. *See also* Front organizations; MAQĪ; RAQAḤ
Companies' Law, 97
Compulsory Education Law, 39, 42
Co-operation and Brotherhood (electoral slate), 128, 133, 138, 147, 174, 259, 273
Co-operation and Reward (electoral slate), 174
Co-operatives, 81. *See also* Economic co-operation
Congress of Arab Workers, 200, 212
Copts, 4 n., 8, 209 n.
Court of Appeal (Druze), 14. *See also* Druze courts
Courts, 8, 11, 27, 229. *See also* Bedouin courts; Christian courts; District courts; Druze courts; Rabbinical courts; Sharī'a courts; Supreme Court
Cultural Identification, 2, 29, 36, 40, 47 ff., 67, 221, 223
Cyprus, 266–7
Dabbūriyya, 164
Dāliyat al-Karmil, 126, 164, 166, 178, 182
Damascus, 34, 203, 266
al-Darb, 63
Dā'ūd, Sam'ān, 177 n.
Davar, 38, 265
Dayyan, Moshe, 139, 140, 267
Defence, Ministry of, 50, 74 n., 99, 101
Democratic List of the Arabs of Israel, 75, 113, 115, 117, 121, 199
Democratic List of Nazareth, 110–11
Democratic Party, 73
Democratic Teachers' Association, 92
Demography, 3 ff., 7 ff., 12, 16, 185, 206–7, 212–13, 269. *See also* Population
Development: agricultural, 52, 138, 195, 276; economic, 35, 37, 68, 158, 195, 215, 275; educational, 42, 68, 112, 123, 132, 214, 223, 275; health services, 214; in Arab towns, 69, 207; in Arab villages, 20, 23, 51, 76, 91, 112–13, 123, 135, 138, 142, 168, 214–15; in Druze villages, 15, 237–8; industrial, 132, 195; social, 275–6
Development (electoral slate), 174
Dī-Nūr, Nīna, 37, 38 n., 135 n.
Dibbini, Sami, xi
Dimona, 26
District courts, 100
Dīvōn, S., 106 n.
Dīwān, 195
Druze courts, 13 ff. *See also* Court of Appeal (Druze)
Druze Religious Council, 14
Druzes: centres, 12, 16, 76, 83; judicial autonomy, 14; local elections, 161–2, 166–8; local politics, 14, 17, 46, 47, 161 ff., 202; military service, 30, 53, 184; MKs, 75, 118, 124, 193; modernization, 15, 24; parliamentary elections, 113–4, 126, 131–2, 138–40, 143–4, 148–9, 237, 243; political attitudes, 63, 83, 91, 148, 217, 262, 264, 274; recognition as a community, 9, 13–14; rivalry with other communities, 13; statistics, 7, 12; trade union elections, 181–2, 249
Dunam, 166 & n.

Eban, A., *see* Even
Ecologic groups, 6, 7, 10, 16, 29

Economic co-operation (Arab-Jewish), 43, 48, 78, 114, 116, 206–7
Economic power, 8, 9, 17, 21, 24, 26–27, 48
Economic recession, 20 n., 50, 91, 173, 207, 264
The Economist, 265
Education: activities, 80; Bedouin, 7, 26–27; changes in, 221 ff.; Christian, 16; congregational, 83, 208; Government interference, 90; high schools, 139; *Histadrūt* contribution to, 179–80, 249–50; increase in, 70, 112, 117, 123, 138, 214, 238–9; Jordanian, 30; literacy, 41–42; Ministry of, 92; problems, 39 ff.; sports clubs, 216 ff.; standards of, 23, 37, 44, 102, 104; students, 49 ff., 57–58, 136, 168, 225
Education and Culture, Ministry of, 39, 41–42, 92
Egypt, 2, 32, 57, 83, 86, 90, 123–4, 126, 184, 203, 217, 232, 266–7. *See also* United Arab Republic
Eilat, 15
Election results, *see* Statistics
Elections, *see* Local elections; Parliamentary elections; Trade union elections
Elī'ad, Nissīm, 145
Elites, *see* Leadership
Emigration, Arab, 4, 33, 68, 74 n., 205–6, 269
English (language), 40, 266
Equality (electoral slate), 174
Eshkōl, Levī, 137–8, 226, 267
Etgar, 102
Even, Abbā, 138, 267
Export Bank (Tel-Aviv), xi
Extremism: incitement, 56; intellectual, 43 ff., 54 ff., 187; literary, 51, 57 ff., 64, 67–68, 73, 254; nationalist, 39, 51 ff., 123, 187; political, 61, 64, 74, 100 ff., 180, 200–1, 217, 219–20, 241, 243; propaganda, 210–11, 215, 228–32, 239, 254; rejection of Israel, 37; voting, 144, 151, 245. *See also* Alienation
Eytan, Ya'aqōv, 79

Fāhūm, Yaḥyà, 68
al-Fajr, 63
Faraḥ, Najwa Qa'wār, 66
Fassūṭa, 105, 164
al-Fatḥ, 54, 102
Fayṣal (King of Saudi Arabia), 260, 275
Finance, Ministry of, 267
Flapan, Simḥa, 79
Foci of political activity, 205–19
Foreign Affairs, Ministry of, 50, 267
France, 29, 43, 48
Frank Sinatra *Histadrūt* club, 211
French (language), 266
Front organizations, communist, 92 ff., 131, 169, 201
Furaydīs, 159, 164, 177

GAḤAL, 135, 144, 147, 149, 167, 178, 181, 243, 245, 259, 268, 273, 278
Galilee, 3, 5, 6, 7, 12, 14, 27, 49, 76, 79, 80, 87, 105–6, 113, 117, 138, 140–1, 143, 145, 149, 150, 159, 170, 180–1, 185–6, 193–4, 199, 203, 206–7, 211, 218, 246, 262 n., 264, 267
Gaza Strip, 2–4, 34 n., 98, 129, 189
General Federation of Labour, *see* *Histadrūt*
General Muslim Congress, 83
General Zionists (party), 73, 78, 110, 114–16, 119–22, 125, 127, 129, 132, 135, 155
Germany, 268
al-Ghad, 63, 142
Giv'at Ḥavīva, 38, 81
Government Workers Union, 142
Great Britain, 29, 43
Greek Catholics: characteristics, 16, 202, 208; leadership, 114, 118, 138, 172, 202 ff., 208, 274; local politics, 167–9, 171–2, 208; political activity, 144; political attitudes, 17, 75 n., 105; publications, 62, 253 n.; statistics, 8, 16, 262; voting, 161–2
Greek Orthodox: characteristics, 16, 202, 208; leadership, 202, 208; local politics, 167–9, 171, 208; political activity, 126, 200; political attitudes, 17, 83, 95, 105; statistics, 8, 262; voting, 148, 161
Greeks, 16, 202, 208
Grievances, *see* Alienation

al-Hadaf, 63
Hādhā'l-'ālam, 63, 67, 265
Haifa, 5, 16, 36 n., 38–39, 41, 49, 73–74, 77–78, 88, 94, 98, 100, 105–6, 111, 131, 145, 157, 168, 180, 186, 193–4, 200, 207, 262, 264
al-Hawārī, Nimr, 73, 132, 134, 171
Health services, 4, 7, 138, 179–80, 182, 189, 195, 212, 214, 217, 250, 269–70

Hebrew, x, 40–41, 53, 57, 59, 63, 105, 145, 196–7, 200, 240, 257, 265, 276, 278. *See also* Literature, Hebrew
Hebrew University, Jerusalem, xi, 7 n., 26, 49, 53, 55–56, 105, 225, 261
Herald Tribune, 265
High Court of Justice, 3, 96–99, 229
Histadrūt: attitude to Arabs, 228–9; Arab membership, 134, 142, 178 ff., 212–13; clubs, 211, 216, 250; contacts with Arabs, 24, 38, 47, 137, 186; Druze membership, 178, 181–2; elections, 78, 156, 178 ff., 186, 204; image among Arabs, 257, 264–5, 269, 272, 275, 278; planning for the Arabs, 234, 238; publications, 58, 60, 63, 65–66; resolutions, 249–50; services for the Arabs, 183, 212, 214, 216, 238, 249–50; training the Arabs, 26, 216, 249–50
Honesty and Work (electoral slate), 174
Hope (electoral slate), 174
Huzayl tribe, 27

Ḥabībī, Emīl, 83, 85, 88, 94, 114, 141, 190, 200–1, 241–3, 274
al-Ḥāfiẓ, Amīn, 260, 275
al-Ḥā'ik (family), 144, 172
al-Ḥakīm, George (Archbishop), 16, 62, 73, 114, 120, 137, 167, 202–5, 208, 253 n., 274
al-Ḥalabī (family), 167
al-Ḥalabī, Quftān, 149
Ḥamdān, Fāris, 43, 76 n., 195, 274
Ḥāmid, Ṭāhir, 11
Ḥamūla: characteristics, 8 ff., 188, 278; impact on local politics, 23; leadership, 109, 115, 186, 188, 199; local politics, 80, 92, 159 ff., 165 ff., 174 ff.; loyalties, 70–71, 153, 188, 207 ff.; modernization, 23, 69, 207–10; political alliances of, 14, 77–78, 109, 111, 124, 140, 142, 162 ff., 174 ff., 182, 192, 199; power, 22–24, 69, 111, 115, 140, 146, 160, 207 ff., 214 ff., 270; rivalries, 21 ff., 57, 75, 153, 156, 159 ff., 164, 207 ff., 216, 272; statistics, 139; structure, 14, 15, 24; voting, 70
Ḥaqqāq, Fu'ād, 140 n.
Ḥerūt (party), 110, 115, 121, 126–7, 129, 133, 135, 144, 167, 178, 268, 278
Ḥerūt-Liberals Block, *see* GAḤAL
al-Ḥilū, Charles (President), 275
Ḥurfaysh, 164
al-Ḥurriyya (newspaper), 144
Ḥusayn (King), 226, 260, 274–5
Ḥusayn, Rāshid, 35, 274
al-Ḥusaynī, Amīn, 11, 232
Ḥusaynīs (family), 71
Ḥūshī, Abbā, 40, 77, 131

I'blīn, 164
Ideologies: Arab, 72 ff., 170, 187, 222, 231 ff.; communist, 71, 85 ff., 226–7; nationalist Arab, 106–7, 170, 190, 219, 228 ff.; opportunist, 205; parties, 109 ff., 123, 134, 151, 154, 162, 174, 177; religious, 190; Zionist, 71
Iksāl, 164
Immigration, Jewish, 1, 4, 40, 57, 108
Independent Liberal Party, 135, 144, 147, 149, 172 n., 181, 259, 268, 273
Independent List of the Arabs in Israel, 128
Indifference to politics, ix
Inner organization, 8
Institute for Arab and Afro-Asian Studies, 81
Institutionalism, 8 ff., 69, 210
Intellectuals in politics: aims, 70; components, 45–46; crisis, 48 ff.; extremism, 35, 200; impact on Arabs, 46 ff.; influence, 46; involvement in politics, 92, 95, 105–6, 116, 125, 138, 158, 177, 190; literary contribution, 58–59, 81, 128; non-identification with Israel, 29; partisans of change, 22, 158, 188; political attitudes, 43 ff., 130, 177, 195; search for identity, 35–36; statistics, 44–46. *See also* Students
Interior, Ministry of, 23 n., 143, 158–61, 164–6, 169, 173, 177, 189, 247
Iran, 4 n.
Iraq, 2, 40, 57, 60 n., 94, 266
'Irāqī, Ḥusnī, 217–18, 255 n.
'Īsà, Muḥammad 'Abd al-Raḥmān, 105
'Isfiyya, 78, 164, 166, 182, 262
Islam, 7–11, 83, 214
Israel, *see* under various headings
Israel-USSR Friendship Association, 201, 254
Israeli Arab awareness, 231 ff., 239
Israeli Arab Bank, 43
Israeli Arab Bloc, 74
Israeli Arab Labour Party, 78, 125, 128, 278
Israeli Arab Party, 74

Israeli Committee for Peace, 201
Israeli Labour Party, 135, 278
Israeli Teachers' Federation, 209
Italy, 267
al-Ittiḥād, 35, 61, 63–64, 86–87, 89, 90, 94, 100, 136, 141, 148, 176, 195, 201, 217, 265

Jabbāra, Salīm Khalīl, 191
Jabbārīn, Muḥammad Ḥasan, 85–86
Jabbūr, Jabbūr Yūsuf, 93, 131, 162, 274
al-Jadīd, 63, 100, 142, 265
Jaffa, *see* Tel-Aviv-Jaffa
Jaljūliyya, 164, 177, 217
Jarjūra, Amīn Salīm, 198, 251 n.
Jarjūra, Mun'im, 88
Jatt, 22, 164, 216
Jerusalem, xi, 5, 28, 30, 55–56, 59, 97, 112, 119, 142, 157–8, 186, 200, 262
Jerusalem Post, 265–6
Jewish settlements, 22
Jewish-Arab Convention for Peace and Equality, 200
Jiryis, Ṣabrī, 95, 99, 101, 105–6, 274
Jish, 164
Jisr al-Zarqā', 164
Jordan, Kingdom, 2–4, 16–18, 25, 30, 32, 51, 84, 86, 165, 184, 189, 213–15, 266, 275
Jordan river, 2, 84
Jubrān, Salīm, 28, 78
Judicial system, 8–10, 13–15, 17, 51, 66, 68. *See also* Courts
Juhayna, *see* Ḥabībī, Emīl
Jūlis, 14, 126, 140
Justice, Ministry of, 97, 228

Kabābīr, 262
Kafr Bara, 164
Kafr Kamā, 164
Kafr Kannā, 22, 57
Kafr Mandā, 159–60, 164
Kafr Qara', 164, 217–18
Kafr Qāsim, 87, 122, 124, 164, 177–8, 213
Kafr Yāṣīf, 30 n., 34, 46, 81, 87, 93, 158, 164, 201 n.
Kanafānī, Ghassān, 57
Kanā'ne, Maḥmūd 'Abd al-Qādir, 68
Khalīl, Ibrāhīm, 218
Khamīs, Ṣalībā, 88
Khamīs, Yūsuf, 42, 80, 119–20, 191, 197, 274
al-Khaṭīb, Muḥammad, 85
al-Khaṭīb, Murshid, 30 n., 34
Khayr, 'Abd Allāh, 73
Khneyfeṣ, Ṣāliḥ, 124, 126, 131–2, 139, 246
Khūrī, Dā'ūd, 73
Khūrī, Fu'ād Jābir, 171, 176, 210, 226
Kibbūtz, 38, 67, 79, 80, 116, 120, 132, 165, 167, 173, 182, 207, 209 n., 242, 272, 278
Kināna, As'ad Yūsuf, 169, 170 n.
Kneset: Arab demands in, 89, 196 ff.; groups in, 77, 88, 157, 186, 190 ff.; legislation, 11, 14; speeches in, 198, 226–7, 251–2. *See also* MKs, Arab; Parliamentary elections
Kteylī, Mūsà, 174
Kūsā, Eliyās N., 73–74, 93

Labour, Ministry of, 91, 267
Land Appropriation Law, 117–18, 120
Land problems, 31, 51, 55, 57, 84, 89, 90, 96, 98, 102, 104, 117, 123, 129–30, 135, 138, 150, 204, 214, 223, 270–1
Land registration, 27
Language problems, 2, 33, 40, 41, 53. *See also* Arabic; Hebrew
Latins, 8, 17, 161, 168–9, 208, 262
Lavōn Affair, 130
Law for the Concentration of Land, 129, 134
Leadership, *see* Local leadership; Political leadership; Religious leadership; Tribal leadership
League for National Liberation, 201
League of Arab States, 71, 101
League of Nazareth Workers, 212
Lebanon, 2, 4, 12, 14, 30 n., 32, 86, 123, 150, 184, 203, 266–7, 275
Lerner, Daniel, 261
Liberal Party, 132–3, 135, 144, 178, 278
Life (electoral slate), 174
Līn, Amnōn, vi, 74–75, 201 n., 226, 237
List of Peace, 139–40, 147, 149, 163, 178, 182, 259, 273
List of the Workers of Israel, *see* RAFĪ
List of Arab candidates: allied with *Aḥdūt ha-'avōda*, 78; —with the Alignment, 137 ff., 146 ff., 190, 193, 196, 209, 243 ff., 259, 268, 273; —with the General Zionists, 78, 119; —with MAPAI, 75 ff., 109 ff., 113–15, 117–18, 120 ff., 130 ff., 152 ff., 163 ff., 190, 193, 195 ff., 237, 240; —with MAPAM, 78, 177; —with the National Religious Party, 163, 177; —with RAFĪ, 139–40,

147, 163, 178; Independent, 72, 74, 100–1, 186
Literacy, 41
Literature, Arabic (In Israel), x, 3 n., 35, 40, 51, 56, 57 ff., 81, 89, 97, 105, 112, 128, 151–2, 200, 207, 217, 250, 275, 280–1
Literature, Hebrew, 3 n., 58, 67, 281–3
Little Triangle, 3, 5, 10, 26–27, 30, 43, 70, 76, 79, 80, 87–88, 101, 106, 112–15, 119, 122–3, 125, 138, 140, 145, 149–50, 158, 162–3, 165, 180, 185–6, 193–4, 206, 213–19, 243, 246, 264
Local Councils, 15, 23, 45, 91, 93, 131, 139, 156 ff., 188–90, 195, 210, 216, 218, 249, 270
Local elections: case studies, 165 ff.; Druze participation, 15, 91; introduction into Arab localities, 157 ff.; party participation, 174 ff., 199–200; religious factor in, 208, 213; sign of growing interest in politics, 112, 115; sign of modernization, 70; statistics, 164, 189, 213; versus parliamentary elections, 24, 144 n., 157, 162, 164, 170–2, 175–7; weaken *ḥamūla* influence, 23–24
Local government, 156 ff., 188
Local leadership: alliances with Jewish parties, 77–78, 138, 150, 154, 186 ff., 197; characteristics, 20 ff., 185 ff., 205 ff., 277; image among Arabs, 271; rivalry, 165 ff., 216 ff.; versus intellectuals, 47, 50, 70, 92; versus modernization, 70, 158 ff.; versus workers, 69; versus the young, 150, 188
Local politics, 14, 20 ff., 25, 46, 49, 71, 124, 157 ff., 190, 199, 200, 204, 218–19, 277
Location of Arabs, 5 ff., 72, 257, 262, 264
Loyalties, 69 ff., 91–92, 113, 150, 190–1, 197, 208–9, 221 ff., 231 ff., 239
Loyalty to Israel, x, 9, 30, 33, 35–38, 53, 75, 92, 221 ff., 231 ff., 261. *See also* Subversiveness
Lybia, 86
Lydda, 5, 93

Ma'arīv, 265
Mahr, 24, 271
Ma'īlyā, 81, 164, 195, 262
Majd al-Kurūm, 164
Majdal, 169
Makarios (President), 98
Makr, 105
Ma'lūl, 169
Mandelbaum gate, 30
Mansour, A., 43 n., 44–46, 67, 96 n.
Manṣūr, Kamāl, 78, 274
Manṣūr, Ṣuwayliḥ 'Abd al-Hādī, 139, 182, 243, 246
MAPAI: attitude to Arabs, 38, 74 ff., 80 ff., 229, 237 ff.; elections, 75 ff., 109 ff., 162 ff., 181 ff., 186, 213, 237 ff.; image among Arabs, 259, 267, 272–3; leadership, 190 ff., 199, 204; propaganda, 215; publications, 60, 63, 65; tactics, 89, 237 ff.
MAPAM: Arab membership, 72, 78, 185; attitude to Arabs, 42, 61; elections, 78 ff., 109 ff., 157, 162 ff., 176 ff., 180 ff., 213, 242 ff., 247; image among Arabs, 259, 267–8, 272; leadership, 187 ff., 190 ff., 199–200; propaganda, 215; publications, 60, 63–65; tactics, 89, 210
MAQĪ: Arab membership, 72, 185; attitude to Arabs, 81 ff., 86 ff.; 'cultural homes', 89; elections, 109 ff., 161 ff., 176 ff., 213, 239; image among Arabs, 259, 268, 273; leadership, 94, 186, 190 ff., 200–1; propaganda, 215, 217 n.; publications, 62, 89–90; rivalries, 93 ff.; split, 85 ff.; tactics, 83 ff., 87–88, 100, 106–7, 208–13, 239
Maronites, 8, 17, 105, 150, 208
Mashhad, 164
Mass communication, 31–32, 34, 70, 111, 232, 265, 272. *See also* Press; Radio; Television
Maṣārwe, Aḥmad, 145
Maṣārwe, Muḥammad, 54
Mazzāwī (family), 144, 172
Mecca, 17
Member of the *Kneset*, *see* MK
Menashe Mountains, 30
Message of the Club, 218, 255
Military administration: Arab attitudes to, 33, 51, 55, 57, 76, 98, 104, 118, 130, 135–6, 138, 195, 197, 270 ff.; Communist opposition to, 61, 84, 89, 90, 109, 114, 124, 132, 226–7; in Arab literature, 66; Jewish attitudes to, 33, 122–3, 139, 144 n., 244; legal basis of, 2–3; MAPAM's opposition to, 61, 119, 125, 132; policies, 6, 32, 94, 102, 129, 148, 189, 210, 218, 220
Military service, 13, 15, 29–30, 53, 114, 148, 166–8, 184, 271

Millet, 8, 278
Minority-majority relations, ix, 2, 13, 28, 32 ff., 36 ff., 42 ff., 48 ff., 52, 55, 62, 70, 72, 77, 79, 82, 84–86, 88, 96, 102–4, 117, 122, 135, 140, 145, 158, 185, 187, 190, 201, 203, 220, 221–4, 229 ff., 238, 251, 253–6, 260, 269–70. *See also* Arab-Jewish social contacts
Mīqūnīs, Shmū'el, 85, 114, 140
al-Mirṣād, 60–61, 64, 81, 132, 143, 176, 195, 200, 265–6
Mish'al, Badrān Jamīl, 51
Mixed towns, 2, 5, 6, 33, 46, 48, 112, 119, 136, 146, 158, 161, 185, 190. *See also* Towns
MKs, Arab: activities, 56, 194 ff.; allied to MAPAI (Alignment), 74, 76–77, 117–18, 124, 126, 137–8, 143, 154, 166–7, 174, 190 ff., 199, 244, 251; characteristics, 191 ff.; Communists, 83, 89, 94, 111, 190 ff., 200–1; MAPAM's, 42, 79–81, 174, 190 ff., 199–200
MKs, Jewish, 56, 77, 89, 137, 144, 192, 194, 267
Mobility, 6, 7, 13–14, 19, 20, 22, 26, 91, 129, 136, 168–9, 207, 214, 224, 275
Modernization, 15, 19 ff., 25, 69 ff., 139, 199, 214, 220–4, 270–1, 276
Morocco, 86
Moscow, 94, 123–4, 266, 268
Mu'addī (*ḥamūla*), 14
Mu'addī, Jabr, 75 n., 118, 138, 193, 197, 246, 274
Mu'ammar, Eliyās, 105
Mu'ammar, Tawfīq, 66–68
Muftī, 11, 278
Mughār, 91, 164, 167
Mukhtār, 21, 23, 30, 67, 126, 150, 158, 188, 247, 278
Mullah (*ḥamūla*), 14
Municipal councils, *see* Local councils
Muqaybala, 31
Muslim Brethren, 12
Muslim Fraternity (electoral slate), 174
Muslims: centres, 10, 264; education, 39 n., 40, 42; emigration, 43; intellectuals, 46, 60; judicial autonomy, 8–10, 279; leadership, 11, 75, 80, 105, 118, 138, 200, 202; MKs, 193; mosques, 12; organization, 9; political participation, 146, 163, 165 ff., 171, 200; religiousness, 213; rivalry with other communities, 16–17, 206; sages, 45; statistics, 4, 7–8; support for Communists, 83, 91, 208–9
al-Muṣawwar, 62, 265
Muthaqqafīn, 43, 278

Nablus, 59
Naḥf, 34 n.
Nakhla, Eliyās, 138, 167, 195, 197, 274
Naqqāra, Ḥannā, 88
Nashāshībī (family), 71
Nāshif, Maḥmūd, 128
National Religious Party: attitude to Arabs, 177; image among Arabs, 259, 267–8, 273; local elections, 162–3, 166–7, 171–2, 174, 177; parliamentary elections, 129, 131–5, 139, 143–4, 177, 243, 247; trade union elections, 181–2
Nationalists, Arab: factor in elections, 118, 123, 129, 134, 136–7, 145–6, 149 ff., 172, 182; Israeli, 29, 32, 37, 40, 70, 77, 187, 190, 222; literary expression, 58–59, 61 ff., 67; Middle Eastern, 11, 32, 238; Palestinian, 1; parties, 75, 92 ff., 101 ff., 210, 219, 241–2, 273; propaganda, 211, 228–30, 238; students, 51 ff., 136; versus communism, 81 ff., 90 ff., 205, 215, 241–2, 273; versus Islam, 11–12; versus religious sentiment, 207–8; versus Zionism, 48, 79, 268
Nazareth, 5, 6, 11–12, 16, 26–27, 29, 44, 45 n., 46, 59, 67, 73–74, 76, 78, 80–81, 83, 87–88, 93, 105, 113–14, 117, 119, 120, 126, 131, 137–8, 140–2, 144–6, 154, 157–8, 161, 164, 168–76, 179–80, 182, 186, 190, 193–4, 199, 200, 204, 206–15, 226, 231, 249, 262, 264
Nazism, 233
Negev, 5–7, 10, 25–28, 79, 115, 123, 139–40, 143, 150, 180, 185, 194, 269
Ner, 117
New Communist List, *see* RAQAḤ
New Outlook, 104–5, 200
New York, xi
Newsweek, 265
Non-aligned States, 35
North Africa, 28

Occupations, 19, 20, 26, 42–46, 55, 80, 92, 105, 113, 132, 192, 194, 206, 257, 263–4
Oggi, 204
ha-'Ōlam ha-zeh, 63, 64 n., 265
Opposition, 23, 42–43, 45, 49–51, 56, 63–64, 66 ff., 86, 118–19, 122, 124,

148, 190, 196, 217, 233, 269, 273. *See also* Extremism
Ottoman rule, 7, 8, 10, 12, 13, 44, 156, 188, 278

Palestine Liberation Organization, 98 n., 275
Palestinian Arabs, ix, x, 1–3, 20, 25, 55, 59, 71–72, 81–82, 88, 102–3, 205, 229, 233, 275
Palmōn, Y., 156
Parliamentary elections: Bedouin participation, 27; Egyptian propaganda, 32; party participation, 72 ff., 86–88, 107–55, 186, 208, 213, 237 ff.; party propaganda, 60, 63, 94, 100; versus local elections, 24, 144 n., 157, 162, 164, 170–2, 175–7; versus trade union elections, 179, 182–3; weaken *ḥamūla* influence, 70
Participation in politics, ix, 20, 23, 32, 50 ff., 55 ff., 62, 64–65, 69 ff., 92 ff., 100, 106, 108 ff., 120 ff., 149 ff., 154, 164, 183, 201, 212, 215–16, 220
Parties of Oriental Jews, 110, 112, 115–16
Party Clubs, 93, 211, 215–16
Patriarch, 18, 62 n., 203. *See also* Greek Orthodox
Peace, Ministry for, 145
Peace and Prosperity (electoral slate), 174
People's Party, 73
Peres, Shim'ōn, 4 n., 139
Personal groups, 76 ff. *See also* Lists of Arab candidates
Petaḥ-Tiqva, 87
Police, 24, 55, 57, 93, 105, 174, 200; Ministry of, 28 n., 267
Political alertness, 1, 17, 42, 50 ff., 55, 64, 70, 83, 97, 109, 112, 118, 120, 130, 136, 152, 170, 185, 187, 194, 215, 232, 239, 257, 264, 272, 276
Political groups, 20 ff., 36, 56, 64, 69 ff., 76 ff., 92 ff., 111, 122, 149, 156 ff., 186, 229
Political integration, 28, 35 ff., 47, 66, 68, 71, 76, 123, 138, 140, 144, 151, 220 ff., 232, 235, 271–2, 276
Political leadership: Arab MKs, 190 ff.; Arabs outside Israel, 260, 269, 274–5; characteristics, 10–11, 184 ff., 205 ff., 222, 232–3, 277; Communist, 83, 90, 92, 131, 196, 200–1; nationalist, 83, 90, 92 ff., 103, 219; political alertness, 72; political responsibility, 66; religious leaders, 201 ff.; versus *ḥamūla* rule, 21 ff., 70–71, 208; versus modernization, 70
Political parties, 20–21, 27, 47, 60, 64–65, 71 ff., 75 ff., 80 ff., 97, 104, 108 ff., 117 ff., 120 ff., 130 ff., 150 ff., 156, 190, 194, 209, 215, 217, 240 ff., 249, 251, 253, 258, 261, 267, 272, 274, 276–7. *See also* Political groups *and under names of parties*
Political polarization, 210–12, 228 ff.
Political power, 20 ff., 48, 69, 70, 103, 157, 175, 215–16, 240 ff.
Polytechnic Institute in Haifa, 49
Pope, 17, 143. *See also* Vatican
Popular Arab Bloc, 110
Popular Arab Front, *see* Popular Front
Popular Front, 74, 93–96, 104, 106, 123, 204, 210
Population ratio, 4 ff., 7 ff., 12, 75, 110 n., 112, 149, 158, 185, 264
Port Said, 94
Posts, Ministry of, 267
Press: Arab, 38, 51, 59 ff., 253–4, 257, 265; Jewish, 38, 265–6; party, 38, 112, 130–2, 136, 140–1, 144–5; political expression, 73–74, 130, 203, 217–9, 228–9, 253–4
Progress and Development (electoral slate), 75, 128, 133, 138, 147, 259, 273
Progress and Work (electoral slate), 113, 115, 118, 121, 128, 133
Progressive Party, 115, 119, 121, 125, 127, 129, 132, 135
Proletariat, 69, 209, 214
Protestants, 8, 201, 262
Public opinion, 33, 38, 112–13, 123, 156, 218, 232, 236–7, 240, 276

Qāḍī, 10, 11, 45, 83, 117, 149, 202, 278
Qāḍīs Law, 11, 83
Qahwajī, Ḥabīb Nawfal, 96, 99, 105, 274
Qalansawa, 141, 164, 217–18
Qardōsh, Manṣūr, 95–96, 99, 102, 105–6
Qāsim, 'Abd al-Karīm, 94–95, 123–4, 126, 128, 208
al-Qāsim, Salīm, 88, 226
Qāsim, Samīḥ, 63, 67, 217
Qasīs, Mas'ad, 75 n., 118, 124, 126, 195
Qa'wār, Jamāl, 65 n.
Qōl ha-'am, 86
Qur'ān, 143

Rabbinical courts, 10
al-Rābiṭa, vi, 62, 203, 253

Radio and broadcasting, 31–32, 45, 53, 60, 70, 106, 122, 126, 140 n., 148, 151, 172, 204, 207–8, 210, 238–9, 242, 257–8, 265–7, 272, 276
RAFĪ party, 4 n., 135, 137, 139, 146–7, 149, 152, 163, 167, 171, 174, 178, 181–2, 240–3, 245–7, 259, 268, 273, 278
al-Rā'id, 62
Rāma, 22, 138, 161, 164, 167–8, 195, 262
Ramle, 5, 16, 93, 141
RAQAḤ, 61, 86 ff., 135–7, 139–43, 146–9, 151–4, 162, 165–6, 170–4, 176–7, 179 n., 180–4, 185–6, 190–5, 199–201, 205, 208–13, 215–17 n., 225 n., 242, 244, 247, 259, 268, 278
Realpolitik, 1
Reform (electoral slate), 174
Reform and Light (electoral slate), 174
Refugee List, 169
Rejwan, Nissim, 60 n.
Religions, Ministry of, 13, 143, 247
Religious belief, 8, 11, 16, 24, 45, 83, 150, 207, 213–14
Religious communities, 7 ff., 13 ff., 16 ff., 24, 60, 64, 69, 70, 76, 83, 91, 94, 112, 148, 150, 161–3, 167–72, 187, 190, 193, 201 ff., 207–10, 262, 264, 274. *See also by community and denomination*
Religious leadership, 11, 13–15, 190, 201 ff., 208, 210
Religious parties (Jewish), 110, 114–15, 121, 126–7, 132–3, 143, 147
Renaissance (electoral slate), 174
Renaissance and Independence (electoral slate), 174
Rěshūmōt, 99
Rhodes (Island), 32, 73, 112
Rhodesia, 55
Rushdī, 'Ārif, 78
Russia, *see* Soviet Union

Sa'd, George, 78, 182, 207 n., 212
Safad, 161, 167
Sakhnayn, 164
al-Salām, 140
al-Salām Mosque, 12
al-Salām wa'l-khayr, 265
Salmān, Faraj Nūr, 66
Samne, 27, 279
Sapīr, Pinḥas, 206, 267
Sartre, J.-P., 56
Sasōn, E., 267
Saudi Arabia, 2, 275
Security considerations, 3, 5, 33–34, 52, 90, 96, 125, 138, 221, 223, 226, 268
Semitic Action, 102 n.
Service to the People (electoral slate), 174
Shafā 'Amr, 5, 6, 16, 83, 93, 124, 131, 139, 158, 161–2, 164, 177, 190, 262, 264, 274
Sharet, Moshe, 118
Sharī'a courts, 10, 11, 17, 279
Shazar, Zalman, 267
Shihāda, 'Azīz, 57
Shīṭrīṭ, Běkhōr, 28 n., 137, 267
ha-Shōmer ha-ṣa'īr, 80, 279
Shonfield, Andrew, xi
al-Shuqayrī, Aḥmad, 275
Simon, Ernst A., 117
Sinai War (1956), 59, 65, 89, 122, 124
Six-days' war (1967), x, 53 n., 59, 84 n., 89, 102, 165, 204, 213, 220
Smith, Ian, 55
Sneh, Moshe, 85, 191, 241
Social change, 19 ff., 25 ff., 43, 47, 65, 154, 158, 189, 205, 207, 213–14, 223, 275–6. *See also* Modernization
Social Services, Ministry of, 143, 247
South Africa, 55
Soviet Union, 29, 48, 61, 82, 85, 90, 94, 109, 169, 201, 208. *See also* Moscow
Sports clubs, 55, 99, 101, 216–19, 225, 255 n.
Statistics, 3 ff., 12, 16, 40, 49, 82, 110, 112, 114–15, 120–1, 126–8, 133, 145 ff., 152, 171, 179–81, 190–4, 206, 241 ff., 262, 276
Stendel, Ori, xi
Students, 4, 11, 45–47, 49–57, 92, 95, 98, 250, 263–4, 275. *See also* Arab Students' Committee; Education; Intellectuals
Subversiveness, 75, 94, 101. *See also* Loyalty
Supreme Court, 3, 97, 99, 100, 102, 136, 242. *See also* High Court of Justice
Supreme Muslim Council, 11
Surūjī, Maḥmūd, 105
Syria, 2, 12, 14, 32, 87 n., 123, 184, 201 n., 267, 275

Ṣābā, Niqūlā, 73
Ṣadā'l-tarbiya, 265
al-Ṣa'īdī, 'Abd al-Muta'āl, 29
Ṣawt al-sha'b, 61, 140

Tamrā, 164, 177
Tarshīḥa, 34, 126
Taxation, 23, 68, 160, 169, 188, 204, 208 n., 268

Tel-Aviv University, 49
Tel-Aviv-Jaffa, xi, 3, 5, 11, 37, 39, 55, 59, 72, 98, 102, 104, 136 n., 143, 157–8, 200, 207, 262, 264, 270
Television, 24, 31–32, 53, 70, 151, 170, 207, 210, 238–9, 242, 258, 265–7, 276
Thant, U, 98
This World—a New Force, 135, 145, 147, 149, 181, 259, 268, 273, 278
Time, 265
Tōmā, Emīl, 83
Towns, 10, 13, 16, 19, 20, 46–47, 50, 69, 91, 121, 123, 127, 129, 131, 133, 141, 143, 147, 176, 179, 189–90, 214–15, 242, 259–60, 264, 275–6
Townspeople, 6, 10, 185, 261
Trade union elections, 92, 178 ff., 185–6. *See also Histadrūt*
Travel-permits, 3, 227, 270
Tribal leadership, 27, 150, 189–90. *See also* Bedouins

al-Ṭabarī, Ṭāhir, 11, 45 n., 117
Ṭaiyyba, 11, 81, 87, 93, 101, 105, 116, 132, 138, 158, 164, 178, 214–17, 262, 264
Ṭanṭā, 203
Ṭarīf, Amīn, 14, 274
Ṭīra, vi, 81, 87, 119, 139–40, 158, 163–6, 177–8, 182, 214, 215 n., 217–19, 243, 255 n., 262, 264
Ṭōleydānō, Sh., 137
Ṭūbī, Tawfīq, vi, 83, 85, 88–89, 111, 114, 141, 190, 200–1, 226, 241–3, 274
Ṭu'ma, Khalīl, 54, 56
Trade and Industry, Ministry of, 206
Ṭur'ān, 22 n., 162, 164

'Ubayd, Diyāb, 138, 195, 197, 246
Umm al-Faḥm, 78, 87, 141, 163–4, 177, 213, 215 n., 216–18
Unemployment, 43, 45–46, 50–51, 66, 84, 90–91, 104, 136, 207 n., 263–5, 269–71. *See also* Occupations
Union (electoral slate), 174
United Arab Republic, 123
United Nations, 2, 29, 55, 82, 98, 119, 228–30, 233, 253, 272
United States, 29, 90, 157
'Urf, 26

Vatican, 16, 203. *See also* Pope
Vietnam, 56
Villages, 10, 12–16, 19 ff., 34 ff., 34 n., 39, 46–47, 49, 51–52, 56, 59, 69, 70, 77, 80–81, 83, 87, 89, 91–92, 112, 119, 121–3, 126–7, 129, 133, 135–6, 138–45, 147, 150, 153–4, 157 ff., 179, 181, 188, 194–5, 213–16, 218–19, 225, 238–9, 242–3, 247, 250, 259–60, 264, 269–71, 275–6, 278
Villagers, 6, 10, 12, 19 ff., 52, 69, 72, 76, 91, 136 n., 158 ff., 168, 185, 206
Voice of America, 266
Voice of the Arabs, 266
Voting, 23, 32, 108 ff., 149 ff., 161 ff., 178 ff., 188–9, 191, 197, 202, 208, 220, 237 ff., 253. *See also* Elections

Wādī Nisnās (Haifa), 93
Waqf, 8, 10 n., 11, 202, 279
Waschitz, Yosef, 81, 151
Wāsṭa, 21, 23–24, 272, 279
Wenner-Gren Foundation, xi
Wīlner, Me'īr, 84, 86, 88, 141
Wītqōn, 101
Women in politics, 23, 80, 87, 146, 150
Workers' Bloc, 110–11
Workers' Councils, 179, 182, 212–13, 249–50
Workers in politics: confrontation with Jews, 37, 136, 158, 183, 249–50; literary expression, 65; political attitudes, 171, 179 ff., 249–50, 264; target for Communist propaganda, 22, 91; ties with MAPAI, 109; — with MAPAM, 81, 177, 242; — with Communists, 84, 91–92, 116, 140; weakening of ties with the village, 69, 148, 158
World War, Second, 2, 26
World Zionist Movement, *see* Zionism

Yāfat al-Nāṣira, *see* Yafī'
Yafī', 163–4, 168–70
Yamma, 262
Yānī, Yānī, 93
Yānūḥ, 13 n.
al-Yawm, 60, 131, 175, 195, 265
Yĕdī'ōt aḥarōnōt, 265
Yĕhōshū'a, Y., 12 n.
Yemen, 2
Yirkā, 14, 15, 22, 126, 138, 164
YMCA, 211
Youth in politics: alienation, 42–43, 220; Druzes, 46–47, 166–7, 202; exposure to modernization, 24, 271; flight across the borders, 34, 122; Greek Orthodox, 208; literary contribution, 59; non-identification with Israel,

Youth in politics—*contd.*
29, 238–9; political attitudes, 130, 150, 166–8, 187 ff., 192, 195, 215–16, 240, 253–4, 264, 277; susceptibility to propaganda, 53; target for *al-Arḍ* propaganda, 99, 103 ff.; ties with MAPAI, 78, 123, 133; —with MAPAM, 80–81, 154, 177; —with Communists, 87, 89, 91–92, 116, 134, 154, 176, 211–12, 242
Yūsuf, Maḥmūd, 15 n.

Zayd, Qāsim, 177
Zayd, Tawfīq, 176, 226
Zionism, 1, 34, 58, 71, 75, 79, 82, 85, 124–5, 134, 142, 146, 228–9, 268, 272–3
Zu'bī (*ḥamūla*), 80, 119, 190
Zu'bī, 'Abd al-'Azīz, 81, 142, 157, 173–4, 191, 199, 200, 274
Zu'bī, Sayf al-Dīn, 37, 75 n., 118, 137–8, 157, 172–4, 193, 197, 199, 200, 226, 231, 274

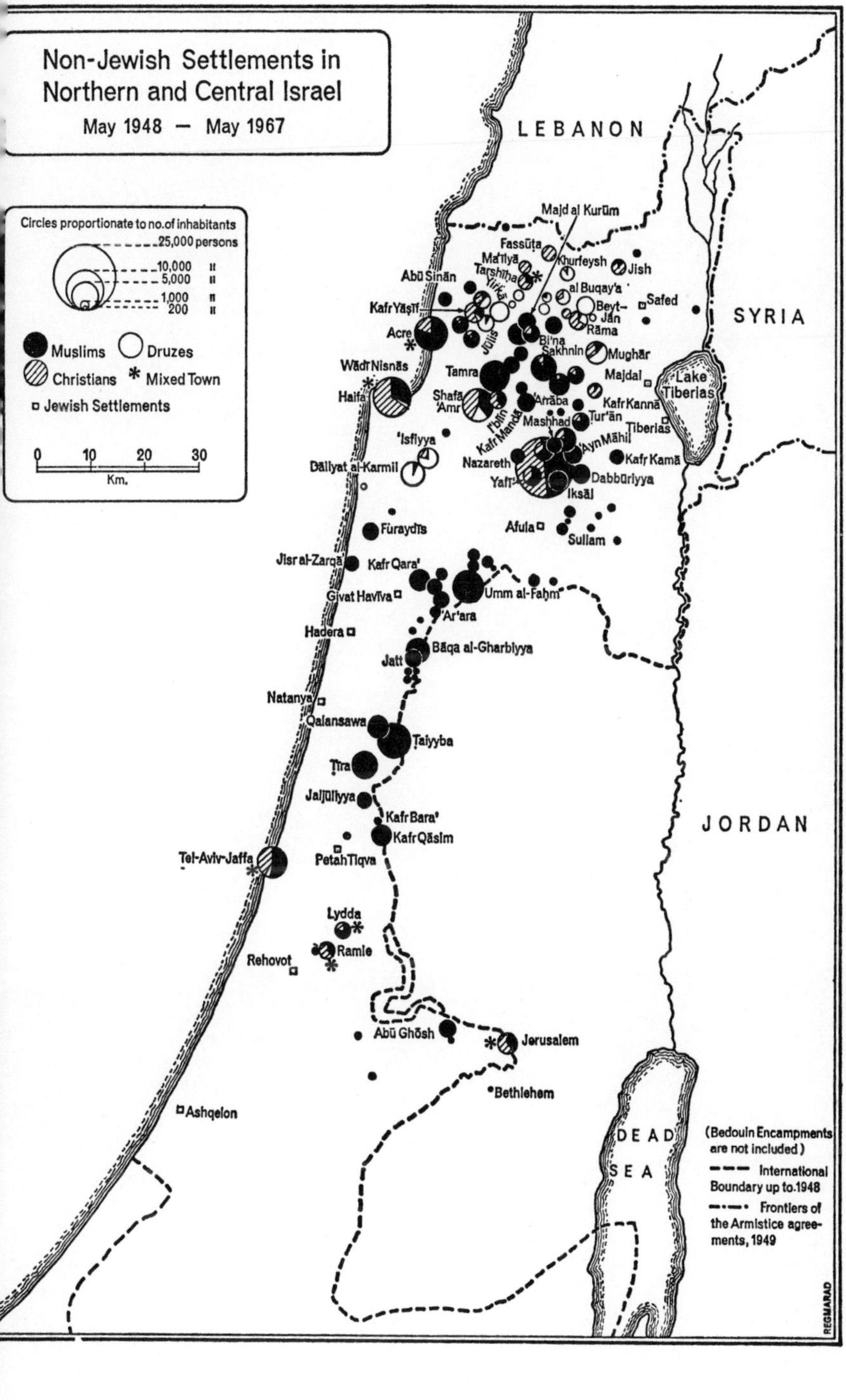
Non-Jewish Settlements in Northern and Central Israel
May 1948 — May 1967
Circles proportionate to no. of inhabitants
25,000 persons
10,000 "
5,000 "
1,000 "
200 "
Muslims
Druzes
Christians
Mixed Town
Jewish Settlements
0 10 20 30
Km.
LEBANON
SYRIA
JORDAN
Majd al Kurūm
Fassūṭa
Ma'ilyā
Tarshīḥa
Khurfeysh
Jish
Abū Sinān
Yirkā
al Buqay'a
Safed
Kafr Yāṣīf
Beyt-Jān
Rāma
Acre
Jūlis
Bi'na
Sakhnīn
Mughār
Wādī Nisnās
Tamra
Majdal
Lake Tiberias
Haifa
Shafā 'Amr
'Arrāba
Kafr Kannā
I'blīn
Kafr Mandā
Mashhad
Tur'ān
Tiberias
'Isfiyya
'Ayn Māhil
Kafr Kamā
Nazareth
Dāliyat al-Karmil
Yāfā
Dabbūriyya
Iksāl
Fūraydīs
Afula
Sūlam
Jisr al-Zarqā
Kafr Qara'
Umm al-Faḥm
Givat Havīva
'Ar'ara
Hadera
Bāqa al-Gharbiyya
Jatt
Natanya
Qalansawa
Ṭaiyyba
Ṭīra
Jaljūliyya
Kafr Bara'
Kafr Qāsim
Tel-Aviv-Jaffa
Petah Tiqva
Lydda
Ramle
Rehovot
Abū Ghōsh
Jerusalem
Bethlehem
Ashqelon
DEAD SEA
(Bedouin Encampments are not included)
International Boundary up to 1948
Frontiers of the Armistice agreements, 1949
REGMARAD

PRINTED IN GREAT BRITAIN BY
HAZELL WATSON AND VINEY LTD
AYLESBURY, BUCKS